14th EDITION

SOUTH-WESTERN

TEACHER'S EDITION FOR WORKBOOK

Applied

BUSINESS

Mathematics

Robert A. Schultheis
Professor, Department of
Management Information Systems
Southern Illinois University
Edwardsville, Illinois

Raymond M. Kaczmarski
Supervisor of Business Education
Detroit Public Schools
Detroit, Michigan

JOIN US ON THE INTERNET
WWW: http://www.thomson.com
EMAIL: findit@kiosk.thomson.com

A service of I(T)P®

SOUTH
WESTERN
EDUCATIONAL
PUBLISHING

I(T)P® An International Thomson Publishing Company

Cincinnati • Albany • Bonn • Boston • Detroit • London • Madrid • Melbourne • Mexico City
• New York • Philadelphia • Pacific Grove • San Francisco • Singapore • Tokyo • Toronto • Washingtoı

gift

TABLE OF CONTENTS

Name: _____ Date: _____

MONEY RECORDS

LESSON 1-1 CASH RECEIPTS RECORDS

Exercise 1. (Cash receipts records)

1. The cash receipts record of Carole Brown is on the right. Carole is an office worker and has a part-time job, also.

   Add the amounts in the "Amount" column and write the total on the line labeled "Total."

Carole Brown
CASH RECEIPTS RECORD

DATE	EXPLANATION	AMOUNT
June 2	Refund on returned purchase	19 95
3	Full-time pay	324 89
7	Part-time pay	65 27
10	Full-time pay	324 89
17	Full-time pay	324 89
21	Interest on savings	17 23
24	Full-time pay	324 89
30	Birthday gift	50 00
	Total	1,452 01

2. The Future Business Leaders of America at Bendix High School sold popcorn at football games to earn money. For five games in the fall, their receipts were $245.71, $133.89, $92.12, $91.45, and $49.30. What were the total receipts for the games? $_____612.47_____

   $245.71 + $133.89 + $92.12 + $91.45 + $49.30 = $612.47

3. The ferris wheel ride at a fair had the following cash receipts during one week: Monday, $512.75; Tuesday, $310.25; Wednesday, $277.50; Thursday, $189.25; Friday, $479.75; Saturday, $535.25; Sunday, $507.75. What were the ride's total receipts for the week? $_____2,812.50_____

   $512.75 + $310.25 + $277.50 + $189.25 + $479.75 + $535.25 + $507.75 = $2,812.50

Exercise 2. (Adding faster)

Add the columns below. Combine two or more numbers when you can.

1. 16	**2.** 96	**3.** 17	**4.** 34	**5.** 56	**6.** 51	**7.** 36	**8.** 79
94	14	21	25	24	37	74	24
71	53	72	51	75	42	69	15
39	57	45	18	35	23	41	95
65	12	21	61	72	14	28	77
15	68	24	11	38	33	16	39
300	300	200	200	300	200	264	329

Exercise 3. (Adding faster)

When you add these problems, combine two or more numbers when you can.

1. 35	**2.** 12	**3.** 32	**4.** 82	**5.** 17	**6.** 25	**7.** 76	**8.** 45
11	65	13	27	83	13	34	65
64	33	65	11	10	72	12	26
17	14	67	65	62	81	98	84
22	83	33	33	17	18	44	12
71	15	19	62	31	11	71	64
45	82	91	44	81	72	15	34
12	67	23	15	29	25	84	83
23	14	67	81	15	13	16	27
300	385	410	420	345	330	450	440

Exercise 4. (Checking addition)

Add these problems and check them by using reverse addition. To do this, add from top to bottom the first time. Then check your work by adding from the bottom up. Put a check mark (✓) at the right of each answer you have checked by reverse addition.

1. $27.02	**2.** $19.10	**3.** $ 1.31	**4.** $35.26	**5.** $49.37	**6.** $ 1.27	**7.** $32.46	**8.** $ 6.05
0.78	5.43	16.39	9.14	1.56	10.48	0.74	13.12
4.36	15.57	3.25	40.76	42.83	15.09	1.26	1.98
12.14	7.75	75.03	0.32	9.03	3.23	16.27	0.19
0.93	0.35	8.42	1.62	42.72	89.35	13.45	86.46
$45.23	$48.20	$104.40	$87.10	$145.51	$119.42	$64.18	$107.80

LESSON 1-2   CASH PAYMENTS RECORDS

Exercise 1.   (Cash payments records)

1. The cash payments record of Mario Talina for the week of March 12 is shown at the right. What were his total payments for the week?

Cash Payments Record				
DATE		EXPLANATION	AMOUNT	
March	*12*	*Rent*	*385*	*00*
	13	*Electric bill*	*102*	*76*
	13	*Contribution*	*25*	*00*
	14	*Groceries*	*46*	*23*
	15	*Concert tickets*	*11*	*50*
	15	*Charge account payment*	*37*	*88*
	16	*Movie*	*6*	*25*
	17	*Clothing*	*118*	*99*
	18	*Monthly bus tokens*	*20*	*00*
		Total	*753*	*61*

2. Elergy Electronic Co. spent these amounts for electric power and natural gas for a year:

January	$2,857.23	July	$2,145.09
February	2,645.72	August	2,904.68
March	1,967.98	September	1,800.40
April	1,421.35	October	1,370.53
May	1,562.49	November	1,811.06
June	1,825.12	December	2,007.38

The total amount Elergy Electronic Co. spent on energy for the year was $ 24,319.03 .

3. The Van Dyke family spent these amounts for May:

Food	$478.21	Transportation	$600.12
Clothing	325.78	Entertainment	145.67
Housing	1,235.98	Education	800.00
Medical	220.07	Savings	300.00

The total amount spent was $ 4,105.83 .

4. An amusement park cashier received the following amounts of money for 10 weeks in the summer:

$1,101.75	$2,117.55
1,507.65	1,780.25
2,007.15	1,603.45
1,813.45	1,803.45
1,967.34	2,350.75

The total amount received by the cashier was $ 18,052.79 _____.

Exercise 2. (Numerals)

Look at each sentence. Is it true or false?

1. 45 + 24 = 79   F

2. 36 = 15 + 21   T

3. 39 − 11 = 27   F

4. 67 − 9 = 58   T

5. 15 + 20 = 17 + 18   T

6. 75 − 35 = 53 − 13   T

7. 12 + 4 + 6 = 7 + 5 + 11   F

8. 8 − 3 + 13 = 24 + 6 − 12   T

9. 34 − 12 + 6 = 18 + 14 − 4   T

10. 15 + 14 − 10 = 25 − 10 + 14   F

Exercise 3. (Numerals)

In the blank space at the right of each open sentence, write the numeral that makes the sentence true.

1. $N + 3 = 10$ ___7___   **5.** 24 − 6 = ? ___18___   **9.** $N − 11 = 21$ ___32___

2. $N − 5 = 15$ ___20___   **6.** ? + 12 = 30 ___18___   **10.** 10 + ? = 26 ___16___

3. 29 − N = 6 ___23___   **7.** 38 + N = 52 ___14___   **11.** 45 − N = 13 ___32___

4. $N − 34 = 7$ ___41___   **8.** 47 + ? = 63 ___16___   **12.** $N − 32 = 18$ ___50___

Exercise 4.   (Reading and writing numbers in the decimal system)

1. In the number 9,136, what digit is in the:

   a. thousands place? _____9_____

   b. hundreds place? _____1_____

   c. tens place? _____3_____

   d. ones place? _____6_____

2. In the number 1,648, the 1 has a value of _____1,000_____; the 6 has a value of _____600_____; the 4 has a value of _____40_____; the 8 has a value of _____8_____.

3. Write the number 10,567 in words: _____Ten thousand, five hundred, sixty-seven_____

4. The table at the right shows that 4,859 is equal to 4,000 + 800 + 50 + 9. Make tables like the one on the right to show the value of each digit and the sum of the digits in each of these numbers.

   4,000
   800
   50
   <u>9</u>
   4,859

   a. 589

   500
   80
   <u>9</u>
   589

   b. 2,407

   2,000
   400
   0
   <u>7</u>
   2,407

5. Write the numbers 497 and 1,798 in words:

   a. 497: _____Four hundred, ninety-seven_____

   b. 1,798: _____One thousand, seven hundred, ninety-eight_____

6. The numbers 687, 786, 768, 867, 678, and 876 are all made up of the same digits.

   a. Which number represents the largest number? _____876_____

   b. Which number represents the smallest number? _____678_____

7. a. Write below in words the largest number you can write with the digits 2, 6, and 5, using each digit only once.

   _____Six hundred, fifty-two_____

   b. Write below in words the smallest number you can write with those same digits.

   _____Two hundred, fifty-six_____

LESSON 1-3   COLUMNAR CASH PAYMENTS RECORDS

Exercise 1.   (Columnar cash payments records)

Complete the cash payments record with special columns below. Check your work by adding horizontally the totals of each of the Type of Payment columns.

Week	Type of Payment					Total Payment
	Rent	Food	Clothing	Other	Savings	
Nov 1–7	625 00	110 79	25 98	102 56	100 00	964 33
8–14		142 51	145 67	12 08		300 26
15–21		75 68		40 81	100 00	216 49
22–28		161 34		201 45		362 79
29–30		15 11		10 77		25 88
Totals	625 00	505 43	171 65	367 67	200 00	1,869 75

Exercise 2.   (Checking horizontal and vertical addition)

Do these problems. Check your work by adding horizontally the sums of the first six columns.

1. 10 + 2 + 4 + 6 + 8 + 9 = _39_

  6 + 9 + 6 + 4 + 1 + 3 = _29_

  12 + 3 + 8 + 7 + 4 + 9 = _43_

  7 + 9 + 5 + 8 + 5 + 5 = _39_

  10 + 4 + 8 + 7 + 6 + 9 = _44_

  45 + 27 + 31 + 32 + 24 + 35 = _194_

2. 3 + 7 + 6 + 5 + 2 + 6 = _29_

  2 + 9 + 8 + 4 + 7 + 3 = _33_

  10 + 8 + 5 + 6 + 5 + 7 = _41_

  12 + 4 + 9 + 8 + 7 + 8 = _48_

  9 + 8 + 7 + 3 + 3 + 2 = _32_

  36 + 36 + 35 + 26 + 24 + 26 = _183_

LESSON 1-4   CHECK REGISTER RECORDS

Exercise 1.   (Deposit slips)

1. Find the total of this deposit and enter it on the last line of the deposit slip.

For DEPOSIT to the Account of **PEG AND HAROLD HOBART**		14-735 / 2810	
		Dollars	**Cents**
Date _December 1_ 19 _ _ _	Bills	263	00
	Coins	12	83
Riverside National Bank St. Louis, MO	Checks as follows Properly Endorsed		
	6-218	786	33
Subject to the Terms and Conditions of this Bank's Collection Agreement	1-121	520	21
	15-610	199	03
⑈02810 0735⑈ 13 61502⑈	Total Deposit	1,781	40

2. The Edgemont Commerce and Growth Association has this deposit to make on August 21 of this year: $2,063 in bills; $167.23 in coins; and checks 14-735, $108.22; 14-740, $456.19; 35-318, $5.09.

    Prepare the deposit slip, using the blank form at the right.

For DEPOSIT to the Account of **EDGEMONT COMMERCE AND GROWTH ASSOC.**		14-621 / 2810	
		Dollars	**Cents**
Date _August 21_ 19 _ _ _	Bills	2,063	00
	Coins	167	23
EDGEMONT BANK AND TRUST COMPANY St. Louis, MO	Checks as follows Properly Endorsed		
	14-735	108	22
Subject to the Terms and Conditions of this Bank's Collection Agreement	14-740	456	19
	35-318	5	09
⑈02810 06219⑈ 15 98632⑈	Total Deposit	2,799	73

3. Amaray Data Systems has these items to deposit on March 21: (bills) $3,035; (coins) $5,812.89; (checks) 1-145, $308.77; 12-701, $7,801.54; 14-306, $407.31.

    Prepare the deposit slip, using the blank form at the right.

For DEPOSIT to the Account of **Amaray Data Systems**		74-396 / 2724	
		Dollars	**Cents**
Date _March 21_ 19 _ _ _	Bills	3,035	00
	Coins	5,812	89
EDGEMONT BANK AND TRUST COMPANY St. Louis, MO	Checks as follows Properly Endorsed		
	1-145	308	77
Subject to the Terms and Conditions of this Bank's Collection Agreement	12-701	7,801	54
	14-306	407	31
⑈02810 06219⑈ 15 98632⑈	Total Deposit	17,365	51

Exercise 2.   (Checks and check registers)

1. On January 30, Alicia Ti must write these checks: No. 1092, for $45.82 to the Dover Water Co. for her water bill; No. 1093, for $289.79, to Sandy's, for dresses; No. 1094, for $50 to the American Cancer Society, for a donation and No. 1095, for $675, to Townsend Apartments, Inc., for her February rent. She has written the first check and recorded it in the check register below. Using the first check as a model, write the other three checks. Record each check in the check register as soon as you write it.

NUMBER	DATE	CHECK ISSUED TO OR DESCRIPTION OF DEPOSIT	(-) CHECK		(+) DEPOSIT		√	BALANCE $ 1,208	45
— —	1/29	*Insurance claim payment*	$		$ 126	72		1,335	17
1092	1/30	*Dover Water Company*	45	82				1,289	35
1093	1/30	*Sandy's*	289	79				999	56
1094	1/30	*American Cancer Society*	50	00				949	56
1095	1/30	*Townsend Apartments, Inc.*	675	00				274	56

Alicia Ti   Date *January 30* 19 _ _   No. *1092*
                                                                    2-2101
                                                                    2260

PAY TO THE ORDER OF ___*Dover Water Company*___ $ _*45.82*_

Forty-five and $\frac{82}{100}$ _____ **Dollars**

For Classroom Use Only

Superior National Bank
    New York, New York   *Alicia Ti*

⑈02260 2101⑈ 6321⑈943⑈

Alicia Ti   Date *January 30* 19 _ _   No. *1093*
                                                                    2-2101
                                                                    2260

PAY TO THE ORDER OF ___*Sandy's*___ $ _*289.79*_

Two hundred eighty-nine and $\frac{79}{100}$ _____ **Dollars**

For Classroom Use Only

Superior National Bank
    New York, New York   *Alicia Ti*

⑈02260 2101⑈ 6321⑈943⑈

Alicia Ti

Date January 30 19 - -   No. 1094
                                   2-2101
                                   2260

PAY TO THE ORDER OF __American Cancer Society__ $ 50.00

Fifty and 00/100 _____ **Dollars**

For Classroom Use Only

Superior National Bank
New York, New York   Alicia Ti

⑈02260 2101⑈ 6321ᵐ943⑊

Alicia Ti

Date January 30 19 - -   No. 1095
                                   2-2101
                                   2260

PAY TO THE ORDER OF __Townsend Apartments, Inc.__ $ 675.00

Six hundred seventy-five and 00/100 _____ **Dollars**

For Classroom Use Only

Superior National Bank
New York, New York   Alicia Ti

⑈02260 2101⑈ 6321ᵐ943⑊

---

2. Karla Steir's check register showed a balance of $201.34 on August 23, 19—. During the week, Karla made these deposits and wrote these checks:

Aug. 23 Check No. 542, for $22.75 to Janus Newspapers, Inc. for the daily newspaper subscription.
      23 Check No. 543, for $45.27 to Warrensburg Telephone Co. for the monthly telephone bill.
      24 Deposit for $4, rebates on camera film purchases.
      25 Check No. 544, for $123.73 to Secors Electric and Gas Co. for electricity and gas for month.
      27 Deposit for $412.38, Karla's pay for the week.

Record the deposits and checks in the check register below. Find the balance of the account after each check and each deposit.

NUMBER	DATE	CHECK ISSUED TO OR DESCRIPTION OF DEPOSIT	(-) CHECK		(+) DEPOSIT		√	BALANCE $	
								201	34
542	8/23	Janus Newspapers, Inc.	$ 22	75	$			178	59
543	8/23	Warrensburg Telephone Co.	45	27				133	32
- - -	8/24	Rebates on film purchases			4	00		137	32
544	8/25	Sears Electric and Gas Co.	123	73				13	59
- - -	8/27	Paycheck			412	38		425	97

3. The Preston Homeowners Association began the month of June with a balance of $3,081.59 in their checking account. In the first week of June, the following deposits were made and checks written:

June 1 Wrote check No. 1088 for $75.42 to American Mowing Company for mowing and trimming.
2 Wrote check No. 1089 for $150 to Nagle and Balsley, Inc. for legal work.
3 Deposit $856, receipts for homeowners assessments.
4 Wrote check No. 1090 for $85.12 to Ellen Archer for lifeguard wages.
5 Deposited $1,035, receipts for homeowners assessments.

Record the beginning balance, the deposits, and the checks in the register below. Find the balance after each deposit and check.

NUMBER	DATE	CHECK ISSUED TO OR DESCRIPTION OF DEPOSIT	(-) CHECK		(+) DEPOSIT		√	BALANCE $ 3,081 59	
1088	6/1	American Mowing Company	$ 75	42	$			3.006	17
1089	6/2	Nagle and Balsley, Inc.	150	00				2,856	17
- - -	6/3	Homeowners assessments			856	00		3,712	17
1090	6/4	Ellen Archer	85	12				3,627	05
- - -	6/5	Homeowners assessments			1,035	00		4,662	05

Exercise 3.   (Checking subtraction)

Do each of the subtractions below. Check your answers by adding the amount subtracted and the difference. The sum should equal the top number.

1. a.   7,259
       367
      6,892

b.   19,864
       5,976
      13,888

c. $18,965.25
       9,876.37
      $9,088.88

d. $47,863.12
       12,608.98
      $35,254.14

e. $76,219.49
       19,146.15
      $57,073.34

2. a.   9,627
       519
      9,108

b.   24,719
       6,348
      18,371

c. $26,214.97
       17,839.58
      $8,375.39

d. $16,399.28
       15,489.49
      $909.79

e. $29,733.18
       11,974.81
      $17,758.37

Exercise 4.   (Gross and net)

1. The Castleton High School Senior Class had a car wash to earn money. The gross income from the car wash was $325. The total expenses were $45.67. What was the net income from the car wash? $279.33

    Gross income $325.00
    Total expense   45.67
    Net income $279.33

2. Fred Andrew bought a jacket originally priced at $145 but was reduced for quick sale by $37.98. What was the net cost of the jacket? $107.02

    Gross price $145.00
    Reduction   37.98
    Net cost $107.02

3. Alice Goh's gross pay for the week was $258.14. A total of $39.28 was deducted from her gross pay. What was her net pay for the week? $218.86

    Gross pay $258.14
    Deductions   39.28
    Net pay $218.86

4. The gross weight of a can of soup is 12.2 ounces. If the can weighs 1.3 ounces, what is the net weight of the soup?
    10.9 oz.

    Gross weight   12.2 ounces
    Weight of can   1.3 ounces
    Net weight   10.9 ounces

Exercise 5.   (Related problems)

1. On April 21, Tyrone Watson had $45.38 on hand. During the week, he earned $105 mowing lawns, $63 trimming shrubbery, and $147 doing odd jobs. (a) What were Watson's total earnings for the week? $315.00 . (b) What total amount did Watson have available to spend during the week? $360.38 . (c) If he had $23.43 on hand at the end of the week, how much money had he spent during the week? $336.95 .

    Balance on April 21 $ 45.38   Available to spend $360.38
    Earned during week   315.00 ($105 + $63 + $147)   Balance, end of week   23.43
    Available to spend   360.38   Spent during week $336.95

2. A town had 1,200 tons of salt on hand at the start of winter. It bought these amounts during the winter: 145, 250, 115, and 279 tons. (a) How many tons of salt did the town buy? 789 tons. (b) How many tons were available for use during the winter? 1,989 tons. (c) If the town had 153 tons left at the end of winter, how many tons did the town use? 1,836 tons.

    145 + 250 + 115 + 279 = 789 tons bought during winter
    1,200 + 789 = 1,989 tons available for use
    1,989 − 153 = 1,836 tons used during winter

LESSON 1-5   ELECTRONIC BANKING

1. On Sunday, Alice Barr used the automatic teller machine to deposit a check for $637.15 and to withdraw $175 in cash for shopping. If her starting bank balance was $413.63, what is her new balance? _____$875.78_____

    $ 413.63   Starting balance
    + 637.15   Deposit
    $1,050.78
    − 175.00
    $ 875.78   New balance

2. Redina Brown uses a debit card to pay for the following 3 purchases: groceries, $82.96; clothing, $230.95; and books, $52.23. If Redina's bank balance was $792.87 at the start of the day, what is her new balance? _____$426.73_____

    $82.96 + $230.95 + $52.23 = $366.14 (Total purchases)
    $792.87   Starting balance
    −366.14   Purchases
    $426.73   New balance

3. On Sunday morning, Ted Wallace deposited a tax refund check for $413.54 in his bank's automatic teller machine at a shopping center. He then used his debit card to make these purchases: shoes, $64.95; electric razor, $83.50; computer diskettes, $36.59. If his starting bank balance was $714.27, what is his new balance? _____$942.77_____

    $ 714.27   Starting balance
    + 413.54   Deposit
    $1,127.81   Total on hand

    $64.95 + $83.50 + $36.59 = $185.04 (Total purchases)

    $1,127.81   Total on hand
    − 185.04   Total purchases
    $ 942.77   New balance

4. Lou Stein started the day with a bank balance of $307.13. He used the automatic teller to deposit a check for $164.14 and his debit card to make these purchases: $63.30, $37.46, and $32.93. What is the balance in his bank account when these transactions are processed by his bank? _____$337.58_____

    $307.13   Starting balance
    +164.14   Deposit
    $471.27   Total on hand

    $63.30 + $37.46 + $32.93 = $133.69 (Total purchases)

    $471.27   Total on hand
    −133.69   Total purchases
    $337.58   New balances

LESSON 1-6   RECONCILING THE CHECK REGISTER BALANCE

Exercise

1. The Triton Company's bank statement balance on January 31 was $2,871.40. On the same date, their checkbook balance was $2,425.47. The bank statement showed a service charge of $5.60 and interest earned of $5.75. The checkbook showed three outstanding checks: No. 1208 for $263.19, No. 1211 for $116.42, and No. 1212 for $66.17. Complete a reconciliation statement in the space below for the Triton Company.

The Triton Company

Reconciliation Statement

January 31, 19--

Checkbook balance	$2,425.47		Bank statement balance		$2,871.40
Deduct:			Deduct:		
Service charge	5.60		Outstanding checks:		
	$2,419.87		#1208	$263.19	
			#1211	116.42	
Add:			#1212	66.17	445.78
Interest earned	5.75				
Correct checkbook balance	$2,425.62		Available bank balance		$2,425.62

2. Tracy Dickerson' checkbook balance on November 30 was $575.23. On the same date, the bank statement showed a balance of $770.68. Included on the statement was a service charge of $4.15 and interest earned of $3.34. Checks outstanding were: No. 106, $25.76; No. 109, $19.10; No. 110, $142.13; and No. 112, $9.27. Prepare a reconciliation statement in the space below.

Tracey Dickerson

Reconciliation Statement

November 30, 19--

Checkbook balance	$575.23		Bank statement balance		$770.68
Deduct:			Deduct:		
Service charge	4.15		Outstanding checks:		
	$571.08		#106	$ 25.76	
			#109	19.10	
Add:			#110	142.13	
Interest earned	3.34		#112	9.27	196.26
Correct checkbook balance	$574.42		Available bank balance		$574.42

---

3. Oscar Brown's check register balance on May 31 was $612.05. His bank statement balance on May 31 was $721.09. When he compared his check register with his bank statement, the statement showed a service charge of $4.30 and interest earned of $4.65. His check register showed that three checks, #357 for $90.21, #359 for $10.91, and #360 for $7.57 were outstanding. Prepare a reconciliation statement for Brown in the space below.

Oscar Brown
Reconciliation Statement
May 31, 19--

Check register balance	$612.05		Bank statement balance		$721.09
Deduct:			Deduct:		
Service charge	4.30		Outstanding checks:		
	$607.75		#357	$90.21	
			#359	10.91	
Add:			#360	7.57	108.69
Interest earned	4.65				
Correct check register balance	$612.40		Available bank balance		$612.40

4. On September 30, Aldo Muldani's check register balance was $305.67 and his bank statement balance was $415.55. The total amount of deposits on the statement was $456.12 and the total amount of checks was $500.23. The statement also showed a service charge of $2.45 and interest earned of $3.06. Outstanding checks were #416 for $71.03, #418 for $34.45, and #419 for $3.79. Prepare a reconciliation statement in the space below.

Aldo Muldani
Reconciliation Statement
September 30, 19--

Check register balance	$305.67		Bank statement balance		$415.55
Deduct:			Deduct:		
Service charge	2.45		Outstanding checks:		
	$303.22		#416	$71.03	
			#418	34.45	
Add:			#419	3.79	109.27
Interest earned	3.06				
Correct check register balance	$306.28		Available bank balance		$306.28

LESSON 1-7   SPECIAL RECONCILIATION PROBLEMS

Exercise   (Special reconciliation problems)

1. On October 31, Frank Torre had a bank balance of $901.35 and a check register balance of $626.92. Comparing the bank statement to the check register Torre found a service charge of $5.26, that check #456 for $5.07 had been recorded in the check register as $7.05, a deposit of $145 made on October 6 had not been recorded in the check register, and check #461 for $8.25 had been recorded twice in the check register. A deposit of $325 was recorded in the check register but was made too late to appear on the bank statement. Outstanding checks were #476 for $136.35 and #478 for $312.66. Complete a reconciliation statement for Torre.

Frank Torre
Reconciliation Statement
October 31, 19--

Check register balance		$626.92	Bank statement balance		$901.35
Deduct:			Deduct:		
Service charge	$5.26		Outstanding checks:		
Correct amount, Check #456	5.07	10.33	#476	$136.35	
		$616.59	#478	312.66	$449.01
					$452.34
Add:			Add:		
Deposit not recorded	$145.00		Late deposit		$325.00
Check #461 recorded twice	8.25				
Incorrect amount, Check #456	7.50	160.75			
Correct check register balance		$777.34	Available bank balance		$777.34

2. On June 30, Jill McKenzie's check register balance was $409.55 and her bank statement balance was $474.73. Comparing the register with the bank statement, she found a service charge for $5.90 and interest earned of $4.24 listed on the statement. She also found that she had failed to record check #3407 for $56.33 in her check register. Outstanding checks were #3412 for $8.45 and #3414 for $179.72. A deposit mailed on June 29 for $65 was not listed on the bank statement. Complete a reconciliation statement for McKenzie.

Check register balance		$409.55	Bank statement balance		$474.73
Deduct: Service charge	$ 5.90		Deduct: Outstanding checks:		
Check omitted	56.33	62.23	#3412	$ 8.45	
		$347.32	#3414	179.72	188.17
					$286.56
Add: Interest earned		4.24	Add: Late deposit		65.00
Correct check register balance		$351.56	Available bank balance		$351.56

3. On February 28, Tom Raschi's register balance was $284.44 and his bank statement balance was $376.88. Upon looking at the statement, Raschi found that there was a service charge of $1.84 and interest earned of $1.34. He also found that he had failed to record a deposit of $48 and had recorded a check for $43.34 as $34.43 in his register. Outstanding checks were #67, $31.75; #70, $22.10. Complete a reconciliation statement.

Check register balance		$284.44	Bank statement balance		$376.88
Deduct: Service charge	$ 1.84		Deduct: Outstanding checks:		
Correct check amount	43.34	45.18	#67	$ 31.75	
		$239.26	#70	22.10	53.85
Add: Interest earned	$ 1.34				
Deposit not recorded	48.00				
Incorrect check amount	34.43	83.77	Available bank balance		$323.03
Correct check register balance		$323.03			

TERM TICKLER

Directions   Some of the terms listed below are in the puzzle. Circle each term when you find it. It may be written downward, upward, sideways, or diagonally. The term "balance" is circled for you as an example. There are nineteen terms in the puzzle. How many can you find?

Terms

addition	automatic teller machines	balance
bank statement	canceled check	cash payments record
cash receipts record	check	check register
debit card	deposit slip	difference
electronic funds transfer	gross	horizontal addition
magnetic ink character	net	number sentence
numeral	outstanding check	place value
recognition	reconciliation statement	reverse addition
service charge	subtraction	sum or total
transit number	vertical addition	

```
N  N  G  N  U  M  B  E  R  S  E  N  T  E  N  C  E  J  V  X  N  P  I
E  U  S  E  U  A  E  C  G  W  I  J  A  T  C  F  M  T  U  U  G  X  J
J  F  L  T  L  M  U  S  E  R  V  I  C  E  C  H  A  R  G  E  V  C  Y
Q  D  U  A  J  Y  E  D  E  P  O  S  I  T  S  L  I  P  S  P  N  I  S
T  S  N  C  Q  B  C  R  C  T  U  S  A  E  C  N  C  G  H  Y  W  A  U
R  C  Y  H  J  B  K  G  A  B  N  A  S  J  C  R  B  N  E  B  G  Y  V
E  G  M  E  X  D  I  Q  T  L  J  H  O  V  E  M  B  B  L  S  M  L  J
V  V  Q  C  A  S  H  R  E  C  E  I  P  T  S  R  E  C  O  R  D  R  Q
E  J  E  K  C  C  A  M  Y  R  I  R  S  R  V  E  G  U  C  A  P  M  A
R  E  C  O  N  C  I  L  I  A  T  I  O  N  S  T  A  T  E  M  E  N  T
S  O  Z  I  T  W  C  K  O  Z  G  J  V  M  P  M  U  B  B  K  W  Q  V
E  B  T  I  O  Q  Q  N  Y  E  Q  C  X  W  B  V  E  W  C  W  X  I  T
A  X  O  M  R  S  C  T  R  A  N  S  I  T  N  U  M  B  E  R  E  H  E
D  N  N  D  B  G  L  K  F  T  S  L  D  J  R  Y  D  T  T  F  J  N  H
D  V  F  C  A  N  C  E  L  E  D  C  H  E  C  K  A  Y  O  E  A  Q  M
I  L  E  O  V  E  R  T  I  C  A  L  A  D  D  I  T  I  O  N  Y  Q  W
T  L  M  V  H  O  R  I  Z  O  N  T  A  L  A  D  D  I  T  I  O  N  N
I  H  B  C  A  S  H  P  A  Y  M  E  N  T  S  R  E  C  O  R  D  M  V
O  U  T  S  T  A  N  D  I  N  G  C  H  E  C  K  X  R  D  M  K  D  B
N  Z  F  Y  E  Y  R  U  H  H  B  S  L  Z  L  H  V  Y  F  F  P  F  L
```

INTEGRATED PROJECT 1

Directions: Read the project through and then complete Steps 1 and 2.

The partially completed check register for Marjorie Abrams for June is shown below.

NUMBER	DATE	CHECK ISSUED TO OR DESCRIPTION OF DEPOSIT	(-) CHECK		(+) DEPOSIT		√	BALANCE	
							$	578	32
397	6/6	Better Clothing, Inc.	$ 87	03	$		√	491	29
398	6/7	Tri-Town Auto, Inc.	134	87			√	356	42
399	6/7	Ridge National Bank	28	56			√	327	86
400	6/7	Edgemont Products Company	4	11			√	323	75
- - -	6/12	Paycheck			356	17	√	679	92
401	6/14	Ticketorama, Inc.	8	98			√	670	94
402	6/14	Computer Book Club of Ames	35	78				635	16
403	6/16	Jay-Mar Catalog Sales	1	45			√	633	71
404	6/20	Shakeel's Gas Stop	20	91			√	612	80
- - -	6/25	Gift			25	00	√	637	80
405	6/25	Kriege Realty Company	500	00			√	137	80
406	6/26	Manila Stores, Inc.	17	75			√	120	05
- - -	6/28	Interest			200	00	√	320	05
407	6/29	Edgemont Water Company	45	08			√	274	97
408	6/29	Midwest Power Company	134	56				140	41
- - -	6/29	Cash and insurance claim			80	33	√	220	74
- - -	6/30	Service charge	4	75				215	99
- - -	6/30	Interest on checking acct.			3	01		219	00

Near the end of June, Marjorie completed these transactions:

June 29   Wrote check #408 for $134.56 to Midwest Power Company for the monthly power bill.
       29   Deposited $25 in bills, $4.35 in coins, and an insurance claim check for $50.98 (transit number 70-431)

Step 1:   Enter these transactions in the check register above and complete the check and deposit slip for Marjorie using the forms supplied.

Marjorie Abrams
2134 S. Charles Street
Belleville, IL 62221

Date _June 29_ 19 - -

No. _408_

70-410
810

PAY TO THE
ORDER OF ___ *Midwest Power Company* ___ $ _134.56_

One hundred thirty-four and 56/100 _____ **Dollars**

For Classroom Use Only

RIDGE NATIONAL BANK
BELLEVILLE, IL 62221

Marjorie Abrams

⑆08100 0410⑆ 254⑉ 11390⑈

For DEPOSIT to the Account of			70-410
Marjorie Abrams			810
2134 S. Charles Street		Dollars	Cents
Belleville, IL 62221	Bills	25	00
Date June 29 19 - -	Coins	4	35
	Checks as follows Properly Endorsed		
RIDGE NATIONAL BANK	70-431	50	98
BELLEVILLE, IL 62221			
Subject to the Terms and Conditions			
of this Bank's Collection Agreement			
⑆0810 0410⑆ 235⑈ 1:390⑈	Total Deposit	80	33

In early July, Marjorie Abrams received her monthly bank statement.

RIDGE NATIONAL BANK
7301 N. belt street
Belleville, IL 62221

[*Marjorie Abrams*
2134 S. Charles Street
Belleville, IL 62221]

Statement for period ending June 30

CHECKS	NUMBER	DEPOSITS	DATE	BALANCE
		Balance Forward	June 1	578.32
28.56	399		7	549.76
87.03	397		9	462.73
134.87	398		9	327.86
4.11	400		10	323.75
		356.17	12	679.92
1.45	403		20	678.47
8.98	401		20	669.49
20.91	404		22	648.58
		25.00	25	673.58
17.75	406		27	655.83
500.00	405	200.00	28	355.83
45.08	407	80.33	29	391.08
4.75 SC		3.01 IN	30	389.34

CC	Certified Check	EC	Error Corrected	OD	Overdraft
CM	Credit Memo	IN	Interest Credited	RT	Returned Item
DM	Debit Memo	NC	Check Not Counted	SC	Service Charge

Step 2:

a. Compare Marjorie's bank statement with her check register. When you find that a check or deposit in the check register is also listed on the bank statement, place a check mark in the [✓] column of the register. This will let Marjorie know that the check has been paid or that the deposit has been recorded by the bank.

b. Prepare a bank reconciliation statement using the space below.

Marjorie Abrams				
Reconciliation Statement				
June 30, 19--				
Check register balance	$220.74		Bank statement balance		$389.34
Deduct:			Deduct:		
Service charge	4.75		Outstanding checks:		
	$215.99		#402	$ 35.78	
			#408	134.56	170.34
Add:					
Interest earned	3.01				
Correct check register balance	$219.00		Available bank balance		$219.00

c. Update Marjorie's check register by entering the service charge and the interest earned.

Name: _____ Date: _____

GROSS AND AVERAGE PAY

LESSON 2-1   MULTIPLICATION AND ESTIMATION

Exercise 1.   (Checking multiplication)

Multiply the two factors in each problem below. Reverse the factors and multiply again to check your work. The answers you get should be the same, providing that the multiplications are correct.

1.	**2.**	**3.**	**4.**	**5.**	**6.**
95	42	275	196	345	286
× 65	× 73	× 125	× 243	× 135	× 572
6,175	3,066	34,375	47,628	46,575	163,592

Check:

1.	**2.**	**3.**	**4.**	**5.**	**6.**
65	73	125	243	135	572
× 95	× 42	× 275	× 196	× 345	× 286
6,175	3,066	34,375	47,628	46,575	163,592

Exercise 2.   (Placing the decimal point in the product)

Do the problems below. Use the space at the right for figuring your answers. Put your answers on the blank lines. Check each product by reversing the factors and multiplying again.

1. 3.24 × 510 = _____1,652.4_____

2. 12.7 × 3.22 = _____40.894_____

3. 24.6 × 40.8 = _____1,003.68_____

4. 70.4 × 1.65 = _____116.16_____

5. 79.8 × 69.25 = _____5,526.15_____

6. 3.6 × $4.20 = _____$15.12_____

7. 6.5 × $8.32 = _____$54.08_____

8. 2.4 × $6.55 = _____$15.72_____

Exercise 3.   (Estimating the product)

In Problems 1 through 7, show the rounded factors and the estimated product. In Problems 8 through 14, give (a) the estimated product and (b) the exact product. Use the Rule of Five Method for rounding factors to estimate the product. Do your calculations on a separate sheet of paper.

	Rounded Factors		Estimated Product				Estimated Product	Exact Product
1. 48 × 87	50	× 90	= 4,500		**8.** 28.7 × 7.15	=	210	205.205
2. 585 × 34	600	× 30	= 18,000		**9.** 28 × $91	=	$2,700	$2,548
3. 129 × 18	100	× 20	= 2,000		**10.** 43 × $575.25	=	$24,000	$24,735.75
4. 70.4 × 62	70	× 60	= 4,200		**11.** 49 × $6.12	=	$300	$299.88
5. 16.1 × 35.6	20	× 40	= 800		**12.** 215 × $20.35	=	$4,000	$4,375.25
6. 27 × $9.15	30	× $9	= $270		**13.** 68 × $9.40	=	$630	$639.20
7. 0.35 × 4.75	0.4	× 5	= 2		**14.** 36 × $32.50	=	$1,200	$1,170

Exercise 4.   (Multiplication by 10, 100, or 1,000)

1. 10 × 483	= 4,830	**7.** 10 × 17¢	= $1.70
2. 100 × $6.45	= $645	**8.** 10 × $8.15	= $81.50
3. 1,000 × 0.0742	= 74.20	**9.** $100 × 5.9	= $590
4. 10 × 39¢	= $3.90	**10.** $1,000 × 16.3	= $16,300
5. $1,000 × 62.1	= $62,100	**11.** 10 × 0.051	= 0.51
6. 1,000 × $0.07	= $70	**12.** 100 × $4.30	= $430

Exercise 5.   (Multiplication by a multiple of 1¢ and 10¢)

1. 55 lb. @ $0.03 = $1.65	**6.** 60 bu. @ $0.40 = $24	**11.** 80 oz. @ 6¢ = $4.80
2. 52 yd. @ $0.06 = $3.12	**7.** 43 qt. @ $0.30 = $12.90	**12.** 70 lb. @ 5¢ = $3.50
3. 85 ft. @ $0.04 = $3.40	**8.** 13 gal. @ $0.60 = $7.80	**13.** 28 qt. @ 40¢ = $11.20
4. 112 yd. @ $0.05 = $5.60	**9.** 25 bu. @ $0.70 = $17.50	**14.** 110 bu. @ 70¢ = $77
5. 35 lb. @ $0.08 = $2.80	**10.** 83 yd. @ $0.20 = $16.60	**15.** 134 items @ 2¢ = $2.68

Chapter ⟨2⟩   Name: _____   Date: _____

Exercise 6. (Review of estimating the product)

In each problem, show the rounded factors and the estimated product.

	Rounded Factors			Estimated Product				Rounded Factors			Estimated Product

1. 34 × 258 __30__ × __300__ = __9,000__   **7.** 7.05 × 4.31 __7__ × __4__ = __28__

2. 22 × 307 __20__ × __300__ = __6,000__   **8.** 81 × 0.47 __80__ × __0.5__ = __40__

3. 208 × 431 __200__ × __400__ = __80,000__   **9.** 72 × 0.83 __70__ × __0.8__ = __56__

4. 72 × 63.1 __70__ × __60__ = __4,200__   **10.** 0.415 × 54 __0.4__ × __50__ = __20__

5. 5.43 × 44 __5__ × __40__ = __200__   **11.** 0.7234 × 0.62 __0.7__ × __0.6__ = __0.42__

6. 76 × 6.09 __80__ × __6__ = __480__   **12.** 0.684 × 1.10 __0.7__ × __1__ = __0.7__

Exercise 7. (Review of multiplication)

In each problem, show the rounded factors, the estimated product, and the exact product.

	Rounded Factors		Estimated Product	Exact Product
1. 604 × 12.02	600	× 10 =	6,000	7,260.08
2. 710 × 520	700	× 500 =	350,000	369,200
3. 1,650 × 3.4	2,000	× 3 =	6,000	5,610
4. 45 × $2.35	50	× $2 =	$100	$105.75
5. 86 × $9.40	90	× $9 =	$810	$808.40
6. 54 × $32	50	× $30 =	$1,500	$1,728
7. 96 × $2.98	100	× $3 =	$300	$286.08
8. 1,015 × $0.96	1,000	× $1 =	$1,000	$974.40
9. 120 × $18.85	100	× $20 =	$2,000	$2,262
10. 1,800 × $3.40	2,000	× $3 =	$6,000	$6,120

Exercise 8. (Review of multiplication)

Use one of the multiplication shortcuts you have been shown to do these problems.

1. 10×24 = ___240___	**7.** 10×135 = ___1,350___	**13.** $732 \times 10¢$ = ___$73.20___
2. $186 \times \$0.01$ = ___$1.86___	**8.** $120 \times \$40$ = ___$4,800___	**14.** $520 \times 30¢$ = ___$156___
3. $15 \times \$0.20$ = ___$3___	**9.** $50 \times \$0.09$ = ___$4.50___	**15.** 200×19 = ___3,800___
4. $100 \times 1,624$ = ___162,400___	**10.** $1,921 \times 1¢$ = ___$19.21___	**16.** $1,000 \times 703$ = ___703,000___
5. 100×90 = ___9,000___	**11.** $1,000 \times 5.2$ = ___5,200___	**17.** $60 \times \$1.50$ = ___$90___
6. 30×211 = ___6,330___	**12.** $23 \times 6¢$ = ___$1.38___	**18.** $187 \times \$0.10$ = ___$18.70___

Exercise 9. (Review of estimation)

1. A student bought 19 packs of paper at a cost of $1.96 a pack. The estimated cost of this purchase is (a)
$___40___. The actual cost is (b) $___37.24___.

    a. $20 \times \$2 = \$40$ estimated cost
    b. $19 \times \$1.96 = \$37.24$ actual cost

2. A total of 231 sheets of paper is used to print a computer prepared report. To print 11 copies of the same report an
estimated (a) ___2,300___ sheets of paper will be needed. The actual number of sheets that will be needed is
(b) ___2,541___.

    a. $230 \times 10 = 2,300$ sheets, estimated number needed
    b. $231 \times 11 = 2,541$ sheets, actual number needed

3. On a 29-day bicycle trip, Arlene Lamberck rode an average of 29 miles a day. The estimated distance she traveled
during the trip was (a) ___900___ miles while her actual mileage was (b) ___841___.

    a. $30 \times 30 = 900$ miles, estimated distance
    b. $29 \times 29 = 841$ miles, actual distance

LESSON 2-2   FINDING GROSS PAY

Exercise

1. Chester Krump worked these hours last week: Monday, 7 hours; Tuesday, 8 hours; Wednesday, 6 hours; Thursday, 7 hours; Friday, 5 hours. Chester is paid $12 an hour. How many hours did Chester work last week? _____33_____. What was his gross pay for the week? _____$396_____.

   7 + 8 + 6 + 7 + 5 = 33 hours worked
   33 × $12 = $396 gross pay

2. Rosemary Karzim earns $9 an hour at her job. The hours she worked during each of the last four weeks are shown at the right. For each week find the gross pay Rosemary earned. Then find her total gross pay for four weeks. Write your answers in the chart.

Week	Hours Worked	Gross Pay
1	40	$ 360
2	31	279
3	37	333
4	39	351
Total Gross Pay		$1,323

   40 × $9 = $ 360 first week
   31 × $9 =   279 second week
   37 × $9 =   333 third week
   39 × $9 =   351 fourth week
                $1,323 total gross pay

3. Sandra Milgor has two jobs. Her full-time job pays $9 an hour. A part-time job pays $5 an hour. Last week Sandra worked 32 hours at her full-time job and 14 hours at her part-time job. Find the

   a. gross pay she earned at her full-time job. $_____288_____

   b. gross pay she earned at her part-time job. $_____70_____

   c. total amount she earned from both jobs. $_____358_____

   a. 32 × $9 = $288 full-time job pay
   b. 14 × $5 = $70 part-time job pay
   c. $288 + $70 = $358 total pay

4. Harrison Cronk earns a weekly salary of $356. How much would Harrison earn in 4 weeks of work? $_____1,424_____ How much would he earn in a 52-week year? $_____18,512_____

   4 × $356 = $1,424 in four weeks
   52 × $356 = $18,512 in a year

LESSON 2-3   DIVISION AND ESTIMATION

Exercise 1.   (Review of division facts)

1. $16 \div 4 = \underline{4}$	11. $77 \div 11 = \underline{7}$	21. $48 \div 12 = \underline{4}$
2. $42 \div 6 = \underline{7}$	12. $8 \div 1 = \underline{8}$	22. $72 \div 9 = \underline{8}$
3. $8 \div 2 = \underline{4}$	13. $18 \div 6 = \underline{3}$	23. $28 \div 4 = \underline{7}$
4. $36 \div 6 = \underline{6}$	14. $54 \div 9 = \underline{6}$	24. $21 \div 7 = \underline{3}$
5. $72 \div 12 = \underline{6}$	15. $12 \div 2 = \underline{6}$	25. $40 \div 5 = \underline{8}$
6. $27 \div 9 = \underline{3}$	16. $8 \div 4 = \underline{2}$	26. $30 \div 6 = \underline{5}$
7. $64 \div 8 = \underline{8}$	17. $9 \div 3 = \underline{3}$	27. $14 \div 2 = \underline{7}$
8. $5 \div 5 = \underline{1}$	18. $81 \div 9 = \underline{9}$	28. $56 \div 8 = \underline{7}$
9. $20 \div 4 = \underline{5}$	19. $35 \div 7 = \underline{5}$	29. $48 \div 6 = \underline{8}$
10. $49 \div 7 = \underline{7}$	20. $24 \div 8 = \underline{3}$	30. $12 \div 3 = \underline{4}$

Exercise 2.   (Finding unknown factors and products)

Above each numeral and letter in the number sentences below, print F or P to show if it is a factor or a product. Then write the unknown number on the blank line.

F F P 1. $15 \times 6 = N$ __90__	F F P 8. $4 \times N = 52$ __13__	F F P 15. $15 \times N = 120$ __8__
P F F 2. $N \div 12 = 6$ __72__	F F P 9. $16 \times 4 = N$ __64__	P F F 16. $N \div 6 = 30$ __180__
F F P 3. $8 \times N = 104$ __13__	P F F 10. $N \div 8 = 16$ __128__	F F P 17. $5 \times N = 80$ __16__
F F P 4. $24 \times 3 = N$ __72__	F F P 11. $7 \times N = 140$ __20__	F F P 18. $12 \times N = 60$ __5__
P F F 5. $N \div 9 = 9$ __81__	P F F 12. $39 \div 3 = N$ __13__	P F F 19. $72 \div 18 = N$ __4__
F F P 6. $N \times 12 = 84$ __7__	F F P 13. $12 \times 5 = N$ __60__	F F P 20. $12 \times N = 48$ __4__
P F F 7. $48 \div N = 16$ __3__	P F F 14. $N \div 12 = 12$ __144__	P F F 21. $N \div 18 = 3$ __54__

Exercise 3.   (Locating the decimal point in the quotient)

Do the problems below. Then check your division.

1. $125\overline{)18.75}$ quotient: 0.15

2. $35\overline{)8.75}$ quotient: 0.25

3. $0.27\overline{)0.2835}$ quotient: 1.05

4. $2.33\overline{)54.755}$ quotient: 23.5

Check:

$0.15 \times 125 = 18.75$

Check:

$0.25 \times 35 = 8.75$

Check:

$1.05 \times 0.27 = 0.2835$

Check:

$23.5 \times 2.33 = 54.755$

5. $0.45\overline{)90.18}$ quotient: 200.4

6. $0.55\overline{)110.}$ quotient: 200

7. $0.18\overline{)4.212}$ quotient: 23.4

8. $1.65\overline{)0.0396}$ quotient: 0.024

Check:

$200.4 \times 0.45 = 90.18$

Check:

$200 \times 0.55 = 110$

Check:

$23.4 \times 0.18 = 4.212$

Check:

$0.024 \times 1.65 = 0.0396$

Exercise 4.   (Dividing to a stated number of decimal places)

Find the quotient correct to the nearest cent for Problems 1 and 2. For Problems 3 and 4, find the quotient correct to one decimal place. Then check your division keeping in mind that the dividend you find will be approximate since your quotient was rounded.

1. $8\overline{)\$126.38}$ quotient: $15.80

2. $36\overline{)\$9311.21}$ quotient: $258.64

3. $65\overline{)2224}$ quotient: 34.2

4. $128\overline{)34391}$ quotient: 268.7

Check:

$8 \times \$15.80 = \$126.40$

Check:

$36 \times \$258.64$
$\quad = \$9,311.04$

Check:

$65 \times 34.2 = 2,223$

Check:

$128 \times 268.7 = 34,393.6$

Exercise 5. (Estimating the quotient)

In each problem, give the estimated answer. Then find and check the exact answer.

		Estimated Answer	Exact Answer	a. Estimated Answer	b. Exact Answer
1.	403.2 ÷ 42 =	10	9.6	1. 400 ÷ 40 = 10	403.2 ÷ 42 = 9.6
2.	$48.64 ÷ 1.9 =	$25	$25.60	2. $50 ÷ 2 = $25	$48.64 ÷ 1.9 = $25.60
3.	23.925 ÷ 2.75 =	8	8.7	3. 24 ÷ 3 = 8	23.925 ÷ 2.75 = 8.7
4.	$5.94 ÷ 0.45 =	$12	$13.20	4. $6.00 ÷ 0.50 = $12	$5.94 ÷ 0.45 = $13.20

Exercise 6. (Dividing by 10, 100, or 1,000)

1. $573 ÷ 10 = $57.30	7. 23.4 ÷ 10 = 2.34	13. 7.5 ÷ 1,000 = 0.0075
2. 1,425 ÷ 1,000 = 1.425	8. 4.2 ÷ 1,000 = 0.0042	14. $80 ÷ 100 = $0.80
3. $608 ÷ 100 = $6.08	9. 2.35 ÷ 100 = 0.0235	15. $6.20 ÷ 10 = $0.62
4. $2,740 ÷ 1,000 = $2.74	10. $30 ÷ 1,000 = $0.03	16. 1.3 ÷ 1,000 = 0.0013
5. 314 ÷ 100 = 3.14	11. $1,620 ÷ 10 = $162	17. 0.87 ÷ 10 = 0.087
6. $905 ÷ 10 = $90.50	12. 0.62 ÷ 100 = 0.0062	18. 0.05 ÷ 100 = 0.0005

Exercise 7. (Dropping end zeros in the divisor)

Give (a) the estimated answer and (b) the exact answer correct to two decimal places.

		Estimated Answer	Exact Answer	a. Estimated Answer	b. Exact Answer
1.	$23,000 ÷ 3,700 =	$6	$6.22	1. $24,000 ÷ 4,000 = $6	$6.216 = $6.22
2.	$5,475 ÷ 270 =	$18	$20.28	2. $5,400 ÷ 300 = $18	$20.277 = $20.28
3.	$56,210 ÷ 4,300 =	$14	$13.07	3. $56,000 ÷ 4,000 = $14	$13.072 = $13.07
4.	49,780 ÷ 1,800 =	25	27.66	4. 50,000 ÷ 2,000 = 25	27.655 = 27.66
5.	18,500 ÷ 510 =	40	36.27	5. 20,000 ÷ 500 = 40	36.274 = 36.27
6.	61,200 ÷ 3,230 =	20	18.95	6. 60,000 ÷ 3,000 = 20	18.947 = 18.95

Exercise 8.   (Division to a stated number of decimal places)

For each problem, first find the estimated answer. Then find the exact answer correct to two decimal places. Check the exact answer by multiplication to see if it is reasonable.

	Estimated Answer	Exact Answer		a. Estimated Answer	b. Exact Answer
1. $127.90 ÷ 42 =	$3	$3.05	**1.**	$120 ÷ 40 = $3	$3.045 = $3.05
2. 37.8 ÷ 2.9 =	13	13.03	**2.**	39 ÷ 3 = 13	13.034 = 13.03
3. $3.56 ÷ 6.7 =	$0.50	$0.53	**3.**	$3.50 ÷ 7 = $0.50	$0.531 = $0.53
4. $44 ÷ 2.7 =	$15	$16.30	**4.**	$45 ÷ 3 = $15	$16.296 = $16.30
5. 49.5 ÷ 68 =	0.7	0.73	**5.**	49 ÷ 70 = 0.7	0.727 = 0.73
6. 38.9 ÷ 5.4 =	8	7.2	**6.**	40 ÷ 5 = 8	7.203 = 7.2
7. $206.50 ÷ 5.2 =	$40	$39.71	**7.**	$200 ÷ 5 = $40	$39.711 = $39.71
8. 1.47 ÷ 2.8 =	0.5	0.53	**8.**	1.5 ÷ 3 = 0.5	0.525 = 0.53

Exercise 9.   (Review of multiplying and dividing by 10, 100, or 1,000)

1. 10 × $3.28   = $32.80

2. 1,000 × 0.049 = 49

3. $745 ÷ 10   = $74.50

4. $630 ÷ 1,000 = $0.63

5. 100 × 5.2   = 520

6. 10 × $0.04   = $0.40

7. 345 ÷ 1,000   = 0.345

8. 0.05 ÷ 10   = 0.005

9. 1,000 × $4.27 = $4,270

10. 6.4 ÷ 100   = 0.064

11. 0.75 ÷ 1,000 = 0.00075

12. 100 × 21.4   = 2,140

13. $37.50 ÷ 1,000 = $0.0375

14. 100 × 0.062   = 6.2

15. 10 × $0.125   = $1.25

16. 0.65 ÷ 100   = 0.0065

17. 4.35 ÷ 100   = 0.0435

18. 1,000 × 0.0075 = 7.5

Exercise 10.

1. A store owner sold 37 discontinued computer games at the same price and received a total of $238.65. (a) At what estimated price did the owner sell each game for? $_____6_____. (b) What was the actual price charged for each game? $_____6.45_____.

   a. $240 ÷ 40 = $6 estimated price
   b. $238.65 ÷ 37 = $6.45 actual price

2. The 78 students in the fourth grade at Coswell Elementary read 1,531 books last summer. (a) What was the estimated average number of books read by each student? _____20_____. (b) What was the actual average number of books read by each student, to the nearest tenth? _____19.6_____.

   a. 1,600 ÷ 80 = 20 estimated books read
   b. 1,531 ÷ 78 = 19.62, or 19.6 on average

3. A worker at a small manufacturing plant cuts holes in steel plates to make parts for boat trailers. When the holes are cut, 0.0186 of each plate becomes scrap metal. Each plate weighs 187 lbs., and 19 plates are used each day. (a) In pounds, what is the estimated weight of each day's scrap metal? _____80 lbs._____. (b) What is the actual weight to the nearest tenth pound of each day's scrap metal? _____66.1 lbs._____.

   a. (200 × 20) × 0.2 = 80 lbs. estimated weight of scrap
   b. (187 × 19) × 0.0186 = 66.08, or 66.1 lbs. actual weight of scrap

Chapter  2   Name: _____   Date: _____

LESSON 2-4   FINDING AVERAGE PAY

Exercise 1.   (Finding simple averages)

1. Quinn LeGrow worked at three jobs in three weeks. In the first week, he earned $310. In the next week, he was paid $334. In the third week, he was paid $307. What average pay per week did Quinn earn for these three weeks?
$_____317_____

$310 + $334 + $307 = $951 total pay for 3 weeks
$951 ÷ 3 = $317 average pay per week

2. The monthly earnings of Cynthia Gragg for May through August were $1,684, $1,752, $1,592, $1,664. What average amount per month did she earn for these four months? $_____1,673_____

$1,684 + $1,752 + $1,592 + $1,664 = $6,692 total earnings for 4 months
$6,692 ÷ 4 = $1,673 average monthly earnings

3. Nestor Gorbea worked five days last week and earned these amounts: $85.63, $79.66, $75.65, $89.28, $90.58. What average amount per day did Nestor earn during these five days, rounded to the nearest dollar?
$_____84_____

$85.63 + $79.66 + $75.65 + $89.28 + $90.58 = $420.80 total earnings for 5 days
$420.80 ÷ 5 = $84.16, or $84 average daily earnings, rounded to nearest dollar

4. Pauline Morse has worked as a loan officer in a bank for the past three years. During her first year, she earned $23,400. Her earnings increased to $26,200 the second year, and to $29,600 the third year. What were her average annual earnings for the three years she worked for the bank? $_____26,400_____

$23,400 + $26,200 + $29,600 = $79,200 total earnings for 3 years
$79,200 ÷ 3 = $26,400 average earnings per year

Exercise 2.   (Finding Weighted Averages)

1. Paul Bailey earns extra money by refinishing wood floors. His charge is based on the size and condition of the floor. Last month, he refinished 6 floors for $80 each, 2 floors for $68 each, and 1 floor for $122. What average amount per floor did he earn for the month? $_____82_____

6 × $80 = $480
2 × $68 = 136
1 × $122 = 122
9            $738 total earnings

$738 ÷ 9 = $82 average amount per floor

2. After working at her new job, Rhonda Bloch found that she had earned the following monthly salaries: $1,600 monthly for the first 3 months; $1,720 monthly for the following 2 months; $1,840 for the sixth month. What average amount per month did Rhonda earn during these six months? $_____1,680_____

$3 \times \$1,600 = \$ 4,800$
$2 \times \ \ 1,720 = \ \ \ \ 3,440$
$\underline{1} \times \ \ 1,840 = \ \ \underline{\ \ 1,840}$
$6 \qquad\qquad \$10,080$ total earnings for 6 months

$\$10,080 \div 6 = \$1,680$ average monthly earnings

3. Four employees of the Micro-Line Company earn $14 an hour. Another 6 employees earn $12 an hour, while 4 other are paid $10 an hour. What is the average pay per hour earned by the employees? $_____12_____

$4 \times \$14 = \ \ \ \ \$ 56$
$6 \times \ \ 12 = \ \ \ \ \ \ 72$
$\underline{4} \times \ \ 10 = \ \ \ \ \ \underline{\ 40}$
$14 \qquad\qquad \$168$ total hourly pay, all employees

$\$168 \div 14 = \$12$ average hourly pay

Exercise 3. (Finding an unknown item in a series)

1. By working for 4 weeks at your part-time job you earned these amounts: $60, $72, $53, $47. What pay will you have to earn in the fifth week to average $56 a week for five weeks of work? $_____48_____

$5 \times \$56 = \$280$ total earnings wanted for 5 weeks of work
$\$60 + \$72 + \$53 + \$47 = \$232$ total earnings for 4 weeks of work
$\$280 - \$232 = \$48$ fifth week earnings

2. The average weekly pay of five employees of the Morris Electrical Supply Company is $473. The weekly pay of four of the employees is $385, $530, $526, $495. What is the weekly pay of the other employee?
$_____429_____

$5 \times \$473 = \$2,365$ total weekly pay of 5 employees
$\$385 + \$530 + \$526 + \$495 = \$1,936$ known weekly pay for 4 employees
$\$2,365 - \$1,936 = \$429$ weekly pay of the fifth employee

3. On Monday, five employees of the Wexel Cartage Company earned an average gross pay of $108 for the day. Four of the employees earned these amounts on that day: $116, $102, $119, $86. How much did the fifth employee earn on Monday? $_____117_____

$5 \times \$108 = \$540$ total pay for 5 employees
$\$116 + \$102 + \$119 + \$86 = \$423$ known pay of 4 employees
$\$540 - \$423 = \$117$ pay of fifth employee

TERM TICKLER

Directions: Complete the crossword puzzle below.

Across

1. The reverse of mulitiplication
6. A single number used to represent a group of numbers
7. A number with digits dropped from the right
8. Find approximate answer
9. The result of multiplication
12. A short way to add two or more equal numbers
13. A wage rate based on amounts produced
15. Sum of numbers divided by the number of items is a (n) _____ average
17. An item made or produced by a worker
18. Shows how many times the divisor is included in the dividend

Down

1. Any number that is to be divided
2. A fixed amount of pay for working a week or a month is a(n) _____ rate
3. A rate of pay earned by the hour
4. The total of all pay earned is called the _____ pay
5. Each of the numbers in multiplication
10. A number left over in division
11. A number that shows the size or number of groups into which a dividend is to be split
14. A person or company that employs workers
16. A person who works for someone else

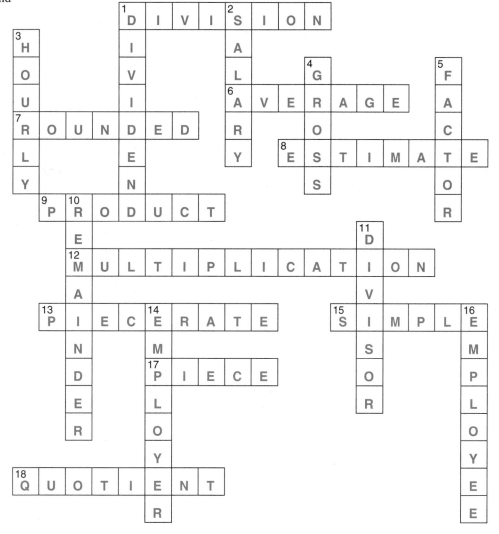

INTEGRATED PROJECT 2

Directions: Read through the entire project before you begin doing any work.

Introduction: The Sten-Med Company builds custom-made medical equipment. Department 15 of the company builds pumps and has 7 workers. The 4 workers who make the pumps are paid on a piece-rate basis. They work as a team and are paid based on the total number of pumps built by the work team; however, they may be paid a different piece rate because their skills differ. The 3 hourly rate workers test the pumps, keep track of supplies, and deliver or ship the pumps to other departments or companies. They also work for other departments of the Sten-Med Company.

The Pay Code Chart shown below lists pay codes and rates. The 7 workers are paid the rate per hour worked or unit produced that corresponds to their pay code. For example, a worker with a "C" pay code earns $8.30 an hour.

A Daily Hours Worked chart shows the hours worked last week by each hourly rate employee. A Daily Unit Production Chart shows the number of pumps produced each day by the work team. Notice that the work team builds different types of pumps during the week.

STEN-MED PRODUCTS PAY CODE CHART

Hourly Rate Employees

Pay Code	Hourly Rate
A	$7.20
B	$7.65
C	$8.30
D	$8.85
E	$9.40

Piece Rate Employees

Pay Code	Rate per Unit
XA	$4.00
XB	$4.80
XC	$5.70
XD	$6.50
XE	$7.00

DAILY HOURS WORKED
Week Ending, March 27, 19--

Employee	Hours Worked					Total Hours Worked for Week
	M	T	W	T	F	
Espinoza, R.	2	6	2	7	8	25
Travis, M.	8	8	8	8	8	40
Zino, G.	0	8	0	7	4	19

DAILY UNIT PRODUCTION
Week Ending, March 27, 19--

Work Team, Department ___15___

Pump Type	Units Produced					Total
	M	T	W	T	F	
11	10	14	0	8	2	34
23	0	2	18	0	19	39
27	12	0	1	13	0	26
Total Weekly Production						99

Step One:

1. Complete the "Daily Hours Worked" chart by adding the hours worked during the week by each employee. Write the sum in the "Total Hours" column.

2. Find the total number of pumps produced for the week. Do this by adding the number of units produced each day for each type of pump. Write the sums in the "Total" column. Add the numbers in the "Total" column and enter their sum on the "Total Weekly Production" line.

Step Two:

Complete the following Time/Job Report forms for each employee.

1. For each piece rate worker, write the total weekly production for the work team on the units produced line.

2. For each hourly rate worker, write the total hours worked for the week from the "Daily Hours Worked" chart on the hours worked line.

3. Look up each employee's pay code in the "Pay Code Chart" and write the dollar amount shown on the pay rate line.

4. Now find the weekly pay for each worker by multiplying the pay rate by either the number of hours worked or by the number of units produced. Write the result on the weekly gross line.

Time/Job Report

Week Ending: _____ 03-27-19-- _____

Employee: Bergman, Lana

Badge No.: __6-115__ Pay Code: __XA__

Pay Rate: _____ $4 _____

Units Produced: _____ 99 _____

Weekly Gross: _____ $396 _____

Time/Job Report

Week Ending: _____ 03-27-19-- _____

Employee: Carrela, Vito

Badge No.: __6-107__ Pay Code: __XB__

Pay Rate: _____ $4.80 _____

Units Produced: _____ 99 _____

Weekly Gross: _____ $475.20 _____

Time/Job Report

Week Ending: _____ 03-27-19-- _____

Employee: Coles, Mildred

Badge No.: __6-110__ Pay Code: __XE__

Pay Rate: _____ $7 _____

Units Produced: _____ 99 _____

Weekly Gross: _____ $693 _____

Time/Job Report

Week Ending: _____ 03-27-19-- _____

Employee: Mosley, Tom

Badge No.: __6-102__ Pay Code: __XC__

Pay Rate: _____ $5.70 _____

Units Produced: _____ 99 _____

Weekly Gross: _____ $564.30 _____

Time/Job Report
Week Ending: _____ 03-27-19-- _____
Employee: Espinoza, Roberto
Badge No.: __6-120__ Pay Code: ___A___
Pay Rate: _____ $7.20 _____
Units Produced: _____ 25 _____
Weekly Gross: _____ $180 _____

Time/Job Report
Week Ending: _____ 03-27-19-- _____
Employee: Travis, Matt
Badge No.: __6-130__ Pay Code: ___D___
Pay Rate: _____ $8.85 _____
Units Produced: _____ 40 _____
Weekly Gross: _____ $354 _____

Time/Job Report
Week Ending: _____ 03-27-19-- _____
Employee: Zino, Grace
Badge No.: __6-122__ Pay Code: ___C___
Pay Rate: _____ $8.30 _____
Units Produced: _____ 19 _____
Weekly Gross: _____ $157.70 _____

Step Three:

The Year-to-Date Earnings report below shows the total pay each employee in Department 15 has received for the current year, From January 1 through March 20. You are to update the Year-to-Date report.

1. For each employee, enter the weekly gross amount from the Time/Job Report into the Earnings This Week Column.

2. Find the New Year-to-Date amount for each employee by adding the amounts in the first two money columns of the Year-to-Date Earnings report. Write the amount in the New Year-to-Date column.

Year-to-Date Earnings, Department 15			
Employee	Earnings Year-to-Date	Earnings This Week	New Year-to-Date
Bergman, Lana	$4,388.00	$396.00	$4,784.00
Carrela, Vito	$5,318.40	$475.20	$5,793.60
Coles, Mildred	$7,756.00	$693.00	$8,449.00
Espinoza, Roberto	$2,217.60	$180.00	$2,397.60
Mosley, Tom	$5,985.00	$564.30	$6,549.30
Travis, Matt	$3,894.00	$354.00	$4,248.00
Zino, Grace	$1,917.30	$157.70	$2,075.00

REGULAR AND OVERTIME PAY

LESSON 3-1   MULTIPLYING, SIMPLIFYING, AND DIVIDING FRACTIONS

Exercise 1.   (Multiplying a fraction by a fraction)

Find each product:

1. $\dfrac{1}{4} \times \dfrac{3}{8} = $ ___$\frac{3}{32}$___

2. $\dfrac{2}{3} \times \dfrac{5}{7} = $ ___$\frac{10}{21}$___

3. $\dfrac{5}{6} \times \dfrac{7}{8} = $ ___$\frac{35}{48}$___

4. $\dfrac{4}{7} \times \dfrac{5}{9} = $ ___$\frac{20}{63}$___

5. $\dfrac{7}{8} \times \dfrac{3}{4} = $ ___$\frac{21}{32}$___

6. $\dfrac{2}{9} \times \dfrac{4}{5} = $ ___$\frac{8}{45}$___

7. $\dfrac{7}{9}$ of $\dfrac{2}{3} = $ ___$\frac{14}{27}$___

8. $\dfrac{5}{8}$ of $\dfrac{1}{4} = $ ___$\frac{5}{32}$___

9. $\dfrac{1}{2}$ of $\dfrac{3}{4} = $ ___$\frac{3}{8}$___

10. $\dfrac{3}{4} \times \dfrac{1}{2} \times \dfrac{3}{5} = $ ___$\frac{9}{40}$___

11. $\dfrac{1}{3} \times \dfrac{5}{8} \times \dfrac{1}{2} = $ ___$\frac{5}{48}$___

12. $\dfrac{1}{2} \times \dfrac{3}{4} \times \dfrac{5}{8} = $ ___$\frac{15}{64}$___

Exercise 2.   (Finding an equivalent fraction)

1. What equivalent fraction do you get by multiplying both the numerator and denominator of the fraction by 3, 6, and 10?

a. $\dfrac{1}{3}$ ___$\frac{3}{9}$___ , ___$\frac{6}{18}$___ , ___$\frac{10}{30}$___

b. $\dfrac{3}{4}$ ___$\frac{9}{12}$___ , ___$\frac{18}{24}$___ , ___$\frac{30}{40}$___

c. $\dfrac{6}{5}$ ___$\frac{18}{15}$___ , ___$\frac{36}{30}$___ , ___$\frac{60}{50}$___

2. What equivalent fraction do you get by dividing the numerator and the denominator of the fraction by the number shown?

a. $\dfrac{5}{10}$ by 5 ___$\frac{1}{2}$___

b. $\dfrac{6}{8}$ by 2 ___$\frac{3}{4}$___

c. $\dfrac{12}{30}$ by 6 ___$\frac{2}{5}$___

d. $\dfrac{27}{72}$ by 9 ___$\frac{3}{8}$___

Exercise 3.   (Simplifying fractions)

Simplify each fraction:

1. $\frac{10}{12} = \underline{\frac{5}{6}}$ 4. $\frac{21}{30} = \underline{\frac{7}{10}}$ 7. $\frac{9}{15} = \underline{\frac{3}{5}}$ 10. $\frac{14}{32} = \underline{\frac{7}{16}}$

2. $\frac{6}{9} = \underline{\frac{2}{3}}$ 5. $\frac{15}{35} = \underline{\frac{3}{7}}$ 8. $\frac{28}{40} = \underline{\frac{7}{10}}$ 11. $\frac{36}{45} = \underline{\frac{4}{5}}$

3. $\frac{12}{20} = \underline{\frac{3}{5}}$ 6. $\frac{24}{36} = \underline{\frac{2}{3}}$ 9. $\frac{12}{28} = \underline{\frac{3}{7}}$ 12. $\frac{30}{80} = \underline{\frac{3}{8}}$

Exercise 4.   (Simplifying the product of fractions)

Find the product in each. Simplify the product when necessary.

1. $\frac{4}{5} \times \frac{5}{16} = \underline{\frac{1}{4}}$ 3. $\frac{4}{5} \times \frac{45}{54} = \underline{\frac{2}{3}}$ 5. $\frac{7}{8} \times \frac{4}{9} \times \frac{3}{4} = \underline{\frac{7}{24}}$ 7. $\frac{5}{8} \times \frac{7}{15} \times \frac{4}{5} = \underline{\frac{7}{30}}$

2. $\frac{3}{4} \times \frac{8}{9} = \underline{\frac{2}{3}}$ 4. $\frac{15}{16} \times \frac{32}{35} = \underline{\frac{6}{7}}$ 6. $\frac{2}{3} \times \frac{3}{4} \times \frac{8}{9} = \underline{\frac{4}{9}}$ 8. $\frac{5}{6} \times \frac{12}{25} \times \frac{3}{4} = \underline{\frac{3}{10}}$

Exercise 5.   (Changing improper fractions to mixed numbers)

1. $\frac{12}{5} = \underline{2\frac{2}{5}}$ 6. $\frac{70}{30} = \underline{2\frac{1}{3}}$ 11. $\frac{172}{14} = \underline{12\frac{2}{7}}$

2. $\frac{19}{4} = \underline{4\frac{3}{4}}$ 7. $\frac{95}{8} = \underline{11\frac{7}{8}}$ 12. $\frac{328}{20} = \underline{16\frac{2}{5}}$

3. $\frac{60}{8} = \underline{7\frac{1}{2}}$ 8. $\frac{100}{15} = \underline{6\frac{2}{3}}$ 13. $\frac{525}{24} = \underline{21\frac{7}{8}}$

4. $\frac{34}{6} = \underline{5\frac{2}{3}}$ 9. $\frac{210}{25} = \underline{8\frac{2}{5}}$ 14. $\frac{390}{25} = \underline{15\frac{3}{5}}$

5. $\frac{111}{10} = \underline{11\frac{1}{10}}$ 10. $\frac{267}{12} = \underline{22\frac{1}{4}}$ 15. $\frac{348}{42} = \underline{8\frac{2}{7}}$

Exercise 6.

1. Marty Zirese bought $\frac{1}{2}$ of a bushel of apples. He used $\frac{2}{3}$ of the apples for baking. What part of a bushel did he use?

   _____ $\frac{1}{3}$ _____

   $\frac{1}{2} \times \frac{2}{3} = \frac{1}{3}$ bushel used

2. A gas tank holds 18 gallons of gasoline. To fill up the tank, Alice Gould bought 15 gallons of gasoline. (a) How much gasoline, as a fractional part of the whole tank, did Alice buy? _____ $\frac{5}{6}$ _____ (b) How much gasoline, as a fractional part of the whole tank, was in the tank before it was filled? _____ $\frac{1}{6}$ _____

   a. $\frac{15}{18} = \frac{5}{6}$ gasoline bought   b. $\frac{3}{18} = \frac{1}{6}$ gas in tank before filling

3. Of the total amount available to pay a bonus to the employees of the Macra Sound Company, Al's share is $\frac{1}{4}$ of the total amount. Irene's share is equal to $\frac{1}{2}$ of Al's share and Reginald's share is equal to $\frac{4}{5}$ of Al's share. Of the total bonus amount, Irene's fractional share was _____ $\frac{1}{8}$ _____ and Reginald's fractional share was _____ $\frac{1}{5}$ _____.

   a. $\frac{1}{4} \times \frac{1}{2} = \frac{1}{8}$ Irene's fractional share   b. $\frac{1}{4} \times \frac{4}{5} = \frac{1}{5}$ Reginald's fractional share

4. The local Parent-Teacher-Student Association had 500 members, 40 of whom were students. What fractional part of the total membership of the PTSA were students? _____ $\frac{2}{25}$ _____

   $\frac{40}{500} = \frac{2}{25}$ part of PTSA membership that are students

Exercise 7. (Multiplying a whole number or a decimal and a fraction)

1. $24 \times \frac{1}{3} = $ _____ 8 _____

2. $16 \times \frac{3}{4} = $ _____ 12 _____

3. $14 \times \frac{3}{7} = $ _____ 6 _____

4. $19 \times \frac{1}{4} = $ _____ $4\frac{3}{4}$ _____

5. $25 \times \frac{5}{9} = $ _____ $13\frac{8}{9}$ _____

6. $33 \times \frac{4}{5} = $ _____ $26\frac{2}{5}$ _____

7. $28 \times \frac{5}{8} = $ _____ $17\frac{1}{2}$ _____

8. $\frac{5}{6}$ of $72 = $ _____ 60 _____

9. $\frac{7}{8}$ of $26 = $ _____ $22\frac{3}{4}$ _____

10. $\frac{2}{7}$ of $\$42 = $ _____ $12 _____

11. $\$22.20 \times \frac{5}{12} = $ _____ $9.25 _____

12. $\$0.75 \times \frac{13}{15} = $ _____ $0.65 _____

LESSON 3-2   ADDING AND SUBTRACTING FRACTIONS

Exercise 1.

1. $\frac{2}{7} + \frac{3}{7} = $ ___$\frac{5}{7}$___

2. $\frac{5}{9} + \frac{2}{9} = $ ___$\frac{7}{9}$___

3. $\frac{7}{10} - \frac{4}{10} = $ ___$\frac{3}{10}$___

4. $\frac{6}{8} + \frac{9}{8} = $ ___$1\frac{7}{8}$___

5. $\frac{7}{12} + \frac{9}{12} = $ ___$1\frac{1}{3}$___

6. $\frac{7}{12} - \frac{5}{12} = $ ___$\frac{1}{6}$___

7. $\frac{21}{18} - \frac{9}{18} = $ ___$\frac{2}{3}$___

8. $\frac{11}{12} + \frac{9}{12} = $ ___$1\frac{2}{3}$___

9. $\frac{18}{16} - \frac{12}{16} = $ ___$\frac{3}{8}$___

10. $\frac{4}{20} + \frac{10}{20} + \frac{5}{20} = $ ___$\frac{19}{20}$___

11. $\frac{5}{16} + \frac{12}{16} + \frac{8}{16} = $ ___$1\frac{9}{16}$___

12. $\frac{14}{24} + \frac{18}{24} + \frac{20}{24} = $ ___$2\frac{1}{6}$___

Exercise 2.   (Raising a fraction to higher terms)

1. Change each fraction to a fraction with a denominator of 16:

   a. $\frac{1}{2} = $ ___$\frac{8}{16}$___   b. $\frac{3}{8} = $ ___$\frac{6}{16}$___   c. $\frac{3}{4} = $ ___$\frac{12}{16}$___   d. $\frac{5}{8} = $ ___$\frac{10}{16}$___

2. Change each fraction to a fraction with a denominator of 24:

   a. $\frac{3}{8} = $ ___$\frac{9}{24}$___   b. $\frac{2}{3} = $ ___$\frac{16}{24}$___   c. $\frac{3}{4} = $ ___$\frac{18}{24}$___   d. $\frac{5}{6} = $ ___$\frac{20}{24}$___

3. Change each fraction to a fraction with a denominator of 30:

   a. $\frac{1}{5} = $ ___$\frac{6}{30}$___   b. $\frac{3}{6} = $ ___$\frac{15}{30}$___   c. $\frac{8}{10} $ ___$\frac{24}{30}$___   d. $\frac{2}{3} = $ ___$\frac{20}{30}$___

Exercise 3.   (Adding and subtracting unlike fractions)

1. $\frac{1}{2} + \frac{3}{4} = $ ___$1\frac{1}{4}$___

2. $\frac{5}{6} - \frac{1}{12} = $ ___$\frac{3}{4}$___

3. $\frac{3}{4} + \frac{5}{8} = $ ___$1\frac{3}{8}$___

4. $\frac{8}{9} - \frac{2}{3} = $ ___$\frac{2}{9}$___

5. $\frac{11}{12} - \frac{5}{8} = $ ___$\frac{7}{24}$___

6. $\frac{5}{6} + \frac{3}{4} = $ ___$1\frac{7}{12}$___

7. $\frac{9}{10} - \frac{5}{6} = $ ___$\frac{1}{15}$___

8. $\frac{1}{2} + \frac{5}{6} + \frac{1}{3} = $ ___$1\frac{2}{3}$___

9. $\frac{1}{5} + \frac{1}{2} + \frac{7}{10} = $ ___$1\frac{2}{5}$___

10. $\frac{1}{4} + \frac{1}{2} + \frac{1}{3} = $ ___$1\frac{1}{12}$___

11. $\frac{3}{4} + \frac{1}{5} + \frac{1}{2} = $ ___$1\frac{9}{20}$___

12. $\frac{1}{4} + \frac{2}{5} + \frac{1}{8} = $ ___$\frac{31}{40}$___

Exercise 4.   (Writing reciprocals)

Write the reciprocal of each:

1. $\dfrac{7}{8}$ $\dfrac{8}{7}$ 3. $\dfrac{8}{3}$ $\dfrac{3}{8}$ 5. 15 $\dfrac{1}{15}$ 7. $\dfrac{6}{5}$ $\dfrac{5}{6}$ 9. 9 $\dfrac{1}{9}$

2. $\dfrac{9}{10}$ $\dfrac{10}{9}$ 4. 7 $\dfrac{1}{7}$ 6. 10 $\dfrac{1}{10}$ 8. $\dfrac{3}{8}$ $\dfrac{8}{3}$ 10. 123 $\dfrac{1}{123}$

Exercise 5.   (Dividing with fractions)

1. $12 \div \dfrac{1}{4} = $ 48 6. $\dfrac{4}{9} \div \dfrac{2}{3} = $ $\dfrac{2}{3}$ 11. $\dfrac{15}{16} \div 5 = $ $\dfrac{3}{16}$

2. $22 \div \dfrac{3}{8} = $ $58\frac{2}{3}$ 7. $\dfrac{7}{12} \div \dfrac{5}{8} = $ $\dfrac{14}{15}$ 12. $\dfrac{27}{32} \div 3 = $ $\dfrac{9}{32}$

3. $12 \div \dfrac{9}{16} = $ $21\frac{1}{3}$ 8. $\dfrac{9}{16} \div \dfrac{7}{12} = $ $\dfrac{27}{28}$ 13. $\dfrac{3}{8} \div 4 = $ $\dfrac{3}{32}$

4. $18 \div \dfrac{16}{25} = $ $28\frac{1}{8}$ 9. $\dfrac{25}{42} \div \dfrac{5}{12} = $ $1\frac{3}{7}$ 14. $\dfrac{4}{5} \div 3 = $ $\dfrac{4}{15}$

5. $\dfrac{5}{8} \div \dfrac{3}{7} = $ $1\frac{11}{24}$ 10. $\dfrac{8}{9} \div 4 = $ $\dfrac{2}{9}$ 15. $\dfrac{3}{4} \div 6 = $ $\dfrac{1}{8}$

Exercise 6.   (Dividing a fraction by a fraction)

1. $\dfrac{1}{3} \div \dfrac{1}{3} = $ 1 6. $\dfrac{4}{15} \div \dfrac{1}{3} = $ $\dfrac{4}{5}$ 11. $\dfrac{6}{15} \div \dfrac{1}{3} = $ $1\frac{1}{5}$

2. $\dfrac{2}{5} \div \dfrac{3}{5} = $ $\dfrac{2}{3}$ 7. $\dfrac{7}{10} \div \dfrac{2}{5} = $ $1\frac{3}{4}$ 12. $\dfrac{11}{12} \div \dfrac{2}{3} = $ $1\frac{3}{8}$

3. $\dfrac{5}{8} \div \dfrac{3}{8} = $ $1\frac{2}{3}$ 8. $\dfrac{3}{4} \div \dfrac{5}{16} = $ $2\frac{2}{5}$ 13. $\dfrac{18}{25} \div \dfrac{2}{5} = $ $1\frac{4}{5}$

4. $\dfrac{1}{2} \div \dfrac{1}{4} = $ 2 9. $\dfrac{2}{3} \div \dfrac{5}{6} = $ $\dfrac{4}{5}$ 14. $\dfrac{13}{39} \div \dfrac{1}{13} = $ $4\frac{1}{3}$

5. $\dfrac{3}{4} \div \dfrac{1}{2} = $ $1\frac{1}{2}$ 10. $\dfrac{5}{6} \div \dfrac{7}{12} = $ $1\frac{3}{7}$ 15. $\dfrac{18}{24} \div \dfrac{5}{6} = $ $\dfrac{9}{10}$

Exercise 7.

1. On Sunday, a shoe store had 264 customers. On Monday, the same store had only $\frac{7}{8}$ of the customers it had on Sunday. How many customers were in the store on Monday? _____231_____

   $\frac{7}{8} \times 264 = 231$ customers on Monday

2. A homeowner spent $54 for 3 gallons of paint. A few days later, she bought another 3 gallons of the same paint on sale for $\frac{5}{6}$ of the cost of the original 3 gallons. How much did the homeowner pay for the last 3 gallons she bought? _____$45_____

   $\frac{5}{6} \times \$54 = \$45$ amount paid for last 3 gallons bought

3. A printing job took $\frac{1}{2}$ of a certain type of paper. Another job took $\frac{1}{6}$ carton of the same paper. The total amount of paper from the carton used for both jobs was _____$\frac{2}{3}$_____ carton.

   $\frac{1}{2} + \frac{1}{6} = \frac{3}{6} + \frac{1}{6} = \frac{4}{6}$, or $\frac{2}{3}$ carton

4. Letitia Fontell bought a box of lettuce (24 heads to the box). She used $\frac{1}{2}$ of the box and threw away $\frac{1}{6}$ of the box which had spoiled. How many heads of lettuce did she have left? _____8_____

   $24 \times \frac{1}{2} = 12$ heads used

   $24 \times \frac{1}{6} = 4$ heads spoiled

   $24 - (12 + 4) = 8$ heads left

LESSON 3-3   RATIO AND PROPORTION

Exercise 1.

Show all ratios as fractions. Simplify the ratio when you are asked to do so.

1. In a class of 34 students, 19 are girls and 15 are boys.

    a. The ratio of girls to boys is ___$\frac{19}{15}$___.   c. The ratio of girls to the total is ___$\frac{19}{34}$___.

    b. The ratio of boys to girls is ___$\frac{15}{19}$___.   d. The ratio of boys to the total is ___$\frac{15}{34}$___.

2. The ratio of 71¢ to $1.53 is ___$\frac{71}{153}$___. (Change the dollars to cents.)

3. The ratio of 7 inches to 2 feet is ___$\frac{7}{24}$___. (Change the feet to inches.)

4. The ratio of 18 ounces to 4 pounds in lowest terms is ___$\frac{9}{32}$___. (Change the pounds to ounces.)

5. As a fraction in lowest terms, the ratio of

    a. 27 to 63 is ___$\frac{3}{7}$___.   c. 5 yards to 5 feet is ___$\frac{3}{1}$___.

    b. 12 inches to 30 inches is ___$\frac{2}{5}$___.   d. 10¢ to $1 is ___$\frac{1}{10}$___.

6. A tennis team won 22 matches and lost 7. The ratio of matches won to matches played is ___$\frac{22}{29}$___.

    22 + 7 = 29 matches played $\frac{22}{29}$ = ratio of matches won to matches played

7. A prize of $20,000 is to be shared by two winners of a contest in the ratio of 6 to 4. The larger share is worth $___12,000___. The smaller share is worth $___8,000___.

    $\frac{3}{5}$ × $20,000 = $12,000 larger share $\frac{2}{5}$ × $20,000 = $8,000 smaller share

8. Isabel Gutierrez, an attorney, and Scott Parcka, an accountant, share an office and agree to pay expenses in the ratio of 5 to 3 with Isabel paying the larger amount. If the office expenses last month were $2,680, Isabel would pay $___1,675___ and Scott would pay $___1,005___.

    $\frac{5}{8}$ × $2,680 = $1,675 Isabel's share $\frac{3}{8}$ × $2,680 = $1,005 Scott's share

9. The ratio of small businesses to large businesses in a city is 75 to 5. If there are 560 businesses in the city, how many are large? ___35___ How many are small? ___525___

    $\frac{5}{80}$ = $\frac{1}{16}$ × 560 = 35 large businesses $\frac{75}{80}$ = $\frac{15}{16}$ × 560 = 525 small businesses

10. Two farmers, Hall and Driscoe, together own 570 acres of land in the ratio of 9 to 10, with Hall owning the smaller share. Hall owns ___270___ acres and Driscoe owns ___300___ acres.

    $\frac{9}{19}$ × 570 = 270 acres, Hall's share $\frac{10}{19}$ × 570 = 300 acres, Driscoe's share

Exercise 2.

1. In 5 hours a truck driver drove 225 miles. At the same rate, the driver could drive _____315_____ miles in 7 hours.

$\frac{N}{225} = \frac{7}{5}$; $5 \times N = 1{,}575$; $N = 1{,}575 \div 5$; $N = 315$ miles

2. At the rate of 10 oranges for $1.50, you can buy _____16_____ oranges for $2.40.

$\frac{N}{10} = \frac{\$2.40}{\$1.50}$; $\$1.50 \times N = \$24$; $N = \$24 \div \$1.50$; $N = 16$ oranges

3. An employee earns $52.50 for 7 hours of work. At the same rate of pay, how much would the employee be paid for 40 hours of work? _____$300_____

$\frac{7}{40} = \frac{\$52.50}{N}$; $7 \times N = \$2{,}100$; $\$2{,}100 \div 7 = \$300$

4. A piece rate worker makes 88 usable parts and 4 unusable parts in one day. At the same rate, the worker would make _____28_____ unusable parts for every 616 usable parts.

$\frac{N}{4} = \frac{616}{88}$; $N \times 88 = 2{,}464$; $N = 2{,}464 \div 88$; $N = 28$ unusable parts

5. A pleasure boat uses $\frac{3}{4}$ gallons of gasoline every 3 miles. At the same rate, how many gallons of gasoline would be used in a 24-mile trip? _____6_____

$\frac{N}{\frac{3}{4}} = \frac{24}{3}$; $3 \times N = 18$; $N = 18 \div 3$; $N = 6$ gallons

6. An office clerk sorts 320 pieces of mail in $\frac{4}{5}$ of an hour. At the same rate, the clerk could sort _____3,200_____ pieces in 8 hours.

$\frac{N}{320} = \frac{8}{\frac{4}{5}}$; $\frac{4}{5} \times N = 2{,}560$; $N = 2{,}560 \div \frac{4}{5}$; $N = 3{,}200$ pieces

LESSON 3-4   REGULAR AND OVERTIME PAY

Exercise 1.

1. Elroy Durell is paid $8.40 an hour for regular time work. He is paid time and half for any hours worked above 40 hours from Monday through Friday. Elroy is also paid double time for weekend work. Elroy's time and a half pay rate is $_____12.60_____ an hour, and his double time pay rate is $_____16.80_____ an hour.

    $1\frac{1}{2} \times \$8.40 = \$12.60$ time and a half rate

    $2 \times \$8.40 = \$16.80$ double time rate

2. Alberta Niswam worked 9 hours at time and a half pay. Her regular pay rate was $14.14 an hour. Alberta's total overtime pay was $_____190.89_____.

    $1\frac{1}{2} \times \$14.14 = \$21.21$ time and a half rate

    $9 \times \$21.21 = \$190.89$ overtime pay

3. On a weekend, Herbert Dupree worked 15 hours at double time pay. His regular pay rate was $10.78. Herbert's overtime pay for the weekend totaled $_____323.40_____.

    $2 \times \$10.78 = \$21.56$ double time pay rate

    $15 \times \$21.56 = \$323.40$ total overtime pay

4. Last week, Ada McFaul earned $320 for regular time work by working 40 regular time hours at $8 an hour. For the week, she was also paid time a half pay for 9 overtime hours and double time pay for another $4\frac{1}{2}$ hours. Her total earnings for the week were $_____500_____.

    $1\frac{1}{2} \times \$8 = \$12$ time and a half pay rate

    $2 \times \$8 = \$16$ double time pay rate

    $(9 \times \$12) + (4\frac{1}{2} \times \$16) + \$320 = \$500$ total earnings for week

5. Sean Weggert's regular time pay rate is $8.73 an hour. Last week he was paid for 37 regular time hours at his regular rate and for 5 overtime hours at a time and a half overtime rate. Sean's gross pay for the week was $_____388.49_____.

    $1\frac{1}{2} \times \$8.73 = \$13.095$ time and a half rate

    $37 \times \$8.73 = \$323.01$ regular time pay

    $5 \times \$13.095 = \$65.475$, or $65.48 overtime pay

    $\$323.01 + \$65.48 = \$388.49$ gross pay

6. Anne Lavelle worked 60 hours last week. Of those hours, 40 hours were paid at the regular time rate of $9.50 an hour, 18 hours at the time and a half rate, and 2 hours at the double time rate. Anne's gross pay for the week was $_____674.50_____.

    $1\frac{1}{2} \times \$9.50 = \$14.25$ time and a half rate

    $2 \times \$9.50 = \$19$ double time rate

    $(40 \times \$9.50) + (18 \times \$14.25) + (2 \times \$19) = \$674.50$ gross pay

Exercise 2.

1. Roger Swartz works for Milrad Carpet Center. He is paid weekly on the basis of a 40-hour week at the rate of $8.98 an hour with time and a half for overtime. During one week he works 49 hours. His total earnings for the week amount to $_____480.43_____.

   40 × $8.98 = $359.20 regular time pay $1\frac{1}{2}$ × $8.98 = $13.47 time and a half rate
   9 × $13.47 = __121.23__ overtime pay
            $480.43 total earnings

2. The Robotek factory usually works 8 hours a day, Monday through Friday. Workers get time and a half for work over 8 hours per day. Olivia Trattner works for Robotek and is paid a regular hourly rate of $9.36. One week she worked these hours: Monday, 7; Tuesday, $8\frac{1}{2}$; Wednesday, 9; Thursday, 10; Friday, 9. During the week Olivia worked (a) _____39_____ hours regular time, and (b) _____$4\frac{1}{2}$_____ hours overtime. (c) Her total earnings for the week were $_____428.22_____.

   a. 7 + 8 + 8 + 8 + 8 = 39 hours regular time   c. $1\frac{1}{2}$ × $9.36 = $14.04 time and a half rate
   b. $\frac{1}{2}$ + 1 + 2 + 1 = $4\frac{1}{2}$ hours overtime   39 × $9.36 = $365.04 regular time pay
                                                            $4\frac{1}{2}$ × $14.04 = __63.18__ overtime pay
                                                                    $428.22 total earnings

3. Sam LaRosa is paid every two weeks. His pay is based on a 40-hour week at a regular pay rate of $8.71 an hour with time and a half for overtime. During the first week of a new pay period, Sam worked 46 hours. In the second week of the pay period, he worked 43 hours. Sam's total gross pay for these two weeks of work is $_____814.39_____.

   $1\frac{1}{2}$ × $8.71 = $13.065 time and a half rate
   Week 1: (40 × $8.71) + (6 × $13.065) = $426.79 gross pay for week
   Week 2: (40 × $8.71) + (3 × $13.065) = __387.60__ gross pay for week
                                        $814.39 total pay for two weeks

4. A part of the payroll record of the Pantel Glass Company is shown below. Overtime is paid when more than 8 hours are worked in a day. Time and a half is paid for overtime. You are to figure these items for each employee and record them in the payroll record: (a) total regular time hours, (b) total overtime hours, (c) total earnings.

PAYROLL RECORD

For Week Ending   July 18, 19—

No.	Name	M	T	W	T	F	Pay Rate	Regular	Overtime	Total Earnings
		Time Record						Total Hours		
1	Jessie Cobb	9	6	8	7	5	$8.56	34	1	$303.88
2	Barbara Lum	6	9	7	9	10	9.14	37	4	$393.02
3	Nedra Trell	7	$6\frac{1}{2}$	9	5	9	9.25	$34\frac{1}{2}$	2	$346.88
4	Harlan Koloff	8	5	9	$9\frac{1}{2}$	10	8.84	37	$4\frac{1}{2}$	$386.75

Exercise 3.

Marge Nicole and Juan Cintron work for a wholesale supply company. At the company, time is figured in units of a quarter hour (15 minutes). All employees who arrive more than 3 minutes late or leave more than 3 minutes early are penalized by losing credit for 15 minutes of work.

The time cards of Marge Nicole and Juan Cintron are shown below. Both work in the telephone sales office. Their regular work day is from 8 A.M. to 12 noon, and from 1 P.M. to 5 P.M. All time worked past 8 hours per day is overtime.

First, figure and record the hours that Marge and Juan worked each day. Then complete the bottom of the time card for both Marge and Juan by showing (a) the regular, overtime, and total hours worked; (b) the regular time pay, overtime pay, and total gross pay.

Dept. _16_   **Badge No.** _212_

Employee: *Marge Nicole*

Week Ending *January 14, 19--*

Morning		Afternoon		Evening		Hours Worked	
In	Out	In	Out	In	Out	Reg.	Over.
7⁵³	12⁰⁴	12⁵⁸	5⁰³			8	
7⁵⁸	12⁰²	1⁰⁰	5⁰⁶			8	
7⁵⁷	12⁰⁵	12⁵⁹	5⁰¹			8	
7⁵⁵	12⁰¹	12⁵⁵	5⁰⁴			8	
7⁵⁹	12⁰²	12⁵⁷	5⁰⁰	5³⁰	7³⁰	8	2

	Hours	Rate	Gross Pay
Regular	40	9.70	388.00
Overtime	2	14.55	29.10
Total	42	---	417.10

Dept. _16_   **Badge No.** _371_

Employee: *Juan Cintron*

Week Ending *January 14, 19--*

Morning		Afternoon		Evening		Hours Worked	
In	Out	In	Out	In	Out	Reg.	Over.
7⁵⁶	12⁰¹	12⁵⁵	5⁰³			8	
7⁵⁸	12⁰²	12⁵⁹	5⁰¹			8	
8⁰⁸	12⁰⁴	12⁵⁸	5⁰²			7$\frac{3}{4}$	
7⁵⁵	12⁰¹	1³⁰	5⁰⁰			7$\frac{1}{2}$	
7⁵⁴	12⁰⁰	12⁵⁷	5⁰¹	5⁵⁹	9⁰⁰	8	3

	Hours	Rate	Gross Pay
Regular	39$\frac{1}{4}$	9.40	368.95
Overtime	3	14.10	42.30
Total	42$\frac{1}{4}$	---	411.25

Exercise 4.

Cassandra Kubik and Kenneth Reiner also work at the wholesale supply company. Their regular working hours are from 6 A.M. to 10 A.M., and from 10:45 A.M. to 2:45 P.M. Their time cards for the week ending January 14 are shown below.

First, figure and record the hours they worked each day. Then complete the bottom of the time card by showing (a) the regular, overtime, and total hours worked; (b) the regular time pay, overtime pay, and total gross pay.

Card 1

Dept. __16__   Badge No. __231__

Employee: *Cassandra Kubik*

Week Ending *January 14, 19--*

Morning		Afternoon		Evening		Hours Worked	
In	Out	In	Out	In	Out	Reg.	Over.
6^{00}	10^{00}	10^{45}	2^{45}	3^{00}	5^{17}	8	$2\frac{1}{4}$
5^{58}	10^{02}	10^{43}	2^{47}			8	
5^{52}	9^{59}	11^{14}	2^{50}			$7\frac{1}{2}$	
5^{59}	10^{00}	10^{43}	2^{43}	2^{45}	4^{31}	8	$1\frac{3}{4}$
6^{01}	10^{01}	10^{45}	2^{16}			$7\frac{1}{2}$	

	Hours	Rate	Gross Pay
Regular	39	10.50	409.50
Overtime	4	15.75	63.00
Total	43	---	472.50

Card 2

Dept. __16__   Badge No. __406__

Employee: *Kenneth Reiner*

Week Ending *January 14, 19--*

Morning		Afternoon		Evening		Hours Worked	
In	Out	In	Out	In	Out	Reg.	Over.
6^{00}	10^{00}	10^{45}	2^{46}	3^{00}	5^{35}	8	$2\frac{1}{2}$
5^{57}	10^{01}	10^{44}	2^{45}			8	
5^{55}	9^{58}	10^{42}	2^{51}	3^{00}	4^{33}	8	$1\frac{1}{2}$
6^{02}	10^{05}	10^{48}	2^{46}			8	
6^{28}	10^{06}	10^{45}	2^{43}			$7\frac{1}{2}$	

	Hours	Rate	Gross Pay
Regular	$39\frac{1}{2}$	10.50	406.85
Overtime	4	15.45	61.80
Total	$43\frac{1}{2}$	---	468.65

Exercise 5.

1. During October, William Korth worked 160 regular time hours at $9.28 an hour and 18 overtime hours at $13.92 an hour. What was William's gross pay for October? $__1,735.36__

    $160 \times \$9.28 = \$1,484.80$ regular time pay
    $18 \times \$13.92 = \underline{\quad 250.56 \quad}$ overtime pay
    $\$1,735.36$ gross pay for October

2. Last year, Ida Zolen worked 2,000 hours at regular time pay of $8.20 an hour. She also worked 75 hours of overtime at $12.30 an hour. What was Ida's gross pay last year? $__17,322.50__

    $2,000 \times \$8.20 = \$16,400.00$ regular time pay
    $75 \times \$12.30 = \underline{\quad 922.50 \quad}$ overtime pay
    $\$17,322.50$ gross pay for year

LESSON 3-5   MIXED NUMBERS

Exercise 1.   (Multiplying a whole number and a mixed number)

Multiply:

1.	36	3.	48	5.	36	7.	$15\frac{1}{8}$	9.	$14\frac{3}{4}$
	$15\frac{1}{3}$		$12\frac{5}{6}$		$17\frac{2}{3}$		13		11
	552		616		636		$196\frac{5}{8}$		$162\frac{1}{4}$

2.	$24\frac{3}{5}$	4.	$13\frac{3}{8}$	6.	20	8.	16	10.	15
	25		24		$7\frac{1}{3}$		$12\frac{2}{3}$		$13\frac{5}{8}$
	615		321		$146\frac{2}{3}$		$202\frac{2}{3}$		$204\frac{3}{8}$

Exercise 2.   (Adding mixed numbers)

Add:

1.	$7\frac{2}{3}$	2.	$9\frac{5}{8}$	3.	$19\frac{5}{6}$	4.	$10\frac{1}{7}$	5.	$26\frac{7}{12}$
	$4\frac{1}{5}$		$6\frac{1}{2}$		$5\frac{2}{3}$		$12\frac{3}{4}$		$84\frac{7}{16}$
	$11\frac{13}{15}$		$16\frac{1}{8}$		$25\frac{1}{2}$		$22\frac{25}{28}$		$111\frac{1}{48}$

6.	$12\frac{7}{8}$	7.	$8\frac{3}{4}$	8.	$14\frac{1}{4}$	9.	$8\frac{5}{6}$	10.	$9\frac{5}{6}$
	$9\frac{3}{4}$		$10\frac{2}{3}$		$11\frac{5}{6}$		$5\frac{1}{4}$		$13\frac{2}{3}$
	$17\frac{5}{8}$		$12\frac{5}{6}$		$13\frac{2}{3}$		$12\frac{7}{8}$		$10\frac{4}{9}$
	$40\frac{1}{4}$		$32\frac{1}{4}$		$39\frac{3}{4}$		$26\frac{23}{24}$		$33\frac{17}{18}$

Exercise 3.   (Subtracting mixed numbers)

Subtract:

1.	$34\frac{2}{7}$	2.	43	3.	121	4.	$15\frac{1}{4}$	5.	$28\frac{3}{8}$	6.	$41\frac{1}{6}$
	27		$27\frac{5}{8}$		$74\frac{5}{6}$		$6\frac{9}{16}$		$10\frac{3}{4}$		$16\frac{7}{8}$
	$7\frac{2}{7}$		$15\frac{3}{8}$		$46\frac{1}{6}$		$8\frac{11}{16}$		$17\frac{5}{8}$		$24\frac{7}{24}$

Exercise 4.   (Changing mixed numbers to improper fractions)

Change each mixed number to an improper fraction:

1. $2\frac{1}{8} = \underline{\quad \frac{17}{8} \quad}$

4. $12\frac{3}{10} = \underline{\quad \frac{123}{10} \quad}$

7. $23\frac{5}{6} = \underline{\quad \frac{143}{6} \quad}$

9. $32\frac{8}{9} = \underline{\quad \frac{296}{9} \quad}$

2. $4\frac{2}{5} = \underline{\quad \frac{22}{5} \quad}$

5. $16\frac{1}{6} = \underline{\quad \frac{97}{6} \quad}$

8. $18\frac{7}{8} = \underline{\quad \frac{151}{8} \quad}$

10. $8\frac{11}{12} = \underline{\quad \frac{107}{12} \quad}$

3. $6\frac{2}{3} = \underline{\quad \frac{20}{3} \quad}$

6. $42\frac{3}{4} = \underline{\quad \frac{171}{4} \quad}$

Exercise 5.   (Multiplying mixed numbers by mixed numbers)

Multiply each by changing the mixed numbers to improper fractions:

1. $7\frac{1}{2} \times 3\frac{2}{3} = \underline{\quad 27\frac{1}{2} \quad}$

4. $1\frac{3}{5} \times 3\frac{1}{8} = \underline{\quad 5 \quad}$

7. $14\frac{2}{3} \times 7\frac{1}{2} = \underline{\quad 110 \quad}$

2. $5\frac{1}{3} \times 3\frac{3}{4} = \underline{\quad 20 \quad}$

5. $15\frac{5}{6} \times 7\frac{1}{2} = \underline{\quad 118\frac{3}{4} \quad}$

8. $15\frac{3}{4} \times 20\frac{2}{3} = \underline{\quad 325\frac{1}{2} \quad}$

3. $2\frac{5}{6} \times 2\frac{1}{2} = \underline{\quad 7\frac{1}{12} \quad}$

6. $4\frac{3}{8} \times 16\frac{2}{5} = \underline{\quad 71\frac{3}{4} \quad}$

Exercise 6.   (Dividing with mixed numbers)

1. $18 \div 8\frac{1}{3} = \underline{\quad 2\frac{4}{25} \quad}$

5. $9\frac{3}{5} \div 64 = \underline{\quad \frac{3}{20} \quad}$

9. $28\frac{7}{8} \div 5\frac{1}{2} = \underline{\quad 5\frac{1}{4} \quad}$

2. $16\frac{3}{4} \div 5 = \underline{\quad 3\frac{7}{20} \quad}$

6. $25 \div 82\frac{1}{2} = \underline{\quad \frac{10}{33} \quad}$

10. $86\frac{1}{4} \div 1\frac{7}{8} = \underline{\quad 46 \quad}$

3. $55\frac{1}{2} \div 15 = \underline{\quad 3\frac{7}{10} \quad}$

7. $43\frac{1}{3} \div 12\frac{1}{2} = \underline{\quad 3\frac{7}{15} \quad}$

11. $5\frac{3}{5} \div 24\frac{1}{2} = \underline{\quad \frac{8}{35} \quad}$

4. $125 \div 7\frac{1}{2} = \underline{\quad 16\frac{2}{3} \quad}$

8. $76\frac{2}{3} \div 9\frac{1}{5} = \underline{\quad 8\frac{1}{3} \quad}$

12. $8\frac{1}{3} \div 32\frac{1}{7} = \underline{\quad \frac{7}{27} \quad}$

LESSON 3-6   FRACTIONAL RELATIONSHIPS

Exercise 1.   (Finding a part of a number)

Do each of these:

1. $\frac{3}{4}$ of 48 = ? ___36___
2. ? = $\frac{2}{5}$ of 25 ___10___
3. ? is $\frac{2}{3}$ as many as 60 ___40___
4. $\frac{5}{6} \times 54$ = ? ___45___

5. ? is $\frac{1}{7}$ as great as $63 ___$9___
6. ? is $\frac{7}{8}$ as much as $56 ___$49___
7. $\frac{3}{8}$ of $40 is ? ___$15___
8. $\frac{2}{9}$ of $108 is ? ___$24___

9. $80 $\times \frac{7}{10}$ = ? ___$56___
10. $\frac{5}{8}$ as much as $60 is ? ___$37.50___
11. $\frac{7}{12} \times 42 = ? ___$24.50___
12. $\frac{3}{16}$ of $96 = ? ___$18___

Exercise 2.   (Finding a number that is a part greater or smaller than another)

Do each of these:

1. ? is $\frac{1}{5}$ greater than 60 ___72___
2. $\frac{1}{6}$ more than 72 is ? ___84___
3. $\frac{5}{8}$ greater than 40 is ? ___65___
4. ? is $\frac{2}{3}$ less than 45 ___15___
5. 42 less $\frac{1}{6}$ of itself is ? ___35___

6. $40 plus $\frac{7}{8}$ of itself is ? ___$75___
7. $\frac{5}{6}$ more than $60 is ? ___$110___
8. $\frac{1}{8}$ less than $44 is ? ___$38.50___
9. ? is $\frac{3}{10}$ less than $70 ___$49___
10. $75 increased by $\frac{2}{5}$ of itself = ? ___$105___

Exercise 3.

1. Sandy Cabell saved $\frac{1}{15}$ of her last year's total earnings of $14,436.15. Last year Sandy saved $___962.41___.

$\frac{1}{15} \times $14,436.15 = 962.41 saved

2. An appliance store sold 360 microwave ovens last year. Of that amount, $\frac{3}{8}$ were apartment-sized models. The number of apartment-sized models sold for the year was ___135___.

$\frac{3}{8} \times 360 = 135$ sold

3. Armando Bakhtar had a full-time job that paid $316.26 a week. He gave up the full-time job and took a part-time job that paid him $\frac{3}{7}$ less per week. The pay he earns at the part-time job is $___180.72___.

$316.26 - (\frac{3}{7} \times $316.26) = $316.26 - $135.54 = 180.72 part-time pay

4. By spending more money on advertising, the Zembo Computer Center's sales receipts in July were $\frac{1}{3}$ more than the previous month's sales of $135,180. The sales in July were $___180,240___.

$135,180 + (\frac{1}{3} \times $135,180) = $135,180 + $45,060 = $180,240$ July sales

Exercise 4.   (Finding what part a number is of another)

Show the number that correctly completes the statement.

1. What part of 36 is 4? __$\frac{1}{9}$__   9? __$\frac{1}{4}$__   3? __$\frac{1}{12}$__   2? __$\frac{1}{18}$__   18? __$\frac{1}{2}$__   24? __$\frac{2}{3}$__

2. 9 is what part of 12? __$\frac{3}{4}$__   18? __$\frac{1}{2}$__   6? __$1\frac{1}{2}$__   3? __$\frac{3}{1}$__   27? __$\frac{1}{3}$__   72? __$\frac{1}{8}$__

3. $4 is what part of $6? __$\frac{2}{3}$__ $2? __$\frac{2}{1}$__ $10? __$\frac{2}{5}$__ $18? __$\frac{2}{9}$__ $1? __$\frac{4}{1}$__ $30? __$\frac{2}{15}$__

4. What part of $10 is $2? __$\frac{1}{5}$__ $20? __$\frac{2}{1}$__ $5? __$\frac{1}{2}$__ $45? __$4\frac{1}{2}$__ $10? __$\frac{1}{1}$__ $25? __$2\frac{1}{2}$__

5. 50¢ is what part of $5? __$\frac{1}{10}$__ $2.50? __$\frac{1}{5}$__ $3? __$\frac{1}{6}$__ $8? __$\frac{1}{16}$__   10¢? __$\frac{5}{1}$__ $50? __$\frac{1}{100}$__

Exercise 5.   (Finding what part a number is greater or smaller than another)

Show the fraction that makes the statement correct.

1. 30 is ? smaller than 40   __$\frac{1}{4}$__

2. 40 is ? greater than 36   __$\frac{1}{9}$__

3. 45 = 40 increased by ? of itself   __$\frac{1}{8}$__

4. 30 increased by ? of itself = 45   __$\frac{1}{2}$__

5. 60 decreased by ? of itself = 40   __$\frac{1}{3}$__

6. 25 increased by ? of itself = 35   __$\frac{2}{5}$__

7. 55 = 40 increased by ? of itself   __$\frac{3}{8}$__

8. 75 decreased by ? of itself = 30   __$\frac{3}{5}$__

9. 30 is ? less than 50   __$\frac{2}{5}$__

10. 50 is ? more than 30   __$\frac{2}{3}$__

Exercise 6.

1. During November, Ezra Wilkins earned a total of $420. Of that amount, $35 was overtime pay. Compared to his total earnings, Ezra's overtime pay was what part? __$\frac{1}{12}$__

$\frac{\$35}{\$420} = \frac{1}{12}$

2. The O'Shea family earned $1,830 last month. Of that amount, they spent $610 for food. What fractional part of their earnings did they spend for food? __$\frac{1}{3}$__

$\frac{\$610}{\$1,830} = \frac{1}{3}$

3. Leona Unger's gross salary increased from $20,250 last year to $22,500 this year. What fractional part of last year's salary was the increase? __$\frac{1}{9}$__

$22,500 - 20,250 = 2,250$ increase
$2,250 \div 20,250 = \frac{1}{9}$ increase

4. Arnie's Golf and Tennis Shop sold 300 tennis racquets this year. Last year, the shop sold 375 racquets. By what fractional part did sales of tennis racquets decrease? __$\frac{1}{5}$__

$375 - 300 = 75$ fewer tennis racquets sold
$\frac{75}{375} = \frac{1}{5}$ decrease

5. The average hourly pay at the Webb Electric Company increased during the past two years from $9.76 an hour to $10.98 an hour. What part was the new pay rate larger than the old pay rate? __$\frac{1}{8}$__

$10.98 - 9.76 = 1.22$ increase
$\frac{\$1.22}{\$9.76} = \frac{1}{8}$ increase

TERM TICKLER

Directions   Each group of scrambled letters can be sorted to spell a word or phrase. Then sort the letters in boxes to form a key word.

a. Sort the scrambled letters below.

1. toira

   [r] a t i o

2. troopronip

   p r o p o r [t] i o n

3. exdim   rebmun

   m i x e d   [n] u m b e r

4. blueod - emit   apy

   [d] o u b l e - t i m e   p a y

5. treamonur

   [n] u m e r a t o r

6. scors   crupodt

   c r [o] s s   p r o d u c t

7. lorripacec

   r e c i p r o c [a] l

8. rraluge   mite

   r [e] g u l a r   t i m e

9. rstem

   t e r [m] s

10. sowelt   strem

    l [o] w e s t   t e r m s

11. meroteiv

    o v e r t [i] m e

b. The key word is _____ denominator _____ .

INTEGRATED PROJECT 3

The Xemar Company stocks replacement parts for all types of household appliances. The company has six employees in the stock department who assemble orders to be shipped to repair shops. As an assistant to an office manager, you have been asked to prepare answers to some questions the manager has asked about the payroll records of the stock department. This is in addition to your job of figuring the time worked and the gross pay for the workers in that department. You are to do the following for each employee:

1. Use the time cards shown on the next page and figure the total hours worked each day. Write the result on the "Daily Totals" line of the time card. Add the daily totals to find the "Weekly Total."

2. For the week, find the number of regular time hours worked and record them in the "R.T. Hours" section. Then figure the overtime hours worked and record the total in the "O.T. Hours" section. The regular work day is from 7:00 A.M. to 3:30 P.M., with a one half hour lunch break from 11:30 A.M. to Noon. Time is figured in 15-minute periods. Workers who are more than 3 minutes late in arriving to work or returning from lunch are penalized 15 minutes. The same penalty applies to workers who leave more than 3 minutes early for lunch or before each 15-minute mark when they leave work at the end of the day.

    All employees in the stock department work on a 40-hour week basis and are paid time and a half for all work over 40 hours in a week.

3. Find the regular time and overtime pay amounts and enter them on the correct "Amount" line in the time card. Then in the "Total" line, write the total number of hours worked and the total gross pay earned by the employee.

4. Write the amount of regular time and overtime hours and the gross pay earned by each employee into the PAYROLL REGISTER shown below. Total the columns.

5. Answer the questions asked by the office manager found on the memo of June 16, 19—.

Xemar Company
PAYROLL REGISTER
Week Ending June 15, 19—

Employee	Hours Worked		Earnings		
	Reg. Time	Overtime	Reg. Time	Overtime	Total
Lu-yin Chu	40	$3\frac{1}{2}$	$ 400	$ 52.50	$ 452.50
Edwin Gault	40	3	400	45.00	445.00
Judy Kirschner	40	$2\frac{1}{4}$	400	33.75	433.75
Tomas Melendez	40	$2\frac{1}{2}$	400	37.50	437.50
Alberta Tinwell	40	5	400	75.00	475.00
Jessie Vanrees	40	$3\frac{3}{4}$	400	56.25	456.25
TOTAL	240	20	$2,400	$300.00	$2,700.00

Xemar Company
Weekly Time Cards

Chu, Lu-Yin

NAME Chu, Lu-Yin — PAY PERIOD ENDING 8-15-XX

	R.T. Hours 40	Rate $10	Amount $400
	O.T. Hours $3\frac{1}{2}$	Rate $15	Amount $52.50
Total	$43\frac{1}{2}$		$452.50

In	7^{00}	6^{59}	6^{55}	6^{56}	7^{01}			
Out	11^{30}	11^{29}	11^{31}	11^{30}	11^{28}			
In	12^{00}	12^{01}	11^{59}	12^{01}	12^{02}			
Out	3^{30}	3^{31}	4^{00}	5^{30}	4^{30}			
Daily Total	1st Day 8	2nd Day 8	3rd Day $8\frac{1}{2}$	4th Day 10	5th Day 9	6th Day 0	7th Day 0	Weekly Totals $43\frac{1}{2}$

Gault, Edwin

NAME Gault, Edwin — PAY PERIOD ENDING 8-15-XX

	R.T. Hours 40	Rate $10	Amount $400
	O.T. Hours 3	Rate $15	Amount $45
Total	43		$445

In	7^{00}	6^{50}	6^{59}	7^{00}	6^{48}	8^{55}		
Out	11^{30}	11^{31}	11^{30}	11^{01}	11^{29}	11^{32}		
In	12^{00}	12^{00}	12^{00}		12^{01}	12^{00}		
Out	3^{30}	3^{33}	3^{32}		4^{31}	3^{35}		
Daily Total	1st Day 8	2nd Day 8	3rd Day 8	4th Day 4	5th Day 9	6th Day 6	7th Day 0	Weekly Totals 43

Kirschner, Judy

NAME Kirschner, Judy — PAY PERIOD ENDING 8-15-XX

	R.T. Hours 40	Rate $10	Amount $400
	O.T. Hours $2\frac{1}{4}$	Rate $15	Amount $33.75
Total	$42\frac{1}{4}$		$433.75

In	6^{54}	7^{00}	6^{55}	6^{50}	6^{58}			
Out	11^{28}	11^{30}	11^{29}	11^{30}	11^{30}			
In	12^{58}	12^{01}	12^{02}	12^{00}	12^{30}			
Out	3^{31}	4^{31}	3^{35}	4^{45}	5^{00}			
Daily Total	1st Day 7	2nd Day 9	3rd Day 8	4th Day $9\frac{1}{4}$	5th Day 9	6th Day 0	7th Day 0	Weekly Totals $42\frac{1}{4}$

Melendez, Tomas

NAME Melendez, Tomas — PAY PERIOD ENDING 8-15-XX

	R.T. Hours 40	Rate $10	Amount $400
	O.T. Hours $2\frac{1}{2}$	Rate $15	Amount $37.50
Total	$42\frac{1}{2}$		$437.50

In	7^{00}		6^{58}	7^{00}	7^{00}	8^{00}		
Out	11^{30}		11^{34}	11^{30}	11^{20}	11^{30}		
In	12^{00}		12^{00}	12^{10}	12^{01}	12^{01}		
Out	3^{30}		4^{30}	4^{45}	5^{45}	3^{00}		
Daily Total	1st Day 8	2nd Day 0	3rd Day 9	4th Day 9	5th Day 10	6th Day $6\frac{1}{2}$	7th Day 0	Weekly Totals $42\frac{1}{2}$

Tinwell, Alberta

NAME Tinwell, Alberta — PAY PERIOD ENDING 8-15-XX

	R.T. Hours 40	Rate $10	Amount $400
	O.T. Hours 5	Rate $15	Amount $75
Total	45		$475

In	6^{52}	7^{02}	7^{00}	6^{47}	7^{36}	7^{00}		
Out	11^{28}	11^{30}	11^{30}	11^{27}	11^{30}	10^{02}		
In	12^{01}	12^{01}	12^{02}	11^{58}	12^{00}			
Out	5^{31}	3^{34}	3^{29}	3^{28}	4^{15}			
Daily Total	1st Day 10	2nd Day 8	3rd Day 8	4th Day 8	5th Day 8	6th Day 3	7th Day 0	Weekly Totals 45

Vanrees, Jessie

NAME Vanrees, Jessie — PAY PERIOD ENDING 8-15-XX

	R.T. Hours 40	Rate $10	Amount $400
	O.T. Hours $3\frac{3}{4}$	Rate $15	Amount $56.25
Total	$43\frac{3}{4}$		$456.25

In	7^{20}	7^{00}	6^{55}	7^{42}	7^{01}	9^{00}		
Out	11^{30}	11^{28}	11^{31}	11^{28}	11^{40}	11^{30}		
In	12^{00}	12^{00}	12^{01}	11^{52}	12^{03}	12^{00}		
Out	3^{31}	2^{05}	4^{30}	3^{34}	4^{32}	2^{01}		
Daily Total	1st Day $7\frac{1}{2}$	2nd Day $6\frac{1}{2}$	3rd Day 9	4th Day $7\frac{1}{4}$	5th Day 9	6th Day $4\frac{1}{2}$	7th Day 0	Weekly Totals $43\frac{3}{4}$

TO: Assistant Office Manager
FROM: Office Manager
SUBJECT: INFORMATION NEEDED FOR MEETING
DATE: June 16, 19—

Use the Payroll Register for this week (the week ending June 15, 19—) to answer the questions found below. I need this information by 9 A.M. tomorrow morning for my department heads' meeting.

1. What part of the total hours worked during the week were regular hours of work? _____$\frac{12}{13}$_____ What part were overtime hours? _____$\frac{1}{13}$_____

2. What part of the total pay for the week was the regular pay? _____$\frac{8}{9}$_____ What part was overtime pay? _____$\frac{1}{9}$_____

3. Which employee worked the most overtime hours? _____Alberta Tinwell_____

4. What part of the total overtime worked by the department did the employee referred to in Question #3 work? _____$\frac{1}{4}$_____

Last week, 232 regular time hours and 30 overtime hours were worked by the department.

5. What part fewer or greater regular time hours were worked for this week compared to last week? _____$\frac{1}{29}$ greater_____

6. What part fewer or greater overtime hours were worked for this week compared to last week? _____$\frac{1}{3}$ fewer_____

During a usual week, one tenth, or 24 hours, of all time worked is overtime. Also, the weekly average of total overtime pay is one-eighth of total pay, or $360.

7. Comparing this week to the average, by what amount were the overtime hours worked less than or greater than the average? _____4 hours less_____

8. What part less or greater than the average does the amount in Question #7 represent? _____$\frac{1}{6}$ less_____

9. Comparing this week to the average, by what amount is the overtime pay less than or greater than the average? _____$60_____

10. What part less or greater than the average does the amount in Question #8 represent? _____$\frac{1}{6}$ less_____

NET PAY, FRINGE BENEFITS, AND COMMISSION

LESSON 4-1   DECIMALS

Exercise 1.   (Expressing fractions as decimals)

		Fraction	Decimal
1.	Six tenths	$\frac{6}{10}$	0.6
2.	Five hundredths	$\frac{5}{100}$	0.05
3.	Nine thousandths	$\frac{9}{1000}$	0.009
4.	Seventy-five hundredths	$\frac{75}{100}$	0.75
5.	Eighteen thousandths	$\frac{18}{1000}$	0.018
6.	One hundred sixteen thousandths	$\frac{116}{1000}$	0.116
7.	Two hundred forty-five ten thousandths	$\frac{245}{10000}$	0.0245
8.	Ninety-five thousandths	$\frac{95}{1000}$	0.095
9.	Two tenths	$\frac{2}{10}$	0.2
10.	Forty-nine hundredths	$\frac{49}{100}$	0.49

Exercise 2.   (Changing a fraction to decimal)

Show the decimal equivalent of the fraction to the nearest:

Tenth: **a.** $\frac{2}{9}$ = ___0.2___   **b.** $\frac{3}{13}$ = ___0.2___   **c.** $\frac{7}{4}$ = ___1.8___   **d.** $\frac{3}{11}$ = ___0.3___

Hundredth: **e.** $\frac{7}{8}$ = ___0.88___   **f.** $\frac{6}{7}$ = ___0.86___   **g.** $\frac{7}{6}$ = ___1.17___   **h.** $\frac{7}{12}$ = ___0.58___

Thousandth: **i.** $\frac{1}{3}$ = ___0.333___   **j.** $\frac{1}{6}$ = ___0.167___   **k.** $\frac{5}{18}$ = ___0.278___   **l.** $\frac{1}{14}$ = ___0.071___

Exercise 3.   (Multiplication by 0.1, 0.01, and 0.001)

Find the product for each problem:

a. $208 \times 0.1 = $ _____20.8_____

b. $83 \times 0.01 = $ _____0.83_____

c. $306 \times 0.001 = $ _____0.306_____

d. $31.7 \times 0.01 = $ _____0.317_____

e. $7.34 \times 0.1 = $ _____0.734_____

f. $193 \times 0.001 = $ _____0.193_____

g. $12.7 \times 0.1 = $ _____1.27_____

h. $7.62 \times 0.01 = $ _____0.0762_____

i. $\$365 \times 0.01 = $ _____\$3.65_____

j. $\$520 \times 0.001 = $ _____\$0.52_____

k. $\$42.60 \times 0.1 = $ _____\$4.26_____

l. $\$2,097 \times 0.01 = $ _____\$20.97_____

Exercise 4.   (Changing a decimal to a fraction)

Change each decimal to a fraction in lowest terms:

a. $0.12 = $ _____$\frac{3}{25}$_____

b. $0.55 = $ _____$\frac{11}{20}$_____

c. $0.365 = $ _____$\frac{73}{200}$_____

d. $0.04 = $ _____$\frac{1}{25}$_____

e. $0.475 = $ _____$\frac{19}{40}$_____

f. $0.008 = $ _____$\frac{1}{125}$_____

g. $0.15 = $ _____$\frac{3}{20}$_____

h. $0.412 = $ _____$\frac{103}{250}$_____

i. $0.068 = $ _____$\frac{17}{250}$_____

j. $0.65 = $ _____$\frac{13}{20}$_____

Exercise 5.   (Division by 0.1, 0.01, and 0.001)

Find the quotient for each problem:

a. $816 \div 0.1 = $ _____8,160_____

b. $51 \div 0.01 = $ _____5,100_____

c. $632 \div 0.001 = $ _____632,000_____

d. $0.08 \div 0.01 = $ _____8.0_____

e. $2.86 \div 0.1 = $ _____28.6_____

f. $0.174 \div 0.001 = $ _____174_____

g. $89.35 \div 0.1 = $ _____893.5_____

h. $0.062 \div 0.1 = $ _____0.62_____

i. $\$4.39 \div 0.001 = $ _____\$4,390_____

j. $\$15.00 \div 0.1 = $ _____\$150_____

k. $\$0.56 \div 0.01 = $ _____\$56_____

l. $\$0.04 \div 0.001 = $ _____\$40_____

LESSON 4-2 PERCENTS

Exercise 1. (Changing a decimal or whole number to a percent)

Change each number to a percent.

1. 0.15 = __15%__   3. 0.07 = __7%__   5. 0.355 = __35.5%__   7. 8.00 = __800%__

2. 0.255 = __25.5%__   4. 0.045 = __4.5%__   6. 2.75 = __275%__   8. 2 = __200%__

Exercise 2. (Changing a fraction to a percent)

Change each fraction to a percent. Round your answers to the nearest *tenth* of a percent.

a. $\frac{3}{7}$ = __42.9%__   b. $\frac{7}{11}$ = __63.6%__   c. $\frac{11}{45}$ = __24.4%__   d. $\frac{13}{14}$ = __92.9%__   e. $\frac{5}{24}$ = __20.8%__

Exercise 3. (Changing a percent to a decimal)

Change each percent to a decimal.

1. 46% = __0.46__   4. 307% = __3.07__   7. 83.4% = __0.834__   10. $8\frac{1}{2}$% = __0.085__

2. $4\frac{1}{4}$% = __0.0425__   5. 250% = __2.5__   8. 3.7% = __0.037__   11. $\frac{3}{4}$% = __0.0075__

3. $\frac{1}{2}$% = __0.005__   6. 189% = __1.89__   9. 0.4% = __0.004__   12. 0.125% = __0.00125__

Exercise 4. (Changing a percent to a fraction)

1. Change each percent to a fraction and simplify:

a. 42% = $\frac{21}{50}$ b. 16% = $\frac{4}{25}$ c. 3% = $\frac{3}{100}$

d. 175% = $\frac{7}{4}$ e. 350% = $\frac{7}{2}$

*2. Change each percent to a fraction and simplify:

a. 8.5% = $\frac{17}{200}$ b. 62.5% = $\frac{5}{8}$ c. 2.5% = $\frac{1}{40}$

d. 12.5% = $\frac{1}{8}$ e. 5.5% = $\frac{11}{200}$

LESSON 4-3   DEDUCTIONS AND TAKE-HOME PAY

Exercise 1.

1. The form below shows the total wages and withholding allowances for eight married workers of the Telestar Co. Use the FICA and withholding tax tables in Chapter 4, Lesson 2, of the textbook to find the withholding tax and FICA tax on each worker's total wages. Write each amount in the proper column in the form.

Name	Allow-ances	Total Wages	Income Tax	FICA Tax
a. Larson, A.	3	$332.07	$10.00	$25.40
b. Mueller, B.	0	$431.59	$47.00	$33.02
c. Nieves, C.	2	$436.32	$32.00	$33.38
d. O'Beron, D.	1	$335.74	$25.00	$25.68

Name	Allow-ances	Total Wages	Income Tax	FICA Tax
e. Pavik, F.	4	$433.14	$18.00	$33.14
f. Quentin, F.	1	$334.90	$25.00	$25.62
g. Rast, G.	0	$331.83	$32.00	$25.38
h. Santoni, H.	2	$436.15	$32.00	$33.37

2. Complete the table below. Show for each married worker (a) the FICA tax (0.0765), (b) total deductions, and (c) net wages. Then find the total of each money column.

Use the column totals to prove your work. The sum of the income tax, FICA tax, and insurance column totals should equal the total deductions column total. The total wages minus the total deductions should equal the total net wages.

Name	Allow-ances	Total Wages	Deductions Income Tax	Deductions FICA Tax	Deductions Insurance	Deductions Total	Net Wages
a. Gibbs, F.	3	$358.33	$13.00	$27.41	$73.23	$113.64	$244.69
b. Hall, F.	0	$497.87	$56.00	$38.09	$39.45	$133.54	$364.33
c. Isom, G.	1	$391.89	$34.00	$29.98	$42.57	$106.55	$285.34
d. Jackson, H.	2	$617.71	$59.00	$47.25	$55.97	$162.22	$455.49
e. Kang, I.	2	$570.95	$53.00	$43.68	$62.59	$159.27	$411.68
	Total	$2,436.75	$215.00	$186.41	$273.81	$675.22	$1,761.53

3. Elaine Kaufman works a 40-hour week at $8.75 an hour with time and a half for overtime. Last week she worked 43 hours. From her earnings, her employer deducted FICA tax at a rate of 0.0765 and income tax of $32.00. Her employer also deducted $33.78 for health insurance and $27.12 for union dues.

Complete Elaine's payroll below.

Regular-time earnings	$ 350.00	
Overtime earnings	39.38	
Total earnings		$ 389.38
Deductions		
Income tax	$ 32.00	
FICA tax	29.79	
Health insurance	33.78	
Union dues	27.12	
Total deductions		122.69
Net earnings		$ 266.69

4. Edwin Nicol earns $6.83 an hour for a 40-hour week. He is paid time and a half for overtime. His employer deducts FICA tax at a rate of 0.0765 and income tax of $26. His employer also deducts $43.72 per week for a family health insurance plan that Edwin carries.

Last week Edwin worked 47 hours. Complete his payroll form below.

Regular-time earnings	$ 273.20	
Overtime earnings	71.72	
Total earnings		$ 344.92
Deductions		
Income tax	$ 26.00	
FICA tax	26.39	
Health insurance	43.72	
Total deductions		96.11
Net earnings		$ 248.81

Name: _____ Date: _____

LESSON 4-4 MORE PERCENTS

Exercise 1. (Finding a percent of a number)

Solve these problems. Show your answer to the nearest cent.

1. 67% of $489 = $ _____327.63_____

2. 15.8% of $250 = $ _____39.50_____

3. 3.5% of $825 = $ _____28.88_____

4. 125% of $83.50 = $ _____104.38_____

5. 400% of $7.50 = $ _____30_____

6. 23.6% of $550 = $ _____129.80_____

Exercise 2. (Finding what percent one number is of another)

Find the missing percents. When you divide, carry the answer to two places of exact value, if the division does not come out evenly at the second decimal place. Simplify any resulting fraction.

1. 42 is _____$8\frac{3}{4}$_____% of 480

2. 150 is _____$20\frac{20}{29}$_____% of 725

3. $10.40 is _____8_____% of $130

4. $27 is _____300_____% of $9

5. $31.50 is _____450_____% of $7

6. $3.50 is _____$3\frac{8}{9}$_____% of $90

7. $2.80 is _____$2\frac{2}{27}$_____% of $135

8. $146.25 is _____325_____% of $45

9. $9.10 is _____$16\frac{1}{4}$_____% of $56

10. $7.50 is _____$66\frac{2}{3}$_____% of $11.25

Exercise 3. (Multiplying by fractional equivalents of parts of 100%)

Use fractional equivalents to find the answers to these problems:

1. 20% of $575 = $ _____115_____

2. 50% of $1,482 = $ _____741_____

3. 75% of $880 = $ _____660_____

4. 40% of $1,200 = $ _____480_____

5. $12\frac{1}{2}$% of $984 = $ _____123_____

6. 25% of $2,240 = $ _____560_____

7. $33\frac{1}{2}$% of $810 = $ _____270_____

8. 60% of $2,500 = $ _____1,500_____

9. $62\frac{1}{2}$% of $480 = $ _____300_____

10. $87\frac{1}{2}$% of $400 = $ _____350_____

11. $66\frac{2}{3}$% of $249 = $ _____166_____

12. $37\frac{1}{2}$% of $1,680 = $ _____630_____

13. 80% of $350 = $ _____280_____

14. $12\frac{1}{2}$% of $640 = $ _____80_____

15. $33\frac{1}{3}$% of $324 = $ _____108_____

Name: _____ Date: _____

Exercise 4. (Finding 1%, 10%, 100%, and 1,000% of a number)

Write the answers rapidly. Round answers to the nearest cent.

1. 1% of $57 = $_____0.57_____
2. 10% of $89 = $_____8.90_____
3. 100% of $76 = $_____76_____
4. 1,000% of $87 = $_____870_____
5. 10% of $31 = $_____3.10_____
6. 1% of $53 = $_____0.53_____
7. 1,000% of $9.77 = $_____97.70_____
8. 10% of $7.48 = $_____0.75_____
9. 1% of $803 = $_____8.03_____

10. 100% of $8.35 = $_____8.35_____
11. 1,000% of $0.05 = $_____0.50_____
12. 1% of $42.98 = $_____0.43_____
13. 100% of $17.39 = $_____17.39_____
14. 10% of $72.19 = $_____7.22_____
15. 1% of $48.39 = $_____0.48_____
16. 1,000% of $17.22 = $_____172.20_____
17. 10% of $638.61 = $_____63.86_____
18. 1% of $713.08 = $_____7.13_____

Exercise 5. (Fractional parts of 1%)

First find 1% and then multiply by the fraction in each problem below. The first one is done to show you how.

1. $\frac{1}{2}$% of $870 = __$\frac{1}{2}$__ × $__8.70__ = $__4.35__
2. $\frac{1}{3}$% of $255 = __$\frac{1}{3}$__ × $__2.55__ = $__0.85__
3. $\frac{1}{8}$% of $1,256 = __$\frac{1}{8}$__ × $__12.56__ = $__1.57__
4. $\frac{1}{4}$% of $680 = __$\frac{1}{4}$__ × $__6.80__ = $__1.70__
5. $\frac{1}{5}$% of $930 = __$\frac{1}{5}$__ × $__9.30__ = $__1.86__
6. $\frac{1}{10}$% of $8,397 = __$\frac{1}{10}$__ × $__83.97__ = $__8.40__
7. $\frac{2}{3}$% of $1,350 = __$\frac{2}{3}$__ × $__13.50__ = $__9.00__
8. $\frac{3}{4}$% of $4,860 = __$\frac{3}{4}$__ × $__48.60__ = $__36.45__
9. $\frac{1}{10}$% of $11,098 = __$\frac{1}{10}$__ × $__110.98__ = $__11.10__

10. $\frac{3}{8}$% of $4,800 = __$\frac{3}{8}$__ × $__48.00__ = $__18.00__
11. $\frac{2}{5}$% of $3,250 = __$\frac{2}{5}$__ × $__32.50__ = $__13.00__
12. $\frac{1}{3}$% of $3,870 = __$\frac{1}{3}$__ × $__38.70__ = $__12.90__
13. $\frac{1}{8}$% of $1,760 = __$\frac{1}{8}$__ × $__17.60__ = $__2.20__
14. $\frac{3}{5}$% of $2,550 = __$\frac{3}{5}$__ × $__25.50__ = $__15.30__
15. $\frac{2}{3}$% of $8,400 = __$\frac{2}{3}$__ × $__84.00__ = $__56.00__
16. $\frac{1}{4}$% of $2,240 = __$\frac{1}{4}$__ × $__22.40__ = $__5.60__
17. $\frac{1}{2}$% of $3,670 = __$\frac{1}{2}$__ × $__36.70__ = $__18.35__
18. $\frac{3}{4}$% of $360 = __$\frac{3}{4}$__ × $__3.60__ = $__2.70__

LESSON 4-5   FRINGE BENEFITS AND JOB EXPENSES

Exercise 1.   (Total job benefits)

1. Shari Traxler is paid $9.75 an hour for a 40-hour week. Her employer also provides these fringe benefits: yearly pension contributions, $1,622.40; health and accident insurance per year, $956; free parking, $520 per year; free tuition for evening classes, $1,200 per year. (a) What is Shari's annual wage? $__20,280.00__ (b) What are her total yearly fringe benefits? $__4,298.40__ (c) What are her total yearly job benefits? $__24,578.40__

   a. $9.75 × 40 = $390 weekly wage
      $390 × 52 = $20,280 annual wage
   b. $1,622.40 + $956 + $520 + $1,200 = $4,298.40 yearly fringe benefits
   c. $20,280 + $4,298.40 = $24,578.40 total yearly job benefits

2. Armand Popoff is paid $1,438 a month. He estimates his yearly fringe benefits to be: pension contributions, $1,035; insurance, $458; free parking, $280; use of company car, $3,480. (a) What is Carl's yearly pay? $__17,256__ (b) What are his total yearly fringe benefits? $__5,253__ (c) What are his total yearly job benefits? $__22,509__

   a. $1,438 × 12 = $17,256 yearly pay
   b. $1,035 + $458 + $280 + $3,480 = $5,253 total yearly fringe benefits
   c. $17,256 + $5,253 = $22,509 total yearly job benefits

Exercise 2.   (Net job benefits)

1. Duane McCoy's job pays him $11.25 per hour for a 40-hour week. He estimates his fringe benefits to be 29% of his yearly wages. His yearly job expenses are estimated to be dues, $375; uniforms, $580; commuting costs, $934. (a) What is Duane's total annual pay? $__23,400__ (b) What is the amount of Duane's fringe benefits per year? $__16,786__ (c) What are Duane's total yearly job benefits? $__30,186__ (d) What are Duane's total yearly job expenses? $__1,889__ (e) What are Duane's net yearly job benefits? $__28,297__

   a. $11.25 × 40 = $450 weekly wage
      $450 × 52 = $23,400 annual pay
   b. $23,400 × 0.29 = $6,786 annual fringe benefits
   c. $23,400 + $6,786 = $30,186 total yearly job benefits
   d. $375 + $580 + $934 = $1,889 total yearly job expenses
   e. $30,186 − $1,889 = $28,297 net yearly job benefits

2. Louella Hatton has a job which pays $1,986 a month. She estimates that her fringe benefits are 32% of her annual wages. She also estimates that her yearly job expenses are special tools, $497; dues, $720; commuting costs, $602; uniforms, $530. (a) What is Louella's total annual pay? $__23,832__ (b) What is the amount of her annual fringe benefits? $__7,626.24__ (c) What are Louella's total annual job benefits? $__31,458.24__ (d) What are Louella's total annual job expenses? $__2,349__ (e) What are Louella's net annual job benefits? $__29,109.24__

   a. $1,986 × 12 = $23,832 annual pay
   b. $23,832 × 0.32 = $7,626.24 annual fringe benefits
   c. $23,832 + $7,626.24 = $31,458.24 total annual job benefits
   d. $497 + $720 + $602 + $530 = $2,349 total annual job expenses
   e. $31,458.24 − $2,349 = $29,109.24 net annual job benefits

Exercise 3.   (Comparing jobs)

1. Benji Enami has just graduated from school and is applying for two jobs. The first job pays $4.50 an hour for a 40-hour week and the second job pays $5.25 an hour for a 40-hour week. The fringe benefits are estimated to be 20% of the annual wage for the first job and 17% for the second. Yearly job expenses are estimated to be $438 for the first job and $762 for the second. (a) Which job has the greater net yearly job benefits? ____Second job____ (b) How much greater? ____$1,220.40____

a.   First Job   Second Job
Weekly wages $4.50 × 40 = $180 $5.25 × 40 = $210
Yearly wages $180 × 52 = $9,360 $210 × 52 = $10,920
Yearly fringe benefits $9,360 × 0.20 = $1,872 $10,920 × 0.17 = $1,856.40
Total yearly job benefits $9,360 + $1,872 = $11,232 $10,920 + $1,856.40 = $12,776.40
Net yearly job benefits $11,232 − $438 = $10,794 $12,776.40 − $762 = $12,014.40

b. Difference $12,014.40 − $10,794 = $1,220.40 greater net yearly job benefits of second job

2. Angela Calgano is comparing the four jobs below. Complete the form for her.

Yearly Job Benefits	Job 1	Job 2	Job 3	Job 4
Hourly wages per 40-hour week	$6.45	$6.20	$6.85	$6.70
Fringe benefits	15% of wages	22% of wages	18% of wages	27% of wages
Yearly job expenses:				
Commuting costs	$380	$758	$543	$180
Uniforms	none	$250	$380	$850
Dues	$175	$480	none	$985
Parking	$350	$200	none	$565
Total Yearly:				
Wages	$13,416.00	$12,896.00	$14,248.00	$13,936.00
Fringe benefits	2,012.40	2,837.12	2,564.64	3,762.72
Job benefits	15,428.40	15,733.12	16,812.64	17,698.72
Job expenses	905.00	1,688.00	923.00	2,580.00
Net job benefits	14,523.40	14,045.12	15,889.64	15,118.72

Name: _____   Date: _____

LESSON 4-6   PERCENT RELATIONSHIPS

Exercise 1.   (Finding the number that is a percent greater or smaller than another number)

1. ____60____ is 20% more than 50.

2. 40 plus 6% of itself = ____42.4____.

3. ____72____ is 10% less than 80.

4. 60 minus 40% of itself = ____36____.

5. $175 increased by 21% = $____211.75____.

6. $____644____ = $736 decreased by $12\frac{1}{2}$%.

7. $1,600 decreased by $62\frac{1}{2}$% = $____600____.

8. $\frac{1}{4}$% more than $240 = $____240.60____.

9. $____270____ = $450 decreased by 40%.

10. $4,500 increased by $\frac{1}{3}$% = $____4,515____.

11. $\frac{1}{5}$% less than $2,500 = $____2,495____.

12. $____386____ is 3.5% less than $400.

13. 175% more than $60 = $____165____.

14. $2,400 decreased by $\frac{3}{4}$% = $____2,382____.

15. Mia Gantt's old employer contributed $24 each week to her pension plan. Her new employer contributes 20% more to her pension plan. The amount her new employer contributes is $____28.80____.

    $24 + ($24 × 0.2) = $28.80

Exercise 2.   (Finding what percent one number is greater or smaller than another)

1. 240 is ____$33\frac{1}{3}$____% more than 180.

2. 45 is ____25____% less than 60.

3. 80 is ____100____% more than 40.

4. 180 is ____200____% more than 60.

5. 200 is ____$33\frac{1}{3}$____% less than 300.

6. 480 is ____20____% more than 400.

7. 75 is ____$37\frac{1}{2}$____% less than 120.

8. 105 is ____30____% less than 150.

9. 400 is ____300____% more than 100.

10. 600 is ____20____% less than 750.

11. 225 is ____80____% more than 125.

12. 125 is ____$66\frac{2}{3}$____% more than 75.

13. 20 is ____$16\frac{2}{3}$____% less than 24.

14. 375 is ____150____% more than 150.

15. Evan Wiley lost his factory job which paid $9.60 an hour. He took a job in an office for $7.50 an hour. By what percent, to the nearest tenth of a percent, is his new hourly pay smaller than his old hourly pay? ____21.9%____

    a. $9.60 − $7.50 = $2.10   The amount smaller
    b. $2.10 ÷ $9.60 = 0.2188, or 21.9%   The percent smaller

Name: _____ Date: _____

LESSON 4-7   COMMISSION

Exercise 1.   (Straight commission and salary plus commission)

1. A salesperson who works on a straight commission basis sold 5 copy machines at $4,500 each. The commission rate was 6%. The amount of commission was $_____1,350_____.

   $4,500 × 5 = $22,500 total sales
   $22,500 × 0.06 = $1,350 amount of commission

2. Sara Blanco is paid a weekly salary of $250 plus a commission of 3% on all sales. Her sales for the last four weeks are shown below. Show her (a) commission for each week, (b) total earnings for each week, (c) total sales, commission, salary and earnings for the four weeks.

Week	Sales	Commission	Salary	Total Earnings
1	$13,500	$ 405	$ 250	$ 655
2	17,200	516	250	766
3	16,200	486	250	736
4	15,400	462	250	712
Total	$62,300	$1,869	$1,000	$2,869

3. Mark Beard sells two types of floor polishers on a straight commission basis. On one polisher which sells for $119, he gets a commission of $24. On the other, which sells for $149, he gets $30. Last month he sold 21 of the $119 polishers and 14 of the $149 polishers. His total commissions for the month were $_____924_____.

   21 × $24 = $504 commission on $119 polishers
   14 × $30 = $420 commission on $149 polishers
   $504 + $420 = total commission on all polishers

4. Mary Banjavic is paid a salary of $200 a week plus $\frac{4}{5}$% commission on weekly sales over $7,500. Her sales last week totaled $14,100. Her total earnings for the week were $_____252.80_____.

   $14,100 − $7,500 = $6,600 amount over $7,500
   $6,600 × $\frac{4}{5}$% = $6,600 × 0.008 = $52.80 commission
   $200 + $52.80 = $252.80 total earnings for week

5. A store pays its salespeople weekly on a salary plus commission basis. The store pays a 3% commission on sales over a weekly quota. The sales of four employees for last week are shown below. Find for each person the (a) amount of commission and (b) total earnings for the week.

Salesperson	Sales	Quota	Commission	Salary	Total Earnings
Ira Feldstein	$9,680	$4,400	$158.40	$215	$373.40
Fara Jain	9,560	5,000	136.40	245	381.80
Ruth Clarke	9,640	4,800	145.20	275	420.20
Tom Bonassi	9,300	4,700	138.00	225	363.00

Exercise 2. (Graduated commission)

1. Tony Bollini sells encyclopedias. His monthly commission is based on the number of sets sold in a month. He earns $45 each for the first 25 sets, $60 each for the next 25 sets, and $75 each for each set over 50 sets he sells. Bollini sold 27 sets in November and 55 in December. His total commission for the two months was $_____4,245_____.

25 sets × $45 = $1,125 commission for first 25 sets   25 sets × $45 = $1,125 commission for first 25 sets
2 sets × $60 = $120 commission for the next 2 sets   25 sets × $60 = $1,500 commission for the next 25 sets
$1,125 + $120 = $1,245 total commission for November   5 sets × $75 = $375 commission for next 5 sets
$1,245 + $3,000 = $4,245 total commission for two months $1,125 + $1,500 + $375 = $3,000 total commission Dec.

2. Northwest Products, Inc. pays it salespersons 5% commission on all sales and 3% more commission on all monthly sales over $10,000. In May Shelly Giannone sold $26,000 worth of goods for Northwest. Her commission for May was $_____1,780_____.

$26,000 − $10,000 = $16,000 amount over quota
$26,000 × 0.05 = $1,300 commission on all sales
$16,000 × 0.03 = $480 commission on sales over quota
$1,300 + $480 = $1,780 total commission for May

3. Ezra Goldbaum is paid a salary of $500 a month, a 1% commission on all sales, and 2% more on monthly sales over $8,500. In June, his sales were $12,500 and in July, $14,300. His total salary and commission was (a) $_____705_____ in June and (b) $_____759_____ in July.

a. $500 + (0.01 × $12,500) + 0.02 × ($12,500 − $8,500) = $705 income for June
b. $500 + (0.01 × $14,300) + 0.02 × ($14,300 − $8,500) = $759 income for July

4. Lisa Schopp is offered a sales job with two firms. Agnew Plastics Co. offers her a salary of $500 a month, a commission of 2% on total monthly sales, and 3% more on monthly sales over $7,500. Randon and Colby, Inc. offers her a commission of 6% on the first $3,000 of monthly sales, 8% on the next $3,000 of monthly sales, and 10% on all monthly sales over $6,000. If Schopp averages $17,000 in sales a month, she will earn (a) $_____395_____ more per month by taking the job with (b) _____Randon and Colby, Inc._____.

a. $500 + (0.02 × $17,000) + 0.03 × ($17,000 − $7,500) = $1,125 income from Agnew Plastics Co.
   (0.06 × $3,000) + (0.08 × $3,000) + (0.10 × $11,000) = $1,520 income from Randon and Colby, Inc.
   $1,520 − $1,125 = $395 more per month
b. Randon and Colby, Inc.

Exercise 3.   (Commission rates)

1. On sales of $34,000, a salesperson earns $2,720 commission. The rate of commission is _____8_____%.

    $2,720 ÷ $34,000 = 0.08 = 8% rate of commission

2. During March, Carl Pozek sold $25,700 worth of goods. His total earnings for the month were $2,356, which included a salary of $300 a month. (a) His commission for the month was $_____2,056_____. (b) The commission rate was _____8_____%.

    $2,356 − $300 = $2,056 commission for month
    $2,056 ÷ 25,700 = 0.08 = 8% rate of commission

3. Jim McAney's total sales last month were $40,800, and his commission was $924. He earns a commission only on monthly sales over $24,000. His rate of commission is _____5.5_____%.

    $40,800 − $24,000 = $16,800 sales over quota
    $924 ÷ $16,800 = 0.055 = 5.5% rate of commission

Exercise 4.

1. Susan Favre sold her home through Tri-Town Realty Company, which charges a 6% sales commission. Her agent was Vince Pineta. Vince had advertised Susan's home for sale at $175,900, but was able to sell it for only $165,500. If Vince's share of the commission was $3\frac{1}{2}$%, he earned $_____5,792.50_____ commission on the sale.

    $165,500 × 0.035 = $5,792.50 commission

2. Ray Oliver was a collection agent for Regents Collections, Inc. The firm charged 25% commission. Ray collected 82% of an overdue account for $23,568 for the Ramsey Corporation. Regents charged $_____4,831.44_____ commission for collecting the account.

    $23,568 × 0.82 = $19,325.76 amount collected
    $19,325.76 × 0.25 = $4,831.44 commission

3. Ester White, a real estate agent, sold a house and lot for the Durrs for $88,000. She charged 6% commission and $275 for expenses. (a) The estimated amount of Ester's commission was $_____5,400_____. (b) The exact amount of her commission was $_____5,280_____. (c) The Durrs received $_____82,445_____ in net proceeds from the sale.

    a. $90,000 × 0.06 = $5,400 estimated commission on sale
    b. $88,000 × 0.06 = $5,280 exact commission on sale
    c. $88,000 − ($5,280 + $275) = $82,445 net proceeds from sale

4. Tom Polanski, a collection agent, collected a bill for $1,850 for Dexeter, Inc. He deducted 35% for commission. (a) His commission was $_____647.50_____. (b) The amount he owed to Dexeter, Inc. was $_____1,202.50_____.

    $1,850 × 0.35 = $647.50 commission
    $1,850 − $647.50 = $1,202.50 amount owed to Dexeter, Inc.

5. Chieko Kato, a collection agent, collected 85% of a debt of $1,780 for Polos Ticket Corporation. She charged 30% to make the collection. The amount owed to Polos Corporation was $_____1,059.10_____.

    $1,780 × 0.85 = $1,513 amount collected
    $1,513 × 0.30 = $453.90 commission
    $1,513 − $453.90 = $1,059.10 amount owed to Polos Ticket Corporation

6. Joe Popoff, a collection agent, collected 90% of a debt of $5,600 which had been overdue 90 days. This collection rate was 5% more than the average collection rate for that agent. The agent charged 25% commission. The net proceeds of the debt were $_____3,780_____.

    $5,600 × 0.90 = $5,040 amount collected
    $5,040 × 0.25 = $1,260 commission
    $5,040 − $1,260 = $3,780 net proceeds

TERM TICKLER

Directions   Find each of the following terms in the puzzle. Circle each term when you find it. It may be written downward, upward, sideways, or diagonally.

Terms

agent	base	decimal
deductions	fica tax	fractional equivalent
fringe benefits	graduated commission	net job benefits
net or takehome pay	net proceeds	percent
principal	quota	straight commission
total job benefits	withholding allowance	withholding tax

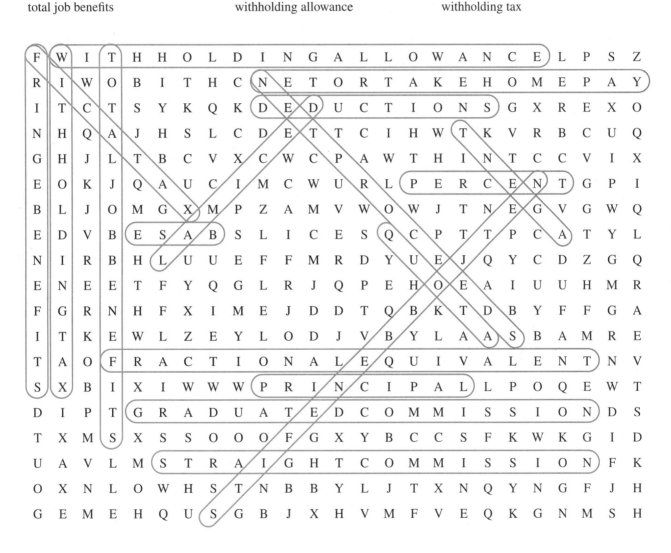

INTEGRATED PROJECT 4

E. Arbruster is the manager of a small architectural firm that employs three architects: R. Benitez, S. Feinstein, and D. Gabronski. J. D'Arcy is a secretary, Y. Chou a bookkeeper and R. Evans a clerk typist. The manager and architects are the professional staff and the secretary, bookkeeper, and clerk typist are the clerical support staff.

1. Complete the payroll sheet below.

Arbuster and Associates
Payroll Sheet for May, 19—

Employee Name	Earnings			Deductions				Net Pay
	Salary	Commission	Gross Pay	Federal With. Tax	FICA Tax (0.0765)	Insurance	Total Deducts	
Arbruster	5,000		5,000	856	382.50	78.12	1,316.62	3,683.38
Benitez	2,500	1,250	3,750	591	286.88	57.40	935.28	2,814.72
Chou	750		750	46	57.38	35.89	139.27	610.73
D'Arcy	890		890	96	68.09	35.89	199.98	690.02
Evans	525		525	41	40.16	32.55	113.71	411.29
Feinstein	2,000	2,775	4,775	788	365.29	78.12	1,231.41	3,543.59
Gabronski	3,000	1,080	4,080	645	312.12	68.45	1,025.57	3,054.43
Totals	14,665	5,105	19,770	3,063	1,512.42	386.42	4,961.84	14,808.16

Analyze the business payroll for May using the completed May payroll sheet.

2. Find the average monthly net pay of employees. $____2,115.45____

$14,808.16 ÷ 7 = $2,115.45 average monthly net pay

3. What is the average yearly gross pay of the professional staff? $____52,815____

$5,000 + $3,750 + $4,775 + $4,080 = $17,605 monthly gross pay of professional staff
$17,605 × 12 = $211,260 yearly gross pay of professional staff
$211,260 ÷ 4 = $52,815 average yearly gross pay of professional staff

4. Find the average weekly gross pay of the clerical staff. $____166.54____

$750 + $890 + $525 = $2,165 total monthly gross pay of clerical staff
$2,165 × 12 = $25,980 total yearly gross pay of clerical staff
$25,980 ÷ 3 = $8,660 average yearly gross pay of clerical staff
$8,660 ÷ 52 = $166.54 average weekly gross pay of clerical staff

5. What is the ratio of the number of professional staff workers to the number of clerical staff workers?

_____4:3_____

4 professional staff workers to 3 clerical staff workers, or 4:3

6. What percent is May's professional staff gross pay of the total gross pay for May, to the nearest whole percent?

_____89%_____

$5,000 + $3,750 + $4,775 + $4,080 = $17,605 total gross pay of professional staff
$17,605 ÷ $19,770 = 0.890, or 89% of professional staff gross pay to total gross pay

7. If Y. Chou gets a 5% raise, find the new salary. _____$787.50_____

$750 × 0.05 = $37.50 raise
$750 + $37.50 = $787.50 new gross pay

Name: _____   Date: _____

METRIC MEASUREMENT

LESSON 5-1   LENGTH

Exercise 1.   (Changing from one metric unit of length to another)

1. 4 m = _____40_____ dm
2. 7 m = ____7 000____ mm
3. 9 km = ____9 000____ m
4. 6 dm = _____600_____ mm
5. 1 cm = _____10_____ mm

6. 70 mm = _____7_____ cm
7. 3 mm = ____0.003____ m
8. 26 m = _____260_____ dm
9. 78 dam = _____7.8_____ hm
10. 8 cm = _____0.8_____ dm

11. 6 700 m = _____6.7_____ km
12. 50 m = ____5 000____ cm
13. 5.4 m = _____54_____ dm
14. 0.3 km = _____300_____ m
15. 5 000 dm = _____500_____ m

Exercise 2.   (Adding, subtracting, multiplying, and dividing metric numbers)

1. Add:

a. 17 km + 9 km = _____26_____ km
b. 7.4 m + 3.8 m = _____11.2_____ m
c. 6.51 m + 4.18 m = _____10.69_____ m
d. 340 m + 1.2 km = _____1.54_____ km

e. 68.73 cm + 6.09 m = ____6.777 3____ m
f. 12 km + 36 km + 6 000 m = _____54_____ km
g. 2 m + 800 cm + 1 000 mm = _____11_____ m
h. 50 000 mm + 20 m + 100 cm = _____71_____ m

2. Subtract:

a. 68 m − 35 m = _____33_____ m
b. 76.73 km − 22.98 km = _____53.75_____ km
c. 140 cm − 101 cm = _____39_____ cm
d. 10 m − 500 cm = _____5_____ m

e. 4 530 mm − 4 m = _____530_____ mm
f. 5 km − 2 000 m = _____3_____ km
g. 755 cm − 4 400 mm = ____3 150____ mm
h. 5 000 mm − 40 cm = ____4 600____ mm

3. Multiply:

a. 34 m × 5 = _____170_____ m
b. 17 cm × 6 = _____102_____ cm
c. 800 m × 30 = _____24_____ km

d. 40 cm × 80 = _____32_____ m
e. 45 km × 3 = ____135 000____ m
f. 19 cm × 7 = _____1,330_____ mm

4. Divide:

a. 72 m ÷ 12 = _____6_____ m
b. 3 500 km ÷ 5 = _____700_____ km
c. 8 000 mm ÷ 100 = _____80_____ mm

d. 84 km ÷ 7 = _____12_____ km
e. 1.5 km ÷ 5 = _____300_____ m
f. 28 cm ÷ 4 = _____70_____ mm

Exercise 3.

1. Alvaro Sandoval has 23 video tape cartridge holders whose average width is 30 mm. How many centimeters wide must a shelf be to store these cartridge holders? _____69_____ cm

   23 × 30 = 690 mm total width of holders in mm
   690 mm ÷ 10 = 69 cm shelf width in cm

2. Plastic tubing 6 meters long was cut into five equal pieces. What was the length of each piece: (a) in centimeters? _____120_____ cm (b) in millimeters? _____1 200_____ mm

   a. 6 m × 100 = 600 cm ÷ 5 = 120 cm length of piece in cm
   b. 600 cm × 10 = 6 000 mm ÷ 5 = 1 200 mm length of piece in mm

3. A store placed on sale a 600-meter roll of nylon rope. These lengths of rope were sold from the roll: 50 m, 75 m, 45 m, 18 m, 23 m.

   a. How many meters of rope were sold from the roll? _____211_____ m

   b. How many meters of rope were left on the roll? _____389_____ m

   a. 50 m + 75 m + 45 m + 18 m + 23 m = 211 m rope sold
   b. 600 m − 211 m = 389 m rope left on roll

4. A charter pilot flew these distances in five trips: 321 km, 280 km, 110 km, 215 km, 384 km.

   a. How many kilometers did the pilot fly in five trips? _____1 310_____ km

   b. What was the average distance flown per trip, in kilometers? _____262_____ km

   c. If there are 0.62 miles in a kilometer, what equivalent distance in miles did the pilot fly on these five trips? _____812.2_____ miles

   a. 321 km + 280 km + 110 km + 215 km + 384 km = 1 310 km distance flown
   b. 1 310 km ÷ 5 = 262 km average distance flown per trip
   c. 1 310 × 0.62 = 812.2 miles flown on five trips

5. A local safety group wants to buy reflective tape for the bicycles of 150 children at a local school. They figure that each bicycle needs these amounts and lengths of tape: 4 strips, each 20 cm long; 2 strips, each 30 cm long.

   a. How many centimeters of tape are needed for each bicycle? _____140_____ cm

   b. How many meters of tape are needed for 150 bicycles? _____210_____ m

   a. 4 × 20 = 80 cm
      2 × 30 = 60 cm
                140 cm total tape needed for one bicycle
   b. 150 × 140 cm = 21 000 cm or 210 m total tape needed for 150 bicycles

6. Eliza Stelig bought 12 boards. Each board was 2.6 meters long. Eliza had to cut 10 cm from the end of 7 boards and 4 cm from the end of the other 5 boards to fit them into place.

   a. How many meters of board did Eliza buy? _____31.2_____ m

   b. How many meters of board did she cut off and not use? _____0.9_____ m

   a. 12 × 2.6 m = 31.2 m total length of boards
   b. (7 × 10 cm) + (5 × 4 cm) = 90 cm or 0.9 m board not used

LESSON 5-2   AREA

Exercise 1.   (Changing from one metric unit of area to another)

1. $8 \text{ km}^2 = \underline{\hspace{0.5cm} 800 \hspace{0.5cm}} \text{ ha}$

2. $1\,000 \text{ cm}^2 = \underline{\hspace{0.5cm} 0.1 \hspace{0.5cm}} \text{ m}^2$

3. $4 \text{ m}^2 = \underline{\hspace{0.5cm} 40\,000 \hspace{0.5cm}} \text{ cm}^2$

4. $600 \text{ mm}^2 = \underline{\hspace{0.5cm} 6 \hspace{0.5cm}} \text{ cm}^2$

5. $15\,000 \text{ m}^2 = \underline{\hspace{0.5cm} 1.5 \hspace{0.5cm}} \text{ ha}$

6. $30\,000 \text{ cm}^2 = \underline{\hspace{0.5cm} 3 \hspace{0.5cm}} \text{ m}^2$

7. $3.6 \text{ ha} = \underline{\hspace{0.5cm} 36\,000 \hspace{0.5cm}} \text{ m}^2$

8. $700 \text{ ha} = \underline{\hspace{0.5cm} 7 \hspace{0.5cm}} \text{ km}^2$

9. $72 \text{ mm}^2 = \underline{\hspace{0.5cm} 0.72 \hspace{0.5cm}} \text{ cm}^2$

10. $0.007 \text{ km}^2 = \underline{\hspace{0.5cm} 7\,000 \hspace{0.5cm}} \text{ m}^2$

11. $4.7 \text{ ha} = \underline{\hspace{0.5cm} 0.047 \hspace{0.5cm}} \text{ km}^2$

12. $2.1 \text{ km}^2 = \underline{\hspace{0.5cm} 2\,100\,000 \hspace{0.5cm}} \text{ m}^2$

13. $13\,000 \text{ mm}^2 = \underline{\hspace{0.5cm} 0.013 \hspace{0.5cm}} \text{ m}^2$

14. $25 \text{ cm}^2 = \underline{\hspace{0.5cm} 2\,500 \hspace{0.5cm}} \text{ mm}^2$

15. $9 \text{ ha} = \underline{\hspace{0.5cm} 90\,000 \hspace{0.5cm}} \text{ m}^2$

Exercise 2.   (Adding, subtracting, multiplying, and dividing metric measures of area)

In each problem, first change to equivalent units, if necessary. Then do the calculations.

1. Add:

 a. $18 \text{ m}^2 + 24 \text{ m}^2 = \underline{\hspace{0.5cm} 42 \hspace{0.5cm}} \text{ m}^2$

 b. $140 \text{ km}^2 + 65 \text{ km}^2 = \underline{\hspace{0.5cm} 205 \hspace{0.5cm}} \text{ km}^2$

 c. $8.3 \text{ cm}^2 + 13.6 \text{ cm}^2 = \underline{\hspace{0.5cm} 21.9 \hspace{0.5cm}} \text{ cm}^2$

 d. $50 \text{ cm}^2 + 700 \text{ mm}^2 = \underline{\hspace{0.5cm} 57 \hspace{0.5cm}} \text{ cm}^2$

 e. $3\,000 \text{ ha} + 20 \text{ km}^2 = \underline{\hspace{0.5cm} 50 \hspace{0.5cm}} \text{ km}^2$

 f. $17 \text{ m}^2 + 300 \text{ dm}^2 = \underline{\hspace{0.5cm} 20 \hspace{0.5cm}} \text{ m}^2$

2. Subtract:

 a. $92 \text{ m}^2 - 30 \text{ m}^2 = \underline{\hspace{0.5cm} 62 \hspace{0.5cm}} \text{ m}^2$

 b. $230 \text{ km}^2 - 70 \text{ km}^2 = \underline{\hspace{0.5cm} 160 \hspace{0.5cm}} \text{ km}^2$

 c. $15.4 \text{ cm}^2 - 11 \text{ cm}^2 = \underline{\hspace{0.5cm} 4.4 \hspace{0.5cm}} \text{ cm}^2$

 d. $60 \text{ cm}^2 - 800 \text{ mm}^2 = \underline{\hspace{0.5cm} 52 \hspace{0.5cm}} \text{ cm}^2$

 e. $1\,600 \text{ mm}^2 - 8 \text{ cm}^2 = \underline{\hspace{0.5cm} 800 \hspace{0.5cm}} \text{ mm}^2$

 f. $27 \text{ km}^2 - 2\,300 \text{ ha} = \underline{\hspace{0.5cm} 4 \hspace{0.5cm}} \text{ km}^2$

3. Multiply:

 a. $34 \text{ ha} \times 8 = \underline{\hspace{0.5cm} 272 \hspace{0.5cm}} \text{ ha}$

 b. $2.3 \text{ km}^2 \times 5 = \underline{\hspace{0.5cm} 11.5 \hspace{0.5cm}} \text{ km}^2$

 c. $700 \text{ cm}^2 \times 40 = \underline{\hspace{0.5cm} 28\,000 \hspace{0.5cm}} \text{ cm}^2$

 d. $2\,000 \text{ mm}^2 \times 0.5 = \underline{\hspace{0.5cm} 0.001 \hspace{0.5cm}} \text{ m}^2$

 e. $27 \text{ cm}^2 \times 3 = \underline{\hspace{0.5cm} 8\,100 \hspace{0.5cm}} \text{ mm}^2$

 f. $900 \text{ ha} \times 2 = \underline{\hspace{0.5cm} 18 \hspace{0.5cm}} \text{ km}^2$

4. Divide:

 a. $250 \text{ m}^2 \div 5 = \underline{\hspace{0.5cm} 50 \hspace{0.5cm}} \text{ m}^2$

 b. $3\,600 \text{ mm}^2 \div 24 = \underline{\hspace{0.5cm} 150 \hspace{0.5cm}} \text{ mm}^2$

 c. $300 \text{ km}^2 \div 4 = \underline{\hspace{0.5cm} 75 \hspace{0.5cm}} \text{ km}^2$

 d. $186 \text{ ha} \div 6 = \underline{\hspace{0.5cm} 31 \hspace{0.5cm}} \text{ ha}$

 e. $200 \text{ cm}^2 \div 20 = \underline{\hspace{0.5cm} 1\,000 \hspace{0.5cm}} \text{ mm}^2$

 f. $800 \text{ km}^2 \div 16 = \underline{\hspace{0.5cm} 5\,000 \hspace{0.5cm}} \text{ ha}$

Exercise 3.

1. A land developer offered for sale 120 hectares of land. One builder bought 45.5 ha of the land to use for single-family houses. Another builder bought 68.2 ha to use for apartment houses. How much land does the developer still own? _____6.3_____ ha

    120 ha − (45.5 ha + 68.2 ha) = 6.3 ha land developer still owns

2. The playing surface of a soccer field is 100 meters by 62 meters. What is the area in square meters? ____6 200____ m²

    62 m × 100 m = 6 200 m² area of field

3. A builder offered to build walls to divide a 200 m × 90 m warehouse into three equal parts. What will be the area in square meters of each part after the walls are built? ____6 000____ m²

    90 m × 200 m = 18 000 m² total area of warehouse
    18 000 m² ÷ 3 = 6 000 m² area of each part

4. A farmer bought two sections of land. One section is 600 m by 150 m; the other is 300 m × 80 m. Wheat was planted on one half of the larger section and soybeans on the other half. The smaller section was left idle.

    a. How many hectares are in these two sections of land? ____11.4 ha____

    b. How many hectares of land are used for growing wheat? ____4.5 ha____

    c. How many hectares of land were left idle? ____2.4 ha____

    d. If one hectare equals 2.5 acres, how many acres of land were left idle? ____6 acres____

    a. (150 m × 600 m) + (80 m × 300 m) = 114 000 m² or 11.4 ha total land bought
    b. (150 m × 600 m) ÷ 2 = 45 000 m² or 4.5 ha land used for growing wheat
    c. 300 m × 80 m = 24 000 m² or 2.4 hectares left idle
    d. 2.4 × 2.5 = 6 acres left idle

5. Katharine Muellander wants to insulate a space 10 m by 13.5 m. She plans to use insulation that covers 4.5 m² per roll.

    a. How many square meters of space does Katharine want to insulate? ____135 m²____

    b. How many rolls of insulation will she have to use? ____30 rolls____

    a. 10 m × 13.5 m = 135 m² area of space to be insulated
    b. 135 m² ÷ 4.5 m² = 30 rolls

6. One wall of an office building measures 6 m by 30 m. Each of the 24 windows in the wall measures 0.8 m by 2.5 m. The rest of the wall surface is brick.

    a. What is the area of the wall in square meters? ____180 m²____

    b. How many square meters of the wall are used for windows? ____48 m²____

    c. How many square meters of the wall surface are brick? ____132 m²____

    a. 6 m × 30 m = 180 m² area of the wall
    b. 0.8 m × 2.5 m = 2 m² area of one window
       24 × 2 m² = 48 m² total window area
    c. 180 m² − 48 m² = 132 m² total brick area

LESSON 5-3   CAPACITY AND MASS

Exercise 1.   (Arithmetic with metric measures of capacity)

1. 17 L + 43 L = ___60___ L = __60 000__ mL
2. 300 mL + 780 mL = __1 080__ mL = __1.08__ L
3. 1 000 L + 500 L = __1 500__ L = __1.5__ kL
4. 25 kL + 35 kL = __60__ kL = __60 000__ L
5. 7.2 L − 5.9 L = __1.3__ L = __1 300__ mL
6. 14 kL − 5 000 L = __9__ kL = __9 000__ L

7. 800 mL − 260 mL = __540__ mL = __0.54__ L
8. 27 L − 600 mL = __26.4__ L = __26 400__ mL
9. 5 × 0.74 kL = __3.7__ kL = __3 700__ L
10. 2 × 10.25 mL = __20.5__ mL = __0.020 5__ L
11. 2.24 L ÷ 14 = __0.16__ L = __160__ mL
12. 6 kL ÷ 120 = __0.05__ kL = __50 000__ mL

Exercise 2.

1. In five days, a lawn-care service used these amounts of gasoline: Monday, 22.65 liters; Tuesday, 26.7 liters; Wednesday, 19 liters; Thursday, 46.85 liters; Friday, 33.7 liters. (a) How many liters of gasoline were used in these five days? __148.9__ L (b) At 0.26 gallons to the liter, how many gallons of gas were used in five days, to the nearest gallon? __39__ gallons

   a. 22.65 L + 26.7 + 19 L + 46.85 L + 33.7 L = 148.9 L
   b. 148.9 × 0.26 = 38.714, or 39 gallons used in five days

2. After a certain chemical is made, it is poured into a 25 mL bottle and sold in that size. How many 25 mL bottles can be filled from one liter of the chemical? __40__

   1 L = 1 000 mL number of mL in one liter
   1 000 mL ÷ 25 mL = 40 number of 25 mL bottles filled from one liter

3. A sugar-free cola can be bought in 354 mL cans or 1 L bottles. If you bought a case of 24 cans, you would buy __8 496__ mL or __8.496__ L of cola. How many one-liter bottles would you have to buy to get at least as much cola as you get in a case of 24 cans? __9__

   24 × 354 mL = 8 496 mL or 8.496 L amount of cola in 24 cans
   8.496 rounded to next highest liter = 9 bottles needed

4. Kinuyo Doi had to use a larger truck than she needed to deliver 100 personal copiers. For the trip, she used 75 liters of gas. If she had used a smaller truck, she would have used 14% less gas. (a) The amount of gas that she would have used in the smaller truck would have been __64.5__ L. (b) If gas costs $0.32 a liter, how much money could she have saved by using a smaller truck? __$3.36__

   a. 14% × 75 L = 0.14 × 75 L = 10.5 L gas that could have been saved
      75 L − 10.5 L = 64.5 L gas usage if smaller truck had been used
   b. $0.32 × 10.5 L = $3.36 money that could have been saved

Exercise 3.   (Arithmetic with metric units of weight)

1. 714 mg + 356 mg = ___1 070___ mg = ___1.07___ g
2. 68 kg + 15 kg = ___83___ kg = ___83 000___ g
3. 3.1 g + 9.7 g = ___12.8___ g = ___0.012 8___ kg
4. 800 g + 7 kg = ___7 800___ g = ___7.8___ kg
5. 6.5 g − 3.9 g = ___2.6___ g = ___2 600___ mg
6. 23 kg − 7 000 g = ___16___ kg = ___16 000___ g

7. 700 mg − 550 mg = ___150___ mg = ___0.15___ g
8. 15 g − 1 500 mg = ___13.5___ g = ___13 500___ mg
9. 0.6 × 90 mg = ___54___ mg = ___0.054___ g
10. 2,000 × 17 mg = ___34 000___ mg = ___0.034___ kg
11. 21 kg ÷ 7 = ___3___ kg = ___3 000___ g
12. 720 g ÷ 0.5 = ___1 440___ g = ___1.44___ kg

Exercise 4.

1. Lionel Mansour loaded this office furniture onto a truck: 6 desks weighing 120 kg each; 14 filing cabinets that weighed 46 kg each; 25 chairs, each weighing 7.2 kg; 2 floor lamps that weighed 18 kg total. (a) The total weight of the furniture that Lionel loaded was _____1 562_____ kg. (b) If the truck weighed 4 300 kg, what was the combined weight of the truck and the furniture? _____5 862_____ kg

    a. (6 × 120 kg) + (14 × 46 kg) + (25 × 7.2 kg) + 18 kg = 1 562 kg weight of furniture
    b. 4 300 kg + 1 562 kg = 5 862 kg combined weight of truck and furniture

2. A case of paint contains 12 one-liter cans packed in a cardboard box. Each can of paint weighs 1.12 kilograms. The cardboard box weighs 520 grams. (a) What is the total weight of the case of paint in kilograms? _____13.96_____ kg (b) What is the total weight of the case of paint to the nearest tenth of a pound, if 1 kilogram = 2.2 pounds? _____30.7_____ pounds

    a. 12 × 1.12 kg = 13.44 kg weight of 12 cans of paint
       520 g = 0.52 kg weight of box in kilograms
       13.44 kg + 0.52 kg = 13.96 kg weight of case of paint
    b. 13.96 × 2.2 = 30.712 pounds, or 30.7 pounds weight of case

3. Omar Steel Products used 600 sheets of steel to make heavy-duty shelving. Each sheet weighed 28.4 kilograms. In making the shelving, 5% of the steel used became scrap. What was the weight of the scrap? _____852_____ kg

    600 × 28.4 kg = 17 040 kg weight of steel used
    5% × 17 040 = 0.05 × 17 040 kg = 852 kg weight of scrap

4. A lawn sprinkler that used to weigh 0.7 kilograms was redesigned to make it lighter. The sprinkler now weighs 455 grams. After being redesigned, the sprinkler's weight is (a) _____245_____ g or (b) _____35_____ % less than its former weight.

    a. 0.7 kg − 455 g = 700 g − 455 g = 245 g amount sprinkler weighs less
    b. 245 g ÷ 700 g = 0.35 or 35% percent of weight reduction in sprinkler

TERM TICKLER

Directions   Complete the crossword puzzle below.

Across

2. One-hundredth of a meter
3. One-thousandth gram
4. One thousand liters
7. One-thousandth meter
8. One-thousandth kilogram
9. Width times length
10. The basic unit of length in the metric system

Down

1. Another name for square hectometer
3. One-thousandth liter
4. One thousand meters
5. Basic measure of weight in the metric system
6. Basic measure of capacity in the metric system

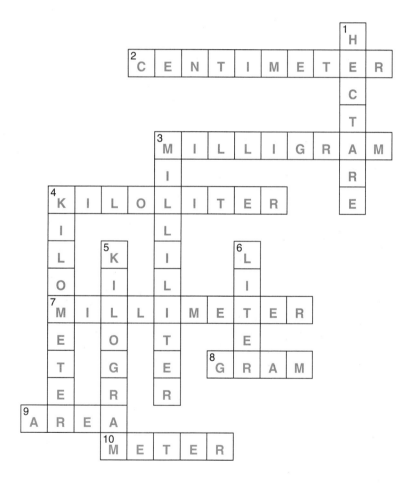

Name: _____ Date: _____

INTEGRATED PROJECT 5

The Wilcore Company buys its office supplies from a local dealer. One of your job duties is to order office supplies. Other employees in the company send their requests to you and often ask detailed questions about the products available. To find answers, you refer to a catalog published by the local office products dealer. A portion of the catalog is shown below. Use the information listed to help you provide an answer to the questions that follow.

Partial List
OFFICE SUPPLY CATALOG

Item	Description	Price
Chair Mat	Clear plastic, 120 cm by 150 cm, weight 12.6 kg	$89.50 each
Copier Paper, Roll	Roll of paper, 216 mm by 253 m, weight 5.2.kg	$47 per roll
Copier Toner	Sold in cartons of six 100 mL bottles. Each carton good for 15,000 copies	$64 per carton
Rubber Cement	125 mL jar with brush	$1.35 per bottle
	1 liter jar with brush	$5.19 per bottle
Shelving, Steel	Unit consists of supports, side braces, 6 shelves 46 cm deep by 91 cm wide; weight 40.5 kg	$122 per unit
Vinyl Tape	Used for making labels, roll 6.35 mm wide by 375 cm long	$1.82 per roll
Twine, Ball	Cotton twine, length is 244 m per kg, weight 250 g per ball	$2.70 per ball
Wrapping Paper	Light-weight paper, 61 cm wide by 220 m long, weight 12 kg	$34 per roll
	Heavy-weight paper, 61 cm wide by 152 m long, weight 12 kg	$34 per roll

1. What area in square meters is covered by one chair mat? _____ 1.8 _____ m^2

   120 cm $\times$ 150 cm = 1.2 m $\times$ 1.5 m = 1.8 m^2

2. If 3 shelving units and 4 chair mats are ordered, what will be the total weight of the order in kilograms?
   _____ 171.9 _____ kg

   (3 $\times$ 40.5 kg) + (4 $\times$ 12.6 kg) = 171.9 kg total weight

3. How many whole copies measuring 216 mm wide by 279 mm long can be made from one roll of copier paper?
   _____ 906 _____

   253 m $\div$ 279 mm = 253 m $\div$ 0.279 m = 906.8, or 906 whole copies

4. How many meters of twine are in one ball of twine? _____ 61 m _____

   250 g $\div$ 1 kg = 250 g $\div$ 1 000 g = $\frac{1}{4}$
   $\frac{1}{4}$ $\times$ 244 m = 61 m twine

5. Using vinyl tape, an employee plans to make labels 125 mm long. How many labels of that length can be made from one roll of vinyl tape? _____30_____

375 cm ÷ 125 mm = 375 cm ÷ 12.5 cm = 30 labels

6. How many photocopies can be made from one bottle of copier toner? _____2,500_____

15,000 ÷ 6 = 2,500 copies

7. If the Wilcore Company makes 60,000 photocopies a year, how much copier toner, in liters, will be used? _____2.4_____ L

60,000 ÷ 15,000 = 4 cartons
6 × 100 mL = 600 mL = 0.6 L in a carton
4 × 0.6 L = 2.4 L to make 60,000 copies

8. How many more meters of wrapping paper are there in a roll of light-weight paper compared to a roll of heavy-weight paper? _____68_____

220 m − 152 m = 68 m

9. a. How many 125 mL jars of rubber cement must be bought to make one liter of rubber cement? _____8_____

b. What would be the total cost of buying that number of 125 mL jars? _____$10.80_____

c. How much could be saved by buying a 1 liter jar of rubber cement instead of buying separate 125 mL jars to make one liter of rubber cement? _____$5.61_____

a. 1L ÷ 125 mL = 1 000 mL ÷ 125 mL = 8 jars
b. 8 × $1.35 = $10.80 cost of 8 jars
c. $10.80 − $5.19 = $5.61 saved

Name: _____ Date: _____

BUYING FOR YOU AND YOUR HOME

LESSON 6-1   PLANNING A BUDGET

Exercise 1.   (Monthly cash record summary)

1. Ellie Compton's monthly cash record summary is shown below. You are to add each column and write the total on the line labeled "Totals." Check your work by adding the totals of the six types of payments columns. The total of these columns should equal the total of the Payments column.

MONTHLY CASH RECORD SUMMARY

Month	Receipts	Payments	Types of Payments (Expenses)					
			Food	Clothing	Housing	Auto	Other	Savings
January	850.00	772.52	138.21	128.87	250.87	156.23	48.34	50.00
February	820.00	763.89	137.53	45.66	275.19	174.22	81.29	50.00
March	875.00	915.38	155.04	72.98	259.61	274.87	102.88	50.00
April	825.00	953.92	135.66	145.32	351.14	173.44	98.36	50.00
May	810.00	732.29	145.33	39.58	250.09	184.21	63.08	50.00
June	890.00	803.89	110.78	28.61	354.71	158.98	100.81	50.00
July	920.00	999.26	125.66	187.32	274.88	207.51	153.89	50.00
August	940.00	853.78	146.90	97.43	289.89	183.74	50.82	85.00
September	910.00	782.45	113.76	31.51	311.10	177.05	99.03	50.00
October	970.00	879.38	131.54	28.95	307.98	161.71	154.20	95.00
November	910.00	984.92	156.99	114.98	314.22	241.98	106.75	50.00
December	980.00	1118.35	164.75	206.74	251.49	163.49	256.88	75.00
Total	10700.00	10560.03	1662.15	1127.95	3491.17	2257.43	1316.33	705.00

2. Based on the totals of the cash summary above, and figured to the nearest tenth of a percent, what percent of the total receipts for the year was Ellie's:

   a. Food payments? _____15.5%_____ $1,662.15 ÷ $10,700 = 0.1553, or 15.5%

   b. Auto payments? _____21.1%_____ $2,257.43 ÷ $10,700 = 0.2109, or 21.1%

   c. Savings? _____6.6%_____ $705 ÷ $10,700 = 0.0658, or 6.6%

3. Ted Kovarik's monthly take-home pay is $900. His expenses last month are shown below. In the blanks provided, write the fractional part of his take-home pay that he spent for each item.

Food $300, or ___$\frac{1}{3}$___ $300 \div \$900 = \frac{1}{3}$ Auto $150, or ___$\frac{1}{6}$___ $150 \div \$900 = \frac{1}{6}$

Clothing $90, or ___$\frac{1}{10}$___ $90 \div \$900 = \frac{1}{10}$ Other $30, or ___$\frac{1}{30}$___ $30 \div \$900 = \frac{1}{30}$

Housing $270, or ___$\frac{3}{10}$___ $270 \div \$900 = \frac{3}{10}$ Savings $60, or ___$\frac{1}{15}$___ $60 \div \$900 = \frac{1}{15}$

Exercise 2.   (Budgeting income)

1. Alma Ortez estimates that her total cash income for the year will be $15,000. She plans to spend her income as shown below. Write in the spaces provided the amounts allowed for each item.

Food 27%, or $___4,050___ $15,000 × 0.27 = $4,050

Auto 18%, or $___2,700___ $15,000 × 0.18 = $2,700

Clothing 7%, or $___1,050___ $15,000 × 0.07 = $1,050

Other 10%, or $___1,500___ $15,000 × 0.10 = $1,500

Housing 30%, or $___4,500___ $15,000 × 0.30 = $4,500

Savings 8%, or $___1,200___ $15,000 × 0.08 = $1,200

2. Paul Schultz is given $500 a month for college living expenses. His budget for this month is shown below. Find what percent of his monthly income is budgeted for each item. Write the answers in the blanks.

Clothing $35, or ___7___% $35 ÷ $500 = 0.07   Housing $200, or ___40___% $200 ÷ $500 = 0.4

Food $135, or ___27___% $135 ÷ $500 = 0.27   Transportation $60, or ___12___% $60 ÷ $500 = 0.12

Recreation $45, or ___9___% $45 ÷ $500 = 0.09   Other $25, or ___5___% $25 ÷ $500 = 0.05

3. Edison Brothers, Inc., a clothing chain, expects to gain extra sales of $450,000 on a sales promotion for next year. The firm plans to spend these percents of the extra sales on the promotion: newspaper advertising, 4.5%; radio advertising, 2.7%; television advertising, 2.3%; other advertising, 0.5%. The firm plans to spend these amounts for each type of advertising: newspapers, $____20,250____; radio, $____12,150____; television, $____10,350____; other, $____2,250____.

$450,000 × 0.045 = $20,250 newspapers; $450,000 × 0.027 = $12,150 radio; $450,000 × 0.023 = $10,350 TV;
$450,000 × 0.005 = $2,250 other advertising

4. Emma and Rod Volmer have a monthly income of $3,600. They plan to spend their income as shown in the chart on the left. Show in the spaces the amount they plan to spend this year for each item in the chart.

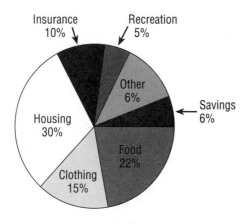

$3,600 × 12 = $43,200 annual income

Food $____9,504____ $43,200 × 0.22 = $9,504 food

Clothing $____6,480____ $43,200 × 0.15 = $6,480 clothing

Housing $____12,960____ $43,200 × 0.30 = $12,960 housing

Insurance $____4,320____ $43,200 × 0.10 = $4,320 insurance

Recreation $____2,160____ $43,200 × 0.05 = $2,160 recreation

Other $____5,184____ $43,200 × 0.12 = $5,184 other

Savings $____2,592____ $43,200 × 0.06 = $2,592 savings

LESSON 6-2   CHECKING SALES SLIPS

Exercise 1.   (Figuring extensions and sales taxes)

1. Complete the sales slip below.

CRAFTS UNLIMITED		803 Oregon Ave., Ogden, UT 84401-3738		
CALL 801-865-8297		**SOLD TO:** Eva Velez		
FROM 8 a.m. to 10 p.m.		**STREET:** 1207 Tracer St.		
DATE June 8 **19** --		**CITY, STATE, ZIP:** Ogden, UT 84404-1341		
SOLD BY I.S.	**CASH** ✓	**CHARGE**	**C.O.D.**	**DELIVER BY** Taken
QUANTITY	**DESCRIPTION**		**UNIT PRICE**	**AMOUNT**
1	Clock kit		44.75	44.75
2 boxes	Mixed sandpaper		2.15	4.30
6 doz.	1" wood screws		1.98	11.88
3	Airplane kits		14.29	42.87
5	Bottles of wood glue		2.88	14.40
CRAFTS ARE FUN! START A PROJECT TODAY!		SUBTOTAL		118.20
		SALES TAX	6%	7.09
		TOTAL		125.29

2. Check each calculation on the sales slip below. If there is an error, cross out the incorrect amount and write the correct amount to the right of the incorrect amount.

AL'S BIKE SHOP		2708 Valley Road, Albuquerque, NM 87114-4094			
CALL 505-348-1888		**SOLD TO:** Benjamin Schwartz			
FROM 8 a.m. to 10 p.m.		**STREET:** 8815 Quail St.			
DATE April 5 **19** --		**CITY, STATE, ZIP:** Albuquerque, NM 87107-9897			
SOLD BY T.M.	**CASH**	**CHARGE** ✓	**C.O.D.**	**DELIVER BY** Taken	
QUANTITY	**DESCRIPTION**		**UNIT PRICE**	**AMOUNT**	
2	All terrain bicycles		139.99	279.98	
2	Saddlebags		22.77	45.54	
8 pr.	Athletic socks		5.98	47.84	
3	Al's Bike Shop T shirts		8.88	26.64	
2	Bicycle caps		3.99	~~7.89~~	7.98
MOUNTAIN BIKETHON EVENT EVERY MAY THIS YEAR JOIN US!		SUBTOTAL		~~406.98~~	407.98
		SALES TAX	3%	12.24	
		TOTAL		~~420.20~~	420.22

3. Check each calculation on the sales slip below. If there is an error, cross out the incorrect amount and write the correct amount next to the incorrect amount.

4. Check each calculation on the sales slip below. If there is an error, cross out the incorrect amount and write the correct amount next to the incorrect amount.

BAKE BAKERY	2291 Pike Drive, Peoria, IL 61609-2454

CALL 309-446-1818   SOLD TO: *Tyrone Brown*

DATE *Nov. 10* 19 --   STREET: *9797 Union St.*

CITY, STATE, ZIP: *Peoria, IL 61604-6755*

SOLD BY A.T.	CASH ✓	CHARGE	

QUANTITY	DESCRIPTION	UNIT PRICE	AMOUNT
1 doz.	Hard rolls	2.29	2.29
3	Loaves whole wheat bread	1.22	3.66
4 doz.	Croissant rolls	6.99	27.96
5	Loaves pumpernickel bread	1.19	5.95
1	Loaf rye bread	1.28	1.28

EVERYTHING BAKED FRESH EVERY DAY!

SUBTOTAL		41.14	
SALES TAX	6%	~~2.46~~	2.47
TOTAL		~~43.60~~	43.61

EVERGREEN GIFTS	56 Broad Street, St. Charles, MO 63303-2008

CALL 314-863-1245   SOLD TO: *Lonnie McNamara*

DATE *Jan. 5* 19 --   STREET: *2407 Lee Ave.*

CITY, STATE, ZIP: *St. Louis, MO 63123-6518*

SOLD BY B.L.	CASH ✓	CHARGE	

QUANTITY	DESCRIPTION	UNIT PRICE	AMOUNT
3 boxes	Cards	7.36	22.08
5 doz.	Party napkins	2.99	14.95
3 decks	Playing cards	5.63	16.89
2	Table covers	8.15	16.30
24	Party hats	2.34	56.16

EVERYTHING BAKED FRESH EVERY DAY!

SUBTOTAL		~~126.36~~	126.38
SALES TAX	5%	~~6.31~~	6.32
TOTAL		~~133.51~~	132.70

Exercise 2.   (Counting change)

1. Show for each item the number of pieces of each kind of money you should give to the customer by completing the form below.

Item	Amount of Sale	Amount Received	Kind of Money							
			1¢	5¢	10¢	25¢	50¢	$1	$5	$10
a.	$3.17	$10	3	1		1	1	1	1	
b.	$0.43	$5	2	1			1	4		
c.	$8.56	$10	4	1	1	1		1		
d.	$1.02	$2	3		2	1	1			
e.	$35.78	2, $20 bills	2		2			4		
f.	$45.25	2, $20 bills 1, $10 bill				1	1	4		
g.	$11.28	$15 check	2		2		1	3		
h.	$82.55	$100 check			2	1		2	1	1

LESSON 6-3   MORE ON EXTENSIONS

Exercise 1.   (Finding the cost of a fraction of a unit)

1. Find the cost of each:

a. $\frac{1}{2}$ doz. rolls	@ $1.19	=	$	0.60
b. $\frac{3}{4}$ lb. sliced turkey	@ $3.99	=	$	2.99
c. $\frac{1}{4}$ yd. rope	@ $0.68	=	$	0.17
d. $\frac{5}{6}$ doz. donuts	@ $4.20	=	$	3.50
e. $\frac{2}{3}$ lb. beef	@ $5.25	=	$	3.50
f. $\frac{5}{8}$ yd. screening	@ $1.19	=	$	0.74
g. $\frac{3}{4}$ lb. fish	@ $4.29	=	$	3.22

2. You bought these items at an office supply store. Find the cost of each item, and the total cost.

a. $\frac{2}{3}$ box of diskettes ($3\frac{1}{2}$")	@ $7.80	=	$	5.20
b. $\frac{5}{6}$ doz. ribbons	@ $169.20	=	$	141.00
c. $\frac{3}{4}$ box of labels	@ $ 4.79	=	$	3.59
d. $\frac{1}{6}$ box of connectors	@ $35.40	=	$	5.90
e. $\frac{1}{4}$ doz. storage boxes	@ $82.44	=	$	20.61
f. Total			$	176.30

Exercise 2.   (Finding the cost when quantities or prices are mixed numbers)

1. Etta White bought the items below. Find the cost of each item, the subtotal, the sales tax, and the total.

a. $18\frac{2}{3}$ sq. yd. carpet	@ $21.99	=	$	410.48
b. $125\frac{1}{2}$ ft. wire	@ $0.20	=	$	25.10
c. $2\frac{1}{4}$ cases oil	@ $12.39	=	$	27.88
d. $4\frac{5}{8}$ cases twine	@ $21.87	=	$	101.15
e. Subtotal			$	564.61
f. Sales tax 5%			$	28.23
g. Total			$	592.84

2. Complete the sales slip below.

1st STREET MARKET		1888 First Street, Albany, NY 12203-7887		
DATE *March 3* **19** --		**SOLD TO:**	*Francis Sudholt*	
		STREET:	*7812 Quail St.*	
		CITY, STATE, ZIP:	*Albany, NY 12203-4511*	

SOLD BY S.R.	CASH ✓	CHARGE	C.O.D.	DELIVER

QUANTITY	DESCRIPTION		UNIT PRICE	AMOUNT
$4\frac{1}{2}$ lb.	Pears		.89	4.01
$2\frac{3}{4}$ lb.	Tangelos		.79	2.17
$2\frac{1}{3}$ lb.	Brussel sprouts		.69	1.61
$1\frac{1}{4}$ lb.	Broccoli spears		1.19	1.49
YOUR CENTER FOR FRESH FRUITS AND VEGETABLES		SUBTOTAL		9.28
		SALES TAX	3%	.28
		TOTAL		9.56

Exercise 3.   (Finding the cost of large quantities)

1. Eloise Vanetta bought 375 concrete blocks for a foundation at 92.29 per C. The total cost of the blocks was $_____346.09_____.

375 ÷ 100 = 3.75 number of 100's
3.75 × $92.29 = $346.09 cost of blocks

2. Vida Groceries bought 11,500 bags at $19.88 per M and 5,750 cartons at $33.58 per C from Denlon, Inc. The cost of the bags was (a) $_____228.62_____. The cost of the cartons was (b) $_____1,930.85_____. The total cost of the purchase was (c) $_____2,159.47_____.

a. 11,500 ÷ 1,000 = 11.5 number of 1,000's
    11.5 × $19.88 = $228.62 cost of bags
c. $228.62 + $1,930.85 = $2,159.47 total cost

b. 5,750 ÷ 100 = 57.5 number of 100's
    57.5 × $33.58 = $1,930.85 cost of cartons

3. Tom Klein bought 18,500 lb. of decorative rock for ground cover at $113.58 per T. The cost of the rock is $_____1,050.62_____.

18,500 ÷ 2,000 = 9.25 Customary tons
9.25 × $113.58 = $1,050.62 cost of rock

4. Elco Delivery Company had three deliveries of gasoline during the summer: 2,566 gallons at $0.999; 2,189 gallons at $1.189; and 2,895 gallons at $1.239. The total cost of the gasoline was $_____8,753.06_____.

2,566 × $.999 = $2,563.43
2,189 × $1.189 = $2,602.72
2,895 × $1.239 = $3,586.91
           $8,753.06 total cost of gasoline

5. At $17.99 a metric ton, the cost of 14 500 kg of sand is $_____260.86_____.

14 500 ÷ 1 000 = 14.5 metric tons
14.5 × $17.99 = $260.86 cost of sand

Exercise 4.

1. Complete the sales slip below. Make extensions mentally. Use exact fractional parts of $1. Find the total sale.

2. Complete the sales slip below. Make extensions mentally. Use exact fractional parts of $1. Find the total sale.

MARKET SQUARE FOODS   1757 Market St., Chesterfield, MO 63017-6612

SOLD TO: *Ted Cowan*

DATE *July 6* **19** --   STREET: *1598 Oak St.*

CITY, STATE, ZIP: *Chesterfield, MO 63017-8571*

SOLD BY A.W.	CASH ✓	CHARGE		C.O.D.	DELIVER
QUANTITY	DESCRIPTION		UNIT PRICE		AMOUNT
12	Cans pumpkin		.40		4.80
24	Boxes cake mix		.80		19.20
15	Lbs. butter		.87 $\frac{1}{2}$		13.13
9	Cans creamed corn		.33 $\frac{1}{3}$		3.00
36	Cans cranberry sauce		.87 $\frac{1}{2}$		31.50
OPEN EVERY DAY OF THE WEEK UNTIL 10:00!	SUBTOTAL				71.63
	SALES TAX	8%			5.73
	TOTAL				77.36

FARREL'S LUMBER YARD   19 Toester Drive, Peru, IN 46970-3398

SOLD TO: *Carlos Ramirez*

DATE *April 3* **19** --   STREET: *21 Old Post Road*

CITY, STATE, ZIP: *Peru, IN 46970-8665*

SOLD BY O.P.	CASH ✓	CHARGE		C.O.D.	DELIVER
QUANTITY	DESCRIPTION		UNIT PRICE		AMOUNT
48	Boxes nails		.87 $\frac{1}{2}$		42.00
75	Wall studs		.80		60.00
85	Brackets		.33 $\frac{1}{3}$		28.33
8	Bottles of glue		.50		4.00
95	Panels		.60		57.00
QUALITY PRODUCTS FOR YOUR HOME	SUBTOTAL				191.33
	SALES TAX	6%			11.48
	TOTAL				202.81

Exercise 5.

1. 368 ft. @ $12\frac{1}{2}$¢ = $ __46__

2. 128 bu. @ 20¢ = $ __25.60__

3. 96 yd. @ 75¢ = $ __72__

4. 36 lb. @ $87\frac{1}{2}$¢ = $ __31.50__

5. 76 lb. @ $0.25 = $ __19__

6. 168 L @ $12\frac{1}{2}$¢ = $ __21__

7. 310 m @ 50¢ = $ __155__

8. 40 cm @ 0.37\frac{1}{2}$¢ = $ __15__

9. 110 kg @ 60¢ = $ __66__

10. 128 m² @ $62\frac{1}{2}$¢ = $ __80__

11. 48 in. @ $33\frac{1}{3}$¢ = $ __16__

12. 48 oz. @ 0.66\frac{2}{3}$ = $ __32__

13. 44 sq. ft. @ $37\frac{1}{2}$¢ = $ __16.50__

14. 80 sq. yd. @ $0.80 = $ __64__

15. 320 qt. @ 0.87\frac{1}{2}$ = $ __280__

Exercise 6.

1. 120 ft. @ $0.20 = $ __24__

2. 84 lb. @ $33\frac{1}{3}$¢ = $ __28__

3. 120 yd. @ $37\frac{1}{2}$¢ = $ __45__

4. 56 yd. @ 0.87\frac{1}{2}$ = $ __49__

5. 42 ft. @ 0.66\frac{2}{3}$ = $ __28__

6. 65 lb. @ $0.60 = $ __39__

7. 45 bu. @ 50¢ = $ __22.50__

8. 42 bu. @ $62\frac{1}{2}$¢ = $ __26.25__

9. 215 lb. @ 40¢ = $ __86__

10. 75 lb. @ 80¢ = $ __60__

11. 70 lb. @ 25¢ = $ __17.50__

12. 186 lb. @ 75¢ = $ __139.50__

Exercise 7.

1. 34 doz. @ $0.25   = $ __8.50__
2. 26 cans @ 0.12\frac{1}{2}$ = $ __3.25__
3. 96 gal @ 0.66\frac{2}{3}$ = $ __64__
4. 50 yd. @ 0.33\frac{1}{3}$ = $ __16.67__
5. 36 cans @ 12$\frac{1}{2}$¢   = $ __4.50__

6. 94 doz. @ 25¢   = $ __23.50__
7. 25 lb. @ 50¢   = $ __12.50__
8. 80 ft. @ 87$\frac{1}{2}$¢   = $ __70__
9. 84 cm² @ 37$\frac{1}{2}$¢ = $ __31.50__
10. 70 kg @ $0.75   = $ __52.50__

11. 130 m @ 60¢   = $ __78__
12. 36 cm @ 0.62\frac{1}{2}$ = $ __22.50__
13. 35 L @ 40¢   = $ __14__
14. 175 m² @ $0.20 = $ __35__
15. 95 kg @ 80¢   = $ __76__

Exercise 8.

1. Doug Rouse, an agent, buys 360, 14 oz. cans of peas @ 0.33\frac{1}{3}$; 240, 10 lb. bags of flour @ 0.87\frac{1}{2}$; and 270, 2 lb. boxes of cheese for 0.66\frac{2}{3}$. The total cost of the purchase is $_____510_____.

$360 \times \frac{1}{3} \times \$1 = \$120$ cost of peas
$240 \times \frac{7}{8} \times \$1 = \$210$ cost of flour
$270 \times \frac{2}{3} \times \$1 = \underline{\$180}$ cost of cheese
$\$510$ total

2. A buyer purchases 560 yd. of fabric @ 0.87\frac{1}{2}$; 2,400 ft. of twine @ 0.33\frac{1}{3}$, and 600 ft. of copper wire @ $0.20. The total cost of the purchase is $_____1,410_____.

$560 \times \frac{7}{8} \times \$1 = \$\ 490$ cost of fabric
$2,400 \times \frac{1}{3} \times \$1 = \$\ 800$ cost of twine
$600 \times \frac{1}{5} \times \$1 = \underline{\$\ 120}$ cost of wire
$\$1,410$ total

3. The following amounts were listed on a sales slip: 24 doz. @ 0.33\frac{1}{3}$; 160 cans @ 0.37\frac{1}{2}$; 240 yd. @ 0.66\frac{2}{3}$; and 575 bu. @ $0.60. The total of the sales slip is $_____573.00_____.

$24 \times \frac{1}{3} \times \$1 = \$\ 8.00$
$160 \times \frac{3}{8} \times \$1 = \$\ 60.00$
$240 \times \frac{2}{3} \times \$1 = \$160.00$
$575 \times \frac{3}{5} \times \$1 = \underline{\$345.00}$
$\$573.00$ total

LESSON 6-4   FINDING UNIT PRICES

Exercise 1.   (Finding a unit price from a group price)

1. A store sells the items below at a special sale. Find the price of one unit of each item.

	Qty.	Item	Total Price	Price of One Unit
a.	3	car batteries	$128.98	$ 43.00
		$128.98 ÷ 3 = $42.993, or $43		
b.	2	Bars of bath soap	2.99	$ 1.50
		$2.99 ÷ 2 = $1.495, or $1.50		
c.	5	Boxes of gelatin	1.89	$ 0.38
		$1.89 ÷ 5 = $0.378, or $0.38		
d.	6	Cans of orange juice	5.95	$ 1.00
		$5.95 ÷ 6 = $0.991, or $1.00		
e.	4	Boxes of cold tablets	4.29	$ 1.08
		$4.29 ÷ 4 = $1.072, or $1.08		
f.	3	Videotapes	14.99	$ 5.00
		$14.99 ÷ 3 = $4.997, or $5.00		
g.	5	Foil roasting pans	6.89	$ 1.38
		$6.89 ÷ 5 = $1.378, or $1.38		

2. Find the price of one unit of each item below.

	Qty.	Item	Total Price	Price of One Unit
a.	5 lb.	Apples	$2.44	$ 0.49
		$2.44 ÷ 5 = $0.488, or $0.49		
b.	4	Sheets	56.98	$ 14.25
		$56.98 ÷ 4 = $14.245, or $14.25		
c.	3	Two-drawer file cabinets	386.00	$ 128.67
		$386.00 ÷ 3 = $128.667, or $128.67		
d.	6	Rolls, wrapping paper	6.15	$ 1.03
		$6.15 ÷ 6 = $1.025, or $1.03		
e.	8	Furnace filters	4.79	$ 0.60
		$4.79 ÷ 8 = $0.598, or $0.60		
f.	3	Packages, color film	8.95	$ 2.99
		$8.95 ÷ 3 = $2.983, or $2.99		
g.	3	Boxes of foil wrap	1.39	$ 0.47
		$1.39 ÷ 3 = $0.463, or $0.47		

Exercise 2.   (Finding the unit price when the item price is for a fractional or mixed number quantity)

1. The price of a 12 oz. box of crackers is $1.22. The price of the crackers per pound is $_____1.63_____.

    12 oz $= \frac{12}{16}$ lb., or $\frac{3}{4}$ lb. $1.22 $\div \frac{3}{4}$ = $1.22 $\times \frac{4}{3}$ = $1.626, or $1.63 per lb.

2. The price of a 15 oz. box of cereal is $3.99. The price of the cereal per pound is $_____4.26_____.

    15 oz. $= \frac{15}{16}$ lb. $3.99 $\div \frac{15}{16}$ = $3.99 $\times \frac{16}{15}$ = $4.256, or $4.26 per lb.

3. A 5 oz. tube of toothpaste costs $1.47. The price of the toothpaste per pound is $_____4.71_____.

    5 oz $= \frac{5}{16}$ lb. $1.47 $\div \frac{5}{16}$ = $1.47 $\times \frac{16}{5}$ = $4.704, or $4.71 per lb.

4. A $7\frac{1}{2}$ oz. jar of liquid makeup costs $3.99. The price of the liquid makeup per pound is $_____8.51_____.

    7.5 oz. $= \frac{7.5}{16}$ lb., or $\frac{15}{32}$ lb. $3.99 $\div \frac{15}{32}$ = $3.99 $\times \frac{32}{15}$ = $8.512, or $8.51 per lb.

5. A $3\frac{1}{4}$ lb. sirloin tip steak costs $8.74. The price per pound is $_____2.69_____.

    $8.74 $\div 3\frac{1}{4}$ = $8.74 $\times \frac{4}{13}$ = $2.689, or $2.69 per lb.

6. $21\frac{1}{2}$ ft. of electric cable costs $4.89. The price per foot is $_____0.23_____.

    $4.89 $\div 21\frac{1}{2}$ = $4.89 $\times \frac{2}{43}$ = $0.227, or $0.23 per ft.

7. A 12 oz. bag of Voran's chocolate chips costs $1.11. A 14 oz. bag of Yount's chocolate chips costs $1.39.

    a. The price per lb. of Voran's chips is $_____1.48_____.

        12 oz. $= \frac{12}{16}$ lb., or $\frac{3}{4}$ lb. $1.19 $\div 4$ = $1.11 $\times \frac{4}{3}$ = $1.48 per lb.

    b. The price per lb. of Yount's chips is $_____1.59_____.

        14 oz. $= \frac{14}{16}$ lb., or $\frac{7}{8}$ lb. $1.39 $\div \frac{7}{8}$ = $1.39 $\times \frac{8}{7}$ = $1.588, or $1.59 per lb.

    c. The difference between the two brands is $_____0.11_____ per lb.

        $1.59 $-$ $1.48 = $0.11 difference

LESSON 6-5   BUYING WISELY

Exercise 1.   (Buying at special prices)

1. A set of three audio tapes is regularly priced at $17.85. If you buy them at a special sale, you get a factory rebate of $6. At the sale price, the net cost per tape is $_____3.95_____.

    ($17.85 − $6) ÷ 3 = $3.95 net cost per tape

2. The price of milk in a gallon jug is $2.19. The same milk in quart containers is $0.59. By buying milk in the gallon jug, you save $_____0.17_____.

    (4 × $0.59) − $2.19 = $0.17

3. As an introductory offer, a cable TV company will install the cable free and charge you $35 a month for the first year's service. The regular price is $70 for installation and $38 a month for the service fee. If you take the introductory offer, you will save $_____106_____ in the first year.

    12 × $35 = $420 for first year at special offer
    (12 × $38) + $70 = $526 regular price for one year
    $526 − $420 = $106 saved

4. At a close-out sale, Ezra Steinfeld bought trousers that were reduced from $69.99 to $48.99. (a) By buying the trousers at the sale, he saved $_____21_____. (b) The reduction in price was a savings of _____30_____%, to the nearest percent.

    a. $69.99 − $48.99 = $21 amount saved
    b. $21 ÷ $69.99 = 30% saved

5. A company wants to buy 8 office chairs. Each chair is priced at $376.97 if from 1 to 5 are bought, and $298.50 if more than 5 are bought at one time. (a) The company will save $_____627.76_____ by buying 8 all at once instead of eight, one at a time. (b) The percent saved by buying all eight now, to the nearest whole percent, is _____21_____%.

    a. 8 × $376.97 = $3,015.76 total cost if bought one at a time
       8 × $298.50 = $2,388 total cost if all eight are bought now
       $3,015.76 − $2,388.00 = $627.76 amount saved
    b. $627.76 ÷ $3,015.76 = 0.208, or 21% saved

Exercise 2.   (Comparing prices)

1. You can buy three tubes of caulk at Foley's Hardware Store for $8.97 or five at Schwartz Fixit Shop for $13.45. (a) The price per tube at Foley's is $_____2.99_____. (b) The price per tube at Schwartz's is $_____2.69_____.

    a. $8.97 ÷ 3 = $2.99 price at Foley's Hardware Store
    b. $13.45 ÷ 5 = $2.69 price at Schwartz Fixit Shop

2. Central Stores offers fluorescent tubes at 2 for $7.50. Hardware Palace offers the same tubes at 3 for $9.75. (a) If you needed 6 tubes, the price at Central Stores would be $_____22.50_____; (b) the price at Hardware Palace would be $_____19.50_____. (c) By buying at the less expensive store, you would save $_____3.00_____.

   a. (6 ÷ 2) × $7.50 = $22.50 Central Stores price
   b. (6 ÷ 3) × $9.75 = $19.50 Hardware Palace price
   c. $22.50 − $19.50 = $3.00 you would save by buying at Hardware Palace

3. The Chesterfield Department Store is selling an automatic coffee brewer for $49.50, with a factory rebate of $10. Barry Discount Markets is selling a similar coffee brewer for $44.99, with a discount of 10%. (a) The net cost of the brewer from Chesterfield's is $_____39.50_____; (b) from Barry's, $_____40.49_____. (c) If you bought the brewer from the less expensive store, you would save $_____0.99_____.

   a. $49.50 − $10 = $39.50 net cost at Chesterfield's
   b. $44.99 − ($44.99 × 0.10) = $40.49 net cost at Barry's
   c. $40.49 − $39.50 = $0.99 you would save by buying at Barry's

Exercise 3.   (Renting vs. buying)

1. A tourist can rent a 35 mm camera for $30 a day or for $6 an hour. (a) If the tourist rents the camera for two days and two extra hours, the charge would be $_____72_____. (b) The same camera costs $150 to buy. At the day rate, the number of days the tourist could rent the camera before the cost of renting exceeded the cost of buying would be _____5_____.

   a. (2 × $30) + (2 × $6) = $72 total charge
   b. $150 ÷ $30 = 5 days

2. A homeowner wants to rent a trencher to install an electric line to an outside light. Tri-County Rentals will rent the trencher for $55 for one whole day. The Suburban Rental Store will rent it for $60 a day or $8 an hour. If the homeowner estimates that the trencher will be needed for 6 hours, $_____7_____ will be saved by renting from the least expensive dealer.

   6 × $8 = $48 rental cost from The Suburban Rental Store
   $55 − $48 = $7 saved by renting from The Suburban Rental Store

3. In your town, bicycles rent for $40 a week or $8.00 a day. (a) By renting for a week instead of one day at a time, you would save $_____16.00_____. (b) If the same bicycle can be bought for $180, the number of weeks it would take before the cost of weekly rentals would be more than buying is _____4.5_____.

   a. $8.00 × 7 = $56.00 rent for one week, a day at a time
      $56.00 − $40.00 = $16.00 saved by renting for the week
   b. $180 ÷ 40 = 4.5 weeks before rental costs are more than buying

LESSON 6-6   CHECKING ENERGY COSTS

Exercise 1.   (Checking electric bills)

1. The monthly bills of the Long River Power Company are based on the rate schedule at the right. The Company also charges a fuel adjustment rate of $0.0026 per KWH, and a sales tax of 7%. Norma Rivera uses 948 KWH of electricity in March. Her total bill will be $____116.51____.

First 400 KWH	$0.128 per KWH
Next 400 KWH	$0.107 per KWH
Over 800 KWH	$0.084 per KWH

First 400 KWH @ $0.128   = $ 51.20
Next 400 KWH @ $0.107   = $ 42.80
Next 148 KWH @ $0.084   = $ 12.43
948 KWH @ $0.0026   = $ 2.46 fuel adjustment cost
                             $108.89 charge for electricity

$108.89 × 0.07 = $7.62 sales tax
$108.89 + $7.62 = $116.51 total electric bill

2. Mike Huel is also a customer of the Long River Power Company. His electric bill for May shows an April 30 meter reading of 1,368 KWH and a May 31 reading of 1,910 KWH. During May he used (a) ____542____ KWH of electricity. Using the rate schedule, fuel adjustment rate, and sales tax rate of the Company above, the charge for electricity is (b) $____67.80____. His total electric bill is (c) $____72.55____.

a. 1,910 KWH − 1,368 KWH   =   542 KWH used
b. First 400 KWH @ $0.128   = $51.20
   Next 142 KWH @ $0.107   = $15.19
   542 KWH @ 0.0026   = $ 1.41 fuel adjustment cost
                                $67.80

c. $67.80 × 0.07 = $4.75 sales tax
   $67.80 + $4.75 = $72.55 total electric bill

3. Carol Levy used 644 KWH of electricity in May. Her electric power company uses this rate schedule: first 300 KWH @ $0.167; next 300 KWH @ $0.208; over 600 KWH @ $0.237. The company also charges a monthly facilities fee of $8.19, a fuel adjustment rate of $0.0022 per KWH, and a utility tax of 5.5%. Carol's electric power bill for May is $____139.83____.

First 300 KWH @ $0.167   = $ 50.10
Next 300 KWH @ $0.208   = $ 62.40
Next 44 KWH @ $0.237   = $ 10.43
644 KWH @ $0.0022   = $ 1.42 fuel adjustment cost
                             $124.35 charge for electricity

$124.35 + $8.19 = $132.54
$132.54 × 0.055 = $7.29 utility tax
$132.54 + $7.29 = $139.83 total electric bill

Exercise 2.   (Checking gas bills)

1. Ed Duval's January 31 gas meter reading was 368 and on February 28 was 580. His gas company used a 1.4278 therm factor and charged a $10.50 facilities fee. The company's rates were as follows: first 50 therms @ $0.62; over 50 therms @ $0.45. There was also a 5% regulatory tax on the total gas charge. (a) Ed used ____212____ hundred cubic feet of gas during February. (b) He used ____303____ therms. (c) The total charge for the gas used was $____144.85____. (d) The total bill, including facilities fee and regulatory tax was $____163.12____.

a. 580 − 368 = 212 hundred cubic feet of gas used
b. 212 × 1.4278 = 302.6, or 303 therms
c. First 50 therms @ $0.62   = $ 31.00
   Next 253 therms @ $0.45   = $113.85
                                   $144.85 total charge for gas used

d. $144.85 + $10.50 = $155.35
   $155.35 × 0.05 = $7.77 regulatory tax
   $155.35 + $7.77 = $163.12 total bill

2. The meter readings of four customers are shown in the chart below. Use the rates shown at the right to complete the chart by showing (a) the hundred cubic feet of gas used, (b) the number of therms used, (c) the charge for the gas used, (d) the amount of sales tax at 6%, and (e) the total bill.

First 40 therms $0.4375 per therm
Next 40 therms $0.6712 per therm
Over 80 therms $0.7683 per therm
Therm factor rate 1.5084

Customers	Meter Readings		Hundred Cubic Feet Gas Used	Therms Used	Charge for Gas Used	Sales Tax	Total Bill
	Aug. 31	Sept. 30					
a. D. Day	792	853	61	92	$ 53.57	$3.21	$ 56.78
b. G. Gauling	377	512	135	204	139.62	8.38	148.00
c. R. Morse	539	588	49	74	40.32	2.42	42.74
d. L. Barron	683	764	81	122	76.62	4.60	81.22

a. 853 − 792 = 61 hundred cubic feet used
   61 × 1.5084 = 92.0, or 92 therms used
   (40 × $0.4375) + (40 × $0.6712) +
   (12 × $0.7683) = $53.57 gas charge
   $53.57 × 0.06 = $3.21 sales tax
   $53.57 + $3.21 = $56.78 total bill

b. 512 − 377 = 135 hundred cubic feet used
   135 × 1.5084 = 203.6, or 204 therms used
   (40 × $0.4375) + (40 × $0.6712) +
   (124 × $0.7683) = $139.62 gas charge
   $139.62 × 0.06 = $8.38 sales tax
   $139.62 + $8.38 = $148.00 total bill

c. 588 − 539 = 49 hundred cubic feet used
   49 × 1.5084 = 73.9, or 74 therms used
   (40 × $0.4375) + (34 × $0.6712) = $40.32 gas charge
   $40.32 × 0.06 = $2.42 sales tax
   $40.32 + $2.42 = $42.74 total bill

d. 764 − 683 = 81 hundred cubic feet used
   81 × 1.5084 = 122.2, or 122 therms used
   (40 × $0.4375) + (40 × $0.6712) +
   (42 × $0.7683) = $76.62 gas charge
   $76.62 × 0.06 = $4.60 sales tax
   $76.62 + $4.60 = $81.22 total bill

LESSON 6-7   REDUCING ENERGY COSTS

Exercise

1. Luan lowers the setting on her furnace thermostat from 72 degrees to 68 degrees. She estimates that this will save her 4% of her heating costs for each degree she set it back. If her heating costs last February were $172, she will save $_____28_____ this February.

    72 − 68 = 4 degrees set back
    4 × 4% = 16% saved
    0.16 × $172 = $27.52 will save in February

2. Jules replaced a partial-defrost refrigerator-freezer which used 115 KWH per month with an automatic defrost refrigerator-freezer which uses 210 KWH per month. At 12.5 cents per KWH, the new unit will cost
    (a) $_____11.87_____ more per month, and (b) $_____142.44_____ more per year.

    a. 115 KWH per month @ $0.125 per KWH = $14.38 cost of running old unit
       210 KWH per month @ $0.125 per KWH = $26.25 cost of running new unit
       $26.25 − $14.38 = $11.87 more per month
    b. $11.87 × 12 = $142.44 more per year

3. Bess had a more efficient water heater installed for $410. She estimates that the heater will save her $8.30 each month. The payback period for the water heater, to the nearest whole year, is _____4_____ years.

    12 × $8.30 = $99.60 a year saved
    $410 ÷ $99.60 = 4.12, or 4 years, payback period

4. Tom paid $635 to install insulation around his water heater and in his attic and floors. He estimates that this will save him $97 a year in heating costs. (a) His net savings over a ten-year period are $_____335_____. (b) The payback period, to the nearest tenth of a year, of the insulation is _____6.5_____ years.

    a. 10 × $97 = $970 amount saved in ten years
       $970 − $635 = $335 net savings over ten years
    b. $635 ÷ $97 = 6.5 years, payback period

5. A freezer uses 519 watts per hour and is automatically turned on for an average of 1,250 hours per year. At $13\frac{1}{4}$ cents per KWH, the average cost of running the freezer for a year is $_____85.96_____.

    519 watts per hour ÷ 1,000 = 0.519 KW
    0.519 KW × 1,250 hours = 648.75 KWH
    648.75 KWH @ $13\frac{1}{4}$ cents = $85.96 average annual cost of running the freezer

6. John is considering buying a central air conditioner. In John's area, it is estimated that a central air conditioning unit will run for 1,100 hours at full-load during the summer season. Coldland's central air conditioning unit has an EER rating of 6 and uses 7,200 watts per hour. Freezer King's central unit has an EER rating of 9 and uses only 3,200 watts per hour. (a) At 11 cents per KWH, John estimates that Coldland's unit will cost $_____871.20_____ per season and (b) Freezer King's unit will cost $_____352_____ per season. (c) The yearly estimated savings by buying the more efficient unit are $_____519.20_____.

    a. 7,200 watts per hour ÷ 1,000 = 7.2 KW
       7.2 KW × 1,100 hours = 7,920 KWH
       7,920 KWH @ $0.11 = $871.20 cost of Coldland's unit per season
    b. 3,200 watts per hour ÷ 1,000 = 3.2 KW
       3.2 KW × 1,000 hours = 3,200 KWH
       3,200 KWH @ $0.11 = $352 cost of Freezer King's unit per season
       $871.20 − $352 = $519.20 saved by buying more efficient unit

Chapter 6   Name: _____   Date: _____

LESSON 6-8   CHECKING AND REDUCING WATER COSTS

Exercise 1.   (Checking water bills)

1. The Evanston Water Company charges $13.50 for the first 2,000 cu. ft. of water used, $0.785 per 100 cu. ft. for the next 5,000 cu. ft., and $0.655 for all water used over 7,000 cu. ft. Clara Vicker's meter read 45,670 cu. ft. on July 1 and 53,210 cu. ft. on October 1. Her water bill for the quarter was $_____56.29_____.

    53,210 − 45,670 = 7,540 cu. ft. used during quarter
    First 2,000 cu. ft. $13.50
    Next 5,000 cu. ft.   39.25   (5,000 ÷ 100) × $0.785 = $39.25
    Next 540 cu. ft.   3.54   (540 ÷ 100) × $0.655 = $3.54
    Bill for quarter $56.29

2. Use the Evanston Water Company water rates listed in Problem 1 above to find the total amounts owed by these customers:

    a. Last reading, 45,690; present reading, 57,330; $_____83.16_____.

        57,330 − 45,690 = 11,640 cu. ft. used
        First 2,000 cu. ft. $13.50
        Next 5,000 cu. ft.   39.25   (5,000 ÷ 100) × $0.785 = $39.25
        Next 4,640 cu. ft.   30.39   (4,640 ÷ 100) × $0.655 = $30.39
        Amount owed by customer $83.14

    b. Last reading, 78,310; present reading, 88,240; $_____71.94_____.

        88,240 − 78,310 = 9,930 cu. ft. used
        First 2,000 cu. ft. $13.50
        Next 5,000 cu. ft.   39.25   (5,000 ÷ 100) × $0.785 = $39.25
        Next 2,930 cu. ft.   19.19   (2,930 ÷ 100) × $0.655 = $19.19
        Amount owed by customer $71.94

Exercise 2.   (Reducing water costs)

1. Lyle watered his lawn four times during August. His lawn sprayer uses 10 gallons of water per minute. He left the sprayer on for three hours each time he watered. If Lyle pays $0.783 per thousand gallons of water, he could have saved $_____6.29_____ by not watering his lawn during August.

    60 min. × 10 gal. = 600 gal. per hr.
    600 gal. per hr. × 3 hr. = 1,800 gal. per watering
    4 × 1,800 = 7,200 gal. used during August
    $0.873 × (7,200 ÷ 1,000) = $6.29 he could have saved by not watering lawn

2. Farah leaves the water running while she washes her car. By so doing she wastes 140 gallons each time she washes the car. She washes her car once each week. At $1.28 per 1,000 gallons, she wastes $_____9.32_____ each year by not turning off the water when she does not need it.

    52 × 140 = 7,280 gallons wasted each year
    (7,280 ÷ 1,000) × $1.28 = $9.32 wasted each year

 Chapter 6   Name: _____   Date: _____

LESSON 6-9   CHECKING AND REDUCING TELEPHONE COSTS

Exercise

1. Clyde Williams paid $8.50 a month for his phone line, $3 for call forwarding, $3.50 for call waiting, and $2.75 for speed dialing. He also paid a $12 access charge and made local calls costing $23.88. He paid a federal tax of 3% and a state tax of 6% on his phone bill. The total cost of his phone service for the month is $____58.46____.

Charge for services	$8.50 + $3 + $3.50 + $2.75 =	$17.75
Federal tax on service and equipment	0.03 × $17.75 =	0.53
State tax on service and equipment	0.06 × $17.75 =	1.07
Access charge	=	12.00
Federal tax on access charge	0.03 × $12 =	0.36
State tax on access charge	0.06 × $12 =	0.72
Charge for local calls	=	23.88
Federal tax on local calls	0.03 × $23.88 =	0.72
State tax on local calls	0.06 × $23.88 =	1.43
Total bill for month		$58.46

2. Li-ming pays $4.75 a month for her phone line, $5.50 for caller ID, and $3.50 for call waiting. She paid $31.44 in local calls this month. Her access charges are $10. The total cost of her phone service for the month, including 3% federal and 7% state taxes, is $____60.70____.

Charge for local service	$4.75 + $5.50 + $3.50 =	$13.75
Federal tax on service	0.03 × $13.75 =	0.41
State tax on service	0.07 × $13.75 =	0.96
Access charge	=	10.00
Federal tax on access charge	0.03 × $10.00 =	0.30
State tax on access charge	0.07 × $10.00 =	0.70
Charge for local calls	=	31.44
Federal tax on local calls	0.03 × $31.44 =	0.94
State tax on local calls	0.07 × $31.44 =	2.20
Total bill for month		$60.70

3. Janice uses Supernet Communications Co. as her long-distance company (see Illustration 6-9.2 in text). Janice made a direct-dial, 20-minute call to a friend who lived 200 miles away at 2:45 P.M. on Thursday. (a) The call cost her $____5.11____. (b) If she had waited until 5:01 P.M. to make the call, she would have saved $____2.03____. (c) If she made the call after 11 P.M., she would have saved $____2.50____.

a. $0.2810 + (19 × $0.2540) = $5.11 cost of call at 2:45 p.m.
b. $0.1670 + (19 × $0.1531) = $3.08
   $5.11 − $3.08 = $2.03 saved by calling at 5:01 p.m.
c. $0.1380 + (19 × $0.1299) = $2.61
   $5.11 − $2.61 = $2.50 saved by calling after 11 p.m.

4. The cost of three long-distance calls that Ted made on a weekday was $12.56, $8.30, and $2.99. If he had made his calls on the weekend, he would have saved 60% of the total. The amount he would have saved by making the calls on the weekend is $____14.31____.

$12.56 + $8.30 + $2.99 = $23.85 total amount of long distance charges
0.60 × $23.85 = $14.31 amount saved by calling on weekend

TERM TICKLER

Directions: Each group of scrambled letters can be sorted to spell a key word in Chapter 6. Place the sorted letters for the key word in the spaces given. The first one has been done for you.

a.   Sort the scrambled letters below.

1. c o l a l   c i v e r s e

      l   o   c | a | l   s   e   r   v   i   c   e

2. n o n t e e s i x

      | e | x   t   e   n   s   i   o   n

3. t r e e a p   g a l i d i n

      r   e   p   e   a   t | d | i   a   l   i   n   g

4. m e r t h

      t   h | e | r   m

5. t u i n   i c p e r

      u   n   i   t   p   r | i | c   e

6. l e a s s   s p i l

      s   a   l   e   s   s   l   i | p |

7. l e a s s   a t x

      s   a | l | e   s   t   a   x

8. l a c l   n i t g i w a

      c   a   l   l   w   a   i   t | i | n   g

9. l a c l   g e n e c r i n s

      c   a   l   l   s   c   r   e   e   n | i | n   g

10. b a t u t s o l

      | s | u   b   t | o | t   a   l

11. s e c s a c   g r e a c h

      a   c   c.   e   s   s   c   h   a   r | g | e

12. c a p a b y k   d r o p e i

      p   a   y | b | a   c   k   p   e   r   i   o | d |

b.   The letters in the boxes can be sorted to spell a two-word term used in Chapter 6. Place that term in the spaces below.

      | s | | p | | e | | e | | d | | d | | i | | a | | l | | i | | n | | g |

INTEGRATED PROJECT 6

Claudia and Jose Greco have just been married. They plan to move to a small apartment in Mobile where they work.

Directions: Read the project through and then complete Steps 1 to 6.

Step 1:   Claudia and Jose Greco want to budget their income. They estimate that their net income this year will be $36,000. The percentages below show how they plan to spend their net income. Find the dollar amount they plan to spend on each type of expense.

Expenses	Percent	Amount	
Food	26%	$ _____$9,360_____	$36,000 × 0.26 = $9,360
Clothing	12%	$ _____$4,320_____	$36,000 × 0.12 = $4,320
Housing	25%	$ _____$9,000_____	$36,000 × 0.25 = $9,000
Transportation	16%	$ _____$5,760_____	$36,000 × 0.16 = $5,760
Other	15%	$ _____$5,400_____	$36,000 × 0.15 = $5,400
Savings	6%	$ _____$2,160_____	$36,000 × 0.06 = $2,160

Step 2:   The couple needs to move the furniture Jose has in his three-room apartment to their apartment. Jose called two different moving companies to get estimates on the cost of moving. The Suburban Moving Company said that Jose had 2,450 cu. ft. of furniture to move at a cost of $10.45 per hundred cu. ft. The Olympia Moving Company said that they would do the job for a flat fee of $275.

a. Estimate the moving costs to be charged by Suburban Moving Co. $_____250_____

(2,500 cu. ft. ÷ 100) × $10 = $250 estimated moving costs for Suburban Moving Co.

b. Which company offers the better price? _____Suburban Moving Company_____

(2,450 cu. ft. ÷ 100) × $10.45 = $256.03 Suburban Moving Co. offers best price

c. How much less is the better price? $_____18.97_____

$275.00 − $256.03 = $18.97 less

Step 3:   The Grecos wish to clean the rugs in the apartment before moving in. They estimate that they can clean the rugs in five hours. They can rent a steam-cleaning machine from Denby's Hardware for $8 an hour or $30 a day. They can also buy a similar machine for $240, or have Tom's Cleaning Service do the job for $150.

a. If they rent the machine for the time estimated, is hourly or daily renting cheaper, and by how much?
_____Daily renting $10 cheaper_____

$8 × 5 = $40, cost by the hour; $40 − $30 = $10 saved by renting by the day

b. If they rent by the cheaper method, how much will they save over Tom's Cleaning Service's price? $____120____

$150 − $30 = $120 saved by renting by the day vs. using Tom's Cleaning Service

c. For how many days can they rent the machine before the daily rent is more than the machine's cost? ____8____

$240 ÷ $30 = 8 days

Step 4:   Claudia buys curtains and other items for the new apartment from Vicker's Department Store. The sales slip for her purchase is shown below. Check the sales slip to make sure that it has been completed accurately. If you find any mistakes, cross out the incorrect amounts and write the correct amounts to the right.

VICKER'S DEPARTMENT STORE		4590 Main St., Mobile, AL 36606-2323			
205-415-0089		**SOLD TO:**	*Claudia Greco*		
SINCE 1878		**STREET:**	*1704 Oak St., Apt. 5a*		
		CITY, STATE, ZIP:	*Mobile, AL 36609-4007*		

SOLD BY L ✓	CASH ✓	CHARGE	C.O.D.	DELIVER BY	Taken
QUANTITY	**DESCRIPTION**			**UNIT PRICE**	**AMOUNT**
1	*Picture hanging set*			1.89	1.89
2	*Pairs, kitchen curtains*			9.89	19.78
6	*Pairs, curtains*			2 for 34.89	104.67
2	*Curtain rod sets*			4.59	9.18
6	*Curtain rod sets*			8.99	53.94
3	*Mats*			2 for 8.99	~~17.98~~ *13.49*
MOBILE'S OLDEST AND FINEST DEPARTMENT STORE		SUBTOTAL			~~207.44~~ *202.95*
		SALES TAX 5%			~~10.37~~ *10.15*
		TOTAL			~~217.81~~ *213.10*

Step 5:   To make sure that they have budgeted enough money for utilities, the Grecos would like to estimate their energy and water bills. To make these estimates, they call the customer service departments of their water and electric companies.

a. The Falcon Water Company estimates that they are likely to use about 3,500 cu. ft. of water each month. The company charges are: basic monthly service fee, $5.87; first 3,000 cu. ft., $0.676 per hundred; anything over 3,000 cu. ft., $0.452 per hundred. There is a 3% state tax. What is their estimated water bill for the next year? $_____351.12_____

Basic fee:	$ 5.87	
First 3,000 cu. ft. @ $0.676 per hundred =	20.28	
Next 500 cu. ft. @ $0.452 per hundred =	2.26	
Subtotal	$28.41	
Tax	0.85	($28.41 × 0.03)
Total	$29.26	

$29.26 × 12 = $351.12 estimated water bill for year

b. The Coastal Electric Company estimates that the Grecos will use about 800 KWH during each of the eight months of hot weather and 400 KWH monthly during the other months. Their rates for each KWH are: first 500 KWH, $0.118; next 500 KWH, $0.093; fuel adjustment rate, $0.0032. Taxes are 3%. What is the Grecos' estimated electric bill for the year? $_____936.84_____

Hot Months

500 KWH × $0.118   = $59.00
300 KWH × $0.093   = $27.90
800 KWH × $0.0032   = $ 2.56
Subtotal $89.46
Tax @ 0.03   2.68
Total $92.14

Other Months

400 KWH × $0.118   = $47.20
400 KWH × $0.0032   = $1.28
$48.48
1.45
$49.93

($92.14 × 8) + ($49.93 × 4) = $936.84
estimated electric bill for year

Step 6: After estimating their electric and water bills, Claudia and Jose decide to reduce these bills so that they can save more money to make a downpayment on a house in the near future. They are considering a number of ways to save extra money:

a. In the cool months, they plan to turn down the heat in the rooms they are not using, and use a space heater to warm the room they are in. The space heater they are looking at sells for $45. They estimate that they can save 10% of their winter heating costs this way. Their winter heating costs are estimated to be $200.

1. What will be the net savings for five years if they buy and use the space heater? $_____55_____

$200 × 0.10 = $20 annual savings using the space heater
$20 × 5 = $100 saved in five years
$100 − $45 = $55 net savings for five years

2. What will the payback period be for the heater in years? _____$2\frac{1}{4}$_____ years

$45 ÷ $20 = $2\frac{1}{4}$ years

b. During the hot months, they plan to buy three fans to keep the house cool whenever possible without using air conditioning. The fans cost $35 each and they estimate that they will save 15% of their cooling costs this way. They estimate their cooling costs to be $590 for the year.

1. What will be the net savings for five years if they buy and use the fans? $_____337.50_____

$590 × 0.15 = $88.50 annual savings using the fans
$88.50 × 5 = $442.50 savings over five years
$442.50 − (3 × $35) = $337.50 net savings over five years

2. What will be the payback period for the fans, to the nearest hundredth of a year? _____1.19 year_____

$105 ÷ $88.50 = 1.19 of a year, payback period

Chapter 7

Name: _____ Date: _____

BUYING, LEASING, AND RUNNING A HOME OR MOTOR VEHICLE

LESSON 7-1   BUYING A HOME

Exercise 1.

1. Louisa wants to buy a house priced at $57,000. She will need to make a down payment of 25% and pay closing costs of 2.8% of the purchase price. Louisa will need (a) $_____14,250_____ for the down payment and (b) $_____1,596_____ for the closing costs.

   a. 0.25 × $57,000 = $14,250 amount needed for down payment
   b. 0.028 × $57,000 = $1,596 amount needed for closing costs

2. The Simpsons are buying a used mobile home for $34,000. The seller wants a down payment of 30%, which amounts to (a) $_____10,200_____. Closing costs of 3.2% of the purchase price will amount to (b) $_____1,088_____. The total amount of cash needed by the Simpsons to buy the mobile home is (c) $_____11,288_____.

   a. 0.3 × $34,000 = $10,200 down payment
   b. 0.032 × $34,000 = $1,088 closing costs
   c. $10,200 + $1,088 = $11,288 total cash needed to buy mobile home

3. Rico Mendel buys a condominium for $42,600. He makes a 15% down payment, and pays these closing costs: property survey, $225; insect inspection, $110; points, $852; legal fees, $450; and title insurance, $286. The down payment is (a) $_____6,390_____. The total closing costs are (b) $_____1,923_____. The closing costs are (c) _____4.5_____% of the purchase price, to the nearest tenth of a percent.

   a. 0.15 × $42,600 = $6,390 down payment needed
   b. $225 + $110 + $852 + $450 + $286 = $1,923 total closing costs
   c. $1,923 ÷ $42,600 = 0.0451, or 4.5% percent, closing costs

4. The Rutherfords bought a home for $38,240. They made a 20% down payment and paid these closing costs: legal fees, $270; survey costs, $170; title insurance, $253; loan origination fees, $634; and points, $382. The Rutherfords made a (a) $_____7,648_____ down payment and paid (b) $_____1,709_____ in closing costs. The closing costs were (c) _____4.5_____% of the purchase price, to the nearest tenth percent.

   a. 0.20 × $38,240 = $7,648 down payment
   b. $270 + $170 + $253 + $634 + $382 = $1,709 total closing costs
   c. $1,709 ÷ $38,240 = 0.0446, or 4.5%, closing costs

Exercise 2.

1. Martha Zeller has an agreement with a bank for a $70,000, 30-year mortgage at 11.5% interest. Interest rates have fallen recently, and Martha would have paid an interest rate of 12% if she had taken out a mortgage loan six months ago. Her monthly payment at 11.5% will be $711.53, and would have been $771.46 at 12%. The difference between the two monthly payments is (a) $_____59.93_____ for a month, and (b) $_____719.16_____ for a year. If Martha had to take the mortgage at 12%, she would have paid (c) $_____21,574.80_____ more in interest over the life of the loan.

   a. $771.46 − $711.53 = $59.93 difference per month
   b. 12 × $59.93 = $719.16 difference per year
   c. 30 × $719.16 = $21,574.80 more paid over 30 years if mortgage was taken at 12%

2. Dewayne McCombs bought a $50,000 home. He made a 20% down payment and borrowed the rest on a 25-year, 12.25% fixed rate mortgage. His monthly mortgage payment was $428.70. The down payment Dewayne made was (a) $____10,000____. The amount of the mortgage that he borrowed was (b) $____40,000____. The total amount of monthly payments for the life of the loan is (c) $____128,610____. The amount of interest Dewayne will pay over the life of the loan is (d) $____88,610____.

    a. $0.2 \times \$50,000 = \$10,000$ down payment
    b. $\$50,000 - \$10,000 = \$40,000$ amount of mortgage
    c. $(12 \times 25) \times \$428.70 = \$128,610$ total of all monthly payments
    d. $\$128,610 - \$40,000 = \$88,610$ amount of interest paid

3. The Blaines bought a home for $100,000. They made a 10% down payment and borrowed the rest on a 9%, 30-year fixed rate mortgage. Their monthly payment was $724.17. The down payment they made was (a) $____10,000____ and the amount of their mortgage was (b) $____90,000____. The total amount of their monthly payments over 30 years was (c) $____260,701.20____. The amount of interest they paid over the life of the loan was (d) $____170,701.20____.

    a. $0.1 \times \$100,000 = \$10,000$ down payment
    b. $\$100,000 - \$10,000 = \$90,000$ amount of mortgage
    c. $(12 \times 30) \times \$724.17 = \$260,701.20$ total of monthly payments
    d. $\$260,701.20 - \$90,000 = \$170,701.20$ amount of interest paid

4. The interest rate on the Marshall's variable rate mortgage increased from 10% to 12%. Their old monthly payment was $437.24. Their new monthly payment is $496.73. The total increase in monthly payments for one year will be $____713.88____.

    $\$496.73 - \$437.24 = \$59.49$ monthly increase
    $12 \times \$59.49 = \$713.88$ total increase in monthly payments for one year

Exercise 3.

1. Anita Gerber's old mortgage has a monthly payment of $463.07. The monthly payment on a new mortgage will be $337.92. To refinance the old mortgage, Anita must pay $741 in closing costs and $520 in prepayment penalties. The net amount she will pay less in the first year with the new mortgage is $____240.80____.

    $12 \times (\$463.07 - \$337.92) = \$1,501.80$ difference in payments in first year
    $\$1,501.80 - (\$741 + \$520) = \$240.80$ net amount paid less in first year

2. The Gylsons' old mortgage payment was $811.09 a month. Their new monthly payment is $687.31. To refinance their old mortgage, they had to pay $396 in closing costs and $500 in prepayment penalties. The net amount they paid less in the first year with the new mortgage was $____589.36____.

    $12 \times (\$811.09 - \$687.31) = \$1,485.36$ difference in payments in first year
    $\$1,485.36 - (\$396 + \$500) = \$589.36$ net amount paid less in first year

LESSON 7-2   THE COST OF OWNING A HOME

Exercise

1. Abigail O'Rourke estimates that her home depreciates at the rate of 1.75% each year. If her home cost her $59,620, the amount she estimates it will depreciate this year is $___1,043.35___.

   0.0175 × $59,620 = $1,043.35 depreciation

2. The Haydens want to buy a condominium. They estimate that their expenses in the first year will be mortgage interest, $3,819; real estate taxes, $1,381; insurance, $257; depreciation, $1,370; maintenance and repairs, $425; lost income on cash invested, $985. They also estimate that they will save $1,400 in income taxes because of home expenses. (a) The total home expenses for the first year are $___8,237___. (b) The net cost of owning the home in the first year is $___6,837___.

   a. $3,819 + $1,381 + $257 + $1,370 + $425 + $985 = $8,237 total home expenses
   b. $8,237 − $1,400 = $6,837 net cost of home ownership

3. Iris Velez can rent an apartment for $620 a month, or she can buy a home with about the same space. If she buys the home, Iris estimates that the net cost of owning the home for the first year will be $8,115. In one year the amount that she will save by renting is $___675___.

   12 × $620 = $7,440 rent for one year
   $8,115 − $7,440 = $675 saved by renting in first year

4. The Selzman family rents a home for $900 a month. They could buy a similar home for $89,200. To make the down payment, they must withdraw $17,500 from a savings account that earns $1,365 interest. They estimate that their other first year expenses would be mortgage interest, $6,200; depreciation at 2.25% of the purchase price; maintenance and repairs, $780; insurance, $370; property taxes, $1,780. They estimate they would save $2,560 income taxes from home expenses. (a) The depreciation for the year is $___2,007___. (b) The net cost of owning the home the first year would be $___9,942___. (c) The amount saved in the first year by owning is $___858___.

   a. 0.0225 × $89,200 = $2,007 depreciation in first year
   b. $1,365 + $6,200 + $2,007 + $780 + $370 + $1,780 = $12,502 total first year expenses
      $12,502 − $2,560 = $9,942 net cost of owning the home the first year
   c. (12 × $900) − $9,942 = $858 first year savings by owning

LESSON 7-3   DEPRECIATING A CAR OR TRUCK

Exercise

1. Georgina Connor bought a new car for $11,400. She used the car three years and then traded it in for $5,100.
   (a) The total depreciation for the three-year period was $_____6,300_____. (b) The average annual depreciation
   was $_____2,100_____.

   a. $11,400 − $5,100 = $6,300 total depreciation
   b. $6,300 ÷ 3 = $2,100 average annual depreciation

2. In Problem 1, the average annual depreciation is _____18.4_____% of the original cost of the car, to the nearest
   tenth percent.

   $2,100 ÷ $11,400 = 0.1842, or 18.4% of original cost

3. A wholesale company sold one of its trucks for $2,950. The truck cost $19,890 when it was bought seven years
   ago. (a) The total depreciation on the truck for the seven-year period was $_____16,940_____. (b) The average
   annual depreciation was $_____2,420_____. (c) The average annual rate of depreciation was _____12.2_____%,
   rounded to the nearest tenth of a percent.

   a. $19,890 − $2,950 = $16,940 total depreciation
   b. $16,940 ÷ 7 = $2,420 average annual depreciation
   c. $2,420 ÷ $19,890 = 0.1216, or 12.2% rate of depreciation

4. Steven Marcotte bought a four-wheel drive truck for $14,860. He used the truck for five years and then traded it in
   for $3,715. (a) The average annual depreciation was $_____2,229_____. (b) The rate of depreciation was
   _____15_____%.

   a. ($14,860 − $3,715) ÷ 5 = $2,229 average annual depreciation
   b. $2,229 ÷ $14,860 = 15% rate of depreciation

5. Ilene Delakodas estimated that her new car that cost $9,700 would be worth $5,432 after two years and $2,910
   after five years. Based on Ilene's estimate, the annual rate of depreciation (a) for the first two years is
   _____22_____%; (b) for five years, it is _____14_____%.

   a. ($9,700 − $5,432) ÷ 2 = $2,134 average annual depreciation
      $2,134 ÷ $9,700 = 22% rate of depreciation at end of two years
   b. ($9,700 − $2,910) ÷ 5 = $1,358 average annual depreciation
      $1,358 ÷ $9,700 = 14% rate of depreciation at end of five years

LESSON 7-4   COST OF OPERATING A CAR OR TRUCK

Exercise

1. Felix Brewer paid $11,400 cash for a pickup truck. His truck expenses for the first year were: gas and oil, $3,238.74; insurance, $781; repairs and upkeep, $230.22; license plates, $73; loss of interest at $912 on the truck's original cost; and depreciation estimated at 29%. (a) The annual depreciation was $_____3,306_____. (b) The total truck operating expense for the year was $_____8,540.96_____.

    a. 0.29 × $11,400 = $3,306 annual depreciation
    b. $3,238.74 + $781.00 + $230.22 + $73.00 + $912.00 + $3,306.00 = $8,540.96 operating expense

2. In Problem 1, Felix drove the truck 34,000 miles during the year. (a) The average operating expense per mile was _____25.1_____¢, to the nearest tenth of a cent. (b) If Felix purchased 2,830 gallons of gas during the year, his truck got _____12_____ miles per gallon, to the nearest whole gallon.

    a. $8,540.96 ÷ 34,000 = $0.2512, or 25.1¢ per mile
    b. 34,000 ÷ 2,830 = 12 miles per gallon

3. Sabrina Hester leased a car for four years and drove the car 79,000 miles. Her monthly lease charge was $236.01. The leasing company charged $0.13 a mile for all miles driven over 72,000 miles. In addition, Sabrina had to pay a repair charge of $410.56 for a damaged fender. (a) The total of the monthly lease charges was $_____11,328.48_____. (b) Excess mileage charges amounted to $_____910_____. (c) The total cost of leasing the car was $_____12,649.04_____.

    a. (4 × 12) × $236.01 = $11,328.48 total monthly lease charges for four years
    b. (79,000 − 72,000) × 0.13 = $910 excess mileage charge
    c. $11,328.48 + $910.00 + $410.56 = $12,649.04 total cost of leasing

4. Rico leased a car for one year and drove it 21,185 miles. He spent $580 for insurance, $118 for maintenance and repairs, and $1,487 for gas and oil. The leasing company charged $261.32 a month plus 12¢ for each mile driven over 15,000 miles per year. (a) What was the total cost of operating the car for the year? $_____6,063.04_____. (b) What was the operating cost per mile, to the nearest cent? _____29_____¢

    a. 21,185 − 15,000 = 6,185 excess miles
        $580 + $118 + $1,487 + (12 × $261.32) + (6,185 × $0.12) = $6,063.04 total cost of car
    b. $6,063.04 ÷ 21,185 = $0.286, or 29¢ per mile

5. Della can buy a small van for $15,180 including taxes and delivery charges. She expects to keep the van for four years and drive 18,000 miles each year. Della estimates that the van will depreciate $10,600 in four years, and that she will be able to sell the van for the remaining resale value of $4,580. The total estimated cost of insurance, maintenance, repairs and fuel for four years is $8,300. Della will lose $910 interest per year on the amount of the purchase price. (a) The total net cost of owning and operating the van for four years is $_____22,540_____. By leasing the van, Della will pay $280 a month and 11¢ for each mile she drives over 16,000 miles a year. She will have the same expenses for insurance, maintenance, repairs, and fuel while leasing as she would have for buying the van. (b) The cost of leasing and operating the van for four years will be $_____22,620_____. (c) Is it cheaper to buy or lease the van? _____Buy_____

    a. $10,600 + $8,300 + (4 × $910) = $22,540 total cost of owning the van
    b. (4 × 12 × $280) + (4 × 2,000 × $0.11) = $14,320 total lease charges
        $14,320 + $8,300 = $22,620 total cost of leasing and operating
    c. It is cheaper to buy the van.

TERM TICKLER

Directions: **a.**   The statements on the left are definitions of vocabulary words that you have learned in Chapter 7. Write the vocabulary word or words in the blank spaces.

1. Pay off old mortgage with new mortgage

   r   e   f   i   n   a   n   [c]   e

2. The dollar cost of using a lender's money

   f   i   x   e   d

   r   a   t   [e]   m   o   r   t   g   a   g   e

3. Prepaid interest charges

   p   o   [i]   n   t   s

4. The amount borrowed

   p   r   i   n   c   i   [p]   a   l

5. Depreciatiion is spread evenly over time

   s   t   [r]   a   i   g   h   t   -   l   i   n   e

   m   e   t   h   o   d

6. Shows amount of depreciation as a rate

   r   a   t   e   o   f

   d   e   p   r   e   c   [i]   a   t   i   o   n

7. Expenses payable at time of home purchase

   c   l   [o]   s   i   n   g   c   o   s   t   s

8. Amount you get for an old car when buying a new car

   t   r   a   d   e   -   i   [n]   v   a   l   u   e

9. An estimate of a home's value

   [a]   p   p   r   a   i   s   e   d

   v   a   l   u   e

10. Depreciation per year

    a   v   e   r   a   g   e   a   n   n   u   a   l

    [d]   e   p   r   e   c   i   a   t   i   o   n

11. Interest rate may change during term of the loan

    v   a   r   i   a   b   l   e   r   a   t   [e]

    m   o   r   t   g   a   g   e

12. Price at which a home is sold

    m   a   r   k   e   [t]   v   a   l   u   e

b.   Unscramble the blocked letters to form a word from Chapter 7. Write its meaning on the line below.

depreciation: loss of value caused by wear and tear

_____

INTEGRATED PROJECT 7

Directions: Read through the entire project before you begin doing any work.

Introduction: Tracy and Albert Rushwell now rent an apartment for $670 a month. While renting, they saved $17,000 to use for a down payment on a home and other expenses. The Rushwells have been looking at houses, and found one priced at $85,000 that meets their needs. Closing costs on the house would be $2,500. Before signing a contract to buy the home, the Rushwells went to several lenders for home mortgage information. They found three lenders in the area that offer mortgages at these terms:

Lender A requires a 20% down payment for a 14.25%, 20-year mortgage loan. For these terms, the monthly mortgage payment will be $857.97.

Lender B offers a 14.50%, 25-year mortgage loan with a minimum 16% down payment. At this rate, the monthly mortgage payment will be $886.91.

Lender C offers the longest mortgage term, 30 years. To get that term, the borrower must make a minimum down payment of 14% and pay a rate of 14.875%. At these terms, the monthly mortgage payment will be $917.01.

Because they will no longer live near where they work, the Rushwells will have to buy a second car. They have shopped for a new car, and found one they like that sells for $12,600. With a minimum down payment required of 10%, the monthly payments would be $401.49 for a loan of three years and $324.30 for a four-year loan. It is possible to lease the car they want instead of buying. The monthly lease payments would be $289.50, with no money down.

The estimated annual expenses of operating the car they want are as follows: gasoline, 650 gallons at $1.14; insurance, $420; maintenance, $230; license fees, $45. At the time of purchase, only one-fourth of the annual insurance premium must be paid along with the license fee. If the car is purchased, the interest for the first year would be $1,638 on a three-year loan and $1,711 on a four-year loan. If the car is purchased, the depreciation expense the first year will be 22% of the purchase price and the interest lost on money invested in the car will be $101.

The Rushwells' combined gross income is $45,000 a year. If they buy the house, they will have these expenses: property taxes, $2,090; insurance, $320; maintenance and repairs, $1,100; lost interest on the down payment at 8%; depreciation at the rate of 2% a year. The first-year mortgage interest they would pay varies among lenders as follows: Lender A, $9,649; Lender B. $10,333; Lender C, $10,864.

By paying property taxes and mortgage interest, the Rushwells would have these tax benefits, depending on where they got their mortgage: Lender A, $3,290; Lender B, $3,480; Lender C, $3,630.

Step 1: Complete the following tables to summarize the data that the Rushwells gathered.

Money Needed at Time of Home and Car Purchase (assuming minimum down payment is made):

	Lender A	Lender B	Lender C
Home Down Payment	$17,000	$13,600	$11,900
Closing Cost	2,500	2,500	2,500
Subtotal	$19,500	$16,100	$14,400
Car Down Payment	1,260	1,260	1,260
Car Insurance (one-fourth of annual premium)	105	105	105
License Fee	45	45	45
Total Amount Needed	$20,910	$17,510	$15,810

Cost of Owning Home for First Year

	Lender A	Lender B	Lender C
Property Taxes	$ 2,090	$ 2,090	$2,090
Insurance	320	320	320
Maintenance and Repairs	1,100	1,100	1,100
Lost Interest	1,360	1,088	952
Depreciation	1,700	1,700	1,700
Mortgage Interest	9,649	10,333	10,864
Total Gross Cost	$16,219	$16,631	$17,026
Less Tax Savings	3,290	3,480	3,630
Net Cost of Owning	$12,929	$13,151	$13,396

Total Interest Paid Over Term of Original Mortgage Loan (to nearest dollar)

	Lender A	Lender B	Lender C
Amount	$137,913	$194,673	$257,024

Car Operating Cost

Gasoline	$ 741
Insurance	420
Maintenance	230
License Fees	45
Total Operating Costs	$ 1,436

Cost of Leasing and Operating Car for First Year

Annual Lease Cost	$ 3,474
Total Operating Cost	1,436
Total Cost	$ 4,910

Cost of Owning and Operating Car for First Year

	Assuming 3-Year Loan	Assuming 4-Year Loan
Operating Costs	$1,436	$ 1,436
Depreciation	2,772	2,772
Interest Paid	1,638	1,711
Interest Lost	101	101
Total Cost	$5,947	$ 6,020

Total Annual Payment for Mortgage and Car Loan

Mortgage Obtained from	Total Annual Mortgage Payment Plus Annual Payment on 3-Year Car Loan	Total Annual Mortgage Payment Plus Annual Payment on 4-Year Car Loan
Lender A	$15,113.52	$14,187.24
Lender B	$ 15,460.80	$14,534.52
Lender C	$ 15,822.00	$14,895.72

Step 2: Complete the Decision Table below by writing a "yes" or "no" answer using the data from the tables you completed or other facts provided. Then, answer the questions that follow.

Decision Table: Do the Rushwells have enough money saved to buy a house and a car or buy a house and lease a car?

Can they get a mortgage from . . .	And buy a car?	And lease a car?
Lender A	No	No
Lender B	No	Yes
Lender C	Yes	Yes

1. In order to be approved for a mortgage loan by any lender, the purchase price of the house must be less than 2.5 times the buyer's annual income. Do the Rushwells meet this requirement? _____Yes_____

2. Compare the lowest cost of owning the home with the cost of renting. Which is less expensive, and by how much?
   Renting less expensive by $4,889

3. Compare the cost of buying and leasing a car. Which will be less expensive for the Rushwells during the first year?
   Leasing less expensive for first year by $1,037 for 3-year car loan and $1,110 for 4-year car loan.

4. (a) For each lender, give the total amount of money that is needed if both the home and car are purchased: Lender A, $____20,910____; Lender B, $____17,510____; Lender C, $____15,810____. (b) From which lender(s) can the Rushwells get a mortgage loan and still afford to buy a car after making all required down payments and not spending more than they saved? ____Lender C____

5. Assume the Rushwells do not want to spend more than one-third of their annual gross income on mortgage and car payments. Using the decision table and other data, identify the combination(s) that will come closest to this goal of limiting spending. Also give a reason for your answer.

   Although student answers may vary, this is a problem in which only the cash outlay may be considered. For example, non-cash items such as lost interest or depreciation may be excluded from calculations. So borrowing from Lender A and leasing a car produces an annual expenditure of $14,779, which is within the Rushwells' guidelines. To arrive at that figure, start with the $12,929 net cost of owning the home. Then deduct lost interest of $1,360 and depreciation of $1,700 and add the annual costs of leasing and operating a car, $4,910.

6. If you were making this home and buying decision for the Rushwells, describe what you would do and why.

   Student answers will vary. However, they may raise issues such as the greater total cost of interest over the life of the mortgage when Lender C is selected, the possibility of getting extra money from another source to be able to meet down payment requirements of other lenders, waiting until more money is saved, buying a less expensive home or car, or getting a part-time job to be able to afford monthly payments.

Name: _____ Date: _____

PAYING YOUR TAXES

LESSON 8-1 PROPERTY TAXES

Exercise

1. Ivy Amato owns a home in Torrent valued at $85,000. Her property is assessed at $42,500. At the local tax rate of 35 mills, Amato will pay a real estate tax of $_____1,487.50_____.

    35 mills ÷ 1,000 = $0.035
    $42,500 × $0.035 = $1,487.50 tax

2. Alorton's tax rate is $4.125 on each $100 of assessed value. Jun Mori owns a home in Alorton which is valued at $40,000 and assessed at 40%. (a) The assessed value of Mori's home is $_____16,000_____. (b) The tax on Mori's home this year is $_____660_____.

    a. 0.4 × $40,000 = $ 16,000 assessed value
    b. ($16,000 ÷ $100) × $4.125 = $660 amount of tax

3. In each problem, show (a) the assessed value and (b) the tax bill.

	Value of Property	Assessed Value		Tax Rate	Tax Bill
		Percent of Market Value	Amount		
a.	$ 70,000	50%	$35,000	37 mills	$1,295.00
b.	46,500	80%	$37,200	$3.106 on each $100	$1,155.43
c.	129,000	30%	$38,700	$41.208 on each $1,000	$1,594.75
d.	36,800	75%	$27,600	6.13 cents on each $1	$1,691.88
e.	66,500	100%	$66,500	$2.386 on each $100	$1,586.69
f.	225,800	35%	$79,030	$54.297 on each $1,000	$4,291.09

a. ASSESSED VALUE

a. 0.50 × $70,000 = $35,000
b. 0.80 × $46,500 = $37,200
c. 0.30 × $129,000 = $38,700
d. 0.75 × $36,800 = $27,600
e. 1.00 × $66,500 = $66,500
f. 0.35 × $225,800 = $79,030

b. TAX BILL

$35,000 × $0.037 = $1,295
($37,200 ÷ $100) × $3.106 = $1,155.43
($38,700 ÷ $1,000) × $41.208 = $1,594.75
$27,600 × $0.0613 = $1,691.88
($66,500 ÷ $100) × $2.386 = $1,586.69
($79,030 ÷ $1,000) × $54.297 = $4,291.09

Exercise

1. A school district has property with an assessed value of $97,800,000. The school budget for the coming year shows that $3,400,000 will be needed to run the schools. Of this amount, $350,400 will be received from the state and federal governments. (a) The amount to be raised by taxes on the local property owners is $_____3,049,600_____. (b) The tax rate, shown as a decimal rounded to three places, will be _____0.031_____.

   a. $3,400,000 − $350,400 = $3,049,600 to be raised by property taxes
   b. $3,049,600 ÷ $97,800,000 = 0.031 tax rate

2. Tracy Rogers owns a house and lot assessed at $28,500 in the school district in Problem 1. The tax on Rogers' property will be $_____883.50_____.

   $28,500 × 0.031 = $883.50 property tax

3. Complete the chart below by changing the decimal tax rates to the equivalent rates shown.

	Decimal Rate	Equivalent Rate Shown as			
		Dollars per $100	Dollars per $1,000	Cents per $1	Mills per $1
a.	0.032	$3.20	$32	3.2	32 mills
b.	0.0875	$8.75	$87.50	8.75	87.5 mills
c.	0.0063	$0.63	$6.30	0.63	6.3 mills
d.	0.04078	$4.078	$40.78	4.078	40.78 mills

4. Property worth $86,400 is assessed at 35% of its value. The tax rate is $36.123 per $1,000 of assessed value. The tax on the property is $_____1,092.36_____.

   $86,400 × 0.35 = $30,240 assessed value of property
   ($30,240 ÷ $1,000) × $36.123 = $1,092.36 tax on property

5. The tax rate in Barberton is 21.5 mills per dollar of assessed value. The tax on property assessed at $60,000 is $_____1,290_____.

   21.5 mills ÷ 1,000 = $0.0215 tax rate per $1
   $60,000 × $0.0215 = $ 1,290 tax

LESSON 8-2   SALES TAXES

Exercise 1.   (Figuring sales tax with a table)

1. Using the tax table, find the tax and total sale price on each sale below:

Sales Tax Table—5%	
Amount of Sale	**Sales Tax**
$0.01 – $0.10	0
0.11 – 0.25	1 cent
0.26 – 0.45	2 cents
0.46 – 0.65	3 cents
0.66 – 0.85	4 cents
0.86 – 1.10	5 cents
More than $1.10	5¢ on each dollar, plus amount in table for cents

	Subtotal	Tax	Total
a.	$ 0.98	$ 0.05	$ 1.03
b.	0.21	$ 0.01	$ 0.22
c.	1.00	$ 0.05	$ 1.05
d.	1.10	$ 0.05	$ 1.15
e.	4.50	$ 0.23	$ 4.73
f.	3.79	$ 0.19	$ 3.98
g.	12.78	$ 0.64	$ 13.42
h.	46.40	$ 2.32	$ 48.72

LESSON 8-3   SOCIAL SECURITY TAXES AND BENEFITS

Exercise

1. Melanie Olsen's gross wages last week were $237.50. Her employer withheld 7.65% of that amount for FICA tax. The employer withheld $_____18.17_____.

   $237.50 × 0.0765 = $18.17 amount withheld

2. Last month Rollmatic, Inc. paid its employees $24,595.74 in wages. FICA taxes were deducted on that amount at the rate of 7.65%. As an employer, Rollmatic also paid an equal amount of FICA tax on the wages. (a) Rollmatic deducted $_____1,881.57_____ for FICA tax from employees. (b) Rollmatic sent to the government a total of $_____3,763.14_____ in FICA taxes.

   $24,595.74 × 0.0765 = $1,881.57 FICA taxes withheld from employee wages
   $1,881.57 × 2 = $3,763.14 Total amount of FICA taxes remitted to government

3. Sumio Beppu earned $44,393 last year as a self-employed person. Sumio paid FICA self-employment taxes at 15.3% on a maximum of $70,000 of his earnings. Sumio paid $_____6,792.13_____ in FICA tax last year.

   $44,393 × 0.153 = $6,792.13 self-employment taxes paid

4. Sid Bernstein is comparing his retirement benefits at age 62 and age 65. If he retires at age 65, his monthly benefit will be $761. If he retires at age 62, his monthly benefit will be reduced by 20%. (a) The difference in monthly benefits is $_____152.20_____. (b) The monthly benefit at age 62 will be $_____608.80_____.

   a. $761 × 0.20 = $152.20 difference in monthly benefit
   b. $761.00 − $152.20 = $608.80 monthly benefit at 62

5. Lana Drake is retiring at age 63. Her monthly benefit would be $605 if she retired at 65 but will be $13\frac{1}{3}$% less at age 63. The amount of her monthly benefit at 63, to the nearest whole dollar, will be $_____524_____.

   $605 × 0.13$\frac{1}{3}$ = $80.666, or $81
   $605.00 − $81 = $524 amount of her monthly benefit at 63

6. Doris O'Rourke's average covered annual earnings at 65 will be $40,000. (a) Using the table in Illustration 8-3.1 in the text, her monthly benefits will be $_____1,111_____. (b) If she decides to retire at 63 and her monthly earnings stay the same, her monthly benefits, to the nearest whole dollar, will be $_____955_____.

   a. $1,111 monthly benefits amount from table at age 65
   b. $1,111 × 0.14 = $155.54, or $156
      $1,111 − $156 = $955 monthly benefits at age 63

LESSON 8-4   FEDERAL INCOME TAXES

Exercise 1.   (Finding adjusted gross income and taxable income)

1. Eva Gorbea's gross income for a year included salary, $5,400; commission, $14,375; interest, $340. Her adjustments to income were payments to a retirement plan, $1,000, and a penalty from withdrawing savings early, $246. (a) Her gross income for the year was $_____20,115_____. (b) Her adjusted gross income for the year was $_____18,869_____.

    a. $5,400 + $14,375 + $340 = $20,115 gross income for year
    b. $1,000 + $246 = $1,246 total adjustments to income
       $20,115 − $1,246 = $18,869 adjusted gross income for year

2. Find the amounts that are missing from this summary of an income tax return:

Gross income	$42,107
Adjustments to income	2,733
Adjusted gross income	$39,374
Deductions	6,772
	$32,602
Exemptions (4 × $2,500)	10,000
Taxable income	$22,602

3. Tony Reno's adjusted gross income on his federal tax return was $21,488. He claimed $4,700 in deductions, and one exemption at $2,500. Tony's taxable income was $_____14,288_____.

    $21,488 − ($4,700 + $2,500) = $14,288 taxable income

4. The Prezniks' gross income last year was $45,088. They had adjustments to income totaling $2,289. Their deductions totaled $6,903, and they had four exemptions at $2,500 each. Their taxable income was $_____25,896_____.

    $45,088 − $2,289 = $42,799 adjusted gross income
    $42,799 − ($6,903 + $10,000) = $25,896 taxable income

5. Emily Klein earned $14,543 from wages, $3,000 from tips, and $246 in interest last year. She had adjustments to income of $107. She claimed the standard deduction of $4,000 and a personal exemption for herself of $2,500. (a) Emily's gross income was $_____17,789_____. (b) Her taxable income was $_____11,182_____.

    a. $14,543 + $3,000 + $246 = $17,789 gross income
    b. $ 17,789 − $ 107 = $ 17,682 adjusted gross income
       $17,682 − ($4,000 + $2,500) = $11,182 taxable income

Exercise 2.   (Finding the tax with a table)

Use the tax table in Illustration 8-4.1 in the text to do these problems.

1. Find the tax for each taxable income and filing status.

	Taxable Income	Filing status	Tax
a.	$13,590	Single	$ 2,036
b.	$13,800	Married filing jointly	$ 2,074
c.	$13,998	Head of household	$ 2,096
d.	$22,025	Married filing separately	$ 3,697
e.	$22,200	Married filing jointly	$ 3,334

2. Lisa O'Reilly is single and has a taxable income of $22,780. Her tax is $____3,420____.

3. Len Beale's taxable income last year was $22,932. Len qualified as head of a household.

    a. Len's tax last year was $____3,439____.

    b. As head of a household, Len's tax was $____23____ less than it would have been if his status had been "single."

    $3,462 − $3,439 = $23 less tax

4. Jo Ann Russo's employer withheld $2,132 for taxes last year from her wages. On her tax return, Jo's taxable income was $13,875 and her filing status was "married filing separately." Jo should receive a refund of $____51____ from the government when she files her tax return.

    $2,132 − $2,081 = $51 refund she should receive

5. The Hayes are married and are filing a joint tax return. Their gross income is $40,836. They are claiming $1,000 in adjustments to income. They are also claiming $7,606 in deductions and four exemptions of $2,500 each. They have already paid a total of $4,172 in withholding taxes. (a) The Hayes' actual tax is $____3,334____. (b) They are entitled to a refund of $____838____.

    a. $40,836 − $1,000 = $39,836 adjusted gross income
        $39,836 − ($7,606 + $10,000) = $22,230 taxable income
        $3,334 tax on taxable income from table
    b. $4,172 − $3,334 = $838 refund due

Exercise

Use the tax table in Illustration 8-4.1 to solve these problems. Assume that every person was listed on their parents' return as a dependent and will claim the standard deduction rather than itemize.

1. Justine worked as a painter for 20 weeks last year to help earn money for school. She worked 15 hours each week at $6.25 an hour. Her employer deducted $6 each week for federal withholding taxes. Justine also earned $58.22 in interest on her checking account. Complete the form below:

Wages	$_____1,875.00_____
Interest	$_____58.22_____
Adjusted Gross Income	$_____1,933.22_____
Less Deductions	$_____1,875.00_____
Taxable Income	$_____58.22_____
Tax from Illustration 8-4.1	$_____9.00_____
Amount of Tax Withheld	$_____120.00_____
Refund Due	$_____111.00_____

2. Tom earned $4,292 in wages last year as a part-time salesclerk and $116 in interest. His employer withheld $560 in federal income taxes from his wages. (a) Tom's taxable income was $_____408_____. (b) Tom will receive $_____498_____ as a refund from federal taxes.

    a. $4,292 + $116 = $4,408 adjusted gross income
       $4,408 − $4,000 = $408 taxable income
       $62 tax from table
    b. $560 − $62 = $498 refund

3. Linda Seager earned $1,278 working part-time last year. The total federal withholding taxes she paid were $160. Linda also earned $28 in interest and received $285 in gifts. She should receive $_____154_____ as a tax refund from the federal government.

    $1,278 + $28 = $1,306 adjusted gross income
    $1,306 − $1,278 = $28 taxable income
    $6 tax from table
    $160 − $6 = $154 refund

LESSON 8-5   STATE AND CITY INCOME TAXES

Exercise

1. Shirley Stolte's taxable income last year was $22,291. The state income tax rate in her state on that taxable income is $840 plus 6% of the amount over $20,000. Shirley's tax last year was $____977.46____.

   $22,291 − $20,000 = $2,291 amount over $20,000
   $2,291 × 0.06 = $137.46 tax on amount over
   $840 + $ 137.46 = $977.46 Shirley's tax last year

2. Use these state income tax rates to find the income tax for three taxpayers.

TAX RATES	TAXPAYER	TAXABLE INCOME	INCOME TAX
1% of the first $3,000 of taxable income			
2% of the next $5,000 of taxable income	a. Rex Taylor	$ 9,000	$____160____
3% of the next $7,000 of taxable income	b. Thelma Tong	$14,700	$____331____
4% of the next $10,000 of taxable income			
5% of all taxable income over $25,000	c. Keith Tepen	$36,100	$____1,295____

   a. 0.01 × $3,000 = $30
      0.02 × $5,000 = $100
      0.03 × $1,000 = $30
                      $160

   b. 0.01 × $3,000 = $30
      0.02 × $5,000 = $100
      0.03 × $6,700 = $201
                      $331

   c. 0.01 × $3,000 = $30
      0.02 × $5,000 = $100
      0.03 × $7,000 = $210
      0.04 × $10,000 = $400
      0.05 × $11,100 = $555
                      $1,295

3. Yan Wu lives in Claremont. Residents of the city pay a city income tax of 2% of the first $20,000 of taxable income per year, and $1\frac{1}{2}$% on taxable income over $20,000 per year. Yang's tax on a taxable income of $44,500 is $____767.50____.

   $20,000 × 0.02 = $400 tax on first $20,000
   $24,500 × 0.015 = $367.50 tax on income over $20,000
   $400 + $367.50 = $767.50 total city tax

4. These are the state and city income tax rates in St. Anne:

STATE TAX RATES		CITY TAX RATES	
Rate	Taxable Income	Rate	Taxable Income
2%	First $5,000	1%	First $ 15,000
3%	Next $10,000	2%	All over $15,000
4%	All over $15,000		

   Tom Sutton lives in St. Anne and has a taxable income of $21,800 for a year. (a) Tom's state income tax for the year is $____672____. (b) Tom's city income tax is $____286____. (c) Tom's total state and city income tax is $____958____.

   a. 0.02 × $5,000 = $100
      0.03 × $10,000 = $300
      0.04 × $6,800 = $272
      $100 + $300 + $272 = $672 state tax

   b. 0.01 × $15,000 = $150
      0.02 × $6,800 = $136
      $150 + $136 = $286 city tax

   c. $672 + $286 = $958 total tax

TERM TICKLER

Directions: **a** The list of words below are terms that you have learned in Chapter 8. Write the word or words that each statement defines in the blank spaces given.

adjusted gross income	excise tax	income tax return	property tax
assessed value	exemption	Medicare	self-employment tax
estimated tax	federal income tax	mill	taxable income

1. A tax on certain goods and services

 e   x   c   i   s   e   t   a   x

2. Value placed on property by tax assessors

 a   s   s   e   s   s   e   d   v   a   l   u   e

3. Tax on real estate   p   r   o   p   e   r   t   y   t   a   x

4. One tenth of a cent   m   i   l   l

5. An amount of income free from tax   e   x   e   m   p   t   i   o   n

6. Pays for hospital and medical bills   M   e   d   i   c   a   r   e

7. A form for figuring taxes   i   n   c   o   m   e
 t   a   x   r   e   t   u   r   n

8. Adjusted gross income less exemptions and deductions

 t   a   x   a   b   l   e   i   n   c   o   m   e

9. Gross income less adjustments   a   d   j   u   s   t   e   d
 g   r   o   s   s   i   n   c   o   m   e

10. A federal tax on income   f   e   d   e   r   a   l
 i   n   c   o   m   e   t   a   x

11. Tax paid for those who work for themselves
 s   e   l   f   –   e   m   p   l   o   y   m   e   n   t
 t   a   x

12. Income taxes paid quarterly by self employed

 e   s   t   i   m   a   t   e   d   t   a   x

b. One of the answers is repeated in the blocked letters. What is that answer?

estimated tax

Name: _____   Date: _____

INTEGRATED PROJECT 8

Mrs. Eloise Duphane is a head of household with one son. She lives in the town of Elderton.

Directions: Read the project through and complete all steps.

Step 1:   Mrs. Duphane is a member of the Elderton Town Board. At a recent meeting, the Board decided that its final budget for next year will require total expenses of $2,309,000. They expect to receive $78,800 in licensing and other fees and to get the remaining funds through property taxes. The property in the town has a total assessed value of $37,800,000.

    a. What amount of property taxes do they need to raise? $_____2,230,200_____

      $2,309,000 − $78,800 = $2,230,200 amount of property taxes to be raised

    b. What should the property tax rate be per $1,000 of assessed value? $_____59_____

      $2,230,200 ÷ $37,800,000 = 0.059 decimal rate needed
      0.059 × $1,000 = $59 tax rate per $1,000 needed

Step 2:   Mrs. Duphane owns a house and lot in Elderton worth $89,500 and assessed by the Town's assessor at 40% of its worth. How much property tax will Mrs. Duphane owe next year? $_____2,112.20_____

      $89,500 × 0.40 = $35,800 assessed value of house and lot
      ($35,800 ÷ $1,000) × $59 = $2,112.20 property tax owed for next year

Step 3:   Mrs. Duphane must complete her federal income tax return for last year's income. Her gross income last year was $35,500. She had adjustments to income for an approved retirement plan of $2,760. She also itemized her deductions and found a total of $5,680. She claimed two exemptions (one for herself and one for her son) at $2,500 each.

    a. What is her taxable income? $_____22,060_____

      $34,500 − $2,760 = $32,740 adjusted gross income
      $32,740 − ($5,680 + $5,000) = $22,060 taxable income

    b. Using Illustration 8-4.1 in the text, what is the amount of her federal income tax? $_____3,311_____

      From the table: $3,311

    c. Mrs. Duphane's employer deducted $4,316 in federal withholding taxes during the year. Will Mrs. Duphane have to pay more taxes or will she receive a refund, and what is the amount? $____1,005 refund____

      $4,316 − $3,311 = $1,005 amount of federal tax refund

Step 4:   Mrs. Duphane also must complete a state income tax return and pay a tax on the amount of taxable income shown on her federal return.

    a. Using Illustration 8-5.1 in the text, what is the amount of her state income tax? $_____1,323.60_____

      $22,060 − $20,000 = $2,060 amount over $20,000
      $2,060 × 0.06 = $123.60 tax on amount over $20,000
      $1,200 + $123.60 = $1,323.60 amount of her state income tax

b. Mrs. Duphane's employer deducted $1,206 in state withholding taxes during the year. Will she have to pay more state income taxes or will she receive a refund, and what is the amount? $_____117.60 owed_____

$1,323.60 − $1,206 = $117.60 amount of state tax owed

Step 5: Mrs. Duphane's son, Roger, earned $2,350 last summer to help with the cost of his schooling. He also earned $124 in interest through his savings account. His employer deducted $312 in federal and $87 in state withholding taxes. Roger needs to complete state and federal income tax returns in order to get refunds of the taxes that were with-held from his wages.

a. Using Illustration 8-4.1, find the amount of Roger's federal income tax. He claims the standard deduction, which is a minimum of $500 and a maximum of $3,000. $_____17, amount of tax_____

$2,350 + $124 = $2,474 adjusted gross income
$2,474 − $2,350 = $124 taxable income
From Illustration 8-4.1, the tax is $17

b. How much federal income tax refund should Roger expect? $_____295_____

$312 − $17 = $295 federal income tax refund

c. Using Illustration 8-5.1, find the amount of Roger's state income tax. $_____2.48_____

$124 × 0.02 = $2.48 state income tax

d. How much state income tax refund should Roger expect? $_____84.52_____

$87.00 − $2.48 = $84.52 state income tax refund

Step 6: Both Mrs. Duphane and Roger paid FICA taxes at 7.65% on their gross wages.

a. How much FICA taxes did Mrs. Duphane pay? $_____2,715.75_____

$35,500 × 0.0765 = $2,715.75 FICA taxes paid by Mrs. Duphane

b. How much FICA taxes did Roger pay? $_____179.78_____

$2,350 × 0.0765 = $179.78 FICA taxes paid by Roger

c. What is the amount of Mrs. Duphane's total property, state income, federal income, and FICA taxes?
$_____9,462.55_____

$2,112.20 + $3,311.00 + $1,323.60 + $2,715.75 = $9,462.55 total taxes for Mrs. Duphane

d. How much total state income, federal income, and FICA taxes did Roger pay? $_____199.26_____

$2.48 + $17.00 + $179.78 = $199.26 total taxes for Roger

Chapter 9

Name: _____ Date: _____

MANAGING YOUR INSURANCE NEEDS

LESSON 9-1 LIFE INSURANCE

Use the following table of annual premiums for the problems in this section.

ANNUAL PREMIUMS FOR $1,000 OF LIFE INSURANCE

Age if Insured	1-Year Term		Whole Life		20-Payment Life	
	Male	Female	Male	Female	Male	Female
20	$1.53	$1.34	$ 7.77	$ 6.84	$27.82	$25.60
25	1.55	1.36	9.21	8.11	30.55	28.09
30	1.60	1.41	11.18	9.83	33.83	31.12
35	1.78	1.57	13.84	12.18	37.57	34.56
40	2.10	1.85	17.93	15.77	42.78	39.36
45	2.70	2.38	22.04	19.38	49.19	45.24
50	3.45	3.00	28.97	22.62	57.37	52.23

Exercise 1.

For each problem, find the annual premium per $1,000 for the type of policy the customer wants and the total premium for the policy face.

1.

Customer Name: _____Henry Kane_____ Age/Sex __25/M__ Amount of Insurance Wanted: ___$20,000___

Kind of Policy: __X__ 1-Year Term
_____ Whole Life
_____ 20-Payment Life

For Office Use	
a. Annual premium per $1,000	$ ___1.55___
b. Total annual premium for policy face	$ ___31___

a. $1.55 annual premium on $1,000 policy

b. $20,000 ÷ $1,000 = 20
20 × $1.55 = $31 annual premium

2.

Customer Name: _____Clyde Warner_____ Age/Sex __50/M__ Amount of Insurance Wanted: ___$7,500___

Kind of Policy: _____ 1-Year Term
__X__ Whole Life
_____ 20-Payment Life

For Office Use	
a. Annual premium per $1,000	$ ___28.97___
b. Total annual premium for policy face	$ ___217.28___

a. $28.97 annual premium on a $1,000 policy

b. $7,500 ÷ $1,000 = 7.5
7.5 × $28.97 = $217.28 annual premium

3.

Customer Name: _____Kenyada Payne_____ Age/Sex __35/F__ Amount of Insurance Wanted: ___$30,000___

Kind of Policy: _____ 1-Year Term
_____ Whole Life
__X__ 20-Payment Life

For Office Use	
a. Annual premium per $1,000	$ ___34.56___
b. Total annual premium for policy face	$ ___1,036.80___

a. $34.56 annual premium on a $1,000 policy

b. $30,000 ÷ $1,000 = 30
30 × $34.56 = $1,036.80 annual premium

Exercise 2.

Use the table of cash values shown below to do the problems in this exercise.

CASH VALUES PER $1,000 OF INSURANCE

End of Year	Cash and Loan Values	Paid-up Whole Life
5	$ 22.30	$134
10	$ 84.34	$451
15	$195.76	$785

1. Lorna Mills took out a life insurance policy for $7,000. At the end of the tenth year, she turned in the policy for its cash value and received $_____590.38_____ from the insurance company.

   $84.34 cash value for $1,000 policy
   7 × $84.34 = $590.38 cash value for $7,000 policy

2. When he began working at his first full-time job, Guillermo Valdivia took out a whole life policy for $42,000. At the end of five years, Guillermo decided to cancel the policy and take the cash value of the policy in paid-up whole life insurance. The amount of paid-up insurance he received from the insurance company was $_____5,628_____.

   $134 paid-up whole life for $1,000 policy
   42 × $134 = $5,628 amount of paid-up insurance

3. Marlo Yakish has a whole life policy for $30,000. She pays an annual premium rate of $11.54 per $1,000. When she signed her insurance contract she chose to use the annual dividend to reduce the annual premium. When she gets a notice that her insurance premium is due, she is notified that her policy has paid an annual dividend of $57.34. What amount will Marlo need to send the insurance company to pay the balance due on the annual premium? $_____288.86_____

   30 × $11.54 = $346.20 annual premium for $30,000 policy
   $346.20 − $57.34 = $288.86 amount due

4. Larry Hershfield took out a whole life policy for $40,000 at the annual premium rate of $11.18 per $1,000. He paid premiums for 10 years. Over these years, the policy earned dividends totaling $394, and Larry used them to reduce the premiums he paid. The total net payments to the insurance company over 10 years were $_____4,078_____.

   40 × $11.18 = $447.20 annual premium
   10 × $447.20 = $4,472 total premiums for 10 years
   $4,472 − $394 = $4,078 total net premium

5. At the end of the fifteenth year, Larry (Problem 4) turned in the policy for its cash value. (a) He received $_____7,830.40_____ from the insurance company. (b) Had he chosen to do so, Larry could have turned in the policy for $_____31,400_____ of paid-up whole life insurance.

   a. 40 × $195.76 = $7,830.40 cash value
   b. 40 × $785 = $31,400 paid-up life insurance Larry could have had

---

LESSON 9-2   HEALTH INSURANCE

Exercise

1. Roland Gribbs was hospitalized for four days. He received these bills: hospital, $2,370; doctor, $1,700. Roland's insurance company paid $1,275 of the doctor's bill and all but $255 of the hospital bill. (a) The amount paid by the company was $_____3,390_____. (b) The amount paid by Roland was $_____680_____.

    a. ($2,370 − $255) + $1,275 = $3,390 paid by company   b. ($2,370 + $1,700) − $3,390 = $680 paid by Roland

2. Ellen Deroian was charged these amounts for the six days she spent in the hospital: $270, $405, $260, $301, $256, $242. These amounts included a daily hospital room charge of $150. Ellen's insurance paid only $120 a day for a room, but covered all other expenses. Ellen's insurance company paid $_____1,554_____ of the total bill.

    $270 + $405 + $260 + $301 + $256 + $242 = $1,734 total charge for 6 days
    6 × ($150 − $120) = $180 amount of room charge not covered
    $1,734 − $180 = $1,554 amount paid by insurance company

3. Nobuaki Watanabe missed 50 days of work because of illness. His disability income insurance policy paid 65% of daily wages after the first 30 days of absence. Nobuaki earned $120 a day. His insurance paid him (a) $_____78_____ a day for (b) _____20_____ days, which was a total disability income payment of (c) $_____1,560_____.

    a. 0.65 × $120 = $78 daily payment beginning with day 31
    b. 50 − 30 = 20 days covered
    c. 20 × $78 = $1,560 total disability payments

4. Magdelena Figueroa's covered medical care bills for a recent illness were $8,440. Her major medical policy had a coinsurance feature that paid 80% of all covered expenses above a $400 deductible. (a) The amount paid by the major medical policy was $_____6,432_____. (b) The total amount paid by Figueroa was $_____2,008_____.

    a. $8,440 − $400 = $8,040 amount to be shared through insurance
       0.80 × $8,040 = $6,432 amount major medical paid
    b. $400 + (0.20 × $8,040) = $2,008 amount Figueroa paid

5. Art Georges was charged $35 per visit for 26 visits to his doctor for acne treatment. His major medical policy paid 90% of doctors' fees, except for a deductible of $5 per visit. (a) Of the total bill, Art paid $_____208_____. (b) The insurance company paid $_____702_____.

    a. 26 × $35 = $910 total bill
       26 × $5 = $130 deductible
       $910 − $130 = $780 covered expenses
       (0.10 × $780) + $130 = $208 amount Art paid
    b. 0.90 × $780 = $702 amount insurance company paid

LESSON 9-3   PROPERTY INSURANCE

Exercise

Round the annual insurance premiums to the nearest dollar for problems in this exercise.

1. Gregory Duggal insures his house for $55,200. The contents of the house are automatically insured for 50% of the total insurance on the house, or (a) $_____27,600_____. If Gregory's insurance company charges $0.46 per $100 for the policy, he will pay an annual premium of (b) $_____254_____.

   a. 0.5 × $55,200 = $27,600 total insurance on contents
   b. $55,200 ÷ $100 = 552
       552 × $0.46 = $253.92, or $254 annual premium

2. Monica Benedaret's insurance company, the Wellford Group, charges $346 a year for $105,000 insurance coverage on her home. The Stephens Insurance Company quoted Monica a rate of $0.36 per $100 for the same coverage. (a) The annual premium for insurance from Stephens will be $_____378_____. (b) By taking the less expensive policy, Monica will save $_____32_____ a year.

   a. ($105,000 ÷ $100) × $0.36 = $378 annual premium for insurance from Stephens
   b. $378 − $346 = $32 annual savings

3. Randall Simpkins insures his home for its full value of $57,000. The annual rate for the policy is $0.62 per $100. Increased coverage on the contents of the home will cost $48 more. Special coverage on a computer system used at home will cost $67 more. The total annual premium for all this coverage is $_____468_____.

   ($57,000 ÷ $100) × $0.62 = $353.40, or $353 cost of standard coverage
   $353 + $48 + $67 = $468 total annual premium

4. Susanna Driscoll's home is insured for its value of $62,500, at a rate of $0.40 per $100. (a) The total annual premium for this coverage is $_____250_____. Her insurance company will deduct 2% from her annual premium if she installs smoke detectors or deduct 6% if she installs a fire alarm system connected to the local fire station. (b) If she installs the smoke detectors, Susanna would pay a premium of $_____245_____. (b) If a fire alarm system was installed instead, Susanna's annual premium would be $_____235_____.

   a. ($62,500 ÷ $100) × $0.40 = $250 total annual premium
   b. $250 − (0.02 × $250) = $245 premium if smoke detectors are installed
   c. $250 − (0.06 × $250) = $235 premium if fire alarm system is installed

5. Walter Freeman rents an apartment and insures its contents with a renters policy. The value of the contents is $14,600, and the premium rate is $0.85 per $100. The annual premium Freeman pays is $_____124_____.

   ($14,600 ÷ $100) × $0.85 = $124.10, or $124 annual premium for renters policy

6. A renter insures the contents of an apartment for $15,000. The rate charged on this renters policy is $0.71 per $100. The renter's personal property that is used away from home is insured at 10% of the policy's total coverage, or for (a) $_____1,500_____. Living expense coverage is 20% of the policy's coverage, or (b) $_____3,000_____. For these coverages, the renter pays an annual premium of (c) $_____107_____.

   a. 0.1 × $15,000 = $1,500 coverage away from home
   b. 0.2 × $15,000 = $3,000 living expense coverage
   c. ($15,000 ÷ $100) × $0.71 = $106.50, or $107 annual premium

7. A fire caused $1,370 damage to the Bozena family's kitchen. The Bozenas' homeowners insurance policy had a $250 deductible clause. Of the total damages, the insurance company will pay $_____1,120_____.

   $1,370 − $250 = $1,120 insurance company pays

8. Ernest D'Angelo now pays $180 a year for $20,000 of renters insurance with a $250 deductible. By choosing a $750 deductible he can save 25% of the annual premium. What will be his annual premium for the same policy with the higher deductible? $_____135_____.

   $180 − (0.25 × $180) = $135 annual premium with higher deductible

9. Trina LeGrow insured her home for $48,000. On this homeowners insurance policy, which carried a $100 deductible, a rate of $0.30 per $100 was charged. (a) The annual premium paid was $_____144_____. By choosing a $250 deductible, the policy's cost would be reduced by 15%. For a policy with the higher deductible, the annual premium would be $_____122_____.

   a. ($48,000 ÷ $100) × $0.30 = $144 annual premium
   b. $144 − (0.15 × $144) = $122.40, or $122 annual premium with higher deductible

10. The insurance premium on a homeowners policy dropped from $652 to $489 when the deductible was increased from $250 to $750. What percent of discount was given for taking the higher deductible? _____25%_____

   $652 − $489 = $163 saving per year
   $163 ÷ $652 = 0.25, or 25% discount

11. A homeowners insurance policy that had an annual premium of $730 a year was canceled by the insurance company after being in effect for 30 days. The insurance company gave a pro rata refund of $_____670_____.

   $\frac{30}{365} = \frac{6}{73}$
   $730 \times \frac{6}{73} = $60 insurance cost for 30 days
   $730 − $60 = $670 refund

LESSON 9-4 AUTOMOBILE INSURANCE

Annual Insurance Premiums for Cars and Trucks

Type of Insurance	Limits	Type of Driving		
		Pleasure Only	Driving to Work	Business
Bodily Injury and Property Damage	$25/50,000 $75/100,000 $150/300,000	$108 $132 $153	$122 $146 $170	$160 $189 $218
Collision	$100 deductible $250 deductible $500 deductible	$466 $328 $256	$520 $363 $285	$676 $472 $370
Comprehensive	$50 deductible $100 deductible	$82 $61	$90 $68	$118 $88

Exercise

Use the annual insurance premium table above to do the problems in this exercise.

1. Three cars are used as shown below. Each car is insured for the basic limit of $25/50,000 for combined bodily injury and property damage coverage. All have collision and comprehensive coverage with the deductibles shown. Find the annual premium for each coverage and the total annual premium.

Car Usage and Deductibles	Annual Premium			
	Bodily Injury & Property Damage	Collision	Compre-hensive	Total
a. For driving to work; collision, $250 deductible; comprehensive, $100 deductible	$122	$363	$68	$553
b. For pleasure driving only; $100 deductible for both collision and comprehensive	$108	$466	$61	$635
c. For business; collision, $500 deductible; comprehensive, $50 deductible	$160	$370	$118	$648

2. Danjiro Nishimura uses his truck to drive to work. He wants to carry bodily injury/property damage coverage of $150/300,000, collision coverage with a $500 deductible, and comprehensive with a $50 deductible. The annual premium for the insurance coverage he wants will be (a) bodily injury/property damage, $_____170_____; (b) collision, $_____285_____; (c) comprehensive, $_____90_____.

3. Priscilla McGhee owns a computer repair company and uses her truck for business. She carries bodily injury/property damage insurance of $150/300,000 and a $100 deductible on collision and a $50 deductible on comprehensive. (a) For this coverage, she pays an annual premium of $_____1,012_____. (b) If she chose a $500 deductible for collision and $100 deductible for comprehensive, her annual premium would be $_____676_____. (c) By taking the higher deductibles she would save $_____336_____ annually on truck insurance.

    a. $218 + $676 + $118 = $1,012 annual premium
    b. $218 + $370 + $88 = $676 annual premium with higher deductibles
    c. $1,012 − $676 = $336 amount saved annually

4. Before he retired, Bill Young drove his car to work and carried this insurance coverage: $25/50,000 bodily injury/property damage, $100 deductible for collision, and $50 deductible for comprehensive. (a) For this coverage, Bill paid an annual premium of $_____732_____. After he retired, Bill used his car only for pleasure driving and kept the same insurance coverage. (b) For this coverage, Bill pays $_____656_____ a year.

    a. $122 + $520 + $90 = $732 annual premium, driving to work
    b. $108 + $466 + $82 = $656 annual premium, pleasure driving

5. A truck used for working on a farm and delivering produce to markets is insured as being used in business. The truck is insured for the least amount of bodily injury/property damage coverage and with a $250 deductible for collision coverage and a $100 deductible for comprehensive coverage. Because it is a farm vehicle, a 20% discount is given off the regular annual premium. The premium before any discounts are given is (a) $_____720_____, the discount amount is (b) $_____144_____, and the annual premium to be paid is (c) $_____576_____.

    a. $160 + $472 + $88 = $720 regular premium
    b. 0.2 × $720 = $144 discount amount
    c. $720 − $144 = $576 annual premium to be paid

6. Melissa Franks drives her car for pleasure and carries bodily injury/property damage coverage of $75/100,000 and the highest deductible amounts for collision and comprehensive coverages. (a) At the rates found in the table, her annual premium would be $_____449_____. As a young driver under the age of 25, however, Melissa is charged a total annual premium that is 1.4 times the total premium figured from the table. (b) The annual premium that Melissa will be charged is $_____628.60_____.

    a. $132 + $256 + $61 = $449 annual premium from table
    b. 1.4 × $449 = $628.60 amount Melissa is charged as a young driver

7. Because he was convicted of drunk driving, Courtney Doakes has to pay 4 times the regular rate if he wants to keep driving his car only to work. Courtney wants to keep his bodily injury/property damage coverage at $75/100,000. However, he feels that he can afford collision and comprehensive coverage only if he takes the highest deductibles. For this insurance coverage, what annual premium will Courtney pay? $_____1,996_____.

    4 × ($146 + $285 + $68) = $1,996 annual premium

TERM TICKLER

Directions: **a.** The statements on the left are definitions of vocabulary words that you have learned in Chapter 9. Write the word or words in the blank spaces.

1. Person to whom policy is paid when you die

   b e n e f i c i [a] r y

2. Pay premiums for lifetime

   w [h] o l e l i f e

3. This type of insurance protects owner and owner's dwelling and other property

   [h] o m e o w n e r s

4. Amound paid for insurance

   p r [e] m i u m

5. Covers damage to own car from accident

   c o [l] l i s i o n

6. You pay for first part of health cost

   d e d u c [t] i b l e

7. A return of part of the premium

   d i v [i] d e n d

8. Borrowing cash value of life insurance policy is a policy

   l o [a] n

9. An insurance company

   i n [s] u r e r

10. Offers protection only for a fixed period of time

    t e r m l i f [e]

11. When the insured and the insurer share losses and costs

    c o i n s [u] r a n c e

12. Property loss is paid at the amount needed to buy it new or to build it new with a replacement

    [l] o s s p o l i c y

13. Type of policy that provides property insurance for tenants

    [r] e n t e r s

14. Person whose life is insured

    i [n] s u r e d

15. Type of insurance that covers damage to own car from causes other than an accident

    c o m p r e h e [n] s i v e

16. Amount you get if you cancel a policy [c] a s h v a l u e

b. Unscramble the letters in boxes to form a two-word phrase from Chapter 9. The first six letters of the solution form the first word.

   h e a l t h

   i n s u r a n c e

INTEGRATED PROJECT 9

Directions: Read through the entire project before you begin doing any work.

Introduction: Bill and Helen Cooper, a married couple, recently agreed to adopt Scott, a school-age child. To be able to spend the time with Scott that she feels is necessary, Helen has decided to quit her job. Since Scott will be in school for most of the day, Helen also decided to return to college to complete work on her degree. She will take classes while Scott is at school.

Helen's decision will make a difference in the family's lifestyle, and they will have to save money in different ways to get by. To make it easier for Helen to attend school, the Coopers plan to sell their house outside the city and buy another house near the college Helen will be attending. When the Coopers move, they will be charged less for their property insurance because of improved fire protection.

The Coopers now pay insurance on two cars at the "driving to work" rate. Both cars have identical coverage: $50/100,000 bodily injury, $50,000 property damage, $100 deductible on collision, and $50 deductible on comprehensive. By changing their coverage, they will save money.

Bill's employer provides basic health insurance for the Cooper family. The employer pays for this insurance at a total annual cost of $2,800. Major medical coverage must be paid by the employee at these monthly rates: employee only, $34; each additional dependent, $28. However, because he will have another dependent, Bill will have to pay an additional amount for major medical health coverage.

Both Bill and Helen have life insurance. Helen carries $120,000 of term life insurance while Bill carries $100,000 of term life insurance and $20,000 of 20-payment life. They both pay the 30-year-old rate for term insurance. Bill pays the 20-year-old rate on the 20-payment life policy, which was his age at the time the policy was issued.

Step One: In addition to the information given, use the data from the following tables in your textbook to answer questions about the Coopers' life insurance coverage:

     Illustration 9-1.1. Sample life insurance premiums
     Illustration 9-1.2. Sample cash value table
     Illustration 9-4.1. Sample car and truck insurance premiums

1. The Coopers now pay $0.53 per $100 of value for homeowners insurance. If their current house is insured for its full value of $70,000, what annual premium do they pay? $_____371_____

     $70,000 ÷ $100 = 700 number of $100 units
     700 × $0.53 = $371 annual premium

2. For the insurance on only one car, the Coopers pay these annual premiums:

     a.   bodily injury, $_____126_____

     b.   property damage, $_____16_____

     c.   collision, $_____612_____

     d.   comprehensive, $_____101_____

     e.   The total annual premium for one car is $_____855_____.

     f.   Since the two cars they own carry the same coverage, the total annual premium for insuring both cars is (f) $_____1,710_____.

     e. $126 + $16 + $612 + $101 = $855 annual premium for one car
     f. 2 × $855 = $1,710 annual premium for both cars

3. The total annual cost of major medical insurance paid by the Coopers is (a) $_____744_____. Of this amount, (b) $_____408_____ is paid to cover Bill and (c) $_____336_____ to cover Helen.

   a. $408 + $336 = $744 total annual cost
   b. 12 × $34 = $408 cost of Bill's coverage
   c. 12 × $28 = $336 cost of Helen's coverage

4. For their life insurance coverage, the Coopers pay these amounts: Helen's term policy, (a) $_____153.60_____; Bill's term policy, (b) $_____145_____; (c) Bill's 20-payment life policy, $_____505.80_____. The total of the annual life insurance premiums they pay is (d) $_____804.40_____. After being in effect for ten years, Bill's 20-payment life policy has a cash value of (e) $_____1,521.80_____.

   a. ($120,000 ÷ $1,000) × $1.28 = $153.60 cost of Helen's term insurance
   b. ($100,000 ÷ $1,000) × $1.45 = $145.00 cost of Bill's term insurance
   c. ($20,000 ÷ $1,000) × $25.29 = $505.80 cost of Bill's 20-payment life policy
   d. $153.60 + $145.00 + $505.80 = $804.40 total annual premiums
   e. ($20,000 ÷ $1,000) × $76.09 = $1,521.80 policy cash value

Step Two: Answer the following questions that show how the Coopers can save money on their insurance coverage.

1. The Cooper's new home will be located in a new rate territory where they will be charged $0.47 per $100 of the property's value. Assuming that their new home's value will also be $70,000, (a) the Coopers will pay an annual premium of $_____329_____ for homeowners insurance. (b) This is an annual saving of $_____42_____ over their old policy.

   a. ($70,000 ÷ $100) × $0.47 = $329 annual premium on new home
   b. $371 − $329 = $42 annual saving

2. Since only one car will be driven to work, the second car the Coopers own can be rated for pleasure driving. With the same dollar coverages for bodily injury and property damage and the same deductibles for collision and comprehensive, the total premium they will pay for insuring the second car at the pleasure driving rate is (a) $_____770_____. This is a saving of (b) $_____85_____ over the former rate.

   If the Coopers decide to change the coverage on the second car and take the lowest limits on bodily injury and property damage and take the highest deductibles on collision and comprehensive, the annual premium for that car will be (c) $_____462_____. This is a saving of (d) $_____393_____ over the original rate.

   a. $114 + $14 + $550 + $92 = $770 premium
   b. $855 − $770 = $85 saved
   c. $82 + $10 + $302 + $68 = $462 premium
   d. $855 − $462 = $393 saved

3. When Scott is added to the Major Medical Coverage plan, the additional annual premium that Bill will have to pay is $_____336_____.

   12 × $28 = $336 premium to cover Scott

4. To provide extra life insurance coverage, Bill and Helen agree to each take out an additional $75,000 of term life insurance and to cancel Bill's 20-payment policy. The annual premium that Bill pays for this additional coverage is (a) $_____108.75_____, while Helen pays (b) $_____96_____. The total change in the life insurance premiums they pay each year will be (c) $__301.05 less per year__.

   a. ($75,000 ÷ $1,000) × $1.45 = $108.75 annual premium
   b. ($75,000 ÷ $1,000) × $1.28 = $96.00 annual premium
   c. $505.80 − ($108.75 + $96.00) = $301.05 less per year

Name: _____   Date: _____

SAVING AND BORROWING MONEY

LESSON 10-1   PASSBOOK SAVINGS ACCOUNTS

Exercise 1.   (Keeping a passbook)

For the savings account passbook shown below, find the account balance after each transaction and write it in the balance column.

MID-CITY SAVINGS BANK				
IN ACCOUNT WITH: *ROSEMARIE LEVITT*				
Date	**Withdrawal**	**Deposit**	**Interest**	**Balance**
19__ Jan. 2				827.30
Jan. 15		135.00		962.30
Feb. 9	75.00			887.30
Mar. 26		63.70		951.00
Apr. 1			13.44	964.44
May 7		110.00		1,074.44
June 12	100.00			974.44
June 26		80.17		1,054.61
July 1			15.67	1,070.28

Exercise 2.   (Finding interest on savings accounts)

Figure the interest for one period for each problem. Round your answers to the nearest cent. Write your answers in the table.

Account Balance	Annual Rate of Interest	Interest Period	Amount of Interest
1. $742	5%	quarterly	$ 9.28
2. $813	7%	semiannual	28.46
3. $987	6%	quarterly	14.81
4. $471	$5\frac{1}{2}\%$	quarterly	6.48
5. $394	$6\frac{1}{2}\%$	semiannual	12.81
6. $847	$6\frac{1}{4}\%$	quarterly	13.23
7. $514	$5\frac{3}{4}\%$	semiannual	14.78
8. $963	6%	quarterly	14.44
9. $195	7.2%	quarterly	3.51
10. $327	8.4%	semiannual	13.73

1. $742 \times 0.05 \times \frac{1}{4}$ = $9.28 interest

2. $813 \times 0.07 \times \frac{1}{2}$ = $28.46 interest

3. $987 \times 0.06 \times \frac{1}{4}$ = $14.81 interest

4. $471 \times 0.055 \times \frac{1}{4}$ = $6.48 interest

5. $394 \times 0.065 \times \frac{1}{2}$ = $12.81 interest

6. $847 \times 0.0625 \times \frac{1}{4}$ = $13.23 interest

7. $514 \times 0.0575 \times \frac{1}{2}$ = $14.78 interest

8. $963 \times 0.06 \times \frac{1}{4}$ = $14.44 interest

9. $195 \times 0.072 \times \frac{1}{4}$ = $3.51 interest

10. $327 \times 0.084 \times \frac{1}{2}$ = $13.73 interest

Exercise 3.   (Compounding interest)

Find the interest and balance for each date listed in each savings account. Write your answers in the table. Interest is compounded quarterly on January 2, April 1, July 1, and October 1. Semiannual interest is paid on January 2 and July 1.

1.

Annual interest rate, 7%
Paid: quarterly

Date	Interest	Balance
Oct. 1		600.00
Jan. 2	10.50	610.50
Apr. 1	10.68	621.18
Jul. 1	10.87	632.05
Oct. 1	11.06	643.11

2.

Annual interest rate, 6%
Paid: quarterly

Date	Interest	Balance
Jan. 2		820.00
Jul. 1	24.60	844.60
Jan. 2	25.34	869.94
Jul. 1	26.10	896.04

3.

Annual interest rate, $6\frac{1}{2}$%
Paid: quarterly

Date	Interest	Balance
Apr. 1		550.00
Jul. 1	8.94	558.94
Oct. 1	9.08	568.02
Jan. 2	9.23	577.25
Apr. 1	9.38	586.63

4.

Annual interest rate, $5\frac{1}{4}$%
Paid: quarterly

Date	Interest	Balance
Jul. 1		1,400.00
Jan. 2	36.75	1,436.75
Jul. 1	37.71	1,474.46
Jan. 2	38.70	1,513.16

Exercise 4.   (Finding interest on minimum balances)

Find each missing balance and the interest to be paid quarterly on January 2, April 1, July 1, and October 1. Figure interest on the minimum balance on deposit during the interest period.

1.

		Annual interest rate, $4\frac{1}{2}$%		
Date	Deposit	Withdrawal	Interest	Balance
Jul. 1				643.00
Jul. 9	67.00			710.00
Aug. 11	155.00			865.00
Sep. 22		45.00		820.00
Sep. 29		80.00		740.00
Oct. 1			7.23	747.23

2.

		Annual interest rate, $5\frac{3}{4}$%		
Date	Deposit	Withdrawal	Interest	Balance
Oct. 1				870.00
Oct. 3	93.00			963.00
Nov. 9		212.00		751.00
Nov. 17		75.00		676.00
Dec. 14	47.00			723.00
Jan. 2			9.72	732.72

COMPOUND INTEREST TABLE FOR $1

Interest Periods	$1\frac{1}{4}$%	$1\frac{1}{2}$%	2%	5%	6%	8%	9%
Annual 1	1.012500	1.015000	1.020000	1.050000	1.060000	1.080000	1.090000
2	1.025156	1.030225	1.040400	1.102500	1.123600	1.166400	1.188100
3	1.037971	1.045678	1.061208	1.157625	1.191016	1.259712	1.295029
4	1.050945	1.061364	1.082432	1.215506	1.262477	1.360489	1.411582
5	1.064082	1.077284	1.104081	1.276282	1.338226	1.469328	1.538624
6	1.077383	1.093443	1.126162	1.340096	1.418519	1.586874	1.677100
7	1.090850	1.109845	1.148686	1.407100	1.503630	1.713824	1.828039
8	1.104486	1.126493	1.171659	1.477455	1.593848	1.850930	1.992563
9	1.118292	1.143390	1.195093	1.551328	1.689479	1.999005	2.171893
10	1.132270	1.160541	1.218994	1.628895	1.790848	2.158925	2.367364
11	1.146424	1.177949	1.243374	1.710339	2.898299	2.331639	2.580426
12	1.160754	1.195618	1.268242	2.795856	2.012197	2.518170	2.812665
Daily 30	—	—	—	1.004175	1.005012	1.006688	1.007527
90	—	—	—	1.012578	1.015112	1.020199	1.022752
180	—	—	—	1.025313	1.030452	1.040806	1.046022
365	—	—	—	1.051998	1.062716	1.084482	1.095530

Exercise 5.   (Figuring annual and daily interest)

For each problem use the compound interest table to find the compound amount and compound interest.

Beginning Principal	Rate	Time	Compounding Period	Compound Amount	Compound Interest
1. $3,000	8%	5 years	annually	$4,407.98	$1,407.98
2. $1,200	6%	9 years	annually	$2,027.37	$827.37
3. $800	9%	180 days	daily	$836.82	$36.82
4. $2,400	5%	30 days	daily	$2,410.02	$10.02
5. $500	10%	4 years	semiannually	$738.73	$238.73
6. $700	9%	11 years	annually	1,806.30	$1,106.30

1. 3,000 × $1.469328 = $4,407.98 compound amount $4,407.98 − $3,000 = $1,407.98 interest
2. 1,200 × $1.689479 = $2,027.37 compound amount $2,027.37 − $1,200 = $827.37 interest
3. 800 × $1.046022 = $836.82 compound amount $836.82 − $800 = $36.82 interest
4. 2,400 × $1.004175 = $2,410.02 compound amount $2,410.02 − $2,400 = $10.02 interest
5. 500 × $1.477455 = $738.73 compound amount $738.73 − $500 = $238.73 interest
6. 700 × $2.580426 = $1,806.30 compound amount $1,806.30 − $700 = $1,106.30 interest

Exercise 6.   (Figuring daily, quarterly, and semiannual interest)

For each problem use the compound interest table to find the compound amount and compound interest.

	Beginning Principal	Rate	Time	Compounding Period	Compound Amount	Compound Interest
1.	$650	5%	1 year	daily	$683.80	$33.80
2.	$420	12%	5 years	semiannually	$752.16	$332.16
3.	$500	6%	3 years	quarterly	$597.81	$97.81
4.	$760	5%	2 years	quarterly	$839.41	$79.41
5.	$910	10%	$5\frac{1}{2}$ years	semiannually	$1,556.41	$646.41

1. 650 × $1.051998 = $683.80 compound amount $683.80 − $650 = $33.80 interest
2. 420 × $1.790848 = $752.16 compound amount $752.16 − $420 = $332.16 interest
3. 500 × $1.195618 = $597.81 compound amount $597.81 − $500 = $97.81 interest
4. 760 × $1.104486 = $839.41 compound amount $839.41 − $760 = $79.41 interest
5. 910 × $1.710339 = $1,556.41 compound amount $1,556.41 − $910 = $646.41 interest

Exercise 7.   (Figuring the effective rate of interest)

For each problem use the compound interest table to find the annual interest earned and the effective rate of interest.

1. Elmer Sharry made a deposit of $860 to open a savings account that pays interest at an annual rate of 8%, compounded quarterly. If he keeps his original deposit in the savings account and is paid interest for four quarters, he will earn interest in the first year of (a) $_____70.89_____. His deposit will earn an effective rate of interest of (b) _____8.24%_____, to the nearest hundredth percent.

   a. 860 × $1.082432 = $930.89 compound amount
      $930.89 − $860 = $70.89 interest for one year
   b. $70.89 ÷ $860 = 8.24% effective rate of interest

2. Viola Rosonak's bank pays 6% annual interest on savings accounts, compounded quarterly. On October 1, she made a deposit of $1,200 to her savings account, which had a balance of $300. If she makes no other deposits or withdrawals to the account for one year, her account balance will be (a) $_____1,592.05_____. She will have earned interest of (b) $_____92.05_____, which represents a (c) _____6.14%_____% effective rate of interest, to the nearest tenth percent.

   a. $300 + $1,200 = $1,500 savings account balance on October 1
      $1,500 × $1.061364 = $1,592.05 account balance one year from now
   b. $1,592.05 − $1,500 = $92.05 interest earned for one year
   c. $92.05 ÷ $ 1,500 = 0.06136, or 6.14% effective rate of interest

LESSON 10-2   SPECIAL SAVINGS ACCOUNTS

Exercise 1.

For each deposit, find the amount of certificate interest earned. Then find the difference between passbook and certificate interest. Write your answers in the spaces provided.

Amount of Deposit	Time Money Is on Deposit	Passbook Interest		Certificate Interest		Difference Between Passbook and Certificate Interest
		Rate	Amount	Rate	Amount	
1. $7,000	3 months	5.75%	$100.63	12%	$210	$109.37
2. $13,000	6 months	6%	$390.00	8%	$520	$130.00
3. $6,000	12 months	5.25%	$315.00	11%	$660	$345.00
4. $15,000	9 months	5%	$562.50	9.2%	$1,035	$472.50
5. $12,000	3 months	5.5%	$165.00	8%	$240	$75.00

1. $7,000 \times 0.12 \times \frac{1}{4} = $210 certificate interest $210.00 - $100.63 = $109.37

2. $13,000 \times 0.08 \times \frac{1}{2} = $520 certificate interest $520.00 - $390.00 = $130.00

3. $6,000 \times 0.11 \times 1 = $660 certificate interest $660.00 - $315.00 = $345.00

4. $15,000 \times 0.092 \times \frac{3}{4} = $1,035 certificate interest $1,035.00 - $562.50 = $472.50

5. $12,000 \times 0.08 \times \frac{1}{4} = $240 certificate interest $240 - $ 165 = $75.00

Exercise 2.

Find the amount of the penalty based on the amount withdrawn early. Then find the net interest.

Amount of Deposit	Interest Earned to Date	Amount Withdrawn Early	Penalty		Net Interest
			Charge	Amount	
1. $14,000	$945.00	$6,000	1 month's interest at 9%	$45.00	$900.00
2. $7,000	$682.75	$5,000	3 months' interest at 13%	$162.50	$520.25
3. $12,000	$814.20	$7,500	12 months' interest at 10%	$750.00	$64.20
4. $10,000	$641.67	$3,400	2 months' interest at 11%	$62.33	$579.34
5. $6,000	$240.00	$6,000	6 months' interest at 8%	$240.00	-0-

1. $6,000 \times 0.09 \times \frac{1}{12} = $45 penalty $945.00 - $45.00 = $900.00 net interest

2. $5,000 \times 0.13 \times \frac{1}{4} = $162.50 penalty $682.75 - $162.50 = $520.25 net interest

3. $7,500 \times 0.1 \times 1 = $750 penalty $814.20 - $750.00 = $64.20 net interest

4. $3,400 \times 0.11 \times \frac{1}{6} = $62.33 penalty $641.67 - $62.33 = $579.34 net interest

5. $6,000 \times 0.08 \times \frac{1}{2} = $240 penalty $240.00 - $240.00 = $0 net interest

LESSON 10-3   PROMISSORY NOTES

Exercise 1.   (Finding the interest on a loan)

1. Alice Farrell, a store owner, needed money to purchase store equipment. She borrowed the money from Valley Bank, signing the promissory note below. She pledged no collateral on the loan.

$ __7,800.00__	__Keene, N.H.__	__September 12__	19 __96__

__Two years__   AFTER DATE __I__ PROMISE TO PAY TO

THE ORDER OF __Valley Bank__

__Seven thousand, eight hundred and $\frac{no}{100}$__ ———————————— DOLLARS

PAYABLE AT __Valley Bank__

VALUE RECEIVED WITH INTEREST AT __13__ %

NO. __13807__ DUE __September 12__ 19 __98__   __Alice Farrell__

On the due date, Alice paid the Valley Bank ____$9,828____

$7,800 \times 0.13 \times 2 = \$2,028$ interest for two years

$7,800 + \$2,028 = \$9,828$ amount paid on the due date

2. You borrowed $2,800 from your bank for 4 months with interest at 11%. You paid the note in full on its due date, giving the bank a check for ____$2,902.67____ in payment.

$2,800 \times 0.11 \times \frac{1}{3} = \$102.67$ interest

$2,800 + \$102.67 = \$2,902.67$ amount of check

3. Ben Isenberg signed a promissory note for a three and one-half year home equity loan. The principal was $11,600. The interest rate was $9\frac{1}{2}$%. On the maturity date, Ben owed ____$15,457____ for principal and interest.

$11,600 \times 0.095 \times 3\frac{1}{2} = \$3,857$ interest

$11,600 + \$3,857 = \$15,457$ owed at the maturity date

4. Sally Green borrowed $6,000 to buy a used car. The car cost $7,500 and she pledged the car as collateral for the loan from her bank. She signed a promissory note for $2\frac{1}{2}$ years with interest at 16%. The amount due at maturity was ____$8,400____.

$6,000 \times 0.16 \times 2\frac{1}{2} = \$2,400$ interest

$6,000 + \$2,400 = \$8,400$ due at maturity

Exercise 2.   (Finding interest for time in years and months)

Find the interest in each problem below.

PRINCIPAL (P)	RATE (R)	TIME (T)	INTEREST (I)	PRINCIPAL (P)	RATE (R)	TIME (T)	INTEREST (I)
1. $5,000	15%	2 yr	$1,500	**5.** $2,500	11%	6 mo.	$137.50
2. $3,600	8%	3 yr	$864	**6.** $2,000	10%	9 mo.	$150
3. $15,000	10%	1.5 yr	$2,250	**7.** $8,000	9%	3 mo.	$180
4. $3,000	12%	0.5 yr	$180	**8.** $6,000	15%	5 yr.	$4,500

Exercise 3.   (Finding <u>exact</u> interest for time in days)

In each problem, find the exact interest to the <u>nearest cent</u>.

PRINCIPAL (P)	RATE (R)	TIME (T)	INTEREST (I)	PRINCIPAL (P)	RATE (R)	TIME (T)	INTEREST (I)
1. $1,000	10%	90 days	$24.66	**6.** $200	10%	88 days	$4.82
2. $16,000	12%	73 days	$384.00	**7.** $2,500	11%	292 days	$220.00
3. $1,500	18%	30 days	$22.19	**8.** $1,800	17%	200 days	$167.67
4. $4,000	9%	45 days	$44.38	**9.** $14,000	12%	60 days	$276.16
5. $20,000	16%	219 days	$1,920.00	**10.** $2,000	9.5%	180 days	$93.70

Exercise 4. (Finding <u>banker's</u> interest for time in days)

In each problem below, find the banker's interest to the <u>nearest cent</u>.

PRINCIPAL (P)	RATE (R)	TIME (T)	INTEREST (I)		PRINCIPAL (P)	RATE (R)	TIME (T)	INTEREST (I)
1. $2,000	10%	90 days	$50.00	6.	$1,000	10%	144 days	$40.00
2. $2,500	9%	180 days	$112.50	7.	$6,000	8%	40 days	$53.33
3. $14,000	16%	30 days	$186.67	8.	$4,000	15%	120 days	$200.00
4. $5,000	12%	240 days	$400.00	9.	$2,000	11%	45 days	$27.50
5. $20,000	16%	300 days	$2,666.67	10.	$7,200	9.5%	100 days	$190.00

Exercise 5. (Finding the rate of interest)

In each problem below, find the annual rate of interest.

PRINCIPAL (P)	RATE (R)	TIME (T)	INTEREST (I)		PRINCIPAL (P)	RATE (R)	TIME (T)	INTEREST (I)
1. $2,000	3 mo.	$50	10%	7.	$8,000	2 yr.	$1,280	8%
2. $1,500	6 mo.	$60	8%	8.	$6,000	1.5 yr.	$900	10%
3. $6,000	8 mo.	$480	12%	9.	$1,200	2 yr.	$288	12%
4. $2,500	2 yr.	$700	14%	10.	$5,000	8 mo.	$400	12%
5. $3,200	4 mo.	$96	9%	11.	$8,000	4 yr.	$2,560	8%
6. $3,000	3 yr.	$990	11%	12.	$1,200	9 mo.	$90	10%

Exercise 6.   (Discounting a non-interest-bearing note)

1. a. Use these data to fill in the promissory note below: Face of note, $8,500; date, July 14; time, 3 months; payable to Southside Bank; payable at Southside Bank; interest, none; number 339182; maker, Tomasina Rodriquez; collateral, 1995 Sundance 80908090811.

LOAN NO. _____339182_____   DATE _____July 14_____ 19 __--__

LOAN AMOUNT $ ___8,500.00___ MATURITY DATE _____Oct 14_____ 19 __--__

_____3 months_____ AFTER DATE ___I___ PROMISE TO PAY TO

THE ORDER OF ____Southside Bank_____

___Eight thousand, five hundred and___ $\frac{no}{100}$ _____ DOLLARS

PAYABLE AT _____Southside Bank_____ VALUE RECEIVED WITH INTEREST AT

THE RATE OF ___0___ % PER ANNUM, FOR VALUE RECEIVED, GIVING SAID BANK A

SECURITY INTEREST IN THIS COLLATERAL: _____1995 Sundance 80908090811_____

The rights _____I_____ (am, ~~are~~) giving said bank in this property, and the obligations this agreement secures are defined on the reverse side of this note.

_____Tomasina Rodriquez_____

---

b. Tomasina discounts the note above at her bank on July 14. The discount rate is 15%. The bank credits her account for the proceeds, which are ____$8,181.25____.

$8,500 \times 0.15 \times \frac{1}{4} = $318.75 discount

$8,500 - $318.75 = $8,181.25 proceeds

2. On June 2, Lu Shih found that he had overdrawn his checking account by $500. He then discounted at the bank his 2-month, non-interest-bearing note for $1,000 and had the proceeds put into his checking account. The bank's discount rate was 12%. (a) The proceeds were ____$980____. (b) After the proceeds were put into his checking account, his account balance was ____$480____. (c) The real rate of interest he paid, to the nearest hundredth of a percent, was ____12.24%____.

a. $1,000 \times 0.12 \times 6 = $20 discount
    $1,000 - $20 = $980 proceeds
b. $980 - $500 = $480 checking account balance
c. $20 \times 6 = $ 120 annual interest
    $120 \div $980 = 0.12244, or 12.24% real rate of interest

LESSON 10-4   INTEREST AND DATE TABLES

Exercise 1.   (Figuring interest with an interest table)

Use the table in Illustration 10-4.1 in the text to solve problems 1-4.

1. Find the interest for each promissory note:

   a. $600 @ 10.5% for 21 days _____$3.62_____

   $0.6041 × 6 = $3.6246 or $3.62

   b. $750 @ 10% for 19 days _____$3.90_____

   $0.5205 × 7.5 = $3.9038 or $3.90

   c. $6,950 @ 9.5% for 12 days _____$21.70_____

   $0.3123 × 69.5 = $21.7049 or $21.70

   d. $4,200 @ 8.5% for 9 days _____$8.80_____

   $0.2096 × 42 = $8.8032 or $8.80

   e. $340 @ 16.5% for 90 days _____$13.83_____

   ($0.6575 + 0.6986) × 3 = $4.0683
   $4.0683 × 3.4 = $13.8322 or $13.83

   f. $2,500 @ 20% for 15 days _____$20.55_____

   $0.4110 + $0.4110 = $0.8220
   $0.8220 × 25 = $20.55

   g. $1,700 @ 16% for 24 days _____$17.88_____

   $0.5260 + $0.5260 = $1.0520
   $1.052 × 17 = $17.884 or $17.88

   h. $4,300 @ 20% for 12 days _____$28.28_____

   $0.3288 + $0.3288 = $0.6576
   $0.6576 × 43 = $28.2768 or $28.28

   i. $5,780 @ 17.5% for 50 days _____$138.56_____

   $0.5822 + $0.6164 + $0.5822 + $0.6164 = $2.3972
   $2.3972 × 57.8 = $138.5582 or $138.56

2. Carlos Lugo borrowed $1,500 on a note for 45 days with interest at 12%:

   a. What interest did he pay? _____$22.19_____

   $0.9863 + $0.4932 = $1.4795
   $1.4795 × 15 = $22.1925 or $22.19 interest paid

   b. What total amount did he owe when the note was due? _____$1,522.19_____

   $1,500.00 + $22.19 = $1,522.19 total amount owed

3. Elena Cabrera borrowed $18,000 for 60 days at 9% interest. When the note came due, Elena owed _____$18,266.29_____.

   $0.7397 + $0.7397 = $1.4794
   $1.4794 × 180 = $266.292 or $266.29 interest owed
   $18,000.00 + $266.29 = $18,266.29 principal and interest owed

4. Ed Baum needs to borrow $11,000 for 30 days. Bank A will lend him the money at 12.5% interest. Bank B will lend him the money at 10.5% interest. (a) The interest cost at Bank A is _____$113.01_____. (b) The interest cost at Bank B is _____$94.93_____. (c) By borrowing at the lower interest cost, Ed would save _____$18.08_____.

   a. $1.0274 × 110 = $113.014 or $113.01 interest cost at Bank A
   b. $0.8630 × 110 = $94.93 interest cost at Bank B
   c. $113.01 − $94.93 = $18.08 saved by borrowing at lower interest cost

Exercise 2.   (Finding the Due Dates of Notes)

1. On October 31, Elsa Burns borrowed $2,800 from the Moline National Bank. She gave the bank her three-month note for that amount. The note was dated October 31, and the exact interest rate was 11%. (a) The date of maturity of the note was ____January 1____. (b) On that date Elsa paid the note, giving the bank her check for ____$2,877____.

b. $2,800 \times 0.11 \times \frac{1}{4} = 77 interest

   $2,800 + $77 = $2,877$ amount of check

2. Jun Akona needed to borrow money from his bank to remodel his home. To get the loan, he gave the bank his 120-day note for $27,500, dated April 20, bearing exact interest at $12\frac{1}{2}$%. (a) The note came due for payment on ____August 18____. (b) Akona paid the note on its due date, giving the bank a check for ____$28,347.60____ in payment.

b. $27,500 \times 0.125 \times \frac{90}{365} = 847.60 interest

   $27,500 + $847.60 = $28,347.60$ amount of check

3. The Sinclair Bank holds the notes listed below. They show loans to the people named in the "Maker" column. Show for each note (a) the due date of the note, and (b) the amount due at maturity. Use exact interest.

	Maker	Face of Note	Date of Note	Time	Exact Interest Rate	Due Date	Amount Due at Maturity
a.	Terry Ward	$7,500	Mar. 31	3 months	15%	June 30	$7,781.25
b.	Al Geisel	$6,000	July 30	120 days	9%	Nov. 27	$6,177.53
c.	Emil Toffant	$300	April 30	6 months	7%	Oct. 30	$310.50
d.	Hilda Lopez	$4,200	Oct. 14	80 days	10%	Jan. 2	$4,292.05
e.	Tom Aspella	$700	Sept. 20	4 months	12%	Jan. 20	$728.00
f.	Chris Leeds	$2,300	Dec. 12	9 months	8%	Sept. 12	$2,438.00
g.	Yang Shen	$200	Feb. 23	3 months	9.5%	May 23	$204.75

Exercise 3. (Finding the time of a demand note)

1. On October 24, Hector Lowe borrowed $9,000 from the River State Bank on the demand note shown below. He deposited 30 shares of Lidel Company common stock as collateral security. On January 16, he paid the note in full.

<table>
<tr><td rowspan="8">**DEMAND NOTE**</td><td>$ _____9,000.00_____</td><td>_____October 24_____ 19___--___</td></tr>
<tr><td colspan="2">On demand ___I___ promise to pay to _____River StateBank_____</td></tr>
<tr><td colspan="2">or order, at the Banking House of said Bank in current funds, _Nine thousand and $\frac{no}{100}$_ ___ DOLLARS</td></tr>
<tr><td colspan="2">with interest at the rate of ___11___ % per annum, for value received, having deposited with said</td></tr>
<tr><td colspan="2">Bank as collateral security _____30 shares Lidel Co. common stock_____</td></tr>
<tr><td colspan="2">The rights ___I___ (am, ~~are~~) giving said bank in this property, and the obligations this agreement secures are defined on the reverse side of this note.</td></tr>
<tr><td>No. ___10789___   Due ___Oct. 24___ 19 ___--___</td><td>_____Hector Lowe_____</td></tr>
</table>

(a) Interest on the note is charged for _____84_____ days. (b) The amount of the exact interest is $ 227.84.
(c) The amount that Lowe paid on January 16 in payment of the note and interest is $____9,227.84____.

b. $9,000 \times 0.11 \times \frac{84}{365}$ = $227.835 or $227.84 interest

c. $9,000 + 227.84 = $9,227.84 amount of full payment of note

2. During the year, the Ellerville Bank received payment for each of the twelve demand notes listed below. For each note, find the time of the note. Write your answers in the column headed "Time."

	Maker	Date of Note	Date Paid	Time (Days)		Maker	Date of Note	Date Paid	Time (Days)
a.	Arvin Leeds	Mar. 20	April 30	41	**g.**	Ben Bernstein	Jan. 21	May 27	126
b.	Carmen Leon	July 16	Sept. 24	70	**h.**	Laura Coates	June 2	Dec. 15	196
c.	John LaRocca	Dec. 22	Feb. 16	56	**i.**	Sam Levin	Dec. 16	Mar. 14	88
d.	Ed Leipschutz	Oct. 12	Dec. 29	78	**j.**	Barbara Olin	July 12	Aug. 30	49
e.	Anna O'Malley	May 30	Sept. 16	109	**k.**	Zeb Grey	Nov. 23	Jan. 6	44
f.	Ralph Winslow	April 2	Sept. 15	166	**l.**	Joyce Allen	Aug. 12	Oct. 18	67

Name: _____   Date: _____

3. For each of the demand notes below, find the time in days, the interest to the nearest cent, and the amount due. Use the P × R × T formula and a 365-day year.

	Face	Date of Note	Date Paid	Time (Days)	Interest Rate	Exact Interest	Amount Due
a.	$4,000	May 15	July 14	60	8%	$52.60	$4,052.60
b.	$300	Feb. 19	May 10	80	14%	$9.21	$309.21
c.	$1,000	Dec. 18	Feb. 21	65	10%	$17.81	$1,017.81
d.	$8,500	Sept. 2	Dec. 31	120	15%	$419.18	$8,919.18
e.	$5,000	April 1	July 3	93	12%	$152.88	$5,152.88

a. $4,000 × 0.08 × $\frac{60}{365}$ = $52.602, or $52.60 interest

$4,000 + $52.60 = $4,052.60 amount due

b. $300 × 0.14 × $\frac{80}{365}$ = $9.205, or $9.21 interest

$300 + $9.21 = $309.21 amount due

c. $1,000 × 0.10 × $\frac{65}{365}$ = $17.808, or $17.81 interest

$1,000 + $17.81 = $1,017.81 amount due

d. $8,500 × 0.15 × $\frac{120}{365}$ = $419.178, or $419.18 interest

$8,500 + $419.18 = $8,919.18 amount due

e. $5,000 × 0.12 × $\frac{93}{365}$ = $152.876, or $152.88 interest

$5,000 + $152.88 = $5,152.88 amount due

4. Inez Frisch needed $2,500 to pay a $3,200 bill which was due. On August 14, she borrowed the money from her bank and gave it a $2,500 demand note with 15% interest. She paid the note back in full on December 12 of the same year. (a) The interest on the note was charged for _____120_____ days. (b) The amount of interest Inez paid was _____$123.29_____. (c) The total amount Inez paid her bank on December 12 was _____$2,623.29_____.

a. 120 days time of note

b. $2,500 × 0.15 × $\frac{120}{365}$ = $123.287, or $123.29 interest

c. $2,500 + $ 123.29 = $2,623.29 total amount paid

5. Everett Longfellow needed $12,400 to buy a boat. He gave the Marine Bank and Trust Company a demand note for that amount with 14% interest on July 23. He paid the note in full on November 8. (a) The interest on the note was charged for _____108_____ days. (b) The amount of interest Everett paid was _____$513.67_____. (c) The total amount he paid on November 8 was _____$12,913.67_____.

a. 108 days

b. $12,400 × 0.14 × $\frac{108}{365}$ = $513.665, or $513.67 interest

c. $12,400 + $513.67 = $12,913.67 total amount paid

LESSON 10-5   INSTALLMENT BUYING

Exercise 1.   (Finding the finance charge and total amount paid)

1. Brad Farlow borrowed $900 from his credit union. He agreed to repay the principal in six equal monthly payments, with a finance charge of $1\frac{1}{2}$% a month on the unpaid balance. Complete the schedule below to show (a) the unpaid balance, the finance charge, the payment on principal, and the total payment for each month. Also show (b) the total finance charge, total payments on principal, and total payments for the six months.

End of	Unpaid Balance	Finance Charge at $1\frac{1}{2}$%	Payment on Principal	Total Payment
1st month	$900	$13.50	$150	$163.50
2d month	750	11.25	150	161.25
3d month	600	9.00	150	159.00
4th month	450	6.75	150	156.75
5th month	300	4.50	150	154.50
6th month	150	2.25	150	152.25
		$47.25	$900	$947.25

2. Katherine Colombo wants to borrow $3,000 for six months. She can get the loan from her credit union by repaying it in 6 equal monthly payments plus interest at $1\frac{1}{4}$% per month on the unpaid balance. She can also get the loan from another lender by repaying it in 6 monthly payments of $524.50 each, including the finance charge. (a) If she borrows from the credit union, the finance charge for 6 months will be _____$131.25_____. (b) If she borrows from the other lender, the total finance charge will be _____$147_____. (c) By borrowing from the credit union, she will save _____$15.75_____.

a.   End of   Unpaid   Finance Charge
                   Balance   at $1\frac{1}{4}$%

   1st month $3,000 $37.50
   2d month   2,500   31.25
   3d month   2,000   25.00
   4th month   1,500   18.75
   5th month   1,000   12.50
   6th month   500   6.25
                            $131.25

b. 6 × $524.50 = $3,147 total payments
    $3,147 − $3,000 = $147 finance charge

c. $147.00 − $131.25 = $15.75 she will save

3. Yang Shih borrows $3,500 from a finance company. He repays the loan in 24 equal installments of $180.80 each. (a) The total amount that was paid by Yang is _____$4,339.20_____. (b) The total finance charge on the loan is _____$839.20_____.

a. $180.80 × 24 = $4,339.20 total amount paid
b. $4,339.20 − $3,500 = $839.20 total finance charge

Exercise 2. (Finding installment payments)

Find the equal monthly payment amounts for each loan:

	Principal	Rate of Interest	Term of Loan	Amount of Interest	Total Amount To Be Repaid	Monthly Payment
a.	$5,000	11%	12 months	$550.00	$5,550.00	$462.50
b.	$2,800	13%	6 months	$182.00	$2,982.00	$497.00
c.	$300	17%	6 months	$25.50	$325.50	$54.25
d.	$12,000	9%	24 months	$2,160.00	$14,160.00	$590.00

Exercise 3. (Finding the annual percentage rate)

For each problem, use Illustration 10-5.2 in the textbook to find the annual percentage rate.

1. Ted Ingram borrows $5,200 from the loan department of his bank. Ted repays the loan in 15 equal installments of $416. (a) The total amount that Ted repaid to the bank is __$6,240__. (b) The total finance charge for the loan is __$1,040__. (c) The finance charge per $100 of the amount financed is __$20__. (d) The annual percentage rate is __$28\frac{1}{2}\%$__.

   a. $416 × 15 = $6,240 total amount he will repay
   b. $6,240 − $5,200 = $1,040 total finance charge
   c. ($1,040 × 100) ÷ $5,200 = $20 finance charge per $100 of amount financed
   d. Annual percentage rate from table, $28\frac{1}{2}\%$

2. Eleanor Verseman borrows $600 from a loan company. She must repay the loan in 6 equal installments of $104. (a) The total amount to be repaid is __$624__. (b) The total finance charge on the loan is __$24__. (c) The finance charge per $100 of the amount financed is __$4__. (d) The annual percentage rate is __$13\frac{1}{2}\%$__.

   a. $104 × 6 = $624 total amount to be repaid
   b. $624 − $600 = $24 total finance charge
   c. ($24 × 100) ÷ $600 = $4 finance charge per $100 of amount financed
   d. Annual percentage rate from table, $13\frac{1}{2}\%$

3. A loan of $4,000 is repaid in 12 monthly installments of $360 each. (a) The total amount repaid is __$4,320__. (b) The finance charge on the loan is __$320__. (c) The finance charge per $100 of the amount financed is __$8__. (d) The annual percentage rate is __$14\frac{1}{2}\%$__.

   a. $360 × 12 = $4,320 total amount to be repaid
   b. $4,320 − $4,000 = $320 finance charge
   c. ($320 × 100) ÷ $4,000 = $8 finance charge per $100 of amount financed
   d. Annual percentage rate from table, $14\frac{1}{2}\%$

4. You get a personal loan at a bank for $3,500 which you repay in 15 equal monthly installments of $253.75. (a) The total amount you repay is __$3,806.25__. (b) The total finance charge on the loan is __$306.25__. (c) The finance charge per $100 of the amount financed is __$8.75__. (d) The annual percentage rate is __$12\frac{3}{4}\%$__.

   a. $253.75 × 15 = $3,806.25 total amount to be repaid
   b. $3,806.25 − $3,500 = $306.25 finance charge
   c. ($306.25 × 100) ÷ $3,500 = $8.75 finance charge per $100 of amount financed
   d. Annual percentage rate from table, $12\frac{3}{4}\%$

Exercise 4.

1. The cash price of a piano is $3,500. It can be bought on the installment plan for $350 down and $108.50 a month for 36 months. (a) The installment price of the piano is $_____4,256_____. (b) The finance charge is $_____756_____. (c) The amount financed is $_____3,150_____.

   a. $350 + ($108.50 × 36) = $4,256 installment price
   b. $4,256 − $3,500 = $756 finance charge
   c. $3,500 − $350 = $3,150 amount financed

2. You can buy a clock for $900 in cash or for $90 down and $39.15 each month for 24 months. (a) The installment price of the clock is $_____1,029.60_____. (b) The finance charge is $_____129.60_____. (c) The percent by which the installment price exceeds the cash price, to the nearest tenth of a percent, is _____14.4 %_____.

   a. $90 + ($39.15 × 24) = $1,029.60 installment price
   b. $1,029.60 − $900 = $129.60 finance charge
   c. $129.60 ÷ $900 = 14.4% installment price exceeds cash price

3. A fur coat can be bought for $3,000 cash or on the installment plan by paying $300 down and $108 a month for 30 months. (a) The installment price of the coat is $_____3,540_____. (b) The finance charge is $_____540_____. (c) The amount financed is $_____2,700_____. (d) The finance charge per $100 of the amount financed is $_____20_____. (e) The annual percentage rate, using the tables on page 165 of this workbook, is _____14.75%_____.

   a. $300 + ($108 × 30) = $3,540 installment price
   b. $3,540 − $3,000 = $540 finance charge
   c. $3,000 − $300 = $2,700 amount financed
   d. ($540 × 100) ÷ $2,700 = $20 finance charge per $100 of amount financed
   e. Table value = 14.75%

4. For each of these installment purchases, show (a) the total monthly payments, (b) the installment price, (c) the finance charge, (d) the amount financed, (e) the finance charge per $100 of the amount financed, and (f) the annual percentage rate, using the tables on page 165 of this workbook.

		Cash Price	Down Payment	Monthly Payments			Install-ment Price	Finance Charge	Amount Financed	Finance Charge Per $100	Annual Percentage Rate
				Number	Each	Total					
a.	Guitar	$400	$40	30	$14.40	$432.00	$472.00	$72.00	$360.00	$20.00	14.75%
b.	Chandelier	$600	$75	12	47.60	571.20	646.20	46.20	525.00	8.80	15.75%
c.	Door	$280	$28	6	43.89	263.34	291.34	11.34	252.00	4.50	15.25%
d.	Furnace	$1,400	$140	36	44.03	1,585.08	1,725.08	325.08	1,260.00	25.80	15.50%

Total Mo. Payments	Installment Price	Finance Charge	Amount Financed	FC/100	APR
a. 30 × $14.40 = $432.00	$40 × $432.00 = $472.00	$472.00 − $400.00 = $72.00	$400 − $40 = $360	($72.00 × 100) ÷ $360 = $20.00	14.75%
b. 12 × $47.60 = $571.20	$75 × $571.20 = $646.20	$646.20 − $600.00 = $46.20	$600 − $75 = $525	($46.20 × 100) ÷ $525 = $8.80	15.75%
c. 6 × $43.89 = $263.34	$28 × $263.34 = $291.34	$291.34 − $280.00 = $11.34	$280 − $28 = $252	($11.34 × 100) ÷ $252 = $4.50	15.25%
d. 36 × $44.03 = $1,585.08	$140 × $1,585.08 = $1,725.08	$1,725.08 − $1,400 = $325.08	$1,400 − $140 = $1,260	($325.08 − 100) ÷ $1,260 = $25.80	15.50%

LESSON 10-6   CREDIT CARDS

Exercise 1.   (Finding net receipts from credit card sales)

1. Databank card company charges 5% to store owners who take the Databank credit card. If the Montrose Department store sells $87,500 in a month through the Databank card: (a) how much will Databank deduct from the credit card sales? $_____4,375_____; (b) how much will the store receive from Databank? $_____83,125_____.

   a. $87,500 × 0.05 = $4,375 amount deducted by Databank
   b. $87,500 − $4,375 = $83,125 net receipts from Databank

2. Olsen's takes both Global and General credit cards. Global charges 3% of sales made with its card; General charges 5%. Olsen's total sales last month were $1,250,000. Of that amount, $200,000 was made in cash, $730,000 was made using the Global card, and $320,000 was made using the General card. Of the total sales last month, (a) Global deducted $_____21,900_____ and (b) General deducted $_____16,000_____. (c) Olsen's had total net receipts from sales of $_____1,212,100_____.

   a. $730,000 × 0.03 = $21,900 amount deducted by Global
   b. $320,000 × 0.05 = $16,000 amount deducted by General
   c. $1,250,000 − ($21,900 + $16,000) = $1,212,100 Olsen's net receipts from sales

3. Basler's is considering accepting Megacard. Megacard would charge the store 5% of all Megacard sales. The store estimates that the total sales next year will be $1,400,000 if it does not take the credit card. If the store takes Megacard, the total sales are expected to be $1,850,000. Of that total, $1,600,000 will be made using the card. (a) What are Basler's expected net receipts from sales if it takes Megacard? $_____1,770,000_____. (b) By what amount will their net sales increase if the store takes the credit card? $_____370,000_____.

   a. $1,600,000 × 0.05 = $80,000 amount deducted by Megacard
      $1,850,000 − $80,000 = $1,770,000 net receipts from sales using Megacard
   b. $1,770,000 − $1,400,000 = $370,000 increase in net sales using credit card

Exercise 2.   (Saving money by paying cash)

1. Francelli's Service Stations sells regular gasoline at $1.19 a gallon, cash. If you use a credit card, 3% is added to the total sale. You buy 20 gallons of regular gas at Francelli's and use your credit card. (a) You would have saved $_____0.71_____ by paying cash. (b) The gasoline costs $_____24.51_____ using the credit card.

   a. 20 × $1.19 = $23.80 cash price of gas
      $23.80 × 0.03 = $0.71 amount saved by paying cash
   b. $23.80 + $0.71 = $24.51 cost of gas using credit card

2. Libby can buy a patio set for $1,300 using a credit card. If she pays cash, the store will give her a 4% discount. (a) Libby will save $_____52_____ by paying cash. (b) The cash price of the set is $_____1,248_____.

   a. $1,300 × 0.04 = $52 he will save by paying cash
   b. $1,300 − $52 = $1,248 cash price of set

3. Gary is buying a color TV set priced at $475. If he pays cash instead of using his credit card, he will get a 5% discount from the price. (a) He will save $____23.75____ by buying the TV set for cash. (b) The cash price of the TV set is $____451.25____.

    a. $475 × 0.05 = $23.75 he will save by paying cash
    b. $475 − $23.75 = $451.25 cash price of TV set

Exercise 3.   (Finding the cost of a credit card)

1. Kelly's credit card company charges a $25 annual membership fee and 7¢ for each purchase she makes. If Kelly made 68 purchases last year, how much did her credit card cost her for the year? $____29.76____

    $25 + ($0.07 × 68) = $29.76 cost of card

2. Yancy's card company charges $20 per year for membership and a finance charge of 1.25% a month on any unpaid balance in the account. Last month Yancy's statement showed that he had an unpaid balance of $370 and that the card company charged him for the membership fee. What was the total amount of Yancy's monthly statement?
    $____394.63____

    $370 × 0.0125 = $4.63 finance charge
    $370 + $20 + $4.63 = $394.63 total amount of monthly statement

Exercise 4.   (Borrowing through cash advances)

1. Tammy borrowed $280 for 60 days from her credit card company using a cash advance. The company charged a daily finance charge of 0.05%. What was Tammy's finance charge for the loan? $____8.40____

    $280 × 0.0005 × 60 = $8.40 finance charge

2. Aaron took a $300 cash advance from his credit card company, which charges a daily finance fee of 0.048%. He repaid the advance plus finance fee 40 days later. How much did Aaron repay the company? $____305.76____

    $300 × 0.00048 × 40 = $5.76 finance charge
    $300 + $5.76 = $305.76 total amount repaid

3. Mario's credit card company charges a yearly membership fee of $15, 8¢ for each purchase, and a daily finance charge of 0.045% on all cash advances. Last month, Mario was charged for his annual membership fee, 15 purchases, and a $400 cash advance which he borrowed for 30 days. What was the total amount the credit card company charged Mario? $____21.60____

    $0.08 × 15 = $1.20 charge for purchases
    $400 × 0.00045 × 30 = $5.40 finance charge on cash advance
    $15 + $1.20 + $5.40 = $21.60 total amount company charged

TERM TICKLER

Directions: Complete the crossword puzzle below.

Across

1. A record of receipts and payments
3. The ratio of finance charge to amount financed is the annual _____ rate
5. The amount borrowed
6. Installment _____ is another name for time payment plan
9. A note that must be paid when the bank asks for payment is a(an) _____ note
11. A cash record _____ is used to review income, expenses, and savings for the year
13. The form used to record a credit card sale is called a credit card _____ slip
14. A loan using the borrower's stake in a home as collateral is called a home _____ loan.
16. The day the note is signed is the _____ of note
17. Something you sign when you open a savings account is the _____ card
18. Interest shown as a percent is the _____ of interest
19. A note without an interest rate is called a(an) _____ note
20. The total in a savings account after compound interest is added is the compound _____

Down

2. An agreement to pay back an unpaid balance periodically is called an installment _____
3. What you do when you pay interest on principal plus previous interest
4. Money paid out is called _____
7. Money borrowed on a credit card is called a(an) cash _____
8. Personal property used as security for a loan is called _____
10. A person's stake in property is his _____
12. The yearly charge for having a credit card account is called an annual _____ fee
15. A(an) _____ plan is a way of buying that usually requires a down payment, finance charges, and part payments
16. The rate of _____ is the percent charged on a note and paid in advance

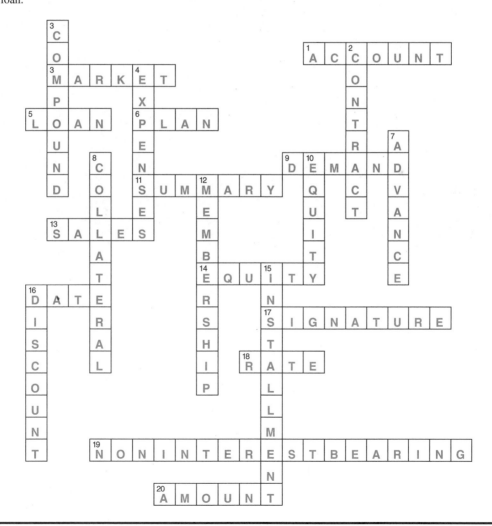

COPYRIGHT © SOUTH-WESTERN EDUCATIONAL PUBLISHING

INTEGRATED PROJECT 10

Jan and Fred Eaton have been shopping for a boat and outboard motor for use on a nearby lake during warm weather. They have shopped very carefully for the boat for several months and believe that they have picked the right boat and motor combination and the right dealer for their needs. The cash price they have bargained for the used boat they want is $6,000. This price includes a used trailer.

The Eatons also shopped around carefully to find the best deal for borrowing the amount of money they will need to buy the boat. They have identified four sources for the funds they need: the dealer, their bank, their credit union, and a special low-interest rate credit card. The information they have gathered about each loan is presented below.

1. Answer these questions about each loan offer.

   The Dealer's Deal: The boat dealer, Water-Craft Sales, Inc., has offered the Eatons these installment plan terms: 10% down and the remainder to be paid in 24 payments of $261 each. Under this plan,

   a. The amount financed is $_____5,400_____.

   $6,000 − ($6,000 × 0.10) = $5,400 amount financed

   b. The installment price of the boat is $_____6,864_____.

   $600 + (24 × $261) = $6,864 installment price of boat.

   c. The total finance charge is $_____864_____.

   $6,864 − $6,000 = $864 finance charge

   d. The total installment plan price of the boat is _____14.4_____% greater than cash price.

   $6,864 − $6,000 ÷ $6,000 = 0.144 or 14.4% installment price greater than cash price

   e. Using the tables below, the annual percentage rate for the dealer's offer is _____14.75_____%.

   ($864 × 100) ÷ $5,400 = $16.00 finance charge per $100 of amount financed
   The nearest value in the table on the 24 payments line is $16.08 in the 14.75% column

No. of Payments	ANNUAL PERCENTAGE RATE										
	14.00	14.25	14.50	14.75	15.00	15.25	15.50	15.75	16.00	17.00	18.00
	(Finance Charge Per $100 of Amount Financed)										
6	4.12	4.20	4.27	4.35	4.42	4.49	4.57	4.64	4.72	5.02	5.32
12	7.74	7.89	8.03	8.17	8.31	8.45	8.59	8.74	8.88	9.45	10.02
18	11.45	11.66	11.87	12.08	12.29	12.50	12.72	12.93	13.14	13.99	14.85
20	12.70	12.93	13.17	13.41	13.64	13.88	14.11	14.35	14.59	15.54	16.49
24	15.23	15.51	15.80	16.08	16.37	16.65	16.94	17.22	17.51	18.66	19.82
30	19.10	19.45	19.81	20.17	20.54	20.90	21.26	21.62	21.99	23.45	24.92
36	23.04	23.48	23.92	24.35	24.80	25.24	25.68	26.12	26.57	28.35	30.15

The Bank's Deal: The Bank of Carlton has offered to the Eatons the promissory note shown below. The Eatons will have to sign the promissory note and pledge the boat, motor, and trailer as collateral. The bank will discount their note at 12.5%. The entire amount is due on March 7, 1997. No monthly payments are required.

Under this plan,

a. The proceeds the Eatons will receive from this note are $_____5,999_____.

$6,856 × 0.125 = $857 bank discount
$6,856 − $857 = $5,999 proceeds of note

b. The real rate of interest on the note, to the nearest tenth of a percent, is _____14.3_____%.

($6,856 − $5,999) ÷ $5,999 = 0.1428, or 14.3%

c. The total price of the boat, to the nearest tenth of a percent, is _____14.3_____% greater than the cash price.

($6,856 − $6,000) ÷ $6,000 = 0.1426, or 14.3%

LOAN NO. __907160__   DATE ___March 7___ 19 __96__

LOAN AMOUNT $ _6,856.00_   MATURITY DATE ___March 7___ 19 __97__

_____One year_____ AFTER DATE __We__ PROMISE TO PAY TO

THE ORDER OF_____The Bank of Carlton_____

__Six thousand, eight hundred fifty-six and $\frac{no}{100}$_____ DOLLARS

PAYABLE AT _____The Bank of Carlton_____ VALUE RECEIVED WITH INTEREST AT

THE RATE OF __none__ % PER ANNUM, FOR VALUE RECEIVED, GIVING SAID BANK A

SECURITY INTEREST IN THIS COLLATERAL: ___1994 Premier Boat, Motor, Trailer___

The rights ___We___ (am, are) giving said bank in this property, and the obligations this agreement secures are defined on the reverse side of this note.

_____Janice Eaton_____   _____Fred Eaton_____

The Credit Union's Deal: The Carlton Credit Union has offered the Eatons these terms: A $6,000, two-year loan with interest on the unpaid balance at the monthly rate of 1.25%. They are to make monthly payments of $250 on the principal along with interest for the month. The Eatons must also sign a promissory note for the loan and pledge the boat, motor, and trailer as collateral.

a. Complete the monthly payment schedule shown at right.

Under this plan,

b. The total price of the boat is
   $ ___6,9737.56___ .

c. The total finance charges are
   $ ___937.56___ .

d. The total installment plan price of the boat is ___15.6___% greater, to the nearest tenth of a percent, than the cash price.

($6,937.56 − $6,000) ÷ $6,000 = 0.1562, or 15.6% installment price greater than cash price

e. The annual rate of interest charged is ___15___%.

1.25% × 12 = 15% annual rate of interest

	CARLTON CREDIT UNION			
	MONTHLY PAYMENT SCHEDULE FOR JANICE AND FRED EATON			
Payment Number	Unpaid Balance	Payment on Principal	Monthly Interest	Total Payment
1	$6,000	$250	$75.00	$325.00
2	5,750	250	71.88	321.88
3	5,500	250	68.75	318.75
4	5,520	250	65.63	315.63
5	5,000	250	62.50	312.50
6	4,750	250	59.38	309.38
7	4,500	250	56.25	306.25
8	4,250	250	53.13	303.13
9	4,000	250	50.00	300.00
10	3,750	250	46.88	296.88
11	3,500	250	43.75	293.75
12	3,250	250	40.63	290.63
13	3,000	250	37.50	287.50
14	2,750	250	34.38	284.38
15	2,500	250	31.25	281.25
16	2,250	250	28.13	278.13
17	2,000	250	25.00	275.00
18	1,750	250	21.88	271.88
19	1,500	250	18.75	268.75
20	1,250	250	15.63	265.63
21	1,000	250	12.50	262.50
22	750	250	9.38	259.38
23	500	250	6.25	256.25
24	250	250	3.13	253.13
		$6,000	$937.56	$6,937.56

Name: _____   Date: _____

The Credit Card Option: The Eatons have just received a new credit card offer. They can charge up to $7,500 on any purchases. The card offers a 7% annual percentage rate until April 30, 199_. After that, an 18% annual percentage rate will be charged. Finance charges are based on the previous balance. If they buy the boat using the credit card, no down payment is required. The Eatons would not make any other purchases with the card until the boat and motor were paid off. Because Mrs. Eaton receives quarterly checks from a devoted aunt, the Eatons know they can make the principal payments shown in the chart below. The first payment is due on April 7.

a. Complete the following chart showing the monthly finance charge, total payment, and new balance.

Date	7% Annual Percentage Rate	Planned Principal Payment	Total Payment	Ending Balance
March 7				6000
April 7	0	950	950.00	5050
May 7	29.46	255	284.46	4795
June 7	27.97	255	282.97	4540
July 7	26.48	255	281.48	4285
Aug 7	25.00	950	975.00	3335
Sept 7	19.45	255	274.45	3080
Oct 7	17.97	255	272.97	2825
Nov 7	16.48	255	271.48	2570
Dec 7	14.99	950	964.99	1620
Jan 7	9.45	255	264.45	1365
Feb 7	7.96	255	262.96	1110
Mar 7	6.48	255	261.48	855
Apr 7	4.99	855	859.99	0
TOTAL	$206.68	$6,000	$6,206.68	0

b. The total credit card price of the boat is $_____6,206.68_____

c. The total finance charges are $_____206.68_____

d. The total credit card price is _____3.4_____% greater, to the nearest tenth of a percent, than the cash price.

($6,206.68 − $6,000) ÷ $6,000 = 0.034 or 3.4% greater

Name: _____   Date: _____

INVESTMENTS

LESSON 11-1   INVESTING IN BONDS

Exercise 1.

Find the market price for each bond.

Bond	Par Value of Bond	Quoted Price	Market Price
1. Garrett Products	$1,000	127	$1,270.00
2. Kortel Spring Co.	$1,000	$82\frac{1}{8}$	$821.25
3. Elden Schools	$500	$92\frac{1}{4}$	$461.25
4. City of Westfield	$500	$106\frac{1}{2}$	$532.50
5. Wexam Office Systems	$1,000	$78\frac{3}{4}$	$787.50
6. Rem Computer Centers	$1,000	$100\frac{5}{8}$	$1,006.25
7. Dort Manufacturing	$500	$95\frac{1}{2}$	$477.50
8. Dressen Mining	$5,000	$68\frac{7}{8}$	$3,443.75

Exercise 2.

1. Sera Nibey bought seven $1,000 par value bonds of the Glade Lawn Products Company at $93\frac{1}{2}$. What was Sera's investment in these bonds? $_____6,545_____.

   $7 \times (0.935 \times \$1,000) = \$6,545$ total investment

2. During the past year, Rick Nortell bought $1,000 par value Ready Solutions Software Company bonds in these quantities and at these prices: 3 at 86; 5 at $79\frac{1}{4}$; 6 at $83\frac{1}{8}$. Rick's total investment in Ready Solution bonds for the past year is $_____11,530_____.

   $3 \times (0.86 \times \$1,000)$ $= \$ 2,580.00$
   $5 \times (0.7925 \times \$1,000)$ $= 3,962.50$
   $6 \times (0.83125 \times \$1,000)$ $= \underline{4,987.50}$
   $\$11,530.00$ total investment for year

3. An insurance company bought these bonds as an investment: 30 Drako County Power, $1,000 bonds at 106; 18 Nemont Mining, $5,000 bonds at $102\frac{1}{2}$; 70 Adams Township Schools, $500 bonds at 85. The investment in each purchase is Drako, $_____31,800_____; Nemont, $_____92,250_____; Adams, $_____29,750_____.

   $30 \times (1.06 \times \$1,000) = \$31,800$ investment in Drako
   $18 \times (1.025 \times \$5,000) = \$92,250$ investment in Nemont
   $70 \times (0.85 \times \$500) = \$29,750$ investment in Adams

---

APPLIED BUSINESS MATHEMATICS   **169**   LESSON 11-1   INVESTING IN BONDS

COPYRIGHT © SOUTH-WESTERN EDUCATIONAL PUBLISHING

Exercise 3.

1. Marty Sorensen buys nine Nordmor Aerospace bonds at $92\frac{3}{4}$, plus $7.50 commission per bond. (a) The market price of the nine bonds is $_____8,347.50_____. (b) The total commission is $_____67.50_____. Marty's total investment in the bonds is $_____8,415_____.

   a. $9 \times (0.9275 \times \$1,000) = \$8,347.50$ market price
   b. $9 \times \$7.50 = \$67.50$ commission
   c. $\$8,347.50 + \$67.50 = \$8,415$ total investment

2. Michelle Whitney buys fourteen $500 bonds at $108\frac{1}{2}$. The commision consists of a $25 transaction charge and a fee of $5 per bond. (a) The total market price of the fourteen bonds is $_____7,595_____. The total cost of the commission is $_____95_____. The total amount Michelle invested in these bonds is $_____7,690_____.

   a. $14 \times (1.085 \times \$500) = \$7,595$ market price
   b. $\$25 + (14 \times \$5) = \$95$ commission
   c. $\$7,595 + \$95 = \$7,690$ total investment

3. Last year, Tim Allard bought these amounts and denominations of U.S. Series EE Savings Bonds: four, $50 bonds; nine, $100 bonds; two, $500 bonds. (a) To make these bond purchases, Tim paid out a total of $_____1,050_____. (b) If all the bonds are redeemed at a future date at exactly their face value, Tim will receive $_____2,100_____.

   a. $(4 \times \$25) + (9 \times \$50) + (2 \times \$250) = \$1,050$ paid for bonds
   b. $(4 \times \$50) + (9 \times \$100) + (2 \times \$500) = \$2,100$ redemption value

Use the bond redemption table at right to do the following problems.

Redemption Values $50 Savings Bond	
End of Year	Redemption Value
1	$26.08
2	$28.14
3	$30.30
4	$32.94
5	$38.38
6	$41.66
7	$45.42
8	$49.32

4. After holding the bonds for four years, Irma redeemed these U.S. Savings Bonds and received these amounts: four, $50 bonds, (a) redemption value, $_____131.76_____; three, $100 bonds, (b) redemption value, $_____197.64_____; one, $500 bond, (c) redemption value, $_____329.40_____. (d) The total amount she received is $_____658.80_____.

   a. $4 \times \$32.94$ = $131.76 redemption value, $50 bonds
   b. $3 \times (2 \times \$32.94)$ = 197.64 redemption value, $100 bonds
   c. $1 \times (10 \times \$32.94)$ = 329.40 redemption value, $500 bond
   d. $658.80 total amount received

5. Lewis Roth bought twelve $50 savings bonds. He redeemed four of these bonds at the end of three years, two bonds at the end of five years, and six bonds at the end of eight years. When they were redeemed, the bonds were worth these values: (a) bonds held three years, $_____121.20_____; (b) bonds held five years, $_____76.76_____; (c) bonds held eight years, $_____295.92_____.

   a. $4 \times \$30.30 = \$121.20$ value of bonds held 3 years
   b. $2 \times \$38.38 = \$76.76$ value of bonds held 5 years
   c. $6 \times \$49.32 = \$295.92$ value of bonds held 8 years

Exercise 4.

1. Elma Latimer owns 24 Plando City $12\frac{1}{2}$%, $1,000 bonds. Her annual income from the 24 bonds is
   $ _____3,000_____ .

   $24 \times (0.125 \times \$1,000) = \$3,000$ annual income

2. Kazumori Fujiwara owns 50 Northeast Line Railway System $1,000 bonds, paying $9\frac{1}{4}$% interest, payable
   March 15 and September 15. Kazumori's semiannual income from the bonds is $_____2,312.50_____ .

   $50 \times (0.0925 \times \$1,000 \times \frac{1}{2}) = \$2,312.50$ semiannual income

3. Joseph Lummenetti bought 12, $500 Arwel Company bonds at 99. These bonds pay 6% annual interest on
   December 31. He also bought 4 Renslow Leasing, 9%, $1,000 bonds at 84. The Renslow bonds pay interest
   semiannually on June 30 and December 31. (a) Joseph's total investment in both bonds is $_____9,300_____ .
   (b) His investment in these bonds will pay interest of $_____720_____ annually if held for one full year.

   a. $12 \times (0.99 \times \$500)$ = $5,940 investment in Arwel bonds
      $4 \times (0.84 \times \$1,000)$ =   3,360 investment in Renslow bonds
                                                $9,300 total investment in both bonds

   b. $12 \times (0.06 \times \$500)$ = $360 annual income from Arwel bonds
      $4 \times (0.09 \times \$1,000)$ =   360 annual income from Renslow bonds
                                                $720 total annual income from both bonds

4. Marcella O'Shea buys a $500, 8% bond at 156, including the broker's commission. (a) Her annual income from
   the bond is $_____40_____ . (b) Her total investment in the bond is $_____780_____ . (c) Her rate of income
   on the investment is _____5.1_____ %, figured to the nearest tenth of a percent.

   a. $0.08 \times \$500 = \$40$ annual income
   b. $1.56 \times \$500 = \$780$ total investment
   c. $\$40 \div \$780 = 5.1\%$ rate of income

5. Sue Arnold buys Esco Electric Company $7\frac{1}{4}$%, $1,000 bonds at $97\frac{3}{4}$, plus $8 commission per bond. Her rate of
   income on the investment, figured to the nearest tenth of a percent, is _____7.4_____ %.

   $(0.9775 \times \$1,000) + \$8 = \$985.50$ investment in one bond
   $(0.0725 \times \$1,000) = \$72.50$ income from one bond
   $\$72.50 \div \$985.50 = 7.4\%$ rate of income on investment

6. Sue wants to earn an annual income of $1,450 from an investment in the bonds described in Problem 5. To do so,
   she must buy (a) _____20_____ bonds and invest (b) $_____19,710_____ .

   a. $\$1,450 \div \$72.50 = 20$ bonds must be bought
   b. $20 \times (\$977.50 + \$8.00) = \$19,710$ investment needed

LESSON 11-2   INVESTING IN STOCK

Exercise 1.

1. Find the total cost of each stock purchase below:

	Number of Shares	Name of Stock	Market Price	Commission	Total Cost
a.	50	Segrin Boat Company	$24\frac{3}{8}$	$48.00	$1,266.75
b.	110	Maxwell Steel Company	$16\frac{1}{4}$	$67.61	$1,855.11
c.	70	Specialty Paints, Inc.	$27\frac{7}{8}$	$56.98	$2,008.23
d.	100	Margold Battery Company	$69\frac{1}{2}$	$97.00	$7,047.00
e.	200	South Coast Power Company	$40\frac{3}{4}$	$192.09	$8,342.09
f.	150	Bower & Company	$19\frac{5}{8}$	$105.21	$3,048.96
g.	100	Sensitel Security Services	$6\frac{1}{8}$	$43.00	$ 655.50

a. (50 × $24.375) + $48 = $1,266.75 total cost Segrin stock
b. (110 × $16.25) + $67.61 = $1,855.11 total cost Maxwell stock
c. (70 × $27.875) + $56.98 = $2,008.23 total cost Specialty stock
d. (100 × $69.50) + $97 = $7,047 total cost Margold stock
e. (200 × $40.75) + $192.09 = $8,342.09 total cost South Coast stock
f. (150 × $19.625) + $105.21 = $3,048.96 total cost Bower stock
g. (100 × $6.125) + $43 = $655.50 total cost Sensitel stock

2. Migda Yasin placed an order with her broker to buy 30 shares of Dow Chemical stock at $94\frac{1}{2}$. The broker bought the stock at that price and charged $68 commission. Her total investment in the stock was $____2,903____.

30 × $94.50 = $2,835 market value of 30 shares
$2,835 + $68 = $2,903 total investment in stock

3. Eddie Johnson bought 300 shares of Inland Steel stock at $46\frac{1}{8}$. On this purchase, the broker charged a commission of $95.33 for each 100 shares. The total investment that Eddie made in Inland Steel stock was $____14,123.49____.

300 × $46.125 = $13,837.50 market value of 300 shares
$13,837.50 + (3 × $95.33) = $14,123.49 total investment in stock

4. Barbara Todd plans to buy 30 shares of Dental-Tek stock at a price of $15 a share. One broker's minimum commission charge on this purchase will be $50. A discount broker's minimum commission charge on this purchase will be $27. If Barbara uses the discount broker, her total investment for this stock purchase will be
$____477____.

(30 × $15) + $27 = $477 total investment

Exercise 2.

1. You make an investment in 120 shares of Lovell Clothiers stock and receive an annual dividend of $0.58 a share. At that rate, your annual income from the investment is $_____69.60_____.

    120 × $0.58 = $69.60 annual income

2. Nina Provencoma owns 200 shares of Western Lumber Products stock, which has a par value of $80 a share. The stock pays a quarterly dividend of $1\frac{1}{2}$%. (a) Each quarter, Nina receives a dividend check from the company for $_____240_____, (b) which amounts to an annual income of $_____960._____

    a. 200 × (0.015 × $80) = $240 amount of quarterly dividend check
    b. 4 × $240 = $960 annual income

3. Cecil McCastner bought 80 shares of stock at a total cost of $2,812. This stock pays a semiannual dividend of $0.78 a share. On the annual dividend income of (a) $_____124.80_____ that Cecil receives, he earns on his investment a rate of (b) _____4.4_____%, figured to the nearest tenth of a percent.

    a. 80 × (2 × $0.78) = $124.80 annual income
    b. $124.80 ÷ $2,812 = 0.0443, or 4.4% rate of income

4. All-Season Sports Company stock pays a quarterly dividend of 3% on its $20 par value stock. Katrina Vola owns 420 shares of this stock which she bought at a total cost of $8,500. To the nearest tenth of a percent, the rate of income Katrina earns on her investment is _____11.9_____%.

    4 × (0.03 × $20) = $2.40 annual income on 1 share
    420 × $2.40 = $1,008 annual income
    $1,008 ÷ $8,500 = 0.1185, or 11.9% rate of income

5. Tempo Intercom Company stock pays a quarterly dividend of $1.19 a share. Drexel buys 60 shares of the stock at $76, and pays $85 commission. On a total investment of (a) $_____4,645_____, Drexel receives an annual income of (b) $_____285.60_____, which is a rate of income of (c) _____6.1_____%, figured to the nearest tenth of a percent.

    a. (60 × $76) + $85 = $4,645 total investment
    b. 60 × (4 × $1.19) = $285.60 annual income
    c. $285.60 ÷ $4,645 = 0.0614, or 6.1% rate of income

Exercise 3.

1. Lester Krell sold 67 shares of Unitrend Data Analysis Company at $15\frac{3}{4}$. His broker charged a commission of $78.66. Other selling charges amounted to $2.14. From this sale, Lester received net proceeds of $ _____974.45_____ .

   $78.66 + $2.14 = $80.80 total selling costs
   (67 × $15.75) − $80.80 = $974.45 net proceeds

2. Winifred Erickson sold 2,000 shares of the 50,000 shares which she holds as the major owner of the Delram Systems Company. She sold the shares at $8\frac{7}{8}$ and paid a total charge of $982.45 for commission and other selling expenses. (a) Winifred received net proceeds of $ _____16,767.55_____ from this sale. (b) Based on the selling price she got for the 2,000 shares, the remaining shares that Winifred owns are worth $ _____426,000_____ .

   a. (2,000 × $8.875) − $982.45 = $16,767.55 net proceeds
   b. 48,000 × $8.875 = $426,000 value of remaining shares

3. Mort Ulmann bought 100 shares of Windsor Imports Company on Monday at a total cost of $3,850. He sold the 100 shares on Wednesday at $46\frac{1}{8}$ and paid a commission of $162. What was the amount of profit or loss from this sale? $ _____600.50_____ profit

   (100 × $46.125) − $162 = $4,450.50 net proceeds from sale
   $4,450.50 − $3,850 = $600.50 profit

4. Marsha Keeghan bought 100 shares of stock at a total cost of $5,310. She received two quarterly dividends of $1.58 each per share and then sold the stock, receiving net proceeds of $6,387. (a) The total dividends she received were $ _____316_____ . (b) Her profit from the sale of the stock was $ _____1,077_____ . (c) Her total gain from owning and selling the stock was $ _____1,393_____ .

   a. 100 × 2 × $1.58 = $316 total dividends received
   b. $6,387 − $5,310 = $1,077 profit on sale
   c. $1,077 + $316 = $1,393 total gain

5. Kent Vernor bought 70 shares of stock at a total cost of $3,492.47. He kept the stock for three years. During this time, he received semiannual dividends of $1.85 per share. He then sold the stock and received net proceeds of $2,874.40. (a) The total dividends he received were $ _____777_____ . (b) His loss on the sale of the stock was $ _____618.07_____ . (c) His net gain from owning and selling the stock was $ _____158.93_____ .

   a. 2 × $1.85 = $3.70 annual dividend from 1 share
       70 × (3 × $3.70) = $777 total dividends
   b. $3,492.47 − $2,874.40 = $618.07 loss
   c. $777 − $618.07 = $158.93 net gain

LESSON 11-3   MUTUAL FUNDS

Exercise

Use the information in the following table to solve all the problems in the exercise.

Fund Name	NAV	Offer Price	Minimum Investment
Wilmont Fund	15.53	16.35	$5,000
Rapid Growth	12.84	N.L.	$3,000
Basic Industry Fund	9.47	9.76	$2,500
Megabank Fund	8.91	N.L.	$1,500

1. Write your answers in the chart below.

Fund Name	Purchase Price	Commission on 100-share Purchase	Number Shares Bought at Minimum Investment Amount
Wilmont Fund	a. $ 16.35	e. $ 82	i. 305.810
Rapid Growth	b. $ 12.84	f. $ 0	j. 233.645
Basic Industry Fund	c. $ 9.76	g. $ 29	k. 256.148
Megabank Fund	d. $ 8.91	h. $ 0	l. 168.350

    a–d. What is the price you will pay to buy one share of each fund listed?

    e–h. What total commission will be charged on a 100-share purchase of each listed fund?

      e. $100 \times (\$16.35 - \$15.53) = \$82$ commission
      f. $0 commission on no-load fund
      g. $100 \times (\$9.76 - \$9.47) = \$29$ commission
      h. $0 commission on no-load fund

    i–l. Correct to the thousandth share, what number of shares of each fund can be bought if the required minimum investment is made?

      i. $5,000 ÷ $16.35 = 305.810 shares
      j. $3,000 ÷ $12.84 = 233.645 shares
      k. $2,500 ÷ $9.76 = 256.148 shares
      l. $1,500 ÷ $8.91 = 168.350 shares

2. The commission rate charged on purchases of these funds, correct to the nearest percent, is (a) Wilmont Fund, _____5_____%; (b) Basic Industry Fund, _____3_____%.

    a. ($16.35 − $15.53) ÷ $16.35 = 0.049, or 5% rate of commission
    b. ($9.76 − $9.47) ÷ $9.76 = 0.029, or 3% rate of commission

3. Latana Mobin's total cost of buying 164.850 shares of the Rapid Growth fund is $1,730.93. She sells all the shares she owns at the price quoted. (a) Her proceeds from the sale are $____2,116.67____, (b) and the profit or loss from this investment is $____385.74 profit____.

    a. 164.850 × $12.84 = $2,116.67 proceeds
    b. $2,116.67 − $1,730.93 = $385.74 profit

LESSON 11-4   INVESTING IN REAL ESTATE

Exercise 1.

1. Ludwik Resa bought a condominium on the beach as an investment. He hired a management company to take care of maintenance and rentals. For this service he pays $90 each month for maintenance and 20% of all rental income. Last year, the condominium was rented for 32 weeks at $900 a week. For the year, he paid $10,680 in interest on the mortgage and $2,670 for taxes, insurance, and other expenses. His (a) gross income was $_____28,800_____; (b) total expenses were $_____20,190_____; and (c) net income was $_____8,610_____.

   a. 32 × $900 = $28,800 gross income
   b. (12 × $90) + (0.2 × $28,800) + $10,680 + $2,670 = $20,190 total expenses
   c. $28,800 − $20,190 = $8,610 net income

2. Lydia Garza bought a house and advertised it for rent at $580 a month. During the first year, she was able to rent it for only 8 months. Even though the house was vacant for the other 4 months, Lydia had to pay average expenses of $165 a month for the whole year. She also paid $3,400 in mortgage interest. For the rental of this house for the first year, Lydia had (a) gross income of $_____4,640_____, and (b) net income or net loss of $_____740 net loss_____.

   a. 8 × $580 = $4,640 gross income

   b. (12 × $165) + $3,400 = $5,380 expenses
      $5,380 − $4,640 = $740 net loss

3. Tom Regan made a cash down payment of $18,000 on a two-unit apartment. In the first year, he rented one of the units for 12 months, the other for 9 months. The monthly rental of each unit was $370. Tom had these expenses for the year: mortgage interest, $1,990; taxes, $830; insurance, $560; repairs, $500; depreciation at 3.5% of the property value of $71,000. When Tom figured his income for the year, he found that he had (a) earned gross income of $_____7,770_____, (b) spent $_____6,365_____ for expenses, and (c) earned a net income of $_____1,405_____.

   a. (12 × $370)+ (9 × $370) = $7,770 gross income
   b. $1,990 + $830 + $560 + $500 + (0.035 × $71,000) = $6,365 total expenses
   c. $7,770 − $6,365 = $1,405 net income

4. Using the information in Problem 3, Tom's rate of income on his cash investment was _____8_____%, figured to the nearest percent.

   $1,405 ÷ $18,000 = 0.078, or 8% rate of income

5. Kuang-ping Jen bought, as an investment, an apartment house which brings in $2,300 a month in rental income. The building cost her $140,000. She paid $50,000 in cash for it and gave a mortgage for the rest. In addition to the $11,740 interest on the mortgage, the expenses of owning the property, including depreciation, average $7,360 a year. (a) If the rent and expenses stay the same, Jen will get from the property an annual net income of $_____8,500_____. (b) This is equivalent to a rate of income of _____17_____% on her cash investment.

   a. 12 × $2,300 = $27,600 gross rental income
      $27,600 − ($11,740 + $7,360) = $8,500 net income
   b. $8,500 ÷ $50,000 = 17% rate of income

Exercise 2.

1. For each problem, find the monthly rent to be charged.

	Type of Rental Property	Value	Owner's Cash Investment	Annual Net Income that Owner Wants	Annual Expenses	Total Monthly Rent from Property
a.	House	$62,000	$17,000	9% of investment	$6,030	$630
b.	Office Building	$87,000	$9,000	14% of investment	$12,420	$1,140
c.	Warehouse	$122,000	$31,000	7.6% of investment	$8,444	$900
d.	Factory	$45,000	$21,000	13% of investment	$4,710	$620
e.	Store	$28,000	$4,000	15% of investment	$3,120	$310
f.	6-Unit Apartment	$205,000	$38,000	11.5% of investment	$49,360	$4,500

a. ($17,000 × 0.09) + $6,030 = $7,560 $7,560 ÷ 12 = $630
b. ($9,000 × 0.14) + $ 12,420 = $ 13,680 $13,680 ÷ 12 = $1,140
c. ($31,000 × 0.076) + $8,444 = $10,800 $10,800 ÷ 12 = $900
d. ($21,000 × 0.13) + $4,710 = $7,440 $7,440 ÷ 12 = $620
e. ($4,000 × 0.15) + $3,120 = $3,720 $3,720 ÷ 12 = $310
f. ($38,000 × 0.115) + $49,630 = $54,000 $54,000 ÷ 12 = $4,500

2. Roy Weitzman made a $34,000 down payment on an apartment that is worth $ 156,000. His total mortgage interest for the first year was $17,080, and other expenses totaled $7,800. In the first year, he also spent $7,500 for a new fire escape, $4,000 for a smoke detection system, and $8,400 for a security alarm system. At the end of the first year, Roy's total investment in the apartment building was $_____53,900_____.

$34,000 + $7,500 + $4,000 + $8,400 = $53,900 total investment

3. Lars Reiner plans to buy a cabin worth $16,000 by making a $4,000 down payment. He estimates that his yearly expenses of owning the cabin will be $3,132. Lars also estimates that he will be able to rent the cabin for only six months a year. What monthly rent must Lars charge if he wants to earn 7% on his investment? $_____602_____

$3,132 + (0.12 × $4,000) = $3,612 annual rental income
$3,612 ÷ 6 = $602 monthly rent

4. Louise Meyer made a $8,000 down payment on a home worth $65,000. To make the home accessible for all potential renters, she paid $2,500 to install ramps at the front and rear entrances. Wall repairs and painting cost $1,500 and another $500 was spent to replace defective wiring. What was Louise's capital investment in the home? $_____10,500_____

$8,000 + $2,500 = $10,500

TERM TICKLER

Directions: Find each of the following terms or phrases in the puzzle. Circle each term or phrase when you find it. It may be written downward, upward, sideways, or diagonally. There are twenty-five terms. How many can you find?

Terms

bond
capital investment
discount
market price
net assets
no par stock
preferred stock
savings bond
yield

broker
common stock
dividends
market value
net proceeds
offer price
premium
shareholder

brokers commission
denomination
load funds
mutual fund
no load funds
par value
redemption value
stock certificate

S	D	N	U	F	D	A	O	L	K	E	I	E	P	D	D	X	S	S	Q	R
T	D	E	N	O	M	I	N	A	T	I	O	N	B	P	D	F	N	V	F	Q
E	I	I	O	X	S	C	K	H	I	Q	F	S	S	I	O	U	O	P	O
S	V	P	S	T	O	C	K	C	E	R	T	I	F	I	C	A	T	E	Z	E
S	I	P	A	C	A	P	I	T	A	L	I	N	V	E	S	T	M	E	N	T
A	D	O	V	J	O	L	T	G	Y	F	B	Y	K	E	P	E	L	P	Y	K
T	E	D	I	Y	I	U	Y	F	J	W	G	T	W	B	U	A	M	M	B	Z
E	N	R	N	W	S	M	N	R	K	R	G	K	N	C	C	G	F	C	M	W
N	D	E	G	O	P	A	Q	T	U	Q	S	P	W	O	T	N	Y	U	E	X
O	S	D	S	C	B	R	O	K	E	R	M	Z	M	D	V	N	F	S	P	V
L	W	E	B	R	O	K	E	R	S	C	O	M	M	I	S	S	I	O	N	C
O	R	M	O	N	M	E	S	F	Q	A	O	R	U	R	B	E	Q	I	V	W
A	K	P	N	E	O	T	D	P	E	N	M	P	L	C	S	G	A	L	U	W
D	K	T	D	T	K	P	T	N	S	R	P	R	E	M	I	U	M	S	C	C
F	R	I	O	P	J	R	A	T	U	H	R	A	H	C	X	K	A	E	B	B
U	B	O	J	R	V	I	O	R	O	F	F	E	R	P	R	I	C	E	Y	P
N	Q	N	V	O	S	C	M	Y	S	J	L	C	D	V	V	S	R	I	M	Q
D	N	V	D	C	K	E	W	Q	E	T	I	A	A	S	A	D	E	H	M	I
S	H	A	R	E	H	O	L	D	E	R	O	K	U	H	T	L	L	V	T	K
M	P	L	W	E	F	D	B	Y	C	B	S	C	U	T	D	O	U	I	P	N
I	D	U	G	D	T	F	Y	N	T	B	J	Z	K	O	U	C	C	E	R	Q
D	K	E	H	S	L	E	U	L	A	V	T	E	K	R	A	M	G	K	V	X

INTEGRATED PROJECT 11

Directions: Read through the entire project before you begin doing any work.

Introduction: Maria Stone began working at the Lindon Tool Company as a bookkeeper after finishing school. Recently, Maria was promoted to office manager and she wants to begin an investment program. In doing research on ways to invest money, Maria found four cases that she would like you to help her analyze.

Maria earns $26,000 a year, is not married, and rents an apartment. She plans to continue taking courses at the local college and expects to get a bachelor's degree in accounting within two years.

Step One: Read each case and analyze the investments by answering the questions that follow.

Case 1. After they both retired, Ted and Laura Swanson sold their house and land for $120,000 and rented an apartment. They invested almost all of the proceeds from the sale of their house in 120, $1,000 par value, 7% bonds of the Resko Corporation. The bonds mature in 8 years. The market price of the bonds was $95\frac{1}{2}$, with a $5 per bond commission charge.

1. What was the total investment in these bonds? ____$115,200____
   $(120 \times 0.955 \times \$1,000) + (120 \times \$5) = \$\,115,200$ total investment

2. Based on the bonds' original purchase price, what rate of income could be earned on this bond investment, to the nearest tenth percent? ____7.3%____
   $(120 \times 0.07 \times \$1,000) \div \$115,200 = 0.0729$, or 7.3% rate of income

3. If interest is paid on these bonds semiannually, what is the amount of the semiannual payment? ____$4,200____
   $(120 \times 0.07 \times \$1,000) \div 2 = \$4,200$ semiannual payment

4. If the Swansons hold the Resko bonds until their maturity date,

   a. What total amount will they receive from the Resko Corporation when they turn in their bonds to be redeemed? (No commission will be charged.) ____$120,000____
      $120 \times \$1,000 = \$120,000$

   b. What total amount of interest will they have earned by holding these bonds and receiving two semiannual interest payments each year? ____$67,200____
      $8 \times (2 \times \$4,200) = \$67,200$

Case 2. Calvin Borzenko deposits money from each paycheck into a credit union savings account. When the savings account balance reaches $2,000, Calvin withdraws $2,000 and invests in the mutual fund shares of the Carter Growth Fund. Calvin has purchased mutual fund shares for the past five years at these prices:

Year	Net Asset Value	Offer	No. of Shares Bought
1	7.27	7.65	261.438
2	7.73	8.14	245.700
3	8.35	8.79	227.531
4	8.74	9.20	217.391
5	9.20	9.68	206.612

1. What total number of Carter Growth Fund shares does Calvin own? ____1,158.672____
   $261.438 + 245.700 + 227.531 + 217.391 + 206.612 = 1,158.672$ shares

2. What average price per share did Calvin pay for the shares he owns? ____$8.63____
   $[(\$7.65 \times 261.438) + (\$8.14 \times 245.700) + (\$8.79 \times 227.53l) + (\$9.20 \times 217.391) + (\$9.68 \times 206.612)] \div 1,158.672$

3. One year after making his last purchase, the Carter Growth Fund has a N.A.V. of 8.93 and a 9.40 offer price. If Calvin sells all the shares he owns,

   a. What will be his net proceeds from the sale? ___$10,346.94___

     1,158,672 × $8.93 = $10,346.94 net proceeds

   b. What will be his net profit or loss from the ownership of these mutual fund shares? ___$346.94 profit___

     $10,346.94 − (5 × $2,000) = $346.94 profit

4. Assume that Calvin makes no additional fund purchases after the fifth year. At what price will Calvin have to sell his shares to double his investment? ___17.26 NAV___

   (2 × 5 × $2,000) ÷ 1,158.672 = 17.26 NAV

Case 3. Loretta Yousef inherited $10,000 which she used to make $5,000 investments in two stocks. She bought 200 shares of Alpen Electric at $25 a share, including commission. The Alpen stock pays a quarterly dividend of $37\frac{1}{2}$¢ per share. She also bought 400 shares of Ryker Chemical Company stock at $12.50 a share, including commission. The Ryker stock paid no dividend for the first four years. In the fifth year, a quarterly dividend of 2¢ a share was paid.

Loretta kept both stocks for five years and then sold them at these net prices after the commission charge was deducted: Alpen, $28; Ryker $18.

1. What total dividend did Loretta receive from both stocks? ___$1,500, Alpen; $32, Ryker___

   Alpen: 5 × (200 × 4 × $0.375) = $1,500   Ryker: (400 × 4 × $0.02) = $32

2. What profit or loss did Loretta make on each sale? ___$600 profit, Alpen; $2,200 profit, Ryker___

   Alpen: (200 × $28) − $5,000 = $600 profit   Ryker: (400 × $18) − $5,000 = $2,200 profit

3. What was the total gain or loss from ownership of these stocks? ___$2,100 gain, Alpen; $2,232 gain, Ryker___

   Alpen: $1,500 + $600 = $2,100 total gain   Ryker: $32 + $2,200 = $2,232 total gain

Case 4. The Wilsons bought eight $500 U.S. Savings Bonds each year for four years. When their daughter began attending college, the Wilsons began redeeming the eight oldest savings bonds each year to help pay for college expenses. The redemption schedule for $500 bonds follows: Year 1, $516.60; Year 2, $519.00; Year 3, $521.40; Year 4, $520.50.

1. What total amount did the Wilsons invest in the bonds? ___$8,000___

   4 × 8 × $250 = $8,000 total investment

2. What total amount did they receive each year for the bonds they redeemed? ___$4,164___

   8 × $520.50 = $4,164 received each year

3. What total interest did they earn on this investment? ___$8,656___

   (4 × $4,164) − $8,000 = $8,656 interest earned

Step Two: Make an investment recommendation for Maria Stone.

1. What type of investment should Maria make if her annual savings are $800? Why?

   Student answers will vary to this open-ended question.

2. Would your recommendation change if Maria's earnings were greater and she could save $2,000 a year? Why?

   Student answers will vary to this open-ended question.

BUSINESS ANALYSIS AND STATISTICS

LESSON 12-1   MEASURES OF CENTRAL TENDENCY

Exercise

1. Sort each group of numbers into ascending order. Then find the mean, median, mode, and range of each group.

Number Group	Mean	Median	Mode	Range
a. 6, 8, 22, 7, 3, 4, 16, 6				
3, 4, 6, 6, 7, 8, 16, 22	9	6.5	6	19
b. 34, 56, 53, 42, 46, 48, 34, 40, 34				
34, 34, 34, 40, 42, 46, 48, 53, 56	43	42	34	22
c. 5.6, 5.4, 6.2, 6.0, 6.8, 5.4, 6.1, 5.7				
5.4, 5.4, 5.6, 5.7, 6.0, 6.1, 6.2, 6.8	5.9	5.85	5.4	1.4

a. Mean = 72 ÷ 8 = 9; median = (6 + 7) ÷ 2 = 6.5; mode = 6; range = (22 − 3) = 19
b. Mean = 387 ÷ 9 = 43; median = 42; mode = 34; range = (56 − 34) = 22
c. Mean = 47.2 ÷ 8 = 5.9; median = (5.7 + 6.0) ÷ 2 = 5.85; mode = 5.4; range = (6.8 − 5.4) = 1.4

2. The daily number of complaints handled by a retail store during one month follow: 12, 7, 9, 14, 8, 7, 9, 11, 13, 12, 9, 10, 12, 14, 15, 9, 9, 12, 15, 9, 10, 8, 11, 12, 15, 11, 14. Use the form below to complete a frequency distribution table for the store. For the number of complaints, the mean is (a) _____11_____, the median is (b) _____11_____, and the mode is (c) _____9_____.

a. 7 × 2 = 14
    8 × 2 = 16
    9 × 6 = 54
    10 × 2 = 20
    11 × 3 = 33
    12 × 5 = 60
    13 × 1 = 13
    14 × 3 = 42
    15 × 3 = 45
            ‾‾‾
            297   297 ÷ 27 = 11 mean

b. 11 median

c. 9 mode

Number of Complaints Frequency Distribution Table		
Item	**Frequency**	**Total**
7	// 2	14
8	// 2	16
9	ℳ / 6	54
10	// 2	20
11	/// 3	33
12	ℳ 5	60
13	/ 1	13
14	/// 3	42
15	/// 3	45
	27	297

LESSON 12-2   PROBABILITY

Exercise

1. A box contains six marbles that are the same size. Four are red and numbered 1, 2, 3, and 4, as shown below. Two are blue and numbered 5 and 6. You are to pick one marble from the box of marbles. In the blank space, write the numeral that shows the probability of each of these events:

    a. Picking a red marble. ___$\frac{2}{3}$___

    b. Picking a green marble. ___0___

    c. Not picking a red marble. ___$\frac{1}{3}$___

    d. Picking a marble marked 4. ___$\frac{1}{6}$___

    e. Picking a marble not marked 2. ___$\frac{5}{6}$___

    f. Picking a marble numbered either 1 or 6. ___$\frac{1}{3}$___

    g. Picking a marble marked with a number less than 7. ___1___

    h. Picking a marble with a number greater than 6. ___0___

    i. Picking a marble marked with an odd number. ___$\frac{1}{2}$___

    j. Picking a marble with a number not greater than 2. ___$\frac{1}{3}$___

RED	BLUE
① ② ③ ④	⑤ ⑥

2. Use the mortality table to find the probability, to the nearest hundredth, of each person living to the projected age.

Name	Present Age	Projected Age	Probability of Reaching Projected Age
a. T. Baird	Born today	60	0.82
b. Y. Shenlo	40	50	0.97
c. A. Angett	10	70	0.68
d. B. Ricardo	30	80	0.41
e. F. Trelin	20	40	0.97

Mortality Table	
Age	Number Living
0	100,000
10	97,000
20	96,000
30	95,000
40	93,000
50	90,000
60	82,000
70	66,000
80	39,000

a. 82,000 ÷ 100,000 = 0.82
b. 90,000 ÷ 93,000 = 0.967, or 0.97
c. 66,000 ÷ 97,000 = 0.680, or 0.68
d. 39,000 ÷ 96,000 = 0.406, or 0.41
e. 94,000 ÷ 97,000 = 0.969, or 0.97

LESSON 12-3   BAR AND LINE GRAPHS

1. The vertical bar graph below shows the sales of Entel Flooring for each quarter of last year. At the right of the graph you are to write the dollar volume of sales shown by each bar.

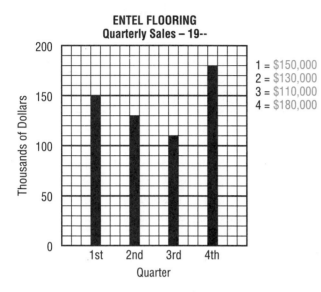

ENTEL FLOORING
Quarterly Sales – 19--

1 = $150,000
2 = $130,000
3 = $110,000
4 = $180,000

3. The horizontal bar graph below shows the sales made by six salespersons for the week ending August 8. At the right of the graph you are to write the amount of each salesperson's sales.

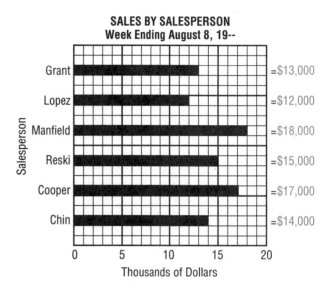

SALES BY SALESPERSON
Week Ending August 8, 19--

Grant =$13,000
Lopez =$12,000
Manfield =$18,000
Reski =$15,000
Cooper =$17,000
Chin =$14,000

2. The monthly sales of Rhome Bag Company for the first four months of the year are January, $24,000; February, $28,000; March, $25,000; April, $36,000. Show these monthly sales figures on the vertical bar graph below.

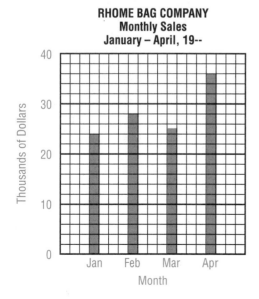

RHOME BAG COMPANY
Monthly Sales
January – April, 19--

4. The sales of Mead Greenhouses for April were shrubs, $35,000; trees, $28,000; seeds, $12,000; fertilizer, $24,000; garden tools, $17,000. Show these facts on the horizontal bar graph below.

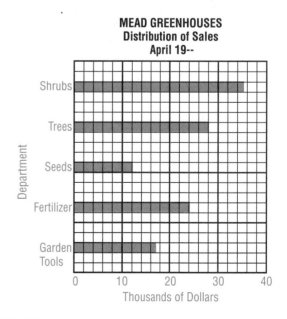

MEAD GREENHOUSES
Distribution of Sales
April 19--

5. The number of airline reservations made by the Tanner Travel Agency last year were these:

January	100	May	170	September	180
February	120	June	240	October	200
March	160	July	320	November	260
April	200	August	230	December	360

Use the graph paper at the right to show these facts in a vertical bar graph.

TANNER TRAVEL AGENCY
Monthly Reservations, 19--

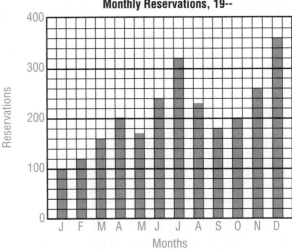

CONWELL VAN CONVERSIONS
Monthly Gross Profit and Expenses
Last Year

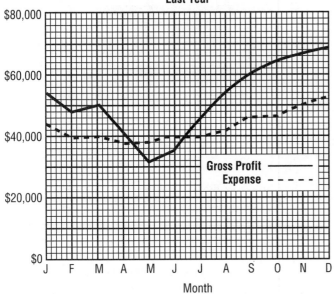

6. The line graph at the left shows Conwell Van Conversion's monthly gross profit and expenses for last year. Answer these questions about the graph.

a. Gross profit was smallest in the month of ___May___.

b. Gross profit was greatest in the month of _December_.

c. In March, gross profit was $_50,000_, expenses were $_40,000_, and net income was $_10,000_.

d. The business had a loss instead of a profit in the months of ___May___ and ___June___.

e. The greatest net income was made in the month of _October_. The amount of the net income was $_18,000_.

7. Rosalie Diaz's total income for the first ten weeks of last year and this year are shown below.

Week	Last Year	This Year	Week	Last Year	This Year
1	$350	$370	6	$550	$530
2	370	400	7	530	580
3	400	340	8	500	520
4	480	390	9	490	470
5	520	450	10	460	430

From these figures make a line graph at the right showing (a) the income for this year, using a solid line; and (b) the income for last year, using a dashed line.

ROSALIE DIAZ'S
Income for First Ten Weeks
Last Year and This Year

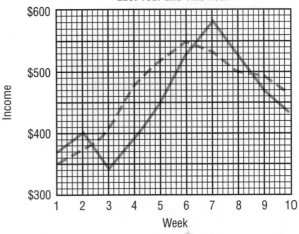

LESSON 12-4   CIRCLE AND RECTANGLE GRAPHS

Exercise 1.

1. The owner of Cutlery Unlimited wants to show the types of sales for last year by making the rectangle graph below. The total sales for last year were $620,000. You are to write in the blank spaces on the graph the amount of the (a) mail-order sales, (b) telephone sales, (c) home demonstration sales, (d) in-store sales.

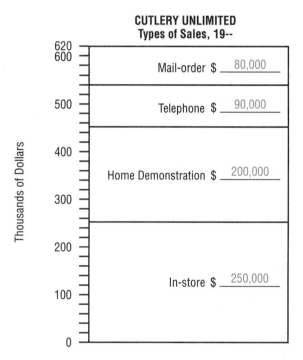

CUTLERY UNLIMITED
Types of Sales, 19--

Mail-order $ 80,000
Telephone $ 90,000
Home Demonstration $ 200,000
In-store $ 250,000

Thousands of Dollars

3. While on a business trip, Nora Cobb spent $1,680. Nora wants to make a circle graph comparing the different expenses of her trip. The sections of the graph are based on these figures taken from her expense record: lodging, $588; meals with customers, $504; samples, $420; car, $134.40; other, $33.60. You are to find the percent relationship of each of these items to the total expenses. Show these percents in the circle graph below.

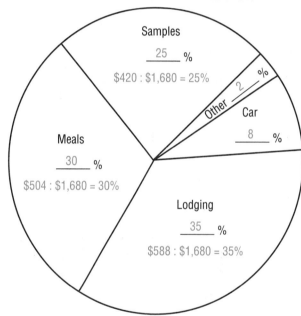

NORA COBB-BUSINESS TRAVEL EXPENSES

Samples 25 %
$420 : $1,680 = 25%

Other 2 %
Car 8 %

Meals 30 %
$504 : $1,680 = 30%

Lodging 35 %
$588 : $1,680 = 35%

$588.00 + $504.00 + $420.00 + $134.40 + $33.60 = $1,680 total expenses

$134.40 ÷ $1,680.00 = 8% for car
$33.60 ÷ $1,680.00 = 2% for other expenses

2. These amounts were spent last year by the Powell Advertising Agency for remodeling their offices: furniture, $8,000; carpeting, $5,000; painting, $4,000; wall hangings, $3,000. Use the form at the right to make a horizontal rectangle graph showing those amounts as percents of the total remodeling expense.

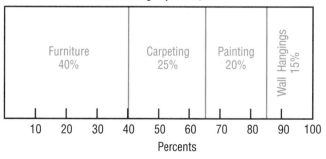

POWELL ADVERTISING AGENCY
Remodeling Expenses, 19--

Furniture 40%   Carpeting 25%   Painting 20%   Wall Hangings 15%

10 20 30 40 50 60 70 80 90 100
Percents

Exercise 2.

1. The owner of Carters Book Exchange estimates that her shop's total annual sales come from these items, stated as percents: fiction books, 45%; nonfiction books, 30%; reference books, 20%; magazines, 5%. Show the items on the circle graph below. Label each part of the circle graph.

**CARTER'S BOOK EXCHANGE
ANNUAL SALES BY TYPE OF ITEM**

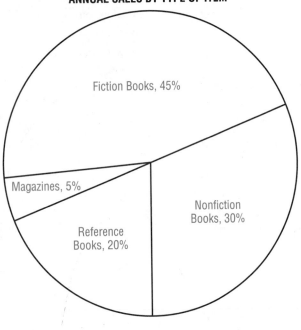

3. The Auto Stop's total sales last year came from installing these items in cars: stereo systems, $150,000; alarms, $100,000; sun roofs, $200,000; phones, $50,000. (a) The total sales last year were $____500,000____. The percent each item represented of the total sales is (b) stereo systems, ____30____%; (c) alarms, ____20____%; (d) sun roofs, ____40____%; (e) phones, ____10____%. Show these percents on the rectangle graph below.

AUTO STOP - PERCENT OF SALES BY ITEM, 19

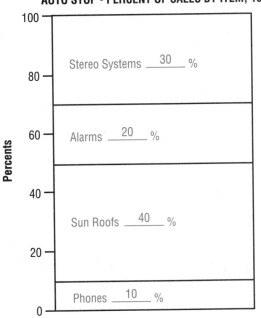

2. The Weller Cleaning Company estimates that its $800,000 in revenue last year came from cleaning the interiors of buildings owned by these customers: retail stores, 25%; insurance companies, 40%; city government, 20%; community college, 15%. Figure the amount of revenue earned from each customer and show those amounts on the horizontal rectangle graph at the right.

**Weller Cleaning Company
Revenue By Customer, 19--**

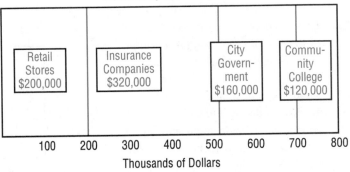

Chapter 12   Name: _____   Date: _____

LESSON 12-5   ECONOMIC STATISTICS

Exercise

1. During a three-year period, these annual inflation rates were recorded: 7.4%, 5.7%, 8.5%. The total inflation over the three years was (a) _____21.6_____%. The average annual (mean) rate of inflation for the three years was (b) _____7.2_____%.

   a. 7.4% + 5.7% + 8.5% = 21.6% total inflation over three years.
   b. 0.216 ÷ 3 = 0.072, or 7.2% average rate of inflation

2. In the base year of a study of prices, a typical family spent $100 a week for groceries. In the fifth year of the study, the purchasing power of the dollar was $0.753. In the sixth year, the purchasing power of the dollar decreased by $0.036. The purchasing power of the dollar in the sixth year was (a) $_____0.717_____, and the $100 in the sixth year would have bought only (b) $_____71.70_____ worth of the same groceries that could have been bought in the base year.

   a. $0.753 − $0.036 = $0.717 purchasing power of the dollar in sixth year
   b. 0.717 × $100 = $71.70 of goods could have been bought

3. The food category of the Consumer Price Index was at 140.9 in 1993. Compared to the base period, by 1993 the cost of food had increased by (a) _____40.9_____%. Assume that the price of a gallon of milk was $1 in the base period. If milk prices increased at the same rate as the prices of all food, the cost of a gallon of milk in 1995 would be (b) $_____1.41_____, rounded to the nearest cent.

   a. 140.9 − 100.0 = 40.9 percent increase in prices
   b. $1 + (0.409 × $1) = $1.409, or $1.41 price of a gallon of milk in 1995 prices

4. In the Consumer Price Index table, the shelter category was 121.3 in 1987 and 155.7 in 1993. Assume that a one-floor house could have been built for $30,000 in the base period. If the cost of building a house identical to the one built in the base period increased at the same rate as did the shelter category in the CPI, the cost of the house would have been (a) $_____36,390_____ in 1987 and (b) $_____46,710_____ in 1993. (c) The cost of the house increased by $_____10,320_____ between 1987 and 1993.

   a. 121.3% × $30,000 = $36,390 cost of identical house in 1987
   b. 155.7% × $30,000 = $46,710 cost of identical house in 1993
   c. $46,710 − $36,390 = $10,320 increase in house cost

5. The unemployment rate among the 180,000 persons in the labor force in Atim County is 8.5%. (a) The number of persons who are unemployed is _____15,300_____. (b) The number of persons who are employed is _____164,700_____.

   a. 0.085 × 180,000 = 15,300 number of persons unemployed
   b. 180,000 − 15,300 = 164,700 number of persons employed

TERM TICKLER

Directions: Complete the crossword puzzle below.

Across

1. Difference between highest and lowest numbers in a group
5. Bars are drawn left to right on the _____ bar graph.
7. The middle number in a group
8. The number that occurs most frequently in a group
9. 100% of a _____ graph is 360 degrees.
12. Sum of numbers divided by the number of items
13. A rise in the prices of good and services

15. A _____ period is a time in the past with which comparisons were made.
16. The percent of the labor force not working is called the _____ rate.

Down

1. A few items selected from the whole group by chance are called _____ samples.
2. The outcome of making a random choice is a _____ event.
3. A way of predicting the outcome of an event

4. A labor _____ includes all persons working or looking for work.
6. A graph that may be shown vertically or horizontally is a _____ graph.
7. The _____ table shows numbers of people living to certain ages.
10. In a _____ bar graph, bars are drawn up and down the graph.
11. Dots show data and lines connect the dots in a _____ graph.
14. A _____ distribution arranges numbers shown in order with a table.

INTEGRATED PROJECT 12

Directions: Read through the entire project before you begin doing any work.

Introduction: The Perlook Company produces custom sweatshirts for resorts, schools, and other companies. The owner of the Perlook Company will soon meet with the manager to review production, sales, and other financial data. As a clerk in the manager's office, you are responsible for keeping statistical records and helping to prepare reports.

For the meeting, a graph of the Perlook Company's operations must be prepared to include the company's third quarter operating results, which are now available. Statistics on employee absences and their cost to the business must also be calculated. In addition, the effect on company costs of pay raises due employees must be calculated.

Step One: Unit production and sales figures for the first three quarters of the year are shown in the worksheet below. Round the actual production and sales figures to the nearest 2,000 units and enter the results in the "rounded" column.

Perlook Company
Quarterly Worksheet

Month	Unit Production		Unit Sales	
	Actual	Rounded	Actual	Rounded
January	79,743	80,000	81,070	82,000
February	61,960	62,000	69,190	70,000
March	66,040	66,000	94,750	94,000
April	99,675	100,000	111,900	112,000
May	141,300	142,000	120,500	120,000
June	139,070	140,000	134,120	134,000
July	157,100	158,000	150,800	150,000
August	130,110	130,000	139,215	140,000
September	109,430	110,000	119,840	120,000

Step Two: Use the graph paper below to make a line graph showing the Perlook Company's unit production and sales figures for the first three quarters of the year. The graph paper has ten blocks to the inch. Follow these steps:

1. Label the graph with the company's name and the title of the graph.

2. Beginning at the left of the horizontal scale, leave the first two blocks empty and mark off every seventh space for the months. Write abbreviations for the names of the months beneath the marks you made.

3. Make each vertical block equal to 2,000 units. Begin with 50,000 units at the bottom of the vertical scale. Label each multiple of 10,000 units in the vertical scale.

4. Use the rounded production and sales figures from the worksheet to make the graph. Use a dashed (---) line for production figures and a solid line (—) for sales.

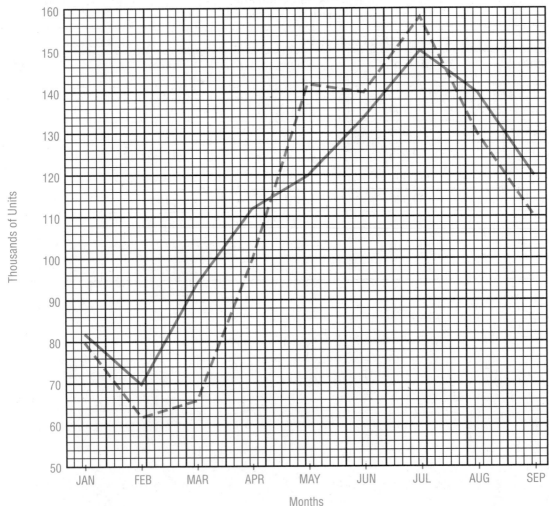

PERLOOK COMPANY
UNIT PRODUCTION AND SALES
Nine Months Ending September 30, 19--

Step Three: The Perlook Company reports data on a quarterly basis on employee absences due to illness. Complete the following frequency distribution table that shows a tally of the times that the number of employees given were absent from work. Then use the data in the table to answer the questions that follow the table.

**Perlook Company
Employee Absence Data
Third Quarter, 19--**

Number of Employees Absent from Work	Number of Times Event Occurred		Total
	Frequency		
0	ⅢⅢ ⅢⅢ	10	0
1	ⅢⅢ ////	9	9
2	ⅢⅢ ⅢⅢ ⅢⅢ ⅢⅢ /	21	42
3	ⅢⅢ ⅢⅢ /	11	33
4	ⅢⅢ /	6	24
5	ⅢⅢ ///	8	40
		65	148

1. The average number of employees absent per day was

   a. _____2.3_____ employees, shown as the mean, to the nearest tenth employee.

   b. _____2_____ employees, shown as the median.

   c. _____2_____ employees, shown as the mode.

   a. 148 ÷ 65 = 2.27, or 2.3 mean number of employees absent per day
   b. median is 2 employees
   c. mode is 2 employees

2. As part of its employee benefits package, the Perlook Company pays its employees for illness-related absences. The average daily wages of employees at the Perlook Company is $69.20. If all employees were paid for the days they were absent, what was the total cost for absent employees' wages during the third quarter?
   $_____10,241.60_____

   148 × $69.20 = $10,241.60 wage cost of absent employees

3. Using the employee absence data from the third quarter, what is the probability that no employees will be absent from work because of illness on any day during the quarter? _____ $\frac{2}{13}$ _____

$\frac{10}{65} = \frac{2}{13}$ probability of no employees being absent

4. What is the probability, stated to the nearest percent, that no more than two employees will be absent from work during the quarter because of illness? _____ 61.5 _____ %

10 + 9 + 21 = 40 total days with two or less employee absences
40 ÷ 65 = 0.6153, or 61.5% probability that no more than two employees will be absent

Step Four: Employee wages are adjusted each quarter for increases in the cost of living as measured by the Consumer Price Index (CPI). During the third quarter, the CPI increased by 1%.

1. **a.** What hourly wage increase, to the nearest cent, would the average employee get if the average hourly pay is $8.65? $ _____ 0.09 _____

   b. How much more would the average employee earn by working a 40-hour week at the new rate of pay? $ _____ 3.60 _____

   a. 0.01 × $8.65 = $0.0865, or $0.09 hourly wage increase
   b. 40 × $0.09 = $3.60 earned more per 40-hour week at new rate

2. The average weekly wages paid by the Perlook Company is $7,266.

   a. How much more will the average weekly wage cost be after employee wages are adjusted for the increase in the CPI? $ _____ 72.66 _____

   b. How much will the Perlook Company's employee wage cost increase over the 13-week period of the fourth quarter after the employee wages are adjusted? $ _____ 944.58 _____

   a. 0.01 × $7,266 = $72.66 more per week
   b. 13 × $72.66 = $944.58 total increase in wage cost for fourth quarter

BUSINESS PROFIT AND LOSS

LESSON 13-1   PROFIT AND LOSS

Exercise 1.

1. For the last month, the total sales of the Discount Tile Shop were $28,972.14. The sales returns and allowances for the month totaled $3,015.72. The shop's net sales for the month were $____25,956.42____.

   $28,972.14 − $3,015.72 = $25,956.42 net sales

2. Kirby's Hospital Supply had total sales of $246,789.50 for the first three months. Sales returns and allowances for that period totaled $7,400.34. The merchandise sold in these three months cost $180,400.12. (a) The net sales were $____239,389.16____. (b) The gross profit on sales was $____58,989.04____.

   a. $246,789.50 − $7,400.34 = $239,389.16 net sales
   b. $239,389.16 − $180,400.12 = $58,989.04 gross profit

3. A sporting goods store figures its cost of merchandise sold every three months. On April 1, the store's merchandise inventory was $186,400. Purchases during the period were $265,219. The ending inventory on June 30 was $231,875. For the three months, the cost of merchandise available for sale was (a) $____451,619____, and the cost of merchandise sold was (b) $____219,744____.

   a. $186,400 + $265,219 = $451,619 cost of merchandise available for sale
   b. $451,619 − $231,875 = $219,744 cost of merchandise sold

4. The Largent Business Forms Company had total sales of $68,400.30 for the month. Sales returns and allowances totaled $2,105.50. The cost of the merchandise sold during the month was $28,692.10. (a) Largent's net sales were $____66,294.80____. (b) The company's gross profit on sales was $____37,602.70.____

   a. $68,400.30 − $2,105.50 = $66,294.80 net sales
   b. $66,294.80 − $28,692.10 = $37,602.70 gross profit

5. The total monthly net sales of a children's clothing store were $45,800. The gross profit on sales was $8,245. Operating expenses for the month totaled $8,895. (a) For the month, the store had a net loss of $____650____. (b) If the amount of the monthly loss continues at the same rate for the whole year, the store will lose $____7,800____.

   a. $8,895 − $8,245 = $650 net loss for month
   b. 12 × $650 = $7,800 possible loss for year

Exercise 2.

1. The Bushnell Audio Company gives you these data for their March operations: net sales, $124,950; inventory at beginning of month, $25,400; purchases during the month, $75,800; inventory at end of month, $29,600; operating expenses, $38,258. Write these figures in the correct spaces of the form below and show the (a) cost of merchandise sold and (b) gross profit on sales. (c) Then figure and indicate whether the company had a net income or loss.

BUSHNELL AUDIO COMPANY

Net Sales $124,950

    Less Cost of Merchandise Sold:

        Inventory, March 1 . . . . $ 25,400

        Add Purchases   75,800

        Merchandise Available for Sale $101,200

        Less Inventory, March 31   29,600

            Cost of Merchandise Sold . . . .   **a.** 71,600

            Gross Profit on Sales . . . .   **b.** 53,350

        Less Operating Expenses   38,258

        Net Income or Loss . . . .   **c.** $15,092 (net income)

2. For the last quarter of the year, the software department of Crest Computer had net sales of $49,750. The beginning inventory was $7,235, and the ending inventory was $5,200. Purchases for the quarter were $21,000. Operating expenses totaled $27,076. Use this information to complete the form below, showing (a) the cost of merchandise sold and (b) the gross profit on sales. (c) Then figure and label the amount of the net income or loss.

CREST COMPUTER
Software Department

Net Sales $49,750

    Less Cost of Merchandise Sold:

        Beginning Inventory . . . . $ 7,235

        Add Purchases   21,000

        Merchandise Available for Sale $28,235

        Less Ending Inventory   5,200

            Cost of Merchandise Sold . . . .   **a.** 23,035

            Gross Profit on Sales . . . .   **b.** $26,715

        Less Operating Expenses   27,076

        Net Income or Loss . . . .   **c.** $ 361 (net loss)

Exercise 3.

1. The owner of a small supermarket had net sales of $135,000 for the month of February. The cost of merchandise sold during the month was $97,250, and the operating expenses were $34,900. (a) The gross profit on sales for February was $____37,750____. (b) For the month, the net income was $____2,850____.

a. $135,000 − $97,250 = $37,750 gross profit on sales
b. $37,750 − $34,900 = $2,850 net income

2. Complete the income statement below by showing (a) total net sales, (b) cost of merchandise sold, (c) gross profit on sales, (d) total operating expenses, and (e) net income.

MARVIN'S SHOE STORE
Income Statement
For the Quarter Ending December 31, 19--

Net Sales:

Dress and Casual Shoes	$153,700	
Sports Footwear	60,340	
Other Merchandise	38,180	
Total Net Sales	**a.**	$252,220

Cost of Merchandise Sold:

Dress and Casual Shoes	$91,250	
Sports Footwear	42,140	
Other Merchandise	22,310	**b.** $155,700

Gross Profit on Sales. . . . . . **c.** $ 96,520

Operating Expenses

Employee Salaries and Wages	$32,100	
Rent	14,900	
Heat, Power, and Light	3,800	
Advertising	4,500	
Taxes	5,820	
Insurance	2,400	
Other Expenses	4,200	
Total Operating Expenses	**d.**	$ 67,720

Net Income . . . . . . **e.** $ 28,800

Exercise 4.

1. The summaries of two income statements follow. For each statement, find what percent each item in the statement is of the net sales.

Income Statement A			Income Statement B		
Major Items	**Amount**	**Percent**	**Major Items**	**Amount**	**Percent**
Net Sales	$150,000	a. ___100___	Net Sales	$32,000	f. ___100___
Cost of Merchandise Sold	90,000	b. ___60___	Cost of Merchandise Sold	14,400	g. ___45___
Gross Profit on Sales	$ 60,000	c. ___40___	Gross Profit on Sales	$17,600	h. ___55___
Operating Expenses	45,000	d. ___30___	Operating Expenses	15,040	i. ___47___
Net Income	$ 15,000	e. ___10___	Net Income	$ 2,560	j. ___8___

2. During the first 13 weeks of the year, a store owner made a gross profit of $54,000 on net sales of $120,000. The operating expenses for the period were $48,000. (a) The net income for the 13-week period was (a) $___6,000___. As a percent of net sales, the gross profit was (b) ___45___% and the net income was (c) ___5___%.

a. $54,000 − $48,000 = $6,000 net income
b. $54,000 ÷ $120,000 = 0.45, or 45% of net sales
c. $6,000 ÷ $120,000 = 0.05, or 5% of net sales

3. Last year, The Wicker Shop's merchandise inventory on January 1 was $21,150; on July 1, $25,750; on December 31, $22,400. The cost of merchandise sold during the year was $86,600. The merchandise turnover rate for the year to two decimal places was ___3.75___.

$21,150 + $25,750 + $22,400 = $69,300 total of inventories
$69,300 ÷ 3 = $23,100 average merchandise inventory
$86,600 ÷ $23,100 = 3.7489, or 3.75 yearly merchandise turnover rate

4. A store's cost of merchandise sold during November was $48,300. The merchandise inventory on November 1 was $62,500 and on November 30 it was $58,100. (a) The store's turnover rate to three decimal places for the month was ___0.801___. (b) For the year, the turnover rate to two decimal places was ___9.61___.

a. $62,500 + $58,100 = $120,600 total of inventories
    $120,600 ÷ 2 = $60,300 average merchandise inventory
    $48,300 ÷ $60,300 = 0.8009, or 0.801 monthly merchandise turnover rate
b. 12 × 0.801 = 9.612, or 9.61 yearly merchandise turnover rate

5. From January through June, the local feed store's cost of merchandise sold was $280,700. The average of three inventories during that six-month period was $75,400. Based on this data, the feed store's yearly merchandise turnover rate to two decimal places was ___7.45___.

$280,700 ÷ $75,400 = 3.7228, or 3.723 merchandise turnover rate for six months
2 × 3.723 = 7.446, or 7.45 yearly merchandise turnover rate

Exercise 5.   (Finding factory costs)

1. During March, the manufacturing costs of Northwest Steel Products were raw materials, $1,278,893; direct labor, $1,458,201; factory expense, $368,125. The total factory cost of the goods produced in March was $____3,105,219____.

$1,278,893 + $1,458,201 + $368,125 = $3,105,219 total factory cost

2. The costs to make 1,440 soccer balls are raw materials, $4,500; direct labor, $3,125; factory expense, $775.
    (a) The total factory cost is $____8,400____. (b) The factory cost per dozen is $____70____.

a. $4,500 + $3,125 + $775 = $8,400 total factory cost
b. 1,440 ÷ 12 = 120 dozen soccer balls
    $8,400 ÷ 120 = $70 cost per dozen

Exercise 6.   (Distributing Factory Expense)

1. The Resco Lens Company pays $100,000 a year rent for its factory. The factory has an area of 20,000 sq. ft. divided into these four departments: Binoculars, 5,000 sq. ft.; Telescopes, 4,000 sq. ft.; Microscopes, 8,000 sq. ft.; Magnifying Lens, 3,000 sq. ft. The amount of rent that should be distributed to the (a) Binoculars Department is $____25,000____, (b) Telescopes Department is $____20,000____, (c) Microscopes Department is $____40,000____, and (d) Magnifying Lens Department is $____15,000____.

a. 5,000 + 4,000 + 8,000 + 3,000 = 20,000 total square feet
    (5,000 ÷ 20,000) × $100,000 = $25,000 rent distributed to Binoculars Dept.
b. (4,000 ÷ 20,000) × $100,000 = $20,000 rent distributed to Telescopes Dept.
c. (8,000 ÷ 20,000) × $100,000 = $40,000 rent distributed to Microscopes Dept.
d. (3,000 ÷ 20,000) × $100,000 = $15,000 rent distributed to Magnifying Lens Dept.

2. The Enloe Manufacturing Company, which employs 1,420 people, spends $72,000 a month on its Human Resources Department. The Company charges its other departments for personnel services on the basis of the number of employees in each department. The amount charged annually for human resource services to the Assembly Department, which has 355 workers, is $____216,000____.

(355 ÷ 1,420) × $72,000 = $18,000 monthly charge for human resource services
$18,000 × 12 = $216,000 annual charge for human resource services

3. The direct costs of producing women's dresses at a factory are raw materials, $8,756; direct labor, $15,350. Factory overhead is estimated at 15% of the total cost of direct labor and materials. The total factory costs for producing the dresses is $____27,721.90____.

$8,756 + $15,350 = $24,106 total direct costs
$24,106 × 0.15 = $3,615.90 factory overhead
$24,106.00 + $3,615.90 = $27,721.90 total factory costs

LESSON 13-2   CALCULATING AND ANALYZING OPERATING COSTS

Exercise 1.

1. Twin Cities Service Corporation budgeted its estimated office costs in this way: employee labor expense, 70%; rent, heat, cooling, light, and insurance, 20%; office supplies, telephone, and postage, 10%. In a yearly budget of $80,000, Twin Cities budgeted (a) $_____56,000_____ for labor; (b) $_____16,000_____ for rent, heat, cooling, light, and insurance; and (c) $_____8,000_____ for office supplies, telephone, and postage.

   a. $80,000 × 0.70 = $56,000 budget for labor
   b. $80,000 × 0.20 = $16,000 budget for rent, heat, cooling, light, and insurance
   c. $80,000 × 0.10 = $8,000 budget for office supplies, telephone and postage

2. A firm stores 500,000 documents in filing drawers and spends $45,000 annually to keep these documents. A study by the firm shows that 35% of the documents are never used after filing and that 5% of the documents are likely to be misfiled. (a) The number of documents kept but never used in this firm is _____175,000_____. (b) The annual cost of keeping the documents not used is $_____15,750_____. (c) The number of documents that are likely to be misfiled is _____25,000_____. (d) If the cost of searching for, finding, or replacing a misfiled document is $22, the firm's estimated cost for misfiled documents is $_____550,000_____.

   a. 500,000 × 0.35 = 175,000 documents never used
   b. (175,000 ÷ 500,000) × $45,000 = $15,750 annual cost of keeping unused documents
   c. 500,000 × 0.05 = 25,000 documents likely to be misfiled
   d. 25,000 × $22 = $550,000 cost of searching for, finding, or replacing misfiled documents

3. Haskins Financial Services, Inc. rents space for a branch office at $2,760 a month. The office is 60 feet long and 40 feet wide. (a) The office has _____2,400_____ square feet of space. (b) The yearly rental cost per square foot is $_____13.80_____.

   a. 60 × 40 = 2,400 square feet of office space
   b. ($2,760 ÷ 2,400) × 12 = $13.80 annual cost per square foot

4. The Delaney Company is studying the cost of copying documents. It estimates that its copier depreciates $4,250 each year. It also estimates that it makes 120,000 copies per year using the copier. Copy paper, bought in large quantities, costs $30 a ream (500 sheets). Toner, or the ink-like material used in the copier, costs $15 a bottle and lasts for 3,000 copies. Insurance on the copier costs $115 per year and the office pays $50 a month for maintenance and repairs. The average cost per copy, to the nearest tenth of a cent, of using the copier is _____10.6_____ cents.

   120,000 ÷ 500 = 240 number of reams per year used
   240 × $30 = $7,200 cost of copy paper per year
   120,000 ÷ 3,000 = 40 number of toner bottles used per year
   40 × $15 = $600 cost of toner per year
   12 × $50 = $600 annual cost of maintenance and repairs
   $4,250 + $7,200 + $600 + $115 + $600 = $12,765 annual cost of copier
   $12,765 ÷ 120,000 = 10.6 cents average cost per copy

5. A local printer offers to make Delaney 100 copies of a 30-page report for $275. (a) Using the facts from Problem 4 and not counting the time and cost of Delaney's copy clerks, is it cheaper for Delaney to use the printer or its own copier? _____printer_____ (b) How much? $_____43_____.

   a. 100 × 30 = 3,000 number of pages
      3,000 × $0.106 = $318 cost of using own copier for report; cheaper to go to printer
   b. $318 − $275 = $43 saved

Exercise 2.   (Payroll register)

1. Complete the payroll record for Huffy Manufacturing Co. Figure overtime at time and a half. Use the FICA and federal income tax tables in Illustrations 21-2 and 21-3 of your textbook, and a state income tax rate of 5%.

	A	B	C	D	E	F	G	H	I	J	K	L
1	HUFFY MANUFACTURING CO.						For the Period Ended May 19, 19--					
2							Deductions					
3		No. of	Total Hours		Hourly	Total	Fed.	FICA	State			Net
4	Employee	Allow.	Reg.	O.T.	Rate	Earn.	Inc. Tax	Tax	Inc. Tax	Other	Total	Pay
5	D. Levy	2	40	5	9.10	432.25	32.00	33.07	21.61	9.48	96.16	336.09
6	E. O'Ryan	0	38	0	8.80	334.40	32.00	25.58	16.72	11.64	85.94	248.46
7	F. Perez	1	40	1	8.10	336.15	36.00	25.72	16.81	10.50	89.03	247.12
8	G. Shih	3	40	3	9.80	436.10	25.00	33.36	21.81	11.64	91.81	344.29
9	H. Tubman	3	40	1	10.40	431.60	25.00	33.02	21.58	10.50	90.10	341.50
10	Total					1,970.50	150.00	150.75	98.53	53.76	453.04	1,517.46
11												
12												
13												

2. Complete the part of a payroll register shown below. Time and a half is paid for time worked over 8 hours in a day.

Name	Time Record M	T	W	T	F	Total Hours Reg.	Over-time	Hourly Rate	Earnings Regular	Over-time	Total
I. Flynn	8	8	8	8	7	39	0	6.50	253.50	0	253.50
J. Gorski	8	9	9	8	8	40	2	7.31	292.40	21.93	314.33
K. Wilson	7	0	9	8	8	31	1	5.80	179.80	8.70	188.50
L. Yang	8	9	9	8	9	40	3	9.42	376.80	42.39	419.19
						Totals			1,102.50	73.02	1,175.52

Exercise 3. (Employee earnings record)

Complete the employee earnings record below. The employee has one withholding allowance, earns $433 each week, and pays a 3% state income tax. The employee also pays $49.90 a week for health insurance. Use the FICA and income tax withholding tables in Illustrations 4-3.2 and 4-3.3 of your textbook.

	A	B	C	D	E	F	G	H	I
1									
2					Deductions				
3			Fed.		State				
4	Week	Gross	Inc.	FICA	Inc.	Health		Net	Accumulated
5	Ended	Pay	Tax	Tax	Tax	Insur.	Total	Pay	Gross Pay
6	1/4	433.00	40.00	33.12	12.99	49.90	136.01	296.99	433.00
7	1/11	433.00	40.00	33.12	12.99	49.90	136.01	296.99	866.00
8	1/18	433.00	40.00	33.12	12.99	49.90	136.01	296.99	1,299.00
9	1/25	433.00	40.00	33.12	12.99	49.90	136.01	296.99	1,732.00
10	2/1	433.00	40.00	33.12	12.99	49.90	136.01	296.99	2,165.00
11	2/8	433.00	40.00	33.12	12.99	49.90	136.01	296.99	2,598.00
12	2/15	433.00	40.00	33.12	12.99	49.90	136.01	296.99	3,031.00
13	2/22	433.00	40.00	33.12	12.99	49.90	136.01	296.99	3,464.00
14	3/1	433.00	40.00	33.12	12.99	49.90	136.01	296.99	3,897.00
15	3/8	433.00	40.00	33.12	12.99	49.90	136.01	296.99	4,330.00
16	3/15	433.00	40.00	33.12	12.99	49.90	136.01	296.99	4,763.00
17	3/22	433.00	40.00	33.12	12.99	49.90	136.01	296.99	5,196.00
18	3/29	433.00	40.00	33.12	12.99	49.90	136.01	296.99	5,629.00
19	Totals								
20	First								
21	Quarter	5,629.00	520.00	430.56	168.87	648.70	1,768.13	3,860.87	

Exercise 4. (Payroll taxes)

Last year, Berstein Bros. paid a total of 40 employees $756,000 in salaries and wages. All employees earned at least $7,000 and not more than $70,000. Berstein paid 7.65% as its share of the FICA taxes, 6.2% of the first $7,000 for FUTA, and 4.2% of the first $7,000 for state unemployment taxes. It is allowed to deduct 90% of its state unemployment taxes from the amount due for FUTA. (a) Its FICA payroll taxes were $___57,834___. (b) Its state unemployment taxes were $___11,760___. (c) Its net FUTA payroll taxes were $___6,776___.

a. $756,000 × 0.0765 = $57,834 FICA payroll taxes
b. 40 × $7,000 = $280,000 taxable wages, SUTA
$280,000 × 0.042 = $11,760 SUTA payroll taxes
c. $280,000 × 0.062 = $17,360 FUTA payroll taxes
$11,760 × 0.90 = $10,584 deductible amount
$17,360 − $10,584 = $6,776 net FUTA payroll taxes

Exercise 5.   (Computer Costs)

1. Calico Products Corporation bought 8 personal computers for the office. Each system was equipped with a central processing unit costing $800, a display screen costing $250, a keyboard costing $80, a hard disk drive costing $400, a CD-ROM drive costing $450, and a floppy disk drive costing $80. Calico also wanted to connect, or network, each computer system. To do that, special equipment, software, and cables costing $3,200 had to be bought. One additional computer system to provide central storage for $3,700 and a printer for $1,800 were also bought. The cost of installing the computers, printers, and cabling was $800. Eight of the nine computers were provided with operating system software costing $80, spreadsheet software costing $395, and word processing software costing $495. The total cost of buying and installing the entire computer system was $_____33,740_____.

```
8 × $800  = $ 6,400 cost of central processing units
8 × $250  = $ 2,000 cost of display screens
8 × $80   = $   640 cost of keyboards
8 × $400  = $ 3,200 cost of hard disk drives
8 × $450  = $ 3,600 cost of CD-ROM drives
8 × $80   = $   640 cost of floppy disk drives
            $ 3,200 cost of networking equipment and cables
            $ 3,700 cost of additional computer
            $ 1,800 cost of printer
            $   800 cost of installing computers and cabling
8 × $80   = $   640 cost of operating system software
8 × $395  = $ 3,160 cost of spreadsheet software
8 × $495  = $ 3,960 cost of word processing software
            $33,740 total cost of entire computer system
```

2. Freebury Corporation wants to equip its salespeople with light, portable computers, called notebook computers. They want their salespeople to use the notebook to enter sales orders and check on inventory levels of products while visiting customers. The price of the notebook they want is $1,395. This includes the central processing units, two disk drives, a display screen, keyboard, and internal memory. In addition, they will need to buy sales order software @ $585, and operating system software @ $45.

To allow the notebooks to send data over telephone lines to the home office, they will need to buy a modem for each notebook. The best price on the modem they want is $225 each. They will also need a program which will tell the notebook how to run the modem. This is called communications software. The communications software costs $178 each. (a) If Freebury has 17 salespeople, the total amount they must spend is $_____51,426_____. (b) The cost per salesperson for the system is $_____3,028_____.

```
a. 17 × $1,395 = $23,715 total cost of notebook computers
   17 × $585   = $ 9,945 total cost of sales order software
   17 × $45    = $   765 total cost of operating system software
   17 × $225   = $ 3,825 total cost of modems
   17 × $178   = $ 3,026 total cost of communications software
                 $41,276 total amount they must spend

b. $41,276 ÷ 17 = $2,428 cost per salesperson
```

3. VP Systems, Inc. can lease 26 personal computers for $133 each per month. They can buy the same system for $3,899 each. (a) The monthly leasing cost of the computers is $_____3,458_____. (b) The number of months that they can lease each system before leasing becomes more expensive than buying, to the nearest whole month, is _____29_____.

a. $133 × 26 = $3,458 monthly leasing cost of hardware
b. $3,899 ÷ $133 = 29.3, or 29 number of months they can lease before leasing is more than buying

4. The environmental protection agency of a state government needs to develop a program which will keep track of the smokestack emissions of each factory in the state. They estimate that the program will require 1,760 lines of computer instructions. They plan to use two programmers to develop the program at an average daily salary of $130 each. Each programmer is expected to produce 20 lines of finished code per day. (a) The number of days that it will take to produce the program is _____44_____. (b) The programming costs to produce the program are $_____11,440_____. (c) The average cost per line of code is $_____6.50_____.

a. 1,760 ÷ (20 × 2) = 44 days to produce program
b. 44 × ($130 × 2) = $11,440 programming costs
c. $11,440 ÷ 1,760 = $6.50 average cost per line of code

5. You want to have 32 MB of internal storage in your personal computer. You can buy 4 MB memory boards for $95 each, 8 MB memory boards for $191 each, and 16 MB memory boards for $439 each. Rounded to the nearest cent, the cost per megabyte of the (a) 4 MB boards is $_____23.75_____, the cost per megabyte of the (b) 8 MB boards is $_____23.88_____, and the cost per megabyte of the (c) 16 MB boards is $_____27.44_____.

a. $95 ÷ 4 = $23.75 cost per MB for 4 MB boards
b. $191 ÷ 8 = $23.88 cost per MB for 8 MB boards
c. $439 ÷ 16 = $27.44 cost per MB for 16 MB boards

6. Ganfield Amusement Company wants to increase the external memory available to its personal computers. It can buy hard disk drives with a storage capacity of 420 MB for a cost of $179 each. It can also buy 850 MB hard disk drives priced at $304 each. (a) The cost per MB of buying 420 MB hard disk drives is $_____0.43_____ rounded to the nearest cent. (b) The cost per MB of buying 850 MB hard disk drives is $_____0.36_____ rounded to the nearest cent.

a. $179 ÷ 420 = $0.426, or $0.43 cost per MB of 420 MB hard disk drives
b. $304 ÷ 850 = $0.357, or $0.36 cost per MB of 850 MB hard disk drive

LESSON 13-3   DEPRECIATION COSTS

Exercise 1.   (Declining-balance method of depreciation)

1. A spraying machine that costs $80,000 is depreciated 10% per year by the declining-balance method. Its book value at the end of three years will be $_____58.320_____.

   $80,000 × 0.10 = $8,000 depreciation, first year
   $80,000 − $8,000 = $72,000 book value, end of first year

   $72,000 × 0.10 = $7,200 depreciation, second year
   $72,000 − $7,200 = $64,800 book value, end of second year

   $64,800 × 0.10 = $6,480 depreciation, third year
   $64,800 − $6,480 = $58,320 book value, end of third year

2. Farlow Micronics buys a fleet of six cars for its salespersons. The cars cost a total of $90,000. After three years, the cars will be traded in for their book value. Using the declining-balance method and a 30% rate, the total book value of the cars at the end of three years will be $_____30,870_____.

   $90,000 × 0.30 = $27,000 depreciation, first year
   $90,000 − $27,000 = $63,000 book value, end of first year

   $63,000 × 0.30 = $18,900 depreciation, second year
   $63,000 − $18,900 = $44,100 book value, end of second year

   $44,100 × 0.30 = $13,230 depreciation, third year
   $44,100 − $13,230 = $30,870 book value, end of third year

3. Yamora Corporation buys 20 computers for a total cost of $45,000. It plans to sell or trade them after five years. Using the declining-balance method and a 25% rate of depreciation, the book value of the computers at the end of two years will be $25,312.50.

   $45,000 × 0.25 = $11,250 depreciation, first year
   $45,000 − $11,250 = $33,750 book value, end of first year

   $33,750 × 0.25 = $8,437.50 depreciation, second year
   $33.750 − $8,437.50 = $25,312.50 book value, end of second year

Exercise 2.   (Sum-of-the years-digits method of depreciation)

1. The Adams Corporation buys a forge for $20,000. It plans to use it for four years and then trade it in for $4,000. (a) Using the sum-of-the-years-digits method, the amount of depreciation for the first year will be $_____6,400_____; (b) second year, $_____4,800_____; (c) third year, $_____3,200_____; (d) fourth year, $_____1,600_____. (e) The total depreciation for four years will be $_____16,000_____. (f) The book value at the end of four years will be $_____4,000_____.

   a. 1 + 2 + 3 + 4 = 10
      $20,000 − $4,000 = $16,000 total depreciation
      $16,000 × $\frac{4}{10}$ = $6,400 depreciation, first year

   b. $16,000 × $\frac{3}{10}$ = $4,800 depreciation, second year

   c. $16,000 × $\frac{2}{10}$ = $3,200 depreciation, third year

   d. $16,000 × $\frac{1}{10}$ = $1,600 depreciation, fourth year

   e. $6,400 + $4,800 + $3,200 + $1,600 = $16,000 total depreciation for four years

   f. $20,000 − $16,000 = $4,000 book value at the end of four years

LESSON 13-4   SHIPPING AND ADVERTISING COSTS

Exercise

1. For each of the shipments below, find the freight charges.

Shipment	Shipment Weight	Rate on 100 lbs.	Freight Charges	
a.	2,560 lb.	$19.50	$_____499.20_____	a. 2,560 ÷ 100 = 25.6
				25.6 × $19.50 = $499.20 freight charges
b.	1,450 lb.	$23.30	$_____337.85_____	b. 1,450 ÷ 100 = 14.5
				14.5 × $23.30 = $337.85 freight charges
c.	880 lb.	$28.75	$_____253_____	c. 880 ÷ 100 = 8.8
				8.8 × $28.75 = $253 freight charges
d.	3,560 lb.	$17.50	$_____623_____	d. 3,560 ÷ 100 = 35.6
				35.6 × $17.50 = $623 freight charges

FOURTH-CLASS MAIL

Inter-Bulk Mail Center Parcel Post Rates								Weight Not Over (lbs.)
Zone								
1 & 2	3	4	5	6	7	8		
$2.63	$2.79	$2.87	$2.95	$2.95	$2.95	$2.95		2
2.76	3.00	3.34	3.68	3.95	3.95	3.95		3
2.87	3.20	3.78	4.68	4.95	4.95	4.95		4
2.97	3.38	4.10	5.19	5.56	5.95	5.95		5
3.07	3.55	4.39	5.67	6.90	7.75	7.95		6
3.16	3.71	4.67	6.11	7.51	9.15	9.75		7
3.26	3.85	4.91	6.53	8.08	9.94	11.55		8
3.33	3.99	5.16	6.92	8.62	10.65	12.95		9
3.42	4.12	5.38	7.29	9.12	11.31	14.00		10

2. Use the table above, find the total cost of sending the shipments below by parcel post.

Package	Zone	Weight	Postage	Value	Insurance	Total Cost
a.	2	8 lb.	$_____3.26_____	$ 50	$_____0.75_____	$_____4.01_____
b.	5	7 lb.	$_____6.11_____	$150	$_____2.50_____	$_____8.61_____
c.	6	4 lb.	$_____10.84_____	$250	$_____3.40_____	$_____14.24_____
					Total	$_____26.86_____

3. An advertiser plans a one year advertising campaign in the magazine whose rate are shown in Illustration 13-4.2 in the text. The advertiser will be billed at the 12x rate for each of the following ads:

    (a) Four– $\frac{1}{2}$ page 2-color ads   a. ($940 + $225) × 4   = $ 4,660

    (b) Two– 4-color covers   b. ($1,860 + $930) × 2   = $ 5,580

    (c) Three– full page ads   c. $1,820 × 3   = $ 5,460

    (d) Three– $\frac{2}{3}$ page ads   d. $1,220 × 3   = $ 3,660

                                                      $19,360 total amount advertiser paid for ads

What total amount did the advertiser pay for the ads? $_____19,360_____

LESSON 13-5 THE BALANCE SHEET

Exercise

1. Jake Stein owns a greeting card store. The store has assets valued at $79,382 and liabilities of $31,070. Jake's
    capital is $_____48,312_____.

    $79,382 − $31,070 = $48,312 capital

2. Josie Hanks owns a pet care shop. On January 1 she has these items in the business: cash of $2,103, merchandise
    worth $19,742, store supplies worth $305, and store equipment valued at $7,294. She owes the Jarvel Supply
    Company $2,806, and Markham Food Products $1,333. (a) The total of Josie's assets is $_____29,444_____.
    (b) The total of her liabilities is $_____4,139_____. (c) The amount of her capital is $_____25,305_____.

    a. $2,103 + $19,742 + $305 + $7,294 = $29,444 assets
    b. $2,806 + $1,333 = $4,139 liabilities
    c. $29,444 − $4,139 = $25,305 capital

3. Lamont Grubbs owns Creative Arts and Crafts and has these assets: cash, $4,977; merchandise inventory, $50,401;
    store supplies, $934; land and building, $102,000; store equipment, $10,732. He owes the Braden Wholesale
    Company $10,275, United Distributing $4,840, and Eastern Shore Crafts $1,950. (a) His total assets are
    $_____169,044_____. (b) His total liabilities are $_____17,065_____. (c) The amount of his capital is
    $_____151,979_____.

    a. $4,977 + $50,401 + $934 + $102,000 + $10,732 = $169,044 total assets
    b. $10,275 + $4,840 + $1,950 = $17,065 total liabilities
    c. $169,044 − $17,065 = $151,979 capital

4. At the end of the year, Marisa Dressner, owner of T-Shirts & Stuff, made a balance sheet. You are to complete
    this balance sheet by showing (a) the total assets, (b) the total liabilities, (c) the capital, and (d) the total liabilities
    and capital.

T-SHIRTS & STUFF
Balance Sheet, December 31, 19--

Assets				Liabilities			
Cash		$5,936	48	Norko Supply Co.		$1,697	64
Accounts Receivable		639	00	Brogan Shirt Supply		982	36
Merchandise Inventory		40,050	50	First State Bank		3,050	00
Store Supplies		2,251	00	Total Liabilities	b.	$ 5,730	00
Store Equipment		8,432	00				
Office Equipment		1,530	00	**Capital**			
Other Assets		2,495	85	Marisa Dressner, Capital	c.	$55,604	83
Total Assets	a.	$61,334	83	Total Liabilities and Capital	d.	$61,334	83

LESSON 13-6   DISTRIBUTING BUSINESS INCOME

Exercise 1.

1. Bard and Nessalla are partners in a lumber yard. Their partnership agreement shows that net income is to be shared in the ratio of 7 to 5 in favor of Bard. If their business produces a net income of $74,400, Bard's share will be (a) $_____43,400_____ and Nessalla's share will be (b) $_____31,000_____.

   a. $\frac{7}{12} \times \$74,400 = \$43,400$ Bard's share

   b. $\frac{5}{12} \times \$74,400 = \$31,000$ Nessalla's share

2. Stokes invests $80,000 and Zimber invests $120,000 in a partnership they form. (a) If they have no written partnership agreement, each partner's share of a $55,600 profit would be $_____27,800_____. If they agree to share profits and losses in proportion to their investments, Stokes' share of a $15,600 loss would be (b) $_____6,240_____, and Zimber's share would be (c) $9,360.

   a. $\$55,600 \div 2 = \$27,800$ each partner's share

   b. $\$80,000 + \$120,000 = \$200,000$ total investment

   $\frac{\$80,000}{\$200,000} \times \$15,600 = \frac{2}{5} \times \$15,600 = \$6,240$ Stokes' share of loss

   $\frac{\$120,000}{\$200,000} \times \$15,600 = \frac{3}{5} \times \$15,600 = \$9,360$ Zimber's share of loss

3. Stinson and Shaw are partners who share profits and losses in proportion to their investments. Stinson's investment is $30,000 and Shaw's is $40,000. A net income of $38,150 is to be divided between them. Stinson's fractional share of the net income, in lowest terms, is (a) _____$\frac{3}{7}$_____, which amounts to (b) $_____16.350_____. Shaw receives a fractional share of (c) _____$\frac{4}{7}$_____, in lowest terms, which amounts to (d) $_____21,800_____.

   $\$30,000 + \$40,000 = \$70,000$ total investment

   a. $\frac{\$30,000}{\$70,000} = \frac{3}{7}$ Stinson's fractional share

   b. $\frac{3}{7} \times \$38,150 = \$16,350$ amount Stinson receives

   c. $\frac{\$40,000}{\$70,000} = \frac{4}{7}$ Shaw's fractional share

   d. $\frac{4}{7} \times \$38,150 = \$21,800$ amount Shaw receives

4. Three partners have these investments in a business: Akabar, $60,000; Fisher, $75,000; and Zack, $45,000. The business makes a profit of $96,000. The partners agree to share profits in proportion to their investment. (a) Akabar's share of the profit is $_____32,000_____; (b) Fisher's share of the profit is $_____40,000_____; and (c) Zack's share is $_____24,000_____.

   $\$60,000 + \$75,000 + \$45,000 = \$180,000$ total investment

   a. $\frac{\$60,000}{\$180,000} \times \$96,000 = \frac{1}{3} \times \$96,000 = \$32,000$ Akabar's share

   b. $\frac{\$75,000}{\$180,000} \times \$96,000 = \frac{5}{12} \times \$96,000 = \$40,000$ Fisher's share

   c. $\frac{\$45,000}{\$180,000} \times \$96,000 = \frac{1}{4} \times \$96,000 = \$24,000$ Zack's share

Exercise 2.

1. Laura Blain and Andy Subram are partners in a business with investments of $240,000 and $40,000, respectively. Their agreement states that net income is to be divided by paying the partners 8% interest annually on their investments and dividing the rest equally. At the end of one year, the net income is $59,800. In the table below, you are to show the interest both partners receive on their investments and their share of the remaining income. Then show the total income received by both and the totals of all three columns.

Partner	Interest on Investment	Share of Remaining Income	Total Share of Net Income
Laura Blain	$19,200	$18,700	$37,900
Andy Subram	3,200	18,700	21,900
Totals	$22,400	$37,400	$59,800

2. Goldman and Roche are business partners who divide their net income as follows: 54% to Goldman and 46% to Roche. Of a net income of $92,455, Goldman's share is (a) $____49,925.70____ and Roche's share is (b) $____42,529.30____.

   a. 0.54 × $92,455 = $49,925.70 Goldman's share
   b. 0.46 × $92,455 = $42,529.30 Roche's share

3. In the partnership of Hsu and Kang, a net income of $67,350 for one year is divided between the partners in a ratio of 8 to 7. Hsu is given 8 parts and Kang is given 7 parts. (a) Hsu's share of the net income is $____35,920____. (b) Kang's share is $____31,430____.

   a. $\frac{8}{15}$ × $67,350 = $35,920 Hsu's share
   b. $\frac{7}{15}$ × $67,350 = $31,430 Kang's share

4. Three partners in a home improvement company invested these amounts: Alexander, $40,000; Breal, $30,000; Garcia, $20,000. Their agreement provides that each will receive 15% interest on their investment with any remaining income to be distributed in proportion to their investments. If the total net income for a year is $168,300, Alexander will get (a) $____74,800____, Breal will get (b) $____56,100____, and Garcia will get (c) $____37,400____.

   (0.15 × $40,000) + (0.15 × $30,000) + (0.15 × $20,000) = $13,500 interest

   $168,300 − $13,500 = $154,800 balance of net income to be distributed

   $40,000 + $30,000 + $20,000 = $90,000 total investment

   a. $6,000 + ($\frac{$40,000}{$90,000}$ × $154,800) = $74,800 Alexander's share

   b. $4,500 + ($\frac{$30,000}{$90,000}$ × $154,800) = $56,100 Breal's share

   c. $3,000 + ($\frac{$20,000}{$90,000}$ × $154,800) = $37,400 Garcia's share

Exercise 3.

1. A corporation has 80,000 shares of $40 par value stock outstanding. Last year the corporation made a net income of $280,000. The board of directors voted to pay out 80% of the net income as dividends. (a) The amount to be paid out in dividends is $_____224,000_____. (b) The per share dividend rate, as a percent, is _____7_____%. (c) In dollars and cents, the amount of dividend paid per share is $_____2.80_____.

    a. 0.8 × $280,000 = $224,000 amount to be paid out as dividends
    b. 80,000 × $40 = $3,200,000 total value of capital stock
       $224,000 ÷ $3,200,000 = 0.07, or 7% per share dividend rate
    c. $224,000 ÷ 80,000 = $2.80 amount of dividend per share

2. The outstanding capital stock of the Greiner Corporation is 100,000 shares, each with a par value of $40. For the first quarter of this year, the corporation's net income is $346,900. The directors vote to pay a quarterly dividend of 1.8% of the capital stock to the shareholders and to keep the rest in a retained earnings account. (a) The total capital value of the 100,000 shares of stock is $_____4,000,000_____. (b) The total dividend paid to the shareholders is $_____72,000_____. (c) The amount of income kept in the retained earnings account is $_____274,900_____.

    a. 100,000 × $40 = $4,000,000 total value of capital stock
    b. 0.018 × $4,000,000 = $72,000 total dividends to be paid
    c. $346,900 − $72,000 = $274,900 amount kept in retained earnings account

3. A corporation with 140,000 shares of capital stock outstanding earns in one quarter a net income of $173,683. The directors vote to pay the regular quarterly dividend of 37.5 cents a share and to keep the rest in the retained earnings account. (a) The total dividend paid to the shareholders is $_____52,500_____. (b) The amount kept in the retained earnings account is $_____121,183_____.

    a. 140,000 × $0.375 = $52,500 total dividend paid
    b. $173,683 − $52,500 = $121,183 amount kept in retained earnings account

4. The outstanding capital stock of a company is 15,000 shares of 6% preferred stock (par value $50) and 140,000 shares of common stock (no-par value). For the first half of the year, the corporation's net income is $472,458. The directors declare the regular 3% semiannual dividend on the preferred stock, a dividend of $0.47 a share on the common stock, and vote to keep the rest of the income in the retained earnings account. (a) The total dividend on the preferred stock is $_____22,500_____. (b) The total dividend on the common stock is $_____65,800_____. (c) The amount kept in the retained earnings account is $_____384,158_____.

    a. 0.03 × (15,000 × $50) = $22,500 total dividend on preferred stock
    b. 140,000 × $0.47 = $65,800 total dividend on common stock
    c. $472,458 − ($22,500 + $65,800) = $384,158 kept in retained earnings

5. At the end of one year, the directors of the Dreggen County Feed Cooperative declare a 9% dividend on the capital stock and a 3% patronage dividend to the cooperative's customers. Carol Hull, a rancher, owns 250 shares of the capital stock, par value $20 per share. During the year she bought $64,300 worth of feed from the cooperative. She should receive a total dividend of $_____2,379_____.

    0.09 × (250 × $20) = $450 dividend on capital stock
    0.03 × $64,300 = $1,929 patronage dividend
    $450 + $1,929 = $2,379 total dividend she should receive

LESSON 13-7   BANKRUPTCY

Exercise

1. Ted Benning owns a retail golf shop. He cannot pay his debts and is forced into bankruptcy. After selling the assets and paying the bankruptcy costs, the trustee has cash to pay creditors 31% of their claims. (a) If Benning owes the Universal Sports Company $26,750, that company should receive $___8,292.50___. (b) Another company, Lite Sports Clothing, has a claim against Benning for $18,460, and should receive $___5,722.60___.

    a. 0.31 × $26,750 = $8,292.50 Universal Sports Company should receive
    b. 0.31 × $18,460 = $5,722.60 Lite Sports Clothing should receive

2. Nell's Surplus Outlet has debts of $120,000. The store goes bankrupt and its assets are sold. After bankruptcy costs are paid, $51,600 is left to pay creditors' claims. (a) The trustee can pay ___43___% of the creditors' claims. (b) The Glade City Electric Company, with a claim of $976, will get $___419.68___.

    a. $51,600 ÷ $120,000 = 0.43, or 43% of creditors' claims can be paid
    b. 0.43 × $976 = $419.68 amount Glade City Electric Company will receive

3. Paine's Custom Shirt Shop is a bankrupt business with debts of $36,000. The trustee has $10,080 cash for payment to creditors. (a) To settle their claims, the creditors will be paid ___28___¢ on the dollar. (b) A creditor with a claim of $1,585 will be paid $___443.80___.

    a. $10,080 ÷ $36,000 = 0.28, or 28% of the claims can be paid
       0.28 × 100¢, = 28¢, on the dollar to be paid
    b. 0.28 × $1,585 = $443.80 paid on creditor's claim

4. Ted Werner's photography studio was declared bankrupt. After selling the company's assets for $8,380, the trustee paid $4,600 for bankruptcy fees and paid creditors' claims of $25,200 with the rest of the money. (a) The amount that was left to pay creditors' claims was $___3,780___. (b) The percent of claims that each creditor got was ___15___%. (c) Kern's Developing, one of the creditors, had a claim for $2,600 and was paid $___390___.

    a. $8,380 − $4,600 = $3,780 amount left to pay creditors
    b. $3,780 ÷ $25,200 = 0.15, or 15% of each claim can be paid
    c. 0.15 × $2,600 = $390 amount Kern's Developing was paid

5. When Unique Designs was declared bankrupt, it owed its creditors $87,500. A trustee sold the assets of Unique Designs for $24,353. From this money, the trustee must first pay court costs and other bankruptcy charges totaling $4,228. Creditors of Unique Designs will be paid from the remaining money. (a) The total amount available to pay creditors' claims is $___20,125___. (b) The total amount of their claims that the creditors will lose is $___67.375___. (c) Each creditor will receive only ___23___¢ on the dollar.

    a. $24,353 − $4,228 = $20,125 amount available to pay creditors' claims
    b. $87,500 − $20,125 = $67,375 amount creditors will lose
    c. $20,125 ÷ $87,500 = 0.23, or 23% of claims can be paid
       0.23 × 100¢ = 23¢ on the dollar to be paid

TERM TICKLER

Directions: Each group of scrambled letters can be sorted to spell a word or phrase in Chapter 13. Place the sorted letters for the key word in the spaces given.

a. Sort out the letters below.

1. tiesialibil
2. rentoviny
3. pactali kcost
4. platica
5. hemriscedan tinynorve

6. tear of viddined
7. na tgoiper nessepex
8. clanabe tehes
9. stases
10. etn monice

11. lose soepphotriprir
12. trecoids
13. phirstanper
14. leass
15. ten sols

1. l i a b i l i t i e [s]
2. i n v e n t [o] r y
3. [c] a p i t a l   s t o c k
4. c a p i [t] a l
5. [m] e r c h a n d i s e
    i n v e n t o r y
6. r a t e   o f   d i v i d e [n] d
7. o p e r a t i n g
    e x p e n [s] e s
8. b a l a n c e   s h e [e] t
9. [a] s s e t s
10. n e t   [i] n c o m e
11. s o l [e]
    p r o p r i e t o r s [h] i p
12. c r e [d] i t o r s
13. p a r t n e [r] s h i p
14. s a [l] e s
15. n e t   l o s [s]

b. The letters in the boxes can be sorted into a term used in Chapter 13. Complete the term started below.

[c] [o] [s] [t]   [o] [f]
[m] [e] [r] [c] [h] [a] [n] [d] [i] [s] [e]   [s] [o] [l] [d]

INTEGRATED PROJECT 13

Directions: Read through the entire project before you begin doing any work.

Introduction: A partially completed annual income statement and balance sheet for the Agotec Company follows. The business was formed by three partners who invested these amounts of money in the business: Gerhard Ling, $40,000; Lenore Snead, $60,000; Stanley Wu, $20,000.

Their partnership agreement to distribute net income calls for these fixed payments to be made to the partners: Ling, $12,000; Snead, $14,500; Wu, $22,000. In addition, each of the partners is paid 7% interest on his/her investments in the business. After deducting the fixed payments and interest payments from the net income, any remaining net income is to be divided in this way: 50% to Ling, 30% to Snead, 20% to Wu.

In comparison to its competitors, the Agotec Company is more profitable because of its repeat business. Because of the company's success and for legal reasons, the partners are planning to form a corporation. When they do, 24,000 shares of stock will be issued. Each partner will receive shares of stock in proportion to the amount of each partner's capital account.

AGOTEC COMPANY
Income Statement, For the Year Ended December 31, 19--

		Percentage Analysis
Sales	$407,800	
Less Sales Returns and Allowances	7,800	
Net Income	$ 400,000	100 %
Cost of Merchandise Sold:		
Merchandise Inventory, January 1	$36,000	
Purchases	237,000	
Merchandise Available for Sale	$273,000	
Less Merchandise Inventory, December 31	33,000	
Cost of Merchandise Sold	240,000	60 %
Gross Profit on Sales	$ 160,000	40 %
Operating Expenses:		
Employee Wages	$32,800	
Rent	13,000	
Taxes	8,850	
Utilities	8,213	
Advertising	8,987	
Depreciation of Equipment	2,470	
Truck Repair and Maintenance	8,530	
Insurance	3,100	
Other Expenses	2,050	
Total Operating Expenses	88,000	22 %
Net Income	$ 72,000	18 %

AGOTEC COMPANY
Balance Sheet, December 31, 19--

Assets			Liabilities		
Cash	$57,600		Anders Company	$50,000	
Accounts Receivable	31,400		Elgor Products	34,000	
Office Supplies	3,775		Total Liabilities		$ 84,000
Merchandise Inventory	33,000		**Capital**		
Office Equipment	14,740				
Warehouse Equipment	34,360		Gerhard Ling, Capital	$40,000	
Delivery Truck	29,125		Lenore Snead, Capital	60,000	
Total Assets	$ 204,000		Stanley Wu, Capital	20,000	
			Total Capital		$ 120,000
			Total Liabilities and Capital		$ 204,000

Step One: Fill in the missing amounts and percentages on the income statement. Also fill in the missing amounts on the balance sheet. Then answer the following questions.

1. Did the Agotec Company have more merchandise on hand at the beginning or end of the year? How much more or less? _____$3,000 more at beginning of year_____

   $36,000 − $33,000 = $3,000 more at beginning of year

2. On the average, what amount of net income did the Agotec Company earn each month? $_____6,000_____

   $72,000 ÷ 12 = $6,000 average monthly net income

3. What was the merchandise turnover rate for the year, correct to two decimal places? _____6.96_____

   ($36,000 + $33,000) ÷ 2 = $34,500 average merchandise inventory
   $240,000 ÷ $34,500 = 6.956, or 6.96 annual turnover rate

Step Two: Complete the following table by figuring each partner's share of the net income under the current partner-ship agreement.

AGOTEC COMPANY
Distribution of Net Income to Partners

Partner	Fixed Payment	Interest on Investment	Share of Remaining Net Income	Total Amount Received
Ling, Gerhard	$12,000	$2,800	$ 7,550	$22,350
Snead, Lenore	$14,500	$4,200	$ 4,530	$23,230
Wu, Stanley	$22,000	$1,400	$ 3,020	$26,420
Total	$48,500	$8,400	$15,100	$72,000

0.07 × $40,000 = $2,800 Ling's interest   0.50 × $15,100 = $7,550 Ling's share
0.07 × $60,000 = $4,200 Snead's interest   0.30 × $15,100 = $4,530 Snead's share
0.07 × $20,000 = $1,400 Wu's interest   0.20 × $15,100 = $3,020 Wu's share
                        $8,400 total

$72,000 − ($48,500 + $8,400) =$15,100 remaining net income to be divided

1. Which partner received the largest amount from the distribution of the company's net income? ___Wu, $26,420___

2. Which partner earned the largest amount of interest on the amount invested in the business? ___Snead, $4,200___

3. Assume that the partners had agreed to change their partnership agreement and divided all net income equally.

   a. What would have been each partner's share of net income? $_____24,000_____

   b. Compared to the original agreement, which partner would have given up the largest amount of net income by dividing income equally? _____Wu_____

   c. How much money would have been given up by that partner? $_____2,420_____

   a. $72,000 ÷ 3 = $24,000 value of equal share
   b. Wu
   c. $26,420 − $24,000 = $2,420 amount given up by Wu

Step Three: Assume that the Agotec Company becomes a corporation and earns the same net income shown on the income statement. Answer these questions about the corporation.

1. List the number of shares of stock each partner would receive when the shares are issued:

   a. Ling, _____8,000_____ shares $\frac{\$40,000}{\$120,000}$ × 24,000 = 8,000 shares

   b. Snead, _____12,000_____ shares $\frac{\$60,000}{\$120,000}$ × 24,000 = 12,000 shares

   c. Wu, _____4,000_____ shares $\frac{\$20,000}{\$120,000}$ × 24,000 = 4,000 shares

2. If all of the net income is distributed as a dividend, what annual per share dividend will be paid? $_____3_____

   $72,000 ÷ 24,000 = $3 dividend per share

   Based on that per share dividend, what amount of net income will be distributed to each of the three shareholders?

   a. Ling, $_____24,000_____   8,000 × $3 = $24,000 Ling's dividend

   b. Snead, $_____36,000_____   12,000 × $3 = $36,000 Snead's dividend

   c. Wu, $_____12,000_____   4,000 × $3 = $12,000 Wu's dividend

3. Assume that 40% of the net income is to be kept in the business as retained earnings in order to help expand the business.

   a. The amount of net income to be kept as retained earnings will be $_____28,800_____.

   0.40 × $72,000 = $28,800 kept as retained earnings

   b. The net income available to be paid out as a dividend is $_____43,200_____. This will be equal to a per share annual dividend of $_____1.80_____.

   $72,000 − $28,800 = $43,200 amount available for dividends
   $43,200 ÷ 24,000 = $1.80 annual dividend per share

Step Four: The balance sheet of the GRA Company, a competitor of the Agotec Company, follows. Any numbers enclosed in parentheses are negative numbers. Use the data in the balance sheet to answer questions about the GRA Company's financial condition.

GRA COMPANY
Balance Sheet, June 30, 19--

Assets			Liabilities	
Cash	$2,340		Armand Delivery Service	$21,100
Accounts Receivable	4,660		Lex Distributing	48,000
Office Supplies	1,200		Kingsbury Electric Co.	4,100
Merchandise Inventory	11,020		Sintel Management Co.	16,800
Office Equipment	8,420		Total Liabilities	$90,000
Stock Handling Equipment	22,360			
Total Assets	$50,000		**Capital**	
			Stuart Lawson, Capital	($40,000)
			Total Liabilities and Capital	$50,000

1. How much greater than its assets are the debts of the GRA Company? $_____40,000_____

    $90,000 − $50,000 = $40,000 amount by which debts are greater

2. If the GRA Company is declared bankrupt, what percent of its debts, to the nearest percent, can be paid to creditors based on the assets on hand on June 30? _____56_____%

    $50,000 ÷ $90,000 = 0.555, or 56% of debts can be paid

3. If a court-appointed receiver can turn into cash only 90% of the total assets of the business, how many cents on the dollar can be paid to each creditor? _____50_____

    0.90 × $50,000 = $45,000 cash value of assets
    $45,000 ÷ $90,000 = 0.50, or 50% of the claims can be paid
    0.50 × 100¢ = 50¢ can be paid on the dollar to creditors

4. How much money would Stuart Lawson, owner of the GRA Company, have to add to the business in order to have enough assets to cover all of the company's debts? $_____40,000_____

    $90,000 − $50,000 = $40,000 must be added to cover debts

Name: _____   Date: _____

DOING BUSINESS IN A GLOBAL ECONOMY

LESSON 14-1   PURCHASING FOR A BUSINESS

Exercise 1.

1. For the purchase invoice shown below, check each extension and the total of the invoice (a–e). Place a check mark on the line provided next to the amount if it is correct. If the amount is wrong, write the correct answer on the line.

990 Barrancas Avenue
Pensacola, FL 32501

BALFOUR
Metal Cookware Company

SOLD TO: **A&M Variety**
        298 Hoover Road
        Hammond, LA 70401

DATE: **March 16, 19--**

TERMS: **n/45**

QUANTITY	UNIT	DESCRIPTION	UNIT PRICE	AMOUNT
48	each	6-inch frying pan	$6.50	$312.00
96	set	measuring spoons	1.75	168.00
24	each	roasting pan, medium	9.25	222.00
36	each	baking sheet, #1218	7.10	255.00
			PAY THIS AMOUNT	$957.00

a. _____✔_____

b. _____✔_____

c. _____✔_____

d. _____255.60_____

e. _____957.60_____

f. What is the due date of the invoice? _____April 30_____

g. Will A & M Variety be given any discount for paying the invoice early? _____No_____

2. During March, A & M Variety's total purchases were $28,800. They returned $350.87 worth of goods as being unusable and received an allowance of $129.50 from the manufacturer for clothing that was soiled. (a) The total sales returns and allowances were $480.37. (b) The net purchases for March were $_____28,319.63_____.

   a. $350.87 + $129.50 = $480.37 total sales returns and allowances
   b. $28,800.00 − $480.37 = $28,319.63 net purchases

3. In each of the following, the unit prices are combinations of fractional equivalents of one dollar. Find each extension by using fractional equivalents.

   a. 40 @ $1.25 = $_____50_____ $(40 \times \$1) + (40 \times \frac{1}{4}) = \$50$

   b. 20 @ $2.75 = $_____55_____ $(20 \times \$2) + (20 \times \frac{3}{4}) = \$55$

   c. 12 @ $4.10 = $_____49.20_____ $(12 \times \$4) + (12 \times \frac{1}{10}) = \$49.20$

   d. 30 @ $3.50 = $_____105_____ $(30 \times \$3) + (30 \times \frac{1}{2}) = \$105$

Exercise 2.

1. A 36% trade discount is given by a manufacturer on an office desk with a list price of $480. (a) The amount of the discount is $_____172.80_____. (b) The invoice price is $_____307.20_____.

   a. $0.36 \times \$480 = \$172.80$ amount of discount
   b. $\$480.00 - \$172.80 = \$307.20$ invoice price

2. Rep-Drives, Inc., a disk drive manufacturer, offers a computer repair dealer a hard drive at a list price of $255, less a $33\frac{1}{3}$% trade discount. (a) The amount to be deducted from the list price as a discount is $_____85_____.
(b) To buy one drive, the retailer must pay an invoice price of $_____170_____.

   a. $0.33\frac{1}{3} \times \$255 = \$85$ amount of discount
   b. $\$255 - \$85 = \$170$ invoice price

3. To clear out old stock, a manufacturer offers retailers a 60% trade discount on a stereo cassette player that lists for $29 in a catalog. After subtracting the discount of (a) $_____17.40_____, the retailers will pay an invoice price of (b) $_____11.60_____ for the cassette players.

   a. $0.6 \times \$29 = \$17.40$ amount of discount
   b. $\$29.00 - \$17.40 = \$11.60$ invoice price

4. A wholesaler offers the following quantity discounts on athletic shoes: 50 pairs, 2.5%; 51–100 pairs, 3.7%; 101–200 pairs, 4.5%; over 200 pairs, 6%. If a retailer buys 150 pairs at an average price of $28.30, the retailer gets a quantity discount of (a) $_____191.03_____ and pays an invoice price of (b) $_____4,053.97_____.

   a. $150 \times \$28.30 = \$4,245$ cost of shoes
     $0.045 \times \$4,245 = \$191.03$ amount quantity discount
   b. $\$4,245.00 - \$191.03 = \$4,053.97$ invoice price

5. A gross of car mats that was sold to an auto parts store for $1,508 has a list price of $2,320. On this purchase, the retailer received a _____35_____% rate of trade discount.

   $(\$2,320 - \$1,508) \div \$2,320 = 0.35$, or 35% rate of discount

6. The Dreller Supply Company sells a lawn chair at an invoice price of $10.08; the catalog price is $24. A retailer who buys the lawn chair at the invoice price receives a _____42_____% rate of discount from the catalog price.

   $(\$24.00 - \$10.08) \div \$24 = 0.42$, or 42% rate of discount

Exercise 3.

1. On August 26, a recently hired office clerk found three invoices in an open file which have not been paid. The dated invoices and their credit terms follow:

Invoice	Invoice Date	Credit Terms
1387	August 24	2/10, n/30
8299	August 9	3/15, 1/30, n/60
5571	August 1	4/20 EOM

The last dates on which the invoices may be paid and a cash discount taken are: (a) Invoice 1387, ____September 3____; (b) Invoice 8299, ____September 8____; (c) Invoice 5571, ____September 20____.

2. You buy merchandise for $822.40 on February 5. The terms are 1/15, n/20. If you pay the invoice by February 20, how much should you pay? $____814.18____

$822.40 − (0.01 × $822.40) = $814.18 you should pay

3. Dreisen Manufacturing sells a snow thrower to the Trent Bay Cooperative for $360, less 20% and 15%. The invoice dated October 3, has credit terms of 3/10, n/30. If the invoice is paid on October 13, the cash price will be $____237.46____.

$360 − $72 = $288
$288.00 − $43.20 = $244.80 invoice price
$244.80 − (0.03 × $244.80) = $237.46 cash price

4. Elgin Distributors allows retail dealers trade discounts of 20% and 10%. Credit terms are 4/10, n/45. Elgin sells and delivers to the Rent-It Shop 160 folding chairs listed at $30 each. The delivery charge for the order is $120. The invoice for the folding chairs and delivery charge, dated July 8, is paid by the Rent-It Shop on July 17. The amount of the payment is $____3,437.76____.

160 × $30 = $4,800 list price of chairs
$4,800 − $960 = $3,840
$3,840 − $384 = $3,456 invoice price of chairs
$3,456 − (0.04 × $3,456) = $3,317.76 cash price of chairs
$3,317.76 + $120.00 = $3,437.76 amount of payment

5. If a retailer paid cash for a purchase, a wholesaler offered to sell a certain style of shoes at $36.10 a pair instead of the usual price of $38. (a) The amount of the cash discount per pair of shoes is $____1.90____. (b) The rate of discount is ____5____%.

a. $38.00 − $36.10 = $1.90 amount of discount
b. $1.90 ÷ $38 = 0.05, or 5% rate of discount

Exercise 4.

1. The Lawn Store buys from Ricardo's Supply the merchandise in the invoice below. The shipment weighs 2,100 pounds, and the cost of truck freight is $14.75 per 100 pounds. Complete the invoice by finding (a) the amount of the trade discount, (b) the invoice price, (c) the freight cost, and (d) the total of the invoice.

RICARDO'S SUPPLY
143 Bowing Avenue
St. Louis, MO 63116-7821

SOLD TO: **The Lawn Store**
1414 Main Street
Belleville, IL 62221-5753

SHIPPED VIA	DATE	INVOICE NO.	YOUR ORDER	F.O.B.	TERMS
Truck	3/6/--	9-1208	589	St. Louis	2/10, n/30

QUANTITY	STOCK NO.	DESCRIPTION	UNIT PRICE	AMOUNT	
15	CS108	Chain saws	125.90	1,888.50	
10	R2265	Power rakes	108.70	1,087.00	
20	B9898	Bag attachments	130.70	2,614.00	5,589.50
		Less 25% and 10%		a. 1,816.59	
				b. 3,772.91	
		Freight		c. 309.75	
		Total		d. 4,082.66	

a. $5,589.50 × 0.25 = $1,397.38 first discount
$5,589.50 − $1,397.38 = $4,192.12
$4,192.12 × 0.10 = $419.21 second discount
$1,397.38 + $419.21 = $1,816.59 total discount

b. $5,589.50 − $1,816.59 = $3,772.91 invoice price
c. (2,100 ÷ 100) × $14.75 = $309.75
d. $3,772.91 + $309.75 = $4,082.66 total of invoice

2. You are a buyer for Marion Sales, Inc. You can buy the items below on the terms shown. Show (a) the invoice price of each item, and (b) the total cost.

	List Price of Item	Discounts	Invoice Price of Item	Freight	Total Cost of Item
a.	$2,560	25%—10%	$1,728.00	$103.50	$1,831.50
b.	$1,080	20%—5%	$820.80	$45.80	$866.60
c.	$960	10%—10%—5%	$738.72	$67.52	$806.24
d.	$420	25%—12$\frac{1}{2}$%—10%	$248.06	$30.30	$278.36

a. $2,560 − ($2,560 × 0.25) = $1,920
$1,920 − ($1,920 × 0.10) = $1,728 invoice price
$1,728 + $103.50 = $1,831.50 total cost

b. $1,080 − ($1,080 × 0.20) = $864
$864 − ($864 × 0.05) = $820.80 invoice price
$820.80 + $45.80 = $866.60 total cost

c. $960 − ($960 × 0.10) = $864
$864 − ($864 × 0.10) = $777.60
$777.60 − ($777.60 × 0.05) = $738.72 invoice price
$738.72 + $67.52 = $806.24 total cost

d. $420 − ($420 × 0.25) = $315
$315 − ($315 × 0.125) = $275.62
$275.62 − ($275.62 × 0.10) = $248.06 invoice price
$248.06 + $30.30 = $278.36 total cost

LESSON 14-2   SERIES DISCOUNTS

Exercise

1. Nora's Lamp Shop buys a floor lamp, listed at $140 less discounts of 20%, 10%, and 5%. The invoice price of the lamp is $_____95.76_____.

   $140 − $28 = $112
   $112 − $11.20 = $100.80
   $100.80 − $5.04 = $95.76 invoice price

2. A paper shredder lists at $260 with discounts to the dealer of 30% and 8%. (a) The shredder costs the dealer $_____167.44_____. (b) The total trade discount is $_____92.56_____.

   a. $260 − $78 = $182
      $182.00 − $14.56 = $167.44 invoice price
   b. $260 − $167.44 = $92.56 trade discount

3. The list price of a fire-resistant filing cabinet is $798. Dealers may buy the filing cabinet at a discount of $33\frac{1}{3}\%$, 5%, and 5%. The invoice price of the filing cabinet is $_____480.13_____.

   $798 − $266 = $532
   $532.00 − $26.60 = $505.40
   $505.40 − $25.27 = $480.13 invoice price

4. A retailer may buy a travel garment bag from the Keller Company for $120 less 25% and 5%. The same bag may be purchased from Belk Distributors for $118, less 20%, 5%, 5%. The invoice price of the bag from Keller is (a) $_____85.50_____ and (b) $_____85.20_____ from Belk. By buying at the lower price, the retailer can save (c) $_____0.30_____ per bag.

   a. $120 − $30 = $90
      $90.00 − $4.50 = $85.50 invoice price from Keller
   b. $118.00 − $23.60 = $94.40
      $94.40 − $4.72 = $89.68
      $89.68 − $4.48 = $85.20 invoice price from Belk
   c. $85.50 − $85.20 = $0.30 amount retailer can save

5. What is the single discount that is equivalent to the trade discount series 32%, 10%, 5%? _____41.86_____ %

   100% − 32% = 68%
   68% − 6.8% = 61.2%
   61.20% − 3.06% = 58.14% invoice price as percent
   100.00% − 58.14% = 41.86% single discount equivalent

6. A retailer can buy a racing bicycle with a list price of $800 at trade discounts of 25%, 15%, 4%. This discount series is equivalent to a single discount of _____38.8_____ %.

   100% − 25% = 75%
   75.00% − 11.25% = 63.75%
   63.75% − 2.55% = 61.2% invoice price as a percent
   100.0% − 61.2% = 38.8% single discount equivalent

LESSON 14-3   PRICING FOR PROFIT

Exercise 1.

1. A newspaper ad reads "Portable stereo radio recorder—was $88—now $52.80." The price of the stereo was reduced by (a) $_____35.20_____. (b) This is _____40_____% of the original marked price.

    a. $88.00 − $52.80 = $35.20 discount amount
    b. $35.20 ÷ $88.00 = 40% discount percent

2. The round-trip first-class fare to a resort city is $350. An economy fare ticket costs $280. If you bought the economy ticket, you would save _____20_____%.

    $350 − $280 = $70 amount of discount
    $70 ÷ $350 = 20% rate of discount

3. At a fast food shop, a seafood dinner that regularly sells for $7.90 is sold on sale at 2 dinners for $11.85. If you buy 2 dinners at the sale price, you get a discount of _____25_____% from the regular price.

    $7.90 × 2 = $15.80 cost of two dinners at regular price
    $15.80 − $11.85 = $3.95 amount of discount
    $3.95 ÷ $15.80 = 25% rate of discount

4. The Wintry Market advertised a pair of skis at a 15% discount from the regular price. The ad included a coupon worth $20 in trade. Russ James bought a cross-country ski outfit regularly priced at $325 and gave the coupon to the clerk. Russ paid $_____256.25_____ for the outfit.

    $325 × 0.15 = $48.75 amount of discount
    $48.75 + $20.00 = $68.75 total discounts
    $325 − $68.75 = $256.25 cost of outfit

5. A discount store catalog tells you that your actual purchase price will be 35% less than the price shown. Your actual price for a set of luggage priced at $428 would be $_____278.20_____.

    $428 × 0.35 = $149.80 amount of discount
    $428 − $149.80 = $278.20 actual price of luggage

6. The sales manager at the music store at which you work tells you to sell all stock at $12\frac{1}{2}$% off the price marked on the tags and to add a 5% sales tax for each sale. For an electronic keyboard that has a price tag marked $4,250, you should charge (a) $_____3,718.75_____ plus a sales tax of (b) $_____185.94_____.

    a. $12\frac{1}{2}$% = $\frac{1}{8}$
        $\frac{1}{8}$ × $4,250 = $531.25
        $4,250 − $531.25 = $3,718.75 sale price of keyboard
    b. $3,718.75 × 0.05 = $185.94 sales tax

Exercise 2.

1. Thrifty Hardware Company buys a line of faucets at $80 each, less 20% and 10%. The store sells them at $90 each. The store's markup is (a) $_____32.40_____ each. This is (b) _____36_____% of the selling price.

   a. $80 × 0.20 = $16 first discount
      $80 − $16 = $64
      $64 × 0.10 = $6.40 second discount
      $64.00 − $6.40 = $57.60 invoice price of faucets
      $90.00 − $57.60 = $32.40
   b. $32.40 ÷ $90.00 = 0.36, or 36% rate of markup based on selling price

2. Abrams Electronics, Inc. bought some speaker systems for $275 each, less 40%. They marked the speakers to sell for $300. At a sale, the store sold the speakers at 20% off the marked price. On each speaker sold at the sale, the store made a markup of (a) $_____75_____. This was (b) _____31.25_____% of the sale price.

   a. $275 − ($275 × 0.40) = $165 invoice price of speakers
      $300 × 0.20 = $60 discount off marked price
      $300 − $60 = $240 sale price
      $240 − $165 = $75 markup price
   b. $75 ÷ $240 = 0.3125, or 31.25% rate of markup based on selling price

3. Kerry Topolo, a wholesale furniture dealer, bought 50 end tables at $89 each and marked them to sell for $140. She sold 36 at that price and then closed out the rest at $110 each. Her average markup per table was $_____42.60_____.

   36 × $140 = $5,040 gross income from first group
   50 − 36 = 14 tables
   14 × $110 = $1,540 gross income from rest
   $5,040 + $1,540 = $6,580 gross income from sales of end tables
   50 × $89 = $4,450 cost of end tables
   $6,580 − $4,450 = $2,130 markup of lot
   $2,130 ÷ 50 = $42.60 average markup per table

4. Tomas's Sporting Center buys hunting bows at $135 and sells them at $200. Operating expenses average $44 per bow. The markup on each bow is (a) $_____65_____. The net income on each bow is (b) $_____21_____. The net income per bow is (c) _____10.5_____% of the selling price.

   a. $200 − $135 = $65 markup on each bow
   b. $200 − ($135 + $44) = $21 net income per bow
   c. $21 ÷ $200 = 0.105, or 10.5% rate of net income on selling price

5. The Corner Store sells a line of sweaters for $52. The sweaters cost the Store $34.32 each. The Store's operating expenses average 25% of the selling price. The Store's net income on each sweater is (a) $_____4.68_____. This is (b) _____9_____% of the selling price.

    a. $52 × 0.25 = $13 operating expenses on each sweater
        $52 − ($13 + $34.32) = $4.68 net income per sweater
    b. $4.68 ÷ $52 = 0.09, or 9% rate of net income on selling price

6. An artist supply store bought 35 easels listed at $160 each, less 20% and 10%, and sold them for $190 each. The store's estimated operating expenses were 15% of the selling price and it paid its salespeople a commission of 3%. The store's net income on the easels was _____21.4_____% of the selling price, to the nearest tenth of a percent.

    $160 × 0.20 = $32 first trade discount
    $160 − $32 = $128
    $128 × 0.10 = $12.80 second trade discount
    $128.00 − $12.80 = $115.20 invoice price
    $190 × (0.15 + 0.03) = $34.20 operating expenses and commission
    $190 − ($115.20 + $34.20) = $40.60 net income per easel
    $40.60 ÷ $190 = 0.2136, or 21.4% rate of net income on selling price

Exercise 3.   (Finding cost price when selling price and rate of markup are known)

1. As the buyer for Kelly's Fitness Store, you are buying exercise bikes for the line that sells at $99.80. The most that you can pay for bikes and maintain a markup of 45% of the selling price is $_____54.89_____

    100% − 45% = 55% cost, as a percent
    $99.80 × 0.55 = $54.89 most you can pay for bikes

2. Your store sells water skis in two price lines. An inexpensive ski set sells for $69.50. A better ski set sells for $95. The highest cost price you can pay for each of these lines and make a markup of 48% of the selling price is (a) $_____36.14_____ for the inexpensive ski set and (b) $_____49.40_____ for the better ski set.

    a. 100% − 48% = 52% cost, as a percent of the selling price
        $69.50 × 0.52 = $36.14 most you can pay for inexpensive ski set
    b. $95 × 0.52 = $49.40 most you can pay for the better ski set

3. You must buy golf bags for a line that sells for $89. The most that you can pay for the bags and make a markup of 34% on the selling price is $_____58.74_____.

    100% − 34% = 66% cost, as a percent of the selling price
    $89 × 0.66 = $58.74 most you can pay for the golf bags

Exercise 4.

1. By buying garage door openers for $128 each and selling them for $176.64 each, the Market Loft made a markup of (a) $_____48.64_____, which was (b) _____38_____% of the cost price.

   a. $176.64 − $128.00 = $48.64 markup
   b. $48.64 ÷ $128.00 = 0.38, or 38% rate of markup based on cost

2. Joselyn's Hardware sold 20 hand trucks at $19.50, and 10 more at $16.50. The store's net markup on the trucks was (a) $_____180_____. The store's rate of net markup was (b) _____48_____% of the cost.

   a. (20 × $19.50) + (10 × $16.50) = $555 total sales dollars received for trucks
   b. $180 ÷ $375 = 0.48, or 48% rate of markup on cost

3. A farm implement dealer buys post hole diggers, delivered, for $249.50 each. The dealer wants to sell them at a price which will yield a gross profit of 60% of the cost. (a) The markup on each digger should be $_____149.70_____. (b) The selling price should be $_____399.20_____.

   a. $249.50 × 0.60 = $149.70 markup on cost
   b. $249.50 + $149.70 = $399.20 selling price of diggers

4. One-Stop Building Supply Company pays $49.94 each for ladders. The company wants a 45% markup on the cost. It should sell the ladders for $_____72.41_____ each.

   $49.94 × 0.45 = $22.473, or $22.47 markup on ladders
   $49.94 + $22.47 = $72.41 price at which ladders should be sold

5. Armco Distributing Company buys air compressors for $1,130. Armco wants a markup of 65% on its cost. The lowest price at which Armco can sell the compressors and make the rate of markup they want is $_____1,864.50_____.

   $1,130 × 0.65 = $734.50 markup on compressors
   $1,130 + $734.50 = $1,864.50 lowest selling price for compressors

LESSON 14-4   FINDING THE BREAK-EVEN POINT

Exercise 1.   (Finding gross profit and net income)

1. Mercer Music Co. made and sold 400 banjos to a wholesaler at $85 each. The manufacturing costs were materials, $6,837; labor, $9,571; overhead, $4,054. (a) The manufacturer's gross profit on the order was $_____13,538_____. (b) The average factory cost per banjo, to the nearest whole cent, was $_____51.16_____.

    400 × $85 = $34,000 selling price
    $6,837 + $9,571 + $4,054 = $20,462 total factory cost
    $34,000 − $20,462 = $13,538 gross profit
    $20,462 ÷ 400 = $51.16 average factory cost per banjo

2. Darts that sell for $1.25 each cost $8.20 a dozen to make. The manufacturer's selling and administrative expenses are 35% of the selling price. The net income per dozen darts is $_____1.55_____.

    $1.25 × 12 = $15 selling price of darts per dozen
    $15 × 0.35 = $5.25 selling and administrative expenses
    $15 − ($8.20 + $5.25) = $1.55 net income per dozen darts

Exercise 2.   (Finding the break-even point)

1. Jackson Sporting Company estimates fixed costs of $19,125 and variable costs of $44,625 to produce and sell 3,000 baseball bases. The selling price of the bases is to be $25 each.

    a.   To break even, the company must have sales income of $_____63,750_____ from this operation.

    b.   At a selling price of $25 each, _____2,550_____ of the bases must be sold to break even.

    c.   If the company sells all 3,000 bases at $25 each, the net income will be $_____11,250_____.

    a. $19,125 + $44,625 = $63,750 break-even point
    b. $63,750 ÷ $25 = 2,550 bases must be sold to break even
    c. 3,000 × $25 = $75,000 gross selling price if all are sold at $25
       $75,000 − $63,750 = $11,250 net income if all are sold at $25

2. A firm plans to sell a new product for $350 each. The fixed cost to produce 1,000 units of the product is estimated to be $133,000. The maximum variable cost the firm can have and break even on the sale of the product is (a) $_____217,000_____ per 1,000 units, or (b) $_____217_____ per unit.

    a. $350 × 1,000 = $350,000 selling price
       $350,000 − $133,000 = $217,000 maximum variable cost
    b. $217,000 ÷ 1,000 = $217 maximum variable cost per unit

3. Albany Fashions, Inc. expects fixed expenses of $2,000 and variable expenses of $6,000 to produce and sell 1,000 shirts. (a) To break even, the company must sell all the shirts for at least $_____8_____ each. (b) To make a net income of 30% of the total cost, the company must sell the shirts for $_____10.40_____ each.

    a. $2,000 + $6,000 = $8,000 total cost
       $8,000 ÷ 1,000 = $8 break-even point per shirt
    b. $8,000 × 0.30 = $2,400 net income on total cost
       ($8,000 + $2,400) ÷ 1,000 = $10.40 selling price

LESSON 14-5   SALES RECORD

Exercise 1.

1. You are a cashier at Dixie's Cafeteria. You started work with a $100 change fund. At the end of your work period, the register readings show cash received, $986.22, and cash paid out, $12.88. Cash in the register drawer totaled $1,072.56. Complete the cash proof form below and find the amount of cash over or short.

Cash Proof		
DIXIE'S CAFETERIA Date *March 16, 19 --*		
Change Fund	100	00
+ Register total of cash received	986	22
Total	1,086	22
− Register total of cash paid out	12	88
Cash that should be in drawer	1,073	34
Cash actually in drawer	1,072	56
Cash short		78
Cash over		

2. You are a cashier at Marcenter Stores. You started a work day with a change fund of $100. At the end of the day, the register totals showed $4,197.22 cash received and $34.57 cash paid out. The money in the drawer included 881 pennies, 247 nickels, 7,410 dimes, 1,855 quarters, 378 one-dollar bills, 52 five-dollar bills, 28 ten-dollar bills, 62 twenty-dollar bills, and $875.88 in checks. Complete the cash proof form below.

Cash Proof		
MARCENTER STORES Date *March 16, 19 --*		
Change Fund	100	00
+ Register total of cash received	4,197	22
Total	4,297	22
− Register total of cash paid out	34	57
Cash that should be in drawer	4,262	65
Cash actually in drawer	4,259	79
Cash short	2	86
Cash over		

3. You are a cashier at the Swan Inn. You started work with a $100 change fund. At the end of your work period, the register readings showed cash received, $922.24, and cash paid out, $28.45. The cash in the register drawer was $992.89. Complete the cash proof form below.

Cash Proof		
SWAN INN Date *March 16, 19 --*		
Change Fund	100	00
+ Register total of cash received	922	24
Total	1,022	24
− Register total of cash paid out	28	45
Cash that should be in drawer	993	79
Cash actually in drawer	992	89
Cash short		90
Cash over		

4. You are a cashier at the Sporting Room. You started the work day with a change fund of $100. At the end of the day, the register totals were $1,136.49 cash received and $18.30 cash paid out. The money in the drawer included 131 pennies, 158 nickels, 213 dimes, 45 quarters, 392 dollars, 21 five-dollar bills, 15 ten-dollar bills, 24 twenty-dollar bills, and $49.56 in checks.

Cash Proof		
SPORTING ROOM Date *March 16, 19 --*		
Change Fund	100	00
+ Register total of cash received	1,136	49
Total	1,236	49
− Register total of cash paid out	18	30
Cash that should be in drawer	1,218	19
Cash actually in drawer	1,218	32
Cash short		
Cash over		13

Exercise 2.

1. David's Video Outlet keeps track of the sales of the six types of videotapes it sells. The table below shows the sales and sales returns for the six types of videos for the week of June 5. You are to

   a. Complete the table.

   b. Prove the total net sales by subtracting the total sales returns from the total sales.

WEEKLY SUMMARY—CASH SALES June 5, 19—			
Video Type	Sales	Returns	Net Sales
Adventure	$1,894	$12	$1,882
Comedy	1,671	22	1,649
Sci-Fi	978	14	964
Horror	677	18	659
Children	990	9	981
Drama	1,618	23	1,595
Totals	$7,828	$98	$7,730

2. The table below shows the daily cash sales for six salespersons who worked at Sandy's Shop for the week of October 5. You are to

   a. Complete the table.

   b. Prove the total of the "Total Sales" column by adding the totals of the daily columns.

WEEKLY SALES SUMMARY October 5, 19—							
Salesperson	Monday	Tuesday	Wednesday	Thursday	Friday	Saturday	Total Sales
H. Herrera	$595.60	$484.30	$679.90	$478.23	$699.33	$824.56	$3,761.92
I. Ivany	376.54	465.46	572.80	207.13	612.89	774.08	3,008.90
J. Joji	466.68	454.23	614.61	431.96	788.49	923.01	3,678.98
K. Krchniak	524.25	415.20	738.65	390.44	766.88	855.61	3,691.03
L. Lasalle	656.80	534.75	813.95	899.39	974.65	945.11	4,824.65
M. Metzenbaum	996.20	596.45	692.65	407.87	710.32	854.20	4,257.69
Totals	$3,616.07	$2,950.39	$4,112.56	$2,815.02	$4,552.56	$5,176.57	$23,223.17

Exercise 3.

1. Thomas Supplies, Inc. keeps records to show how much each customer owes. Open their account with Tri-State Equipment Co. below with a balance of $8,254.20 on April 1 and record the transactions for the rest of the month. Tri-State Equipment Co. is located at 9127 Englewood Avenue, Yakima, WA 98908-1425.

April 7 Sold Tri-State $5,834.90 in merchandise on sales invoice No. 3356
13 Tri-State returned $145.29 of goods from invoice No. 3356; credit memo 867.
17 Tri-State paid the April 1 balance of $8,254.20.
20 Tri-State paid invoice No. 3356, less credit memo 867.
22 Sold Tri-State $4,907.66 in merchandise on sales invoice No. 3783.
25 Tri-State returned $207.88 of goods from invoice No. 3783; credit memo 893.

NAME	Tri-State Equipment Co.							
ADDRESS	9127 Englewood Avenue, Yakima, WA 98908-1425							
Date		Description	Charges		Credits		Balance	
19--								
April	1	Balance					8,254	20
	7	Inv. No. 3356	5,834	90			14,089	10
	13	Credit Memo 867			145	29	13,943	81
	17	Payment			8,254	20	5,689	61
	20	Payment			5,689	61	——	—
	22	Inv. No. 3783	4,907	66			4,907	66
	25	Credit Memo 893			207	88	4,699	78

2. Indoor Lites, Inc. keeps customer records of charge sales. Open their account with Holly Construction Co. below with a balance of $2,864.80 on May 1 and record the sales invoice, credit memo, and payment shown on the next page. Holly Construction Co. is located at 4297 Oberlin Road, Raleigh, NC 27608-8685.

NAME	Holly Construction Co.							
ADDRESS	4297 Oberlin Road, Raleigh, NC 27608-8685							
Date		Description	Charges		Credits		Balance	
19--								
May	1	Balance					2,864	80
	5	Inv. No. 23-890	1,821	79			4,686	59
	18	Credit Memo 288			80	97	4,605	62
	28	Payment			2,864	80	1,740	82

INDOOR LITES, INC.
4100 Grant Avenue
Raleigh, NC 27607-3534

SALES INVOICE NO.:	23-890
DATE:	May 5, 19--
SHIP VIA:	Truck
TERMS:	n/30

SOLD TO: Holly Construction Co.
4297 Oberlin Road
Raleigh, NC 27608-8685

QUANTITY	STOCK NO.	DESCRIPTION	UNIT PRICE	EXTENSION	TOTAL
3	C1077	Chandeliers	282.88	848.64	
15	O3072	Overhead Lights	28.89	433.35	
20	L1883	Lanterns	26.99	539.80	
				————	
		Total			1821.79

CREDIT MEMO   No. 288
INDOOR LITES, INC.
4100 Grant Avenue
Raleigh, NC 27607-3534

Holly Construction Co.
4297 Oberlin Road
Raleigh, NC 27608-8685

DATE: May 18, 19--

We have credited your account as follows:

DESCRIPTION	UNIT PRICE	TOTAL
Returned 3 damaged lanterns; Invoice No. 23-890	26.99	80.97

Holly Construction Co.   No. _4783_
4297 Oberlin Road
Raleigh, NC 27608-8685 $\frac{1\text{-}225}{2478}$

Date _May 28_ 19 _-- --_

PAY TO THE ORDER OF _Indoor Lites, Inc._ $ _2,864.80_

Two thousand, eight-hundred, sixty-four and $\frac{80}{100}$ — _Dollars_

For Classroom Use Only

PACE BANK
Raleigh, NC 27605-9148

|02478 0271| 879|||134|

LESSON 14-6   WHAT IS INTERNATIONAL BUSINESS?

Exercise

1. A country had the following import/export history for three years. The amounts shown are for billions of dollars.

	Year 1	Year 2	Year 3
Imports	$211	$212	$285
Exports	$180	$220	$275

In what year(s) did this country have a trade surplus and how much was the surplus?

There was a surplus in Year 2 of $8 billion dollars.

At the end of three years, did this country have a trade deficit or trade surplus? How much?

Total Imports: $708 billion; Total Exports: $675. At the end of three years: Trade deficit of $33 billion.

2. Following is information on the United State's imports and exports in 1991. The chart shows imports and exports in millions of dollars. Complete the following chart by stating whether there was a trade deficit or surplus with each country and the amount of that deficit or surplus.

	Imports	Exports	Surplus/Deficit	Amount
Canada	$91,141	$85,103	Deficit	$6,038
Japan	$91,583	$48,147	Deficit	$43,436
Mexico	$31,194	$33,276	Surplus	$2,082
Germany	$26,226	$21,317	Deficit	$4,909

LESSON 14-7   INTERNATIONAL TIME, TEMPERATURE, AND MONEY

Exercise

1. It is 7:00 P.M. in Chicago. What time is it in the following cities? Use the time zone chart in Illustration 14-7.1 in the text.

   a. Washington D.C.   _____8 P.M._____

   b. Tokyo   _____10 A.M._____

   c. Tel Aviv   _____3 A.M._____

   d. Vancouver   _____5 P.M._____

2. Show the equivalent Celsius or Fahrenheit temperature for each of the following.

   a. 150° F   a. $\frac{5}{9}(150 - 32) = 65.556°C$

   b. 100°C   b. $1.8\,(100) + 32 = 212°F$

   c. 22°F   c. $\frac{5}{9}(22 - 32) = 5.556°C$

   d. 71°C   d. $1.8\,(71) + 32 = 159.8°F$

   e. 14°F   e. $\frac{5}{9}(14 - 32) = -10°C$

3.

Country	Monetary Unit	Units Per U.S. Dollar
Switzerland	Franc	1.46
England	Pound	0.57

   Use the table to calculate the cost of the following items in francs and pounds or U.S. dollars.

   a. Lunch $15

   b. Shampoo $1.99

   c. A wool sweater $50

   d. A video   25 Swiss francs

Francs	Pounds
a. 15 × 1.46 = 21.90 francs	15 × 0.57 = 8.55 pounds
b. 1.99 × 1.46 = 2.9054 francs	1.99 × 0.57 = 1.134 pounds
c. 50 × 1.46 = 73 francs	50 × 0.57 = 28.5 pounds
d. 25 ÷ 1.46 = 36.50 francs	5 ÷ 0.57 = 43.86 pounds

LESSON 14-8   LOOKING AT CAREERS

Exercise

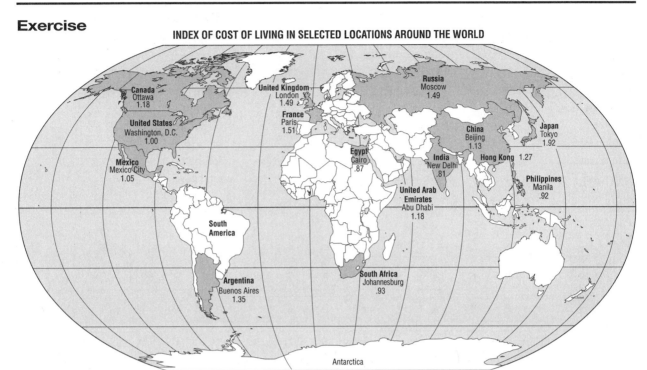

INDEX OF COST OF LIVING IN SELECTED LOCATIONS AROUND THE WORLD

Source: Adapted from *U.S. Department of State Indexes of Living Costs Abroad, Quarters Allowances, and Hardship Differentials—October 1992* (Washington, D.C.: Department of State Publication 9994, Bureau of Administration, Office of Allowances.)

You earn $32,580 in the U.S. Your company is offering incentives to people who move overseas for one year. You get to choose which of the following countries you will move to. Select the best financial offer. Use the Cost of Living Index around the World shown above to determine your base salary in each of the countries.

		Expatriate Bonus	**Base Salary & Raise**
1.	Philippines	$350	3.3% Raise
2.	Argentina	$1,000	0
3.	Ottawa, Canada	$0	1.8% Raise
4.	Moscow	$900	15% Raise

1. ($32,580 × 3.3%) + $350 + $32,580 = $34,005.14
2. $32,580 + $1,000 = $33,580
3. $32,580 × 1.8% = $33,166.44
4. ($32,580 × 115%) + $900 = $38,367 (best offer)

5. Select one of the countries labeled on the international cost of living index. Do some research on the country and identify at least 3 cultural beliefs or practices. Then write a statement about how you would act with someone from this country, if you were doing business with them.   Answers will vary.

TERM TICKLER

Directions: Find each of the following terms in the puzzle. Circle each term when you find it. It may be written downward, upward, sideways, or diagonally. The term "bar code" is circled for you as an example. There are nineteen terms. How many can you find?

Terms

bar code	customer account	prove cash
buying expense	credit memo	retail price
cash over	gross loss	sales invoice
cash proof form	markdown	sales price
cash register	marked price	selling price
cash short	markup	total cost
change fund		

M	A	R	K	D	O	W	N	H	L	X	F	X	D	M	V	K
A	A	G	P	C	A	S	H	P	R	O	O	F	F	O	R	M
R	K	R	E	T	A	I	L	P	R	I	C	E	H	O	X	N
K	W	O	K	C	A	S	H	S	H	O	R	T	W	S	E	Y
E	G	S	F	U	X	C	A	S	H	O	V	E	R	C	C	X
D	H	S	N	Y	P	B	A	R	C	O	D	E	O	U	I	T
P	W	L	S	E	L	L	I	N	G	P	R	I	C	E	R	C
R	T	O	T	A	L	C	O	S	T	C	P	O	H	A	P	A
I	G	S	F	B	L	R	C	M	G	T	R	P	A	C	S	S
C	U	S	T	O	M	E	R	A	C	C	O	U	N	T	E	H
E	Q	C	R	M	Y	D	S	Q	N	P	Y	D	G	B	L	R
Q	K	L	J	A	P	I	A	I	L	P	P	Y	E	Y	A	E
E	R	U	L	D	A	T	J	I	N	S	O	Y	F	X	S	G
C	L	S	W	W	F	M	F	N	B	V	P	I	U	B	U	I
R	Q	E	V	Q	K	E	U	B	S	O	O	L	N	Y	O	S
L	F	E	G	W	K	M	D	R	S	Q	D	I	D	T	M	T
Q	S	I	Z	S	X	O	Y	W	F	J	E	R	C	K	X	E
C	R	B	U	Y	I	N	G	E	X	P	E	N	S	E	S	R

INTEGRATED PROJECT 14

Directions: Read the project through and solve all the problems.

Carlotta Megan is manager of the Office Supplies Department of Oltog's Discount Department Store. The store sells a large variety of merchandise to its customers for cash. The store also provides charge accounts for customers who have good credit ratings.

1. Trent Brown is a cashier for one of the Oltog's two cash registers in the Office Supplies Department. He started his work shift on August 3 with $200 from a change fund and used Register No. 4. At the end of his shift, $4,979.85 was in his cash register. His register's readings are cash received, $4,803.88; cash paid out, $23.88. Complete Trent's cash proof form.

Cash Proof		
OLTOG'S DISCOUNT DEPARTMENT STORE		
Dept. *Office Supplies* Date *August 3, 19 --*		
Change Fund	*200*	*00*
+ **Register total of cash received**	*4,803*	*88*
Total	*5,003*	*88*
− **Register total of cash paid out**	*23*	*88*
Cash that should be in drawer	*4,980*	*00*
Cash actually in drawer	*4,979*	*85*
Cash short		*15*
Cash over		
Cash register No. ___*4*___		
Cash Register Operator		
Trent Brown		

2. John Leemark, a long-time customer of the Department, called Carlotta recently. John thinks that there is an error in his account. His account follows. Check the arithmetic in the account and verify the current balance. If there are any errors, draw a line through the incorrect amount and write the correct amount over it.

NAME	*Leemark Computer Services, Inc.*			
ADDRESS	*3288 Olden Avenue, S.*			
	Trenton, N.J. 08610-2085			

Date		Explanation	Charges		Credits		Balance	
19 -- July	1	*Balance*					2,198	12
	9	*Invoice No. 4989*	2,986	56			5,184	68
	15	*Credit Memo No. 229*			54	88	~~5,129~~ 80 ~~5,138 80~~	
	24	*Payment*			2,198	12	~~2,931~~ 68 ~~2,940 68~~	
	30	*Payment*			2,000	00	~~931~~ 68 ~~940 68~~	

3. The Department bought 700 boxes of $3\frac{1}{2}$-inch computer diskettes from Bradley Computer Supply Co. for $4,200 plus $23.75 in shipping costs. The boxes, priced at $17, have been selling poorly. To move these items rapidly, Carlotta decided to reduce their price to $11.90. The rate of discount Carlotta used on the diskettes was _____30_____%.

$17.00 − $11.90 = $5.10 amount of discount
$5.10 ÷ $17.00 = 0.30, or 30% rate of discount

4. In making her decision to reduce the price of the diskette boxes, Carlotta noted that the Department had only sold 374 boxes at $17 after one month on the shelves.

   a. If the Department sells the rest of the boxes at the new price, the total gross profit will be $_____6,013.65_____.

374 × $17 = $6,358 sales at $17 $6,358 + $3,879.40 = $10,237.40
700 − 374 = 326 boxes remaining $4,200 + $23.75 = $4,223.75 total cost

326 × $11.90 = $3,879.40 $10,237.40 − $4,223.75 = $6,013.65 gross profit on diskettes

   b. The average gross profit per box will be, to the nearest whole cent $_____8.59_____.

$6,013.65 ÷ 700 = $8.59 average gross profit per box

5. Inventory records show that the amount of Swyft-spell, a computer program that the Department stocks, is running low and that it is time to buy more copies of the program. The program sells for $79.95. The store uses a markup of 45% based on the selling price for its computer equipment and supplies. The highest price that Carlotta can pay for each program she buys and still make a 45% markup on the selling price is $_____43.97_____.

$79.95 × 0.45 = $35.98 markup on selling price
$79.95 − $35.98 = $43.97 highest cost price that Carlotta should pay

6. One of the merchandisers the Department buys from wants Carlotta to sell a new computer chair. They'll offer Carlotta a series discount of 20%, 35%, 10% if she'll order 12 chairs. If the retail price is $500 per chair, what is the cost to Carlotta with the series discount? $_____234.00_____

$500 × 80% × 65% × 90% = $234.00

ADDITIONAL REFERENCES AND RESOURCES

* Titles preceded by an asterisk are available from: South-Western Educational Publishing, 5101 Madison Road, Cincinnati, OH 45227.

UNIT 1   MANAGING YOUR MONEY

The American Bankers Association, 1120 Connecticut Avenue, NW, Washington, DC. 20036. Bank services and money management.

Banking: Savings Accounts. Princeton, NJ: Films for the Humanities and Sciences, 14 minutes.

Earning Money. Princeton NJ: Films for the Humanities and Sciences. 14 minutes. Shows how to calculate straight and graduated commissions and piecework.

Go Figure   The Problem Solving Toolkit, 1994–95. Vila Crespo Software, Inc., 1725 McGovern Street, Highland Park, IL 60035-3213, (708)433-0500. An intuitive spreadsheet alternative can be used for finance and banking, general mathematics, and unit conversions.

* Gossage, *Basic Mathematics Review*, 1993.

* Muncaster and Prescott, *Learning Basic Math and Business Math Using the Calculator*, 1992.

Punching In and Out. Princeton NJ: Films for the Humanities and Sciences. 14 minutes. Shows how to calculate hourly wages and overtime pay.

* Schultheis, Kaliski, Passalacqua, *Keeping Financial Records for Business*, 1995.

Secretary's Commission on Achieving Necessary Skills. What Work Requires of Schools: A SCANS Report for American 2000. Washington, DC: US Department of Labor, 1991.

UNIT 2   SPENDING WISELY

American Council of Life Insurance, 1001 Pennsylvania Avenue, NW, 5th Floor South, Washington, DC 20004-2599.

American National Metric Council, 1625 Massachusetts Ave., NW, Washington, D.C. 20036.

Budgeting. Princeton, NJ: Films for the Humanities and Sciences. 14 minutes.

Consumer Information Center, Pueblo, CO 81009. Distributes consumer information on a wide variety of subjects. Catalog available for details.

Consumer Reports Auto Price Service, PO Box 8005, Novi, MI 48376. One of several car pricing services that compares sticker price to dealer's invoice for specific makes and models. A used car price service is also available.

Council of Better Business Bureaus, 4200 Wilson Blvd, Arlington, VA 22203. Among other subjects, has brochures on buying new or used cars, renting cars, credit, etc.

Health Insurance Association of America, 1025 Connecticut Avenue, NW, Suite 1200, Washington, DC 20036.

Highway Loss Data Institute, 1005 N. Glebe Rd., Suite 800, Arlington, VA 22203. Provides insurance information by vehicle type.

Internal Revenue Service, 1111 Constitution Avenue, NW, Washington, DC.

Internet Resources: FinWeb, financial resources; http://riskweb.bus.utexas.edu/finweb.html; GNN Personal Finance Center, managing money, financial planning; http://nearnet.gnn.com/gnn/meta/finance/index.html; Homebuyers Fair, includes other references on subject of home buying; http://www.homefair.com/homepage.html; Taxing Times, federal and state tax information; http://www.scubed.com:8001/tax/tax.html

Mortgage Bankers Association of America, 1125 15th St. NW, Washington, DC 20005. Trade group publishes information on mortgages, interest costs, mortgage refinancing.

National Automobile Dealer's Association, 8400 Westpark Drive, McLean, VA 22102. Publishes *N.A.D.A. Official Used Car Guide*, which contains current used car prices for most automobiles and trucks.

National Center for Financial Education, 2512 Horton St., San Diego, CA 92101. For information on budgeting.

National Vehicle Leasing Association, PO Box 34579, Los Angeles, CA 90034-0579. Provides information on understanding leasing contracts and terms.

* *On Your Own, A Personal Budgeting Simulation*, 1996.

UNIT 3   MAKING MONEY GROW

American Association of Individual Investors, 625 N. Michigan Avenue, Chicago, IL 60611.

American Stock Exchange, 86 Trinity Place, New York, NY 10006. Offers pamphlets on stock investments.

Consumer Bankers Association, 1000 Wilson Blvd., Suite 3012, Arlington, VA 22209. Credit issues.

Equifax Credit Information Services, PO Box 740241, Atlanta GA, 30374-0241. Credit bureau, offers brochures such as "You Have a Right to Know. . . Facts about the Fair Credit Reporting Act.)

Federal Reserve System, 20th St. and C St., NW, Washington, DC 20551. Have numerous booklets on banking and interest, including The ABC's of Figuring Interest and the Arithmetic of Interest Rates.

Investment Company Institute, 1600 M St. NW, Suite 600, Washington, DC 20036. Trade group provides pamphlets on mutual funds.

New York Stock Exchange, 11 Wall St., New York, NY 10005. Has literature on investing in stocks.

Public Securities Association, 40 Broad Street, 12th Floor, New York, NY 1004-2373. Provides information on bonds.

Securities and Exchange Commission, 450 5th St. NW, Washington, DC 20549. The federal agency that regulates stock and bond markets also provides brochures such as "What Every Investor Should Know."

* *The Stock Market*, a Computer Simulation, 1996.

U. S. Department of Health and Human Services, Social Security Administration, Baltimore, MD 21235, or your local Social Security Administration office, can provide material on calculating benefits, getting a social security card, filing claims, etc.

Work of the Stock Exchange, Coronet Films, Inc., 65 East South Water Street, Chicago, IL 60601. A 16-minute film on the exchanges.

UNIT 4   BUSINESS MATHEMATICS

* Cunningham, Alders, Block, *Business in a Changing World, 3E,* 1993

Gonyea, James, C. *The On-Line Job Search Companion*, McGraw-Hill, Inc. New York, 1995.

* Hallman and Johnson, *Building a Professional Life*, 1994.

* *Impact Simulation Software Package*, 1997. Students work in a direct mail agency and learn information management and decision making skills.

Insurance Information Institute, 110 William Street, New York, NY, 10038. Information on probability and statistics.

* Johnson, Dale M., *Probability and Statistics*, 1989.

* Kushner, *How to Find and Apply for a Job*, 6th Edition, 1996.

* Turner and Bottoms, *Marketing in a Global Economy*, 1996.

U.S. Bureau of the Census, Washington, D.C. 20233. Publishes statistical data for a great number of areas, including data related to the Consumer Price Index, purchasing power of the dollar, inflation, and employment.

U.S. Department of Labor, Bureau of Labor Statistics, Washington, D.C. 20212. Has publications on consumer prices and goods and services purchased and employment and earning statistics.

* Wilson and Clark, *South-Western Economics*, 1997.

Working Together: Managing Cultural Diversity. New York: Insight Media. 25 minutes.

* Zedlitz, Robert, *Getting a Job Process Kit*. 1993.

Periodicals   *Business Week; Consumer Reports; Money Magazine; Smart Money; Worth.*

* Titles preceded by an asterisk are available from South-Western Educational Publishing.

PRINT AND MICROEXAM TEST ANSWERS

Chapter 1 Pretest
1. 3,036
2. $3,166.12
3. 3,947
4. $1,395.04
5. $7,020.15; $6,954.43
6. a. 6; b. 3
7. a. 24; b. 20
8. $371.25
9. $1,043.23
10. $509.76
11. 28 ounces
12. a. 275; b. 190

Chapter 1 Test
1. $4,141.07
2. $2,378.67
3. 535
4. 5
5. 14
6. $2,746
7. $78.17
8. $255.24
9. $81.89
10. $670.68
11. 592
12. $225.68
13. $360.90
14. $480.60
15. $248.02

Chapter 2 Pretest
1. a. 2,322; b. 50.22;
   c. $185.20; d. $4,130;
   e. $5
2. a. $68.42; b. $7.69;
   c. $0.0015; d. 1.66;
   e. 9.05
3. a. 18; b. 8; c. 30; d. 8;
   e. 28; f. 48
4. a. $58.63; b. $0.62;
   c. $0.39
5. a. 0.9; b. 1.32; c. 6.79
6. $340.80 gross pay
7. $16,800 yearly pay
8. $44 avg. daily pay
9. 7 avg. minutes late
10. 84 score on third test
11. $46.50 gross pay

Chapter 2 Test
1. $600
2. 16.43
3. 4
4. 75
5. $0.15
6. $311.60
7. $1,658
8. $86
9. $1,640
10. $16,640
11. $79.80
12. $184
13. $7.24
14. 2,900,000
15. $148

Chapter 3 Pretest
1. a. $\frac{5}{8}$; b. $\frac{7}{12}$; c. $6\frac{8}{15}$
2. a. $\frac{7}{12}$; b. $\frac{9}{16}$; c. $4\frac{7}{12}$
3. a. $\frac{2}{5}$; b. $\frac{1}{4}$; c. 35;
   d. 105; e. $30\frac{7}{8}$
4. a. 63; b. $3\frac{6}{7}$; c. 18;
   d. $\frac{3}{32}$; e. $30\frac{7}{8}$
5. a. $\frac{6}{10}$; b. $30; c. $80
   d. $\frac{3}{8}$; e. $2\frac{1}{3}$; f. $\frac{38}{7}$
6. $333.75 gross pay
7. $88 pay for day
8. $\frac{7}{9}$ of earnings spent
9. $36,000 Rose's share of profit

Chapter 3 Test
1. $1\frac{11}{12}$
2. $\frac{11}{24}$
3. 24
4. $\frac{3}{8}$
5. $\frac{1}{4}$
6. $356
7. $270
8. $428
9. $15\frac{5}{12}$
10. $260
11. $30
12. $72
13. $\frac{1}{2}$
14. 15 lbs
15. $\frac{1}{6}$
16. $\frac{1}{5}$
17. $$5\frac{1}{4}$ hours

Chapter 4 Pretest
1. a. 0.8%; b. 300%
   c. $0.14\frac{2}{7}$; d. 0.11
   e. 678.4; f. 6,910
   g. $7.20; h. 0.16
   i. $12\frac{1}{2}$%; j. 64; k. 20%;
   l. $\frac{6}{25}$; m. 2.75; n. 6%
   o. 6%; p. $\frac{5}{8}$
2. a. 41; b. 57; c. 21
   d. 4; e. 48; f. 14
3. $334.49
4. $319.44
5. $17\frac{1}{4}$
6. $395
7. $380
8. $89,108
9. $1,200

Chapter 4 Test
1. 150%
2. 0.43
3. 3.25
4. 0.25%
5. 25
6. $213.71
7. $398.63
8. $6,954
9. $1,571.25
10. $27,000
11. $1,295
12. 6%
13. $28.16
14. 8%
15. 32%
16. $1,400

Chapter 5 Test
1. 98 000 mL
2. 14.67 m
3. 600 g
4. 60 t
5. 25%
6. 61 km
7. 4.8 L
8. 5,200 bottles
9. 409 kg
10. 1 650 t
11. 560 m²
12. 24 m
13. 31.2 km²
14. 11.3 kg
15. 5 panels

Chapter 6 Test
1. $270
2. $2,520
3. $0.48
4. $24.36
5. $525
6. $827.19
7. $10.61
8. $874,835
9. 14
10. $84.68
11. $58.32
12. $4.12
13. 1.2
14. $3.83
15. $39.44

Chapter 7 Test
1. $6,023.89
2. $181,080
3. $9,760
4. $1,710
5. 0.03
6. $1,500
7. $10,880
8. $1,290
9. $80,450
10. $6,044
11. $984
12. 10%
13. $0.25
14. $2,580
15. $9,020

Chapter 8 Test
1. $84.51
2. $350
3. $300
4. $8\frac{1}{4}$
5. $13\frac{2}{3}$
6. $1,088.13
7. $1,021.20
8. $2,022.30
9. $17.19
10. $12.40
11. $5,446.80
12. $16,332.75
13. $20,500
14. $148
15. $429.18; $429 rounded
16. $96

Chapter 9 Test
1. 127.5
2. $132,000
3. $237
4. $\frac{8}{9}$
5. $14,000
6. $390
7. $465.25
8. $190.40
9. $171.60
10. $3,600
11. $6,000
12. $1,030
13. $2,100
14. $2,406
15. $48

Chapter 10 Test
1. $515.11
2. $13.50
3. 0.0525
4. $6\frac{1}{4}\%$
5. $11.25
6. $40
7. $7.50
8. 5.8%
9. $12.04
10. $1,037.50
11. 16%
12. 7%

13. $22
14. $6.10
15. 12.4%

Chapter 11 Test
1. $500
2. $86.625
3. 8%
4. $533.75
5. $350
6. 400
7. $600
8. 4%
9. $98
10. $39,000
11. $6,000
12. 10%
13. $1,100
14. $8,100
15. $2,132
16. $126,250

Chapter 12 Test
1. $4,000
2. 90°
3. $\frac{3}{4}$
4. 20%
5. 12
6. 16 mi
7. 600

8. 12
9. 15.3%
10. $125
11. 1,134
12. 18°
13. $52,000
14. 50%
15. June
16. 180,000

Chapter 13 Test
1. 15%
2. 1.97
3. $\frac{1}{5}$
4. $2,800
5. $0.40
6. 15%
7. $21,000
8. 12%
9. $41,570
10. $2.81
11. 6
12. $1,100; $2,100; $4,100; $700
13. $4,045
14. $7.79
15. $320
16. $812
17. $114,200

Chapter 14 Test
1. Oct 3
2. $1,169.40
3. $127.68
4. $36
5. 27.22°C
6. $377,325
7. 20.75
8. 36%
9. $298.35
10. $1,332.80
11. $1.08 short
12. $1,209.47
13. 18%
14. $31.20
15. $237
16. 25%
17. $332.35
18. $75,033

FIRST SEMESTER TEST

Chapters 1–8
Part I
1. D 2. A 3. D
4. C 5. C 6. A
7. C 8. C 9. D
10. A 11. A 12. C
13. B 14. B 15. D

Part II
1. 2,310 2. 3,349
3. 176 4. 30
5. 28.6% 6. $0.21\frac{3}{7}$
7. $1\frac{11}{12}$ 8. 24
9. 45 10. 28
11. 18 12. 15
13. 36 14. 12.306
15. 20.5g 16. 407,200
17. 40% 18. $30
19. 125% 20. 40%
21. $64 22. $273.60
23. $370.50 24. $39.78
25. $39

Part III
26. 210 27. $2,040
28. $444 29. $256.25
30. $1,088.13 31. $138.18
32. $38,008.32 33. $389.02
34. $75.05 35. $6,044
36. $239.54 37. $309.10

Part IV
38. $20,550
39. $164.35
40. $161.63
41. $82.02
42. $99.09
43. $27.08
44. $333.22
45. $873.38
46. $5.32
47. $818.84
48. $6.04
49. $824.88
50. $68.82
51. $184.54
52. $253.36
53. $824.88

SECOND SEMESTER TEST

Part I
1. D 2. A 3. A
4. C 5. C 6. D
7. C 8. D 9. A
10. B 11. A 12. B
13. A 14. A 15. A

Part II
1. $958.75 2. $2,100
3. 0.007 4. 3%
5. 18.8% 6. $56.25
7. 23 8. $47.78
9. $68,000 10. $\frac{3}{5}$
11. $14,000 12. 1.97
13. $14,560 14. 7%
15. 3% 16. $171.50
17. $12 18. $61.25
19. $4,992 20. 35.2%
21. 1,000 22. $13.67
23. $144 24. 35.2%
25. 8%

Part III
26. $75,361.88 27. $169
28. $6,000 29. $3,840
30. $2,108 31. $675
32. $21,000 33. $812
34. 8 35. $15
36. $48,000

Part IV
37. $1,487.54
38. $1,737.54
39. $185.73
40. $1,551.81
41. $1,552.17
42. $0.36
43. $50,000
44. $53,000
45. $38,000
46. $12,000
47. $4,500
48. 76%
49. 24%
50. 15%
51. 9%
52. $17,000
53. Week 3
54. $59,000
55. 100%
56. 15%

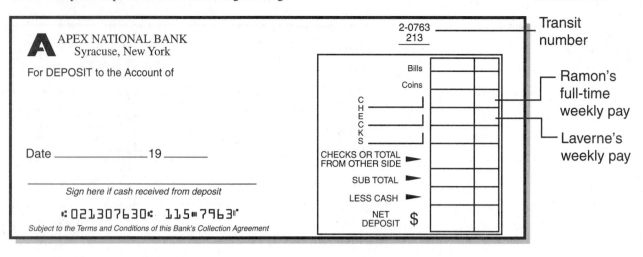

A APEX NATIONAL BANK
Syracuse, New York

For DEPOSIT to the Account of

Date _____ 19 _____

_____
Sign here if cash received from deposit

⑆021307630⑆ 115⑈7963⑈

Subject to the Terms and Conditions of this Bank's Collection Agreement

2-0763
213

	Bills		
	Coins		
C H E C K S			
CHECKS OR TOTAL FROM OTHER SIDE ▶			
SUB TOTAL ▶			
LESS CASH ▶			
NET DEPOSIT $			

Transit number

Ramon's full-time weekly pay

Laverne's weekly pay

Date _____ 19 _____   **1341**

2-0763
213

PAY TO THE ORDER OF _____ $ _____

_____ **Dollars**

A APEX NATIONAL BANK
Syracuse, New York

For Classroom Use Only

Memo _____   _____

⑆021307630⑆ 115⑈7963⑈ 1341

RECORD ALL CHARGES OR CREDITS THAT AFFECT YOUR ACCOUNT

NUMBER	DATE	DESCRIPTION OF TRANSACTION	PAYMENT/DEBIT (-)	√ T	FEE (IF ANY) (-)	DEPOSIT/CREDIT (+)	BALANCE $	
			$		$	$		

	A	B	C	D	E	F	G	H	I	J
1										
2										
3										
4										
5										
6										
7										
8										
9										
10										
11										
12										
13										
14										
15										
16										
17										
18										

No. **63**

Employee: *Paula Steele*

Pay Period Ending
August 7, 19–

Days	In	Out	In	Out	In	Out	Regular Hours	Overtime Hours
		Morning		Afternoon		Overtime		
1 M	8⁰⁵ M	12¹⁰ M	12⁵⁵ M	5⁰² M			$7\frac{3}{4}$	
2 T	7⁵⁶ T	11³² T	1⁰³ T	4⁵⁸ T			$7\frac{1}{2}$	
3 W	8²⁰ W	12⁰⁰ W	1⁰⁰ W	4⁴⁵ W			$7\frac{1}{4}$	
4 Th	7⁵⁹ Th	11⁵⁸ Th	12⁵⁹ Th	5⁰⁰ Th	6⁰⁰ Th	8³⁰ Th	8	$2\frac{1}{2}$
5 F	8⁰¹ F	12⁰² F	12⁵⁵ F	4³⁰ F			$7\frac{1}{2}$	
							Total Regular	Total Overtime
							38	$2\frac{1}{2}$

Arrived Late

Left Early

Overtime

Pay Period Ending

No.

Employee:

Days	Morning In	Morning Out	Afternoon In	Afternoon Out	Overtime In	Overtime Out	Regular Hours	Overtime Hours
1	M	M	M	M				
2	T	T	T	T				
3	W	W	W	W				
4	Th	Th	Th	Th	Th	Th		
5	F	F	F	F				
	In	Out	In	Out	In	Out	Total Regular	Total Overtime
	Morning		Afternoon		Overtime			

CONVERSION BOX

NO.	FRACTION		DECIMAL		PERCENT
Ex.	$\frac{5}{8}$	=	0.625	=	62.5%
1		=		=	12%
2		=	0.8	=	
3	$\frac{3}{4}$	=		=	
4		=	1.5	=	
5		=		=	8%

MARRIED PERSONS—WEEKLY PAYROLL PERIOD												
And the wages are—		And the number of withholding allowances is—										
At least	But less than	0	1	2	3	4	5	6	7	8	9	10
		The amount of income tax to be withhold shall be—										
310	320	29	22	14	7	0	0	0	0	0	0	0
320	330	30	23	16	9	1	0	0	0	0	0	0
330	340	32	25	17	10	3	0	0	0	0	0	0
340	350	33	26	19	12	4	0	0	0	0	0	0
350	360	35	28	20	13	6	0	0	0	0	0	0
360	370	36	29	22	15	7	0	0	0	0	0	0
370	380	38	31	23	16	9	2	0	0	0	0	0
380	390	39	32	25	18	10	3	0	0	0	0	0
390	400	41	34	26	19	12	5	0	0	0	0	0
400	410	42	35	28	21	13	6	0	0	0	0	0
410	420	44	37	29	22	15	8	1	0	0	0	0
420	430	45	38	31	24	16	9	2	0	0	0	0
430	440	47	40	32	25	18	11	4	0	0	0	0
440	450	48	41	34	27	19	12	5	0	0	0	0
450	460	50	43	35	28	21	14	7	0	0	0	0

SOCIAL SECURITY EMPLOYEE TAX TABLE—7.65%

Wages at least	But less than	Tax to be withheld	Wages at least	But less than	Tax to be withheld	Wages at least	But less than	Tax to be withheld
31.05	31.18	2.38	32.88	33.01	2.52	34.71	34.84	2.66
31.18	31.31	2.39	33.01	33.14	2.53	34.84	34.97	2.67
31.31	31.44	2.40	33.14	33.27	2.54	34.97	35.10	2.68
31.44	31.57	2.41	33.27	33.40	2.55	35.10	35.23	2.69
31.57	31.70	2.42	33.40	33.53	2.56	35.23	35.36	2.70
31.70	31.84	2.43	33.53	33.67	2.57	35.36	35.50	2.71
31.84	31.97	2.44	33.67	33.80	2.58	35.50	35.63	2.72
31.97	32.10	2.45	33.80	33.93	2.59	35.63	35.76	2.73
32.10	32.23	2.46	33.93	34.06	2.60	35.76	35.89	2.74
32.23	32.36	2.47	34.06	34.19	2.61	35.89	36.02	2.75
32.36	32.49	2.48	34.19	34.32	2.62	36.02	36.15	2.76
32.49	32.62	2.49	34.32	34.45	2.63	36.15	36.28	2.77
32.62	32.75	2.50	34.45	34.58	2.64	36.28	36.41	2.78
32.75	32.88	2.51	34.58	34.71	2.65	36.41	36.54	2.79

The FICA tax to be withheld on multiples of $100 is:

Wage	Tax to be withheld
100	7.65
200	15.30
300	22.95
400	30.60
500	38.25
600	45.90

Larger ←————— **Base Unit (meter, liter, gram)** —————→ **Smaller**

Prefix + Symbol	Kilo K	hecto h	deca da	m, L, or g	deci d	centi c	milli m
Meaning	thousands 1,000	hundreds 100	tens 10	one 1	tenth 0.1	hundredth 0.01	thousandth 0.001

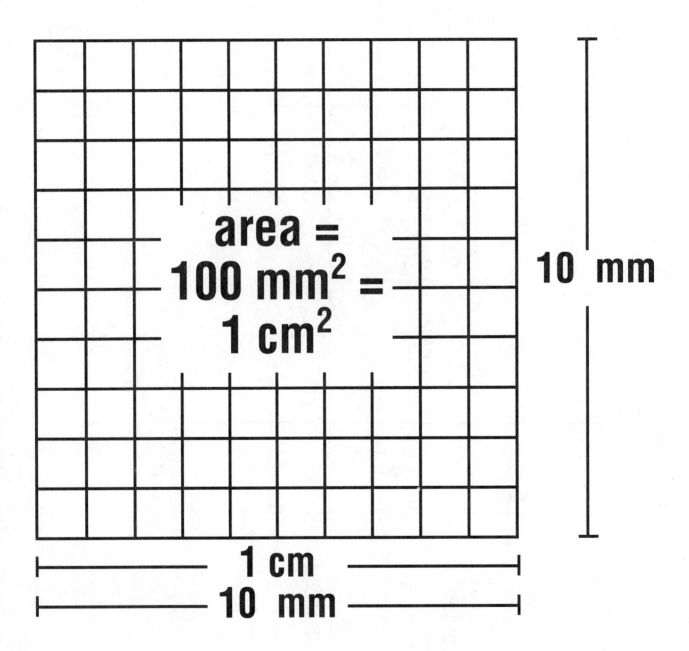

area =
100 mm² =
1 cm²

10 mm

1 cm
10 mm

STATE ELECTRONICS

16 State St., Bellingham, WA 98225-7981
206-555-0100

SOLD TO: _Jessie Podanski_

STREET: _245 South Brevard St._

CITY, STATE, ZIP: _Bellingham, WA 98225-9080_

DATE: _March 22_ 19- -

SOLD BY _RG_

CHARGE √   C.O.D.   DELIVERY BY _Taken_

QUANTITY	CASH DESCRIPTION	UNIT PRICE	AMOUNT
10 boxes	Computer diskettes, 3 1/2"	15 98	159 80
1	Printer cable, parallel	14 95	14 95
12	Diskette caddies	8 95	107 40
2 boxes	Printer paper, white	49 95	99 90
	SUBTOTAL	- - - -	382 05
	SALES TAX	5%	19 10
	TOTAL	- - - -	401 15

Everything
You Ever Wanted
in Electronics!

BUCKEYE POWER COMPANY
16 LANGLEY AVENUE
LIMA, OH   45801-2761

Velma Wense
1756 Bridge St.
Lima, OH   45806-8977

ACCOUNT NO.	DUE DATE	AMOUNT TO BE PAID	150.29
798-334-890	JUL 14		

BILLING SUMMARY

Amount due as of JUN 14	$ 165.06
Payment Received by JUN 13 – Thank You	165.06 CR
Balance (Payments after JUN 13 not included)	0.00

Current Gas Charge	51.77
Current Electric Charge	99.02

AMOUNT TO PAY	$ 150.79
DUE DATE – JUL 14	

TOTAL AMOUNT OWED IS $150.79	AMOUNT DUE IF PAYMENT RECEIVED AFTER JUL 14	$ 152.35

EXPLANATION OF BILLING CHARGES

ITEM	METER NUMBER	BILLING PERIOD From	To	Days	METER READINGS Previous	Present	ENERGY USAGE
Gas	00000	MAY 14	JUN 14	30	802	906	104
Elec	00000	MAY 14	JUN 14	30	4892	5717	825

THERM FACTOR: 1.582   THERMS USED: 165

GAS RATE 202 – Residential Service
Gas Usage Charge: 90 THMs @ $0.2107 =
                                 75 THMs @ $0.1478 =

Facilities Charge	$	19.25
		18.96
		11.09
Current Gas Charge	$	49.30
Taxes @ 0.05		2.47
Current Gas Charge	$	51.77

ELEC RATE KR – Residential Srv – Summer
Elec Usage Charge: 500 kWh @ $0.1011
Elec Fuel Component: 300 kWh @ $0.1216
                 Over 800 kWh @ $0.1471
Fuel Adjustment @ 0.00435

	$	50.55
		36.48
		3.68
		3.59
Total Energy Charge	$	94.30
Taxes @ 0.05		4.72
Current Electric Charge	$	99.02

PLEASE RETURN THIS STUB WITH YOUR PAYMENT

SWANSEA WATER COMPANY
24 Baron Road
Topeka, KS 66604-1872
913-555-0199

DISTRICT	ACCOUNT NO.
4	0829-4913

PRESENT READING	PREVIOUS READING
17780	9280

CU. FT. USED	TOTAL
8500	84.31

Lizbeth Walker
2307 Quail St.
Topeka, KS 66608-3352

RETAIN THIS PART FOR YOUR RECORDS

DATE PAID _____ CHECK NO. _____

SWANSEA WATER COMPANY
24 Baron Road
Topeka, KS 66604-1872
913-555-0199

ACCOUNT NO.		LAST DAY TO PAY
0829-4913		*July 31, 19 - -*

DISTRICT	PREVIOUS READING	CU. FT. USED	AMT. PAST DUE
4	9280	8500	00.00

PRESENT READING	FOR WATER USED TO	YOUR NEXT READING	TOTAL AMOUNT
17780	June 30	December 31	84.31

CUSTOMER
Lizbeth Walker
2307 Quail St.
Topeka, KS 66608-3352

MILEAGE BAND	DAY RATES (D)		EVENING RATES (E)		NIGHT RATES (N)	
	FIRST MIN.	ADDED MIN.	FIRST MIN.	ADDED MIN.	FIRST MIN.	ADDED MIN.
1–124	0.2760	0.2430	0.1560	0.1471	0.1199	0.1099
125–430	0.2810	0.2540	0.1670	0.1531	0.1380	0.1299
431–3000	0.2950	0.2658	0.1780	0.1551	0.1480	0.1389
3001 & over	0.3160	0.2680	0.1830	0.1701	0.1630	0.1420

MONTHLY PAYMENTS NEEDED TO PAY A LOAN

Amount of Loan	Interest Rate 7%			9%			11%		
	Time of Loan								
	20 yrs	25 yrs	30 yrs	20 yrs	25 yrs	30 yrs	20 yrs	25 yrs	30 yrs
$30,000	$232.59	$212.03	$199.59	$269.92	$251.76	$241.39	$309.66	$294.04	$285.70
35,000	271.35	247.37	232.86	314.91	293.72	281.62	361.27	343.04	333.32
40,000	310.12	282.71	266.12	359.90	335.68	321.85	412.88	392.05	380.93
45,000	348.88	318.05	299.39	404.88	377.64	362.09	464.49	441.06	428.55
50,000	387.65	353.39	332.65	449.87	419.60	402.32	516.10	490.06	476.17
55,000	426.41	388.73	365.92	494.85	461.56	442.55	567.71	539.07	523.78
60,000	465.18	424.07	399.18	539.84	503.52	482.78	619.32	588.07	571.40
65,000	503.94	459.41	432.45	584.83	545.48	523.01	670.93	637.08	619.02
70,000	542.71	494.75	465.71	629.81	587.44	563.24	722.54	686.08	666.63
75,000	581.47	530.08	498.98	674.80	629.40	603.47	774.15	735.09	714.25

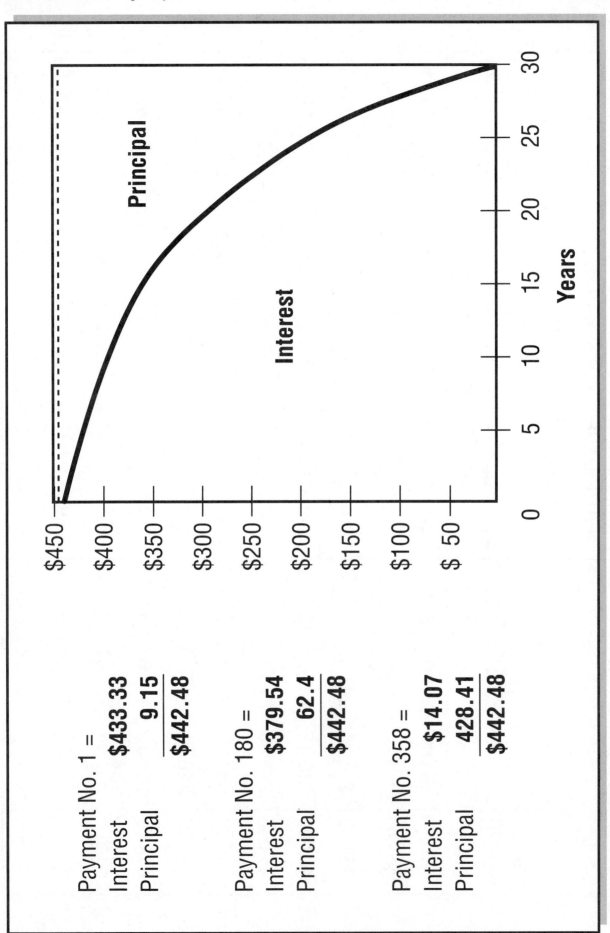

PARCEL I.D. NO.	LOAN I.D. NO.	ASSESSMENT RATE
13-89-47699	3870-7798	33 1/3%

MARKET VALUE	ASSESSED VALUE	TAX RATE PER $100
$150,000	$50,000	$6.20

PROPERTY OWNER AS OF 11/30/94

OTIS & LATONYA JOHNSON

PROPERTY DESCRIPTION

**45 SEVENTH STREET
MADISON, IL 62060-1978**

MAILING ADDRESS

**c/o JOHNSON, OTIS & LATONYA
45 SEVENTH STREET
MADISON, IL 62060-1978**

TAXING DISTRICT	AMOUNT OF TAX
COUNTY	$390.10
TOWN	107.00
ROAD & BRIDGE	105.30
SCHOOL DISTRICT	1,590.60
TOWNSHIP	650.30
FIRE DISTRICT	95.95
COMMUNITY COLLEGE	160.75
TOTAL TAX DUE	$3,100.00

PAY THIS AMOUNT

LAST DAY OF PAYMENT AS EXTENDED WITHOUT PENALTY

2/6/95

= NET GENERAL TAXES
SECOND HALF TAXES
DUE FEBRUARY 6, 1995
OR AS EXTENDED BY LAW

REAL ESTATE TAX
BILL CTL NO.
369669-5

OFFICE PAYMENT HOURS
8:00 A.M. TO 4:00 P.M. MON. THRU FRI.

TAXPAYER'S RECEIPT

YOUR CANCELLED CHECK IS YOUR RECEIPT. FOR AN ADDITIONAL RECEIPT, RETURN ENTIRE STATEMENT AND A SELF-ADDRESSED STAMPED ENVELOPE.

Form 1040 (19) — Page 2

Tax Computation (See page 23.)

32	Amount from line 31 (adjusted gross income)	32
33a	Check if: ☐ You were 65 or older. ☐ Blind; ☐ Spouse was 65 or older, ☐ Blind. Add the number of boxes checked above and enter the total here ▶ 33a ☐	33b ▲ 33c ☐
b	If your parent (or someone else) can claim you as a dependent, check here ▶ 33b	
c	If you are married filing separately and your spouse itemizes deductions or you are a dual-status alien, see page 23 and check here. ▶ 33c ☐	
34	Enter the larger of your: Itemized deductions from Schedule A, line 28, OR Standard deduction shown below for your filing status. But if you checked any box on line 33a or b, go to page 23 to find your standard deduction. If you checked box 33c, your standard deduction is zero. ● Single—$3,900 ● Married filing jointly or Qualifying widow(er)—$6,550 ● Head of household—$5,750 ● Married filing separately—$3,275	34
35	Subtract line 34 from line 32	35
36	If line 32 is $86,025 or less, multiply $2,500 by the total number of exemptions claimed on line 6e. If line 32 is over $86,025, see the worksheet on page 23 for the amount to enter	36
37	Taxable income. Subtract line 36 from line 35. If line 36 is more than line 35, enter -0-	37
38	Tax. Check if from a ☐ Tax Table, b ☐ Tax Rate Schedules, c ☐ Capital Gain Tax Worksheet, or d ☐ Form 8615 (see page 24). Amount from Form(s) 8814 ▶ e	38
39	Additional taxes. Check if from a ☐ Form 4970 b ☐ Form 4972	39
40	Add lines 38 and 39. ▶	40

Credits (See page 24.)

41	Credit for child and dependent care expenses. Attach Form 2441	41	
42	Credit for the elderly or the disabled. Attach Schedule R.	42	
43	Foreign tax credit. Attach Form 1116	43	
44	Other credits (see page 25). Check if from a ☐ Form 3800 b ☐ Form 8396 c ☐ Form 8801 d ☐ Form (specify)	44	
45	Add lines 41 through 44	45
46	Subtract line 45 from line 40. If line 45 is more than line 40, enter -0-. ▶	46

Other Taxes (See page 25.)

47	Self-employment tax. Attach Schedule SE	47
48	Alternative minimum tax. Attach Form 6251	48
49	Recapture taxes. Check if from a ☐ Form 4255 b ☐ Form 8611 c ☐ Form 8828	49
50	Social security and Medicare tax on tip income not reported to employer. Attach Form 4137	50
51	Tax on qualified retirement plans, including IRAs. If required, attach Form 5329	51
52	Advance earned income credit payments from Form W-2	52
53	Household employment taxes. Attach Schedule H.	53
54	Add lines 46 through 53. This is your total tax. ▶	54

Payments Attach Forms W-2, W-2G, and 1099-R on the front.

55	Federal income tax withheld. If any is from Form(s) 1099, check ▶ ☐	55	
56	19 estimated tax payments and amount applied from 19 return.	56	
57	Earned income credit. Attach Schedule EIC if you have a qualifying child. Nontaxable earned income: amount ▶ and type ▶	57	
58	Amount paid with Form 4868 (extension request)	58	
59	Excess social security and RRTA tax withheld (see page 32)	59	
60	Other payments. Check if from a ☐ Form 2439 b ☐ Form 4136	60	
61	Add lines 55 through 60. These are your total payments. ▶	61

Refund or Amount You Owe

62	If line 61 is more than line 54, subtract line 54 from line 61. This is the amount you OVERPAID.	62
63	Amount of line 62 you want REFUNDED TO YOU. ▶	63
64	Amount of line 62 you want APPLIED TO YOUR 19 ESTIMATED TAX ▶ 64	
65	If line 54 is more than line 61, subtract line 61 from line 54. This is the AMOUNT YOU OWE. For details on how to pay and use Form 1040-V, Payment Voucher, see page 33. ▶	65
66	Estimated tax penalty (see page 33). Also include on line 65	66	

Sign Here Keep a copy of this return for your records.

Under penalties of perjury, I declare that I have examined this return and accompanying schedules and statements, and to the best of my knowledge and belief, they are true, correct, and complete. Declaration of preparer (other than taxpayer) is based on all information of which preparer has any knowledge.

Your signature — Date — Your occupation

Spouse's signature. If a joint return, BOTH must sign. — Date — Spouse's occupation

Paid Preparer's Use Only

Preparer's signature		Date	Check if self-employed ☐	Preparer's social security no.
Firm's name (or yours if self-employed) and address			EIN	
				ZIP code

♻ Printed on recycled paper

Form 1040 — U.S. Individual Income Tax Return (19)

Department of the Treasury—Internal Revenue Service

For the year Jan. 1–Dec. 31, 19 , or other tax year beginning , 19 , ending , 19   OMB No. 1545-0074   IRS Use Only—Do not write or staple in this space

Label (See instructions on page 11.) Use the IRS label. Otherwise, please print or type.

- Your first name and initial — Last name — Your social security number
- If a joint return, spouse's first name and initial — Last name — Spouse's social security number
- Home address (number and street). If you have a P.O. box, see page 11. — Apt. no.
- City, town or post office, state, and ZIP code. If you have a foreign address, see page 11.

For Privacy Act and Paperwork Reduction Act Notice, see page 7.

Presidential Election Campaign (See page 11.)

Do you want $3 to go to this fund? — Yes — No — Note: Checking "Yes" will not change your tax or reduce your refund.
If a joint return, does your spouse want $3 to go to this fund?

Filing Status (See page 11.) Check only one box.

1. ☐ Single
2. ☐ Married filing joint return (even if only one had income)
3. ☐ Married filing separate return. Enter spouse's social security no. above and full name here. ▶
4. ☐ Head of household (with qualifying person). (See page 12.) If the qualifying person is a child but not your dependent, enter this child's name here. ▶
5. ☐ Qualifying widow(er) with dependent child (year spouse died ▶ 19). (See page 12.)

Exemptions (See page 12.)

6a	☐ Yourself. If your parent (or someone else) can claim you as a dependent on his or her tax return, do not check box 6a. But be sure to check the box on line 33b on page 2.	No. of boxes checked on 6a and 6b	
b	☐ Spouse		
c	Dependents:		No. of your children on 6c who:

(1) First name — Last name	(2) Dependent's social security number. If born in 19 , see page 13.	(3) Dependent's relationship to you	(4) No. of months lived in your home in 19

If more than six dependents, see page 13.

● lived with you
● didn't live with you due to divorce or separation (see page 14)
Dependents on 6c not entered above
Add numbers entered on lines above ▶

| d | If your child didn't live with you but is claimed as your dependent under a pre-1985 agreement, check here ▶ ☐ | |
| e | Total number of exemptions claimed | |

Income Attach Copy B of your Forms W-2, W-2G, and 1099-R here. If you did not get a W-2, see page 14. Enclose, but do not attach, your payment and payment voucher. See page 33.

7	Wages, salaries, tips, etc. Attach Form(s) W-2	7	
8a	Taxable interest income (see page 15). Attach Schedule B if over $400	8a	
b	Tax-exempt interest (see page 15). DON'T include on line 8a	8b	
9	Dividend income. Attach Schedule B if over $400	9	
10	Taxable refunds, credits, or offsets of state and local income taxes (see page 15)	10	
11	Alimony received	11	
12	Business income or (loss). Attach Schedule C or C-EZ	12	
13	Capital gain or (loss). If required, attach Schedule D (see page 16)	13	
14	Other gains or (losses). Attach Form 4797	14	
15a	Total IRA distributions . 15a	b Taxable amount (see page 16)	15b	
16a	Total pensions and annuities 16a	b Taxable amount (see page 16)	16b	
17	Rental real estate, royalties, partnerships, S corporations, trusts, etc. Attach Schedule E	17	
18	Farm income or (loss). Attach Schedule F	18	
19	Unemployment compensation (see page 17)	19	
20a	Social security benefits 20a	b Taxable amount (see page 18)	20b	
21	Other income. List type and amount—see page 18	21	
22	Add the amounts in the far right column for lines 7 through 21. This is your total income ▶	22	

Adjustments to Income

23a	Your IRA deduction (see page 19)	23a	
b	Spouse's IRA deduction (see page 19)	23b	
24	Moving expenses. Attach Form 3903 or 3903-F	24	
25	One-half of self-employment tax	25	
26	Self-employed health insurance deduction (see page 21)	26	
27	Keogh & self-employed SEP plans. If SEP, check ▶ ☐	27	
28	Penalty on early withdrawal of savings	28	
29	Alimony paid. Recipient's SSN ▶	29	
30	Add lines 23a through 29. These are your total adjustments ▶	30	

Adjusted Gross Income

| 31 | Subtract line 30 from line 22. This is your adjusted gross income. If less than $26,673 and a child lived with you (less than $9,230 if a child didn't live with you), see "Earned Income Credit" on page 27 ▶ | 31 | |

Cat. No. 11320B   Form **1040** (19)

Form 1040EZ

Department of the Treasury—Internal Revenue Service

Income Tax Return for Single and Joint Filers With No Dependents 19--

OMB No. 1545-0675

Use the IRS label here

Your first name and initial   Last name

If a joint return, spouse's first name and initial   Last name

Home address (number and street). If you have a P.O. box, see page 11.   Apt. no.

City, town or post office, state, and ZIP code. If you have a foreign address, see page 11.

Your social security number

Spouse's social security number

See instructions on back and in Form 1040EZ booklet.

Presidential Election Campaign (See page 11.)

Note: *Checking "Yes" will not change your tax or reduce your refund.*

Do you want $3 to go to this fund? ▶

If a joint return, does your spouse want $3 to go to this fund? ▶

Yes   No

Dollars   Cents

Income

Attach Copy B of Form(s) W-2 here. Enclose, but do not attach, any payment with your return.

1   Total wages, salaries, and tips. This should be shown in box 1 of your W-2 form(s). Attach your W-2 form(s).   1

2   Taxable interest income of $400 or less. If the total is over $400, you cannot use Form 1040EZ.   2

3   Unemployment compensation (see page 14).   3

4   Add lines 1, 2, and 3. This is your **adjusted gross income.** If less than $9,230, see page 15 to find out if you can claim the earned income credit on line 8.   4

5   Can your parents (or someone else) claim you on their return?

Note: *You **must** check Yes or No.*

☐ **Yes.** Do worksheet on back; enter amount from line G here.

☐ **No.** If **single,** enter 6,400.00. If **married,** enter 11,550.00. For an explanation of these amounts, see back of form.   5

6   Subtract line 5 from line 4. If line 5 is larger than line 4, enter 0. This is your **taxable income.** ▶   6

Payments and tax

7   Enter your Federal income tax withheld from box 2 of your W-2 form(s).   7

8   **Earned income credit** (see page 15). Enter type and amount of nontaxable earned income below.

Type $ 8

9   Add lines 7 and 8 (don't include nontaxable earned income). These are your **total payments.**   9

10   **Tax.** Use the amount on **line 6** to find your tax in the tax table on pages 29–33 of the booklet. Then, enter the tax from the table on this line.   10

Refund or amount you owe

11   If line 9 is larger than line 10, subtract line 10 from line 9. This is your **refund.**   11

12   If line 10 is larger than line 9, subtract line 9 from line 10. This is the **amount you owe.** See page 22 for details on how to pay and what to write on your payment.   12

I have read this return. Under penalties of perjury, I declare that to the best of my knowledge and belief, the return is true, correct, and accurately lists all amounts and sources of income I received during the tax year.

Sign your return

Keep a copy of this form for your records.

Your signature

Spouse's signature if joint return

Date   Your occupation

Date   Spouse's occupation

For IRS Use Only — Please do not write in boxes below.

1   2   3   4   5

6   7   8   9   10

Cat. No. 11329W

Form 1040EZ (19   )

Partial Federal Tax Table

If your taxable income is —		And your filing status is —			
At least	But less than	Single	Married filing jointly	Married filing separately	Head of a house-hold
		Your tax is —			
22,000	22,050	3,304	3,304	3,697	3,304
22,050	22,100	3,311	3,311	3,711	3,311
22,100	22,150	3,319	3,319	3,725	3,319
22,150	22,200	3,326	3,326	3,739	3,326
22,200	22,250	3,334	3,334	3,753	3,334
22,250	22,300	3,341	3,341	3,767	3,341
22,300	22,350	3,349	3,349	3,781	3,349
22,350	22,400	3,356	3,356	3,795	3,356
22,400	22,450	3,364	3,364	3,809	3,364
22,450	22,500	3,371	3,371	3,823	3,371
22,500	22,550	3,379	3,379	3,837	3,379
22,550	22,600	3,386	3,386	3,851	3,386
22,600	22,650	3,394	3,394	3,865	3,394
22,650	22,700	3,401	3,401	3,879	3,401
22,700	22,750	3,409	3,409	3,893	3,409
22,750	22,800	3,420	3,416	3,907	3,416
22,800	22,850	3,434	3,424	3,921	3,434
22,850	22,900	3,448	3,431	3,935	3,431
22,900	22,950	3,462	3,439	3,949	3,439
22,950	23,000	3,476	3,446	3,963	3,446

If your taxable income is —		And your filing status is —			
At least	But less than	Single	Married filing jointly	Married filing separately	Head of a house-hold
		Your tax is —			
0	5	0	0	0	0
5	15	2	2	2	2
15	25	3	3	3	3
25	50	6	6	6	6
50	75	9	9	9	9
75	100	13	13	13	13
100	125	17	17	17	17
125	150	21	21	21	21
150	175	24	24	24	24
175	200	28	28	28	28
200	225	32	32	32	32
225	250	36	36	36	36
250	275	39	39	39	39
275	300	43	43	43	43
300	325	47	47	47	47
325	350	51	51	51	51
350	375	54	54	54	54
375	400	58	58	58	58
400	425	62	62	62	62
425	450	66	66	66	66
450	475	69	69	69	69
475	500	73	73	73	73
500	525	77	77	77	77
525	550	81	81	81	81
550	575	84	84	84	84
575	600	88	88	88	88

Graduated Income Tax Table

For taxable income Over —	But not over —	The tax is —
$ –0–	$5,000	2% of taxable income
5,000	10,000	$100 plus 3% of taxable income over $5,000
10,000	15,000	250 plus 4% of taxable income over 10,000
15,000	20,000	550 plus 5% of taxable income over 15,000
20,000	25,000	1,200 plus 6% of taxable income over 20,000
25,000	30,000	1,550 plus 7% of taxable income over 25,000
30,000	35,000	1,950 plus 8% of taxable income over 30,000
35,000	40,000	2,400 plus 9% of taxable income over 35,000
40,000	45,000	2,900 plus 10% of taxable income over 40,000

ANNUAL PREMIUMS PER $1,000 UNITS OF LIFE INSURANCE

Age of Insured	1-Year Term		Whole Life		20-Payment Life	
	Male	Female	Male	Female	Male	Female
20	$1.39	$1.22	$ 7.07	$ 6.22	$25.29	$23.27
25	1.41	1.24	8.37	7.37	27.77	25.54
30	1.45	1.28	10.16	8.94	30.75	28.29
35	1.62	1.43	12.58	11.07	34.15	31.42
40	1.91	1.68	16.30	14.34	38.89	35.78
45	2.45	2.16	20.02	17.62	44.72	41.14

*Note: Rates shown are for nonsmokers.

Year	Cash/Loan Values per $1,000 Units	Paid-Up Whole Life per $1,000 Units	Extended Term	
			Years	Days
1	$ 0	$ 0	0	0
5	17.80	119	8	274
10	76.09	403	19	115
15	170.72	716	21	80
20	327.50	1,087	22	107
25	564.33	1,599	22	312

Type of Insurance	Limits	Annual Premiums for:		
		Pleasure Use Only	Driving to Work	Business
Bodily Injury	$20/40,000	$ 82	$ 90	$118
	25/50,000	98	108	140
	50/100,000	114	126	162
Property Damage	$10,000	$10	$12	$16
	25,000	12	14	18
	50,000	14	16	20
Collision	$100 deductible	$550	$612	$796
	250 deductible	386	428	556
	500 deductible	302	336	436
Comprehensive	$ 50 deductible	$ 92	$101	$132
	100 deductible	68	76	98

Interest Periods		$1\frac{1}{4}\%$	$1\frac{1}{2}\%$	2%	$2\frac{1}{2}\%$	4%	5%	6%
Annual	1	1.012500	1.015000	1.020000	1.025000	1.040000	1.050000	1.060000
	2	1.025156	1.030225	1.040400	1.050625	1.081600	1.102500	1.123600
	3	1.037971	1.045678	1.061208	1.076891	1.124864	1.157625	1.191016
	4	1.050945	1.061364	1.082432	1.103813	1.169859	1.215506	1.262477
	5	1.064082	1.077284	1.104081	1.131408	1.216653	1.276282	1.338226
	6	1.077383	1.093443	1.126162	1.159693	1.265319	1.340096	1.418519
	7	1.090850	1.109845	1.148686	1.188686	1.315932	1.407100	1.503630
	8	1.104486	1.126493	1.171659	1.218403	1.368569	1.477455	1.593848
	9	1.118292	1.143390	1.195093	1.248863	1.423312	1.551328	1.689479
	10	1.132270	1.160541	1.218994	1.280084	1.480244	1.628895	1.790848
	11	1.146424	1.177949	1.243374	1.312086	1.539453	1.710339	1.898299
	12	1.160754	1.195618	1.268242	1.344888	1.601032	1.795856	2.012197
Daily	30	—	—	—	1.002087	1.003338	1.004175	1.005012
	90	—	—	—	1.006274	1.010048	1.012578	1.015112
	180	—	—	—	1.012587	1.020196	1.025313	1.030452
	365	—	—	—	1.025688	1.041379	1.051998	1.062716

Date	Withdrawal	Deposit	Interest	Balance
19--				
01-11		300.00		300.00
02-16		400.00		700.00
03-21	150.00			550.00
04-01			4.31	554.31
04-01		70.00		624.31

Date of
Transaction

Amount withdrawn
is *subtracted* from
the balance

The balance tells
how much is in the
savings account

Deposit and interest
amounts are *added*
to the balance

Date	Withdrawal	Deposit	Interest	Balance
19-- Oct. 1				968.40
Nov. 23		300.00		1,268.40
19-- Jan. 2			14.53	1,282.93
Feb. 8	470.00			812.93
Apr. 1			12.19	825.12

First quarter

Second quarter

Minimum balance of the quarter

Time (Days)	8%	8½%	9%	9½%	10%	10½%	11%	11½%	12%	12½%
1	0.0219	0.0233	0.0247	0.0260	0.0274	0.0288	0.0301	0.0315	0.0329	0.0342
2	0.0438	0.0466	0.0493	0.0521	0.0548	0.0575	0.0603	0.0630	0.0658	0.0685
3	0.0658	0.0699	0.0740	0.0781	0.0822	0.0863	0.0904	0.0945	0.0986	0.1027
4	0.0877	0.0932	0.0986	0.1041	0.1096	0.1151	0.1205	0.1260	0.1315	0.1370
5	0.1096	0.1164	0.1233	0.1301	0.1370	0.1438	0.1507	0.1575	0.1644	0.1712
6	0.1315	0.1397	0.1479	0.1562	0.1644	0.1726	0.1808	0.1890	0.1973	0.2055
7	0.1534	0.1630	0.1726	0.1822	0.1918	0.2014	0.2110	0.2205	0.2301	0.2397
8	0.1753	0.1863	0.1973	0.2082	0.2192	0.2301	0.2411	0.2521	0.2630	0.2740
9	0.1973	0.2096	0.2219	0.2342	0.2466	0.2589	0.2712	0.2836	0.2959	0.3082
10	0.2192	0.2329	0.2466	0.2603	0.2740	0.2877	0.3014	0.3151	0.3288	0.3425
11	0.2411	0.2562	0.2712	0.2863	0.3014	0.3164	0.3315	0.3466	0.3616	0.3767
12	0.2630	0.2795	0.2959	0.3123	0.3288	0.3452	0.3616	0.3781	0.3945	0.4110
13	0.2849	0.3027	0.3205	0.3384	0.3562	0.3740	0.3918	0.4096	0.4274	0.4452
14	0.3068	0.3260	0.3452	0.3644	0.3836	0.4027	0.4219	0.4411	0.4603	0.4795
15	0.3288	0.3493	0.3699	0.3904	0.4110	0.4315	0.4521	0.4726	0.4932	0.5137
16	0.3507	0.3726	0.3945	0.4164	0.4384	0.4603	0.4822	0.5041	0.5260	0.5479
17	0.3726	0.3959	0.4192	0.4425	0.4658	0.4890	0.5123	0.5356	0.5589	0.5822
18	0.3945	0.4192	0.4438	0.4685	0.4932	0.5178	0.5425	0.5671	0.5918	0.6164
19	0.4164	0.4425	0.4685	0.4945	0.5205	0.5466	0.5726	0.5986	0.6247	0.6507
20	0.4384	0.4658	0.4932	0.5205	0.5479	0.5753	0.6027	0.6301	0.6575	0.6849
21	0.4603	0.4890	0.5178	0.5466	0.5753	0.6041	0.6329	0.6616	0.6904	0.7192
22	0.4822	0.5123	0.5425	0.5726	0.6027	0.6329	0.6630	0.6932	0.7233	0.7534
23	0.5041	0.5356	0.5671	0.5986	0.6301	0.6616	0.6932	0.7247	0.7562	0.7877
24	0.5260	0.5589	0.5918	0.6247	0.6575	0.6904	0.7233	0.7562	0.7890	0.8219
25	0.5479	0.5822	0.6164	0.6507	0.6849	0.7192	0.7534	0.7877	0.8219	0.8562
26	0.5699	0.6055	0.6411	0.6767	0.7123	0.7479	0.7836	0.8192	0.8548	0.8904
27	0.5918	0.6288	0.6658	0.7027	0.7397	0.7767	0.8137	0.8507	0.8877	0.9247
28	0.6137	0.6521	0.6904	0.7288	0.7671	0.8055	0.8438	0.8822	0.9206	0.9589
29	0.6356	0.6753	0.7151	0.7548	0.7945	0.8342	0.8740	0.9137	0.9534	0.9932
30	0.6575	0.6986	0.7397	0.7808	0.8219	0.8630	0.9041	0.9452	0.9863	1.0274
31	0.6795	0.7219	0.7644	0.8068	0.8493	0.8918	0.9342	0.9767	1.0192	1.0616

At 6%, a $10,000 deposit earns this much interest in one year when compounded:

Daily
$627.16

Quarterly
$613.63

Semiannually
$609.00

Annually
$600.00.

LOAN REPAYMENT SCHEDULE

End of -	Unpaid Balance	Finance Charge: 1.5% of Unpaid Balance	Payment on Principal	Total Payment
1st month	$600.00	$ 9.00	$100.00	$109.00
2d month	500.00	7.50	100.00	107.50
3d month	400.00	6.00	100.00	106.00
4th month	300.00	4.50	100.00	104.50
5th month	200.00	3.00	100.00	103.00
6th month	100.00	1.50	100.00	101.50
Totals		$31.50	$600.00	$631.50

Number of Payments	Annual Percentage Rate										
	12¾%	**13%**	**13¼%**	**13 ½%**	**13¼%**	**14%**	**14¼%**	**14½%**	**14¾%**	**15%**	**15¼%**
	Finance Charge per $100 of Amount Financed										
3	2.13	2.17	2.22	2.26	2.30	2.34	2.38	2.43	2.47	2.51	2.55
6	3.75	3.83	3.90	3.97	4.05	4.12	4.20	4.27	4.35	4.42	4.49
9	5.39	5.49	5.60	5.71	5.82	5.92	6.03	6.14	6.25	6.35	6.46
12	7.04	7.18	7.32	7.46	7.60	7.74	7.89	8.03	8.17	8.31	8.45
15	8.71	8.88	9.06	9.23	9.41	9.59	9.76	9.94	10.11	10.29	10.47

Number of Payments	Annual Percentage Rate										
	15½%	**15¾%**	**16%**	**16¼%**	**16½%**	**16¾%**	**17%**	**17¼%**	**17½%**	**17¾%**	**18%**
	Finance Charge per $100 of Amount Financed										
6	4.57	4.64	4.72	4.79	4.87	4.94	5.02	5.09	5.17	5.24	5.32
12	8.59	8.74	8.88	9.02	9.16	9.30	9.45	9.59	9.73	9.87	10.02

Number of Payments	Annual Percentage Rate										
	18¼%	**18½%**	**18¾%**	**19%**	**19¼%**	**19½%**	**19¾%**	**20%**	**20¼%**	**20½%**	**20¾%**
	Finance Charge per $100 of Amount Financed										
6	5.39	5.46	5.54	5.61	5.69	5.76	5.84	5.91	5.99	6.06	6.14
12	10.16	10.30	10.44	10.59	10.73	10.87	11.02	11.16	11.31	11.45	11.59

Dates	Transaction	Balance at end of Day	Number of Days	Sum of Daily Balances
11/8	+400	$400	1	$400
11/9–11/14	0	$400	6	$2,400
11/15	+$75	$475	1	$475
11/16–11/17	0	$475	2	$950
11/18	–91	$384	1	$384
11/19–11/24	0	$384	6	$2,304
11/25	+$180	$564	1	$564
11/25–12/7	0	$564	13	$7,332
Total			31	$14,809

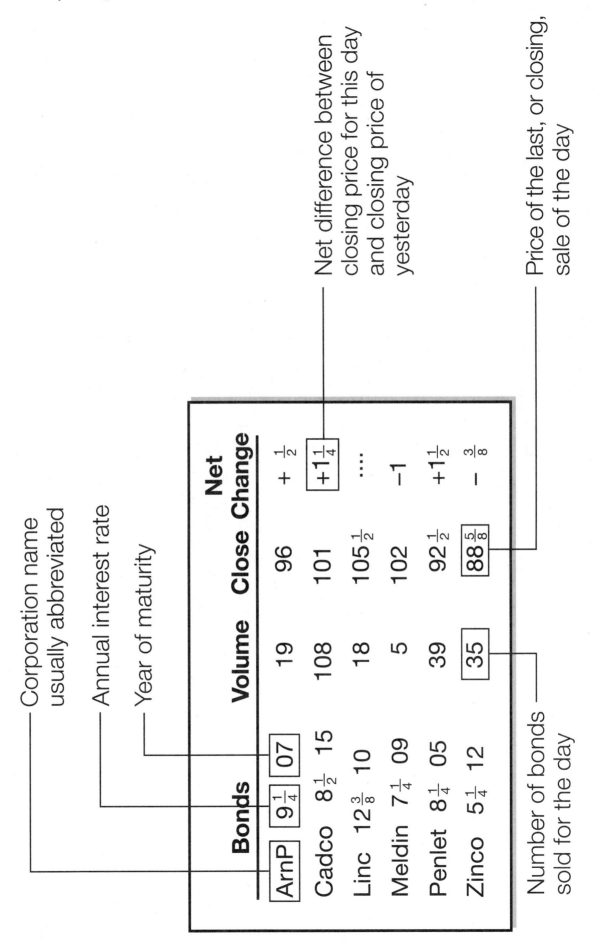

Corporation name usually abbreviated

Annual interest rate

Year of maturity

Net difference between closing price for this day and closing price of yesterday

Price of the last, or closing, sale of the day

Number of bonds sold for the day

Bonds	Volume	Close	Net Change
ArnP $9\frac{1}{4}$ 07	19	96	$+\frac{1}{2}$
Cadco $8\frac{1}{2}$ 15	108	101	$+1\frac{1}{4}$
Linc $12\frac{3}{8}$ 10	18	$105\frac{1}{2}$	....
Meldin $7\frac{1}{4}$ 09	5	102	-1
Penlet $8\frac{1}{4}$ 05	39	$92\frac{1}{2}$	$+1\frac{1}{2}$
Zinco $5\frac{1}{4}$ 12	35	$88\frac{5}{8}$	$-\frac{3}{8}$

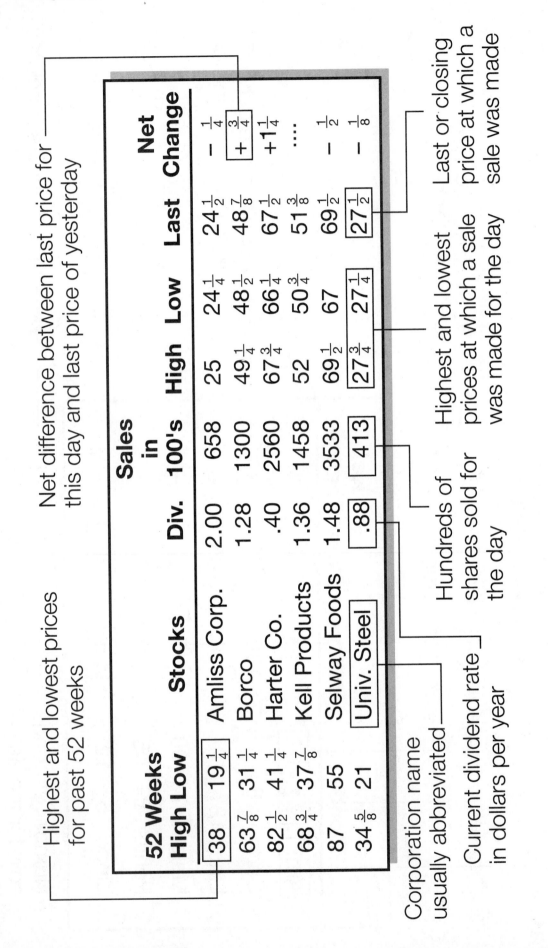

52 Weeks High	Low	Stocks	Div.	Sales in 100's	High	Low	Last	Net Change
38	$19\frac{1}{4}$	Amliss Corp.	2.00	658	25	$24\frac{1}{4}$	$24\frac{1}{2}$	$-\frac{1}{4}$
$63\frac{7}{8}$	$31\frac{1}{4}$	Borco	1.28	1300	$49\frac{1}{4}$	$48\frac{1}{2}$	$48\frac{7}{8}$	$+\frac{3}{4}$
$82\frac{1}{2}$	$41\frac{1}{4}$	Harter Co.	.40	2560	$67\frac{3}{4}$	$66\frac{1}{4}$	$67\frac{1}{2}$	$+1\frac{1}{4}$
$68\frac{3}{4}$	$37\frac{7}{8}$	Kell Products	1.36	1458	52	$50\frac{3}{4}$	$51\frac{3}{8}$	...
87	55	Selway Foods	1.48	3533	$69\frac{1}{2}$	67	$69\frac{1}{2}$	$-\frac{1}{2}$
$34\frac{5}{8}$	21	Univ. Steel	.88	413	$27\frac{3}{4}$	$27\frac{1}{4}$	$27\frac{1}{2}$	$-\frac{1}{8}$

Highest and lowest prices for past 52 weeks

Net difference between last price for this day and last price of yesterday

Last or closing price at which a sale was made

Highest and lowest prices at which a sale was made for the day

Hundreds of shares sold for the day

Corporation name usually abbreviated

Current dividend rate in dollars per year

Fund Name	NAV	Offer Price
Denton Fund	10.03	10.96
Frontier Growth	39.80	41.03
Kaner High Yield	10.58	11.48
Mark International	6.37	N.L.
Newsome Growth	17.87	N.L.
Payne Hall New Hz.	9.27	N.L.
Randall Explorer	17.54	19.17
Walker A-1 Fund	12.21	N.L.

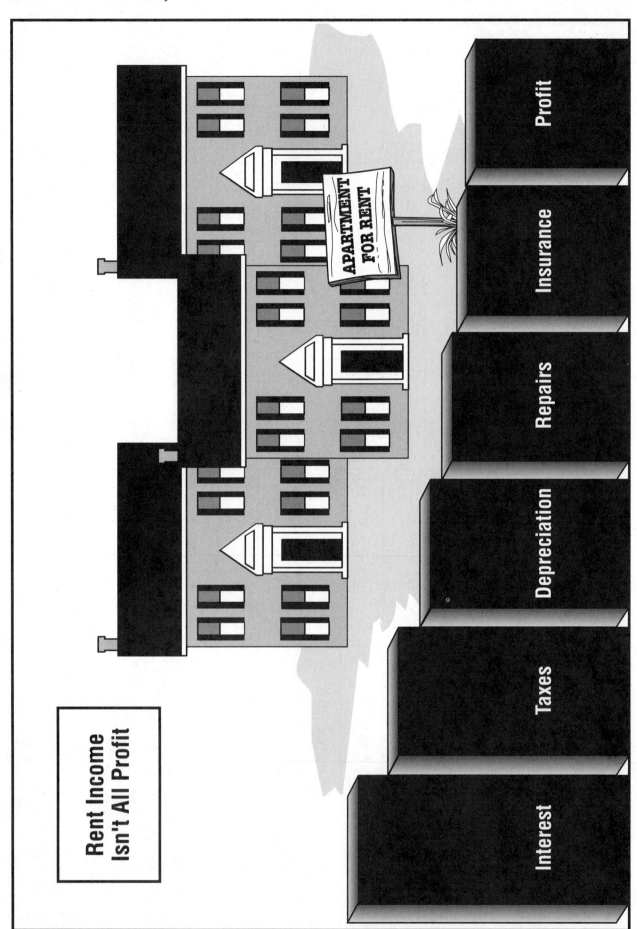

Rent Income Isn't All Profit

Interest

Taxes

Depreciation

Repairs

Insurance

Profit

APARTMENT FOR RENT

Age	Number Living
0	100,000
10	97,000
20	96,000
30	95,000
40	93,000
50	90,000
60	82,000
70	66,000
80	39,000

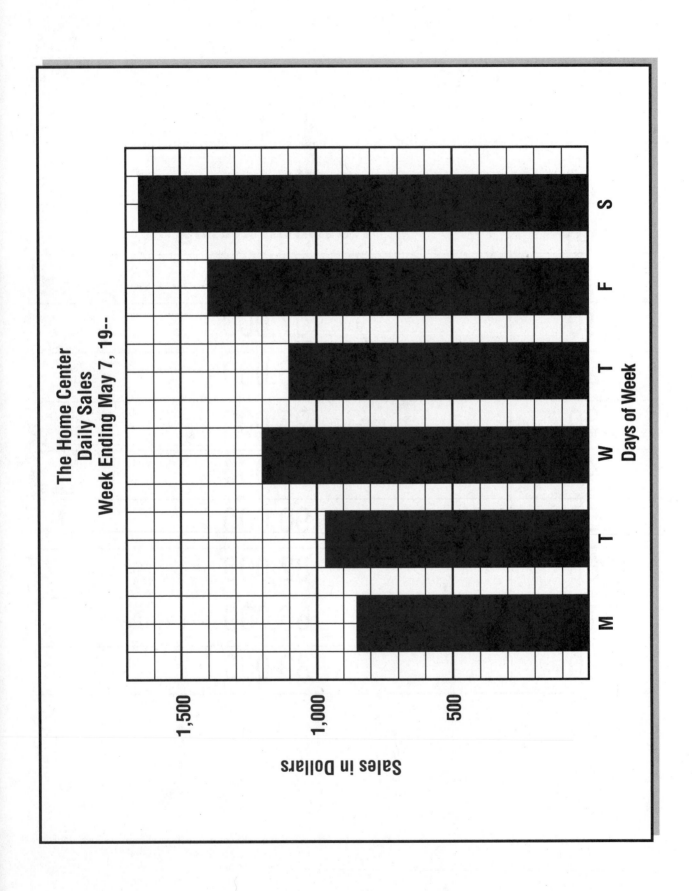

The Home Center
Daily Sales
Week Ending May 7, 19--

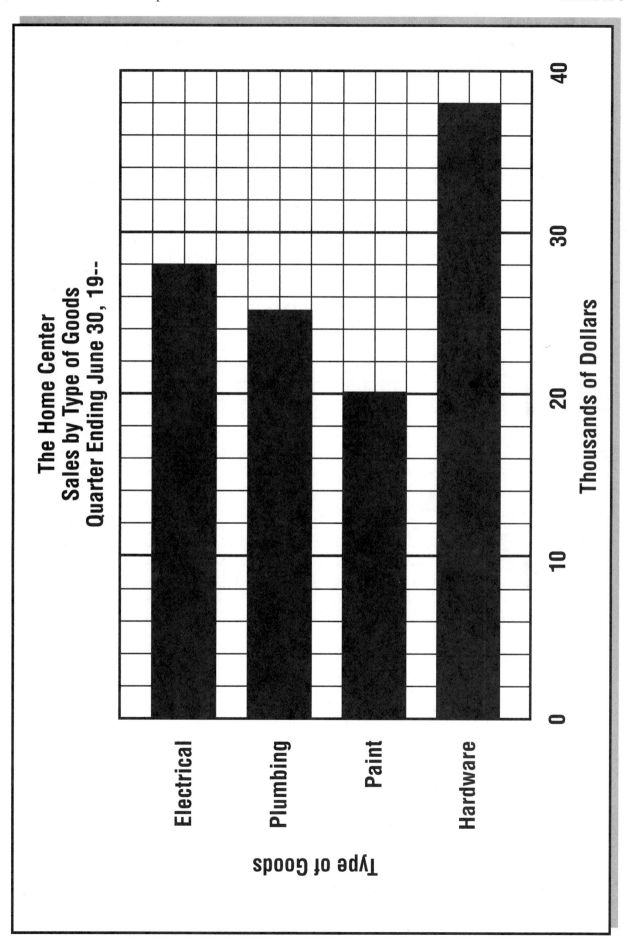

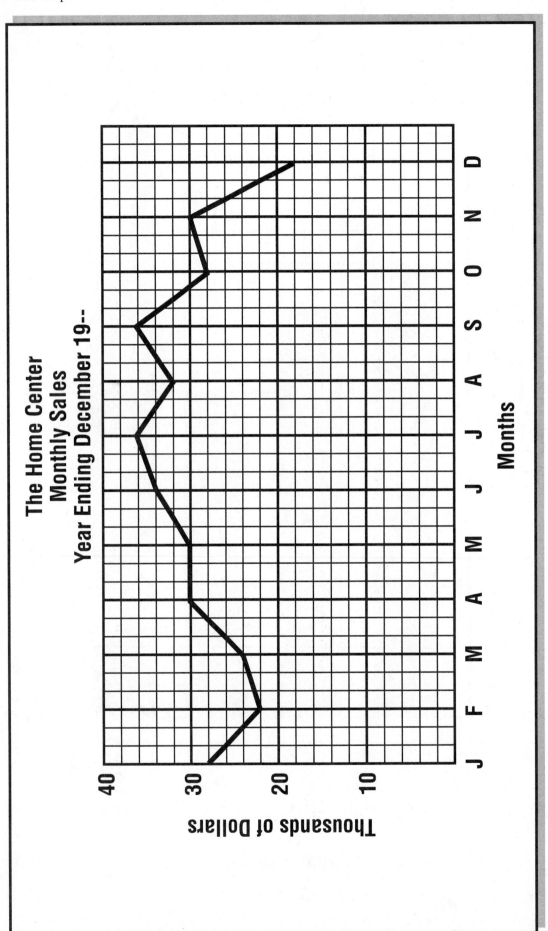

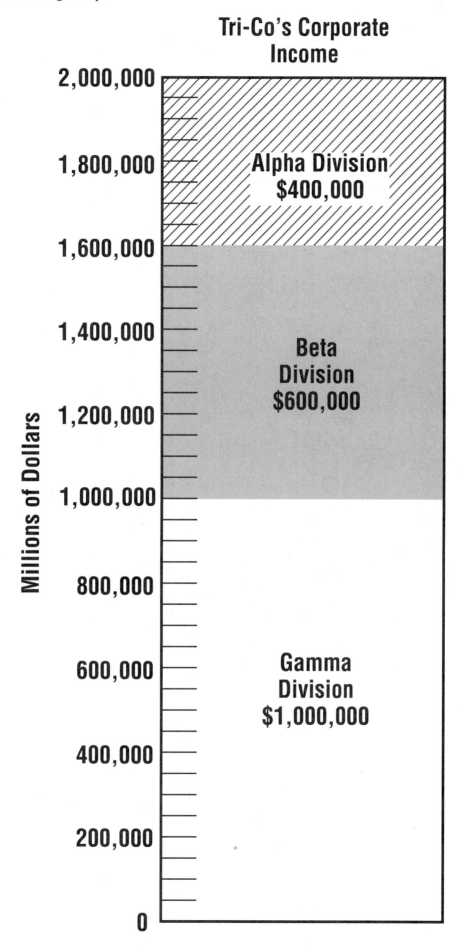

Tri-Co's Corporate Income

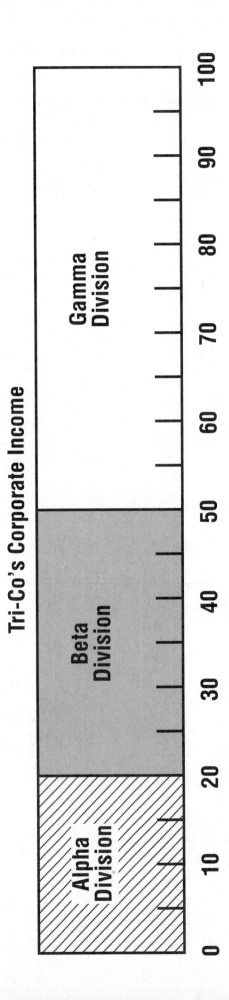

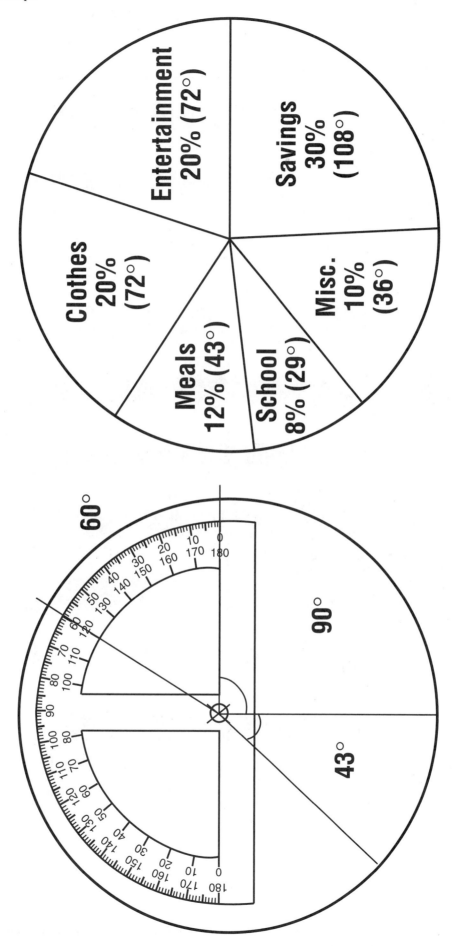

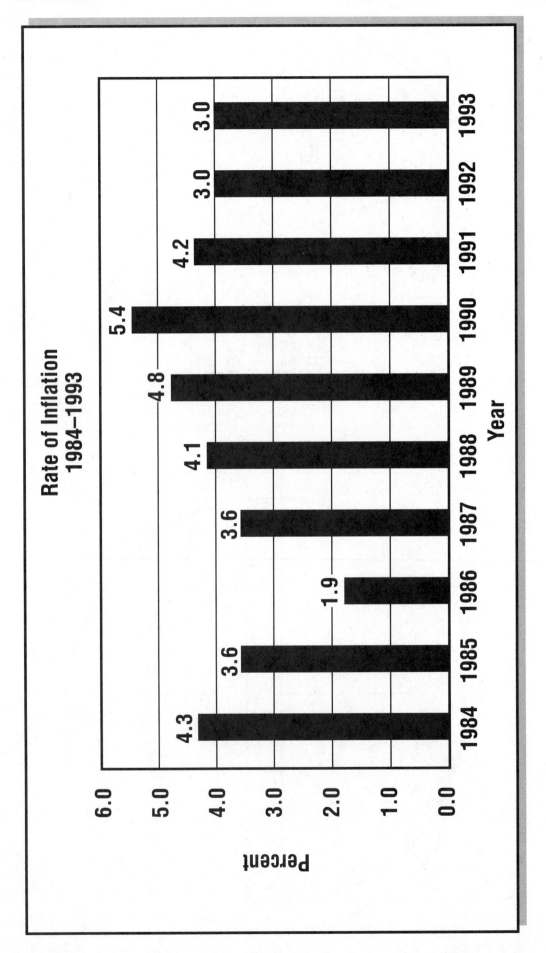

Purchasing Power of the Dollar 1984–1993	
Year	**Purchasing Power**
1982-1984	$1.000
1985	0.928
1986	0.913
1987	0.880
1988	0.846
1989	0.807
1990	0.766
1991	0.734
1992	0.713
1993	0.692

Historical Report — Consumer Price Index, 1984–1993
Categories of Goods and Services

Year	CPI All Items	Energy	Food	Shelter	Apparel and Upkeep	Transpor- tation	Medical Care
1982–84	100.0	100.0	100.0	100.0	100.0	100.0	100.0
1985	107.6	101.6	105.6	109.8	105.0	106.4	113.5
1987	113.6	88.6	113.5	121.3	110.6	105.4	130.1
1989	124.0	94.3	125.1	132.8	118.6	114.1	149.3
1991	136.2	102.5	136.3	146.3	128.7	123.8	177.0
1993	144.5	104.2	140.9	155.7	130.4	130.4	201.4

1993 Unemployment Rates by Race, Sex, and Age	Rate for All…	Rate for 16–19 Year-Old…
Workers	6.8	
Male Workers	7.1	20.4
Female Workers	6.5	17.4
White Workers	6.0	16.2
Black Workers	12.9	38.9
Hispanic Workers	10.6	26.2

Net Sales $10,000	Cost of Merchandise Sold $3,700	
	Gross Profit $6,300	Expenses $4,500
		Net Income $1,800

Total Company Benefit Costs Plus Annual Income
$47,510

Total Company Benefit Costs
$10,968

Total Annual Income
$36,542

Total Company Costs for Your Benefits as a Percent of Your Total Annual Income: 30%

The Company also provides other valuable benefits and programs at no cost to you including:

- Holidays;
- Vacation;
- Personal Days;
- Employee Assistance Program;
- Tuition Reimbursement; and
- Bereavement Days.

Benefit	The Company Pays	You Pay
Health Care	$ 3,912	$ 996
Disability	798	117
Life, Dependent Life, AD&D, and Business Travel Accident Insurance	151	134
Pension Plan	1,326	0
Savings Plan	1,260	2,521
Social Security Tax (FICA)	2,796	2,796
State Unemployment Insurance	249	0
Federal Unemployment Insurance	434	0
Worker's Compensation	42	0
Total Benefit Costs	**$10,968**	**$6,564**

Last Half of	First Year	20.0%
	Second Year	32.0%
	Third Year	19.2%
	Fourth Year	11.5%
	Fifth Year	11.5%
First Half of	Sixth Year	5.8%
	Total	**100.0%**

ADVERTISING RATES

SIZE	1X	3X	5X	12X
Full page	$2,195	$2,070	$1,945	$1,820
$\frac{2}{3}$ page	$1,450	$1,385	$1,285	$1,220
$\frac{1}{2}$ page	$1,115	$1,055	$995	$940
$\frac{1}{3}$ page	$775	$735	$675	$635
Cover Rate	$2,275	$2,145	$2,000	$1,860
Color Charges: Add to per page rate				
2-color	$275	$255	$240	$225
4-color	$1,040	$1,020	$970	$930

Lynn's Books
BALANCE SHEET
March 31, 19--

Assets

Cash	$ 8,300
Merchandise inventory	64,640
Store equipment	16,000
Store supplies	2,100
Total assets	$91,040

Liabilities

Hubbel Book Co.	$19,000
Acril Supply	11,000
Total liabilities	$30,000

Capital

Lynn Gordan, Capital	$64,640
Total liabilities and capital	$91,040

Net Income: $8,400
Shared equally
We share equally

$4,200 $4,200

Net Income: $8,400
Shared in proportion
to investment

I invested   I invested
$10,000. $5,000.

$\frac{10}{15}$ x $8,400 = $\frac{5}{15}$ x $8,400 =

$5,600 $2,800

$5,600 $2,800

Net Income: $8,400
Shared by fixed percent

I get 60%   I get 40%
60% of 8,400 = ?   40% of 8,400 = ?

$5,040 $3,360

Net Income: $8,400
Each earns 8% interest
on investment, rest
is shared equally

I invested   I invested
$10,000. $5,000.
Interest =   Interest =
8% of 10,000 = ?   8% of 5,000 = ?

$ 800 $ 400

The rest we share equally.
$8,400 − $1,200 = $6,200
$6,200/2 = $3,100

+ 3,100   + 3,100
─────────   ─────────
$3,900 $3,500

Remit payment to:

Original invoice   #OJL610

RADEL ADHESIVES COMPANY
1631 Highway 55
Minneapolis, MN 55422-6083

Refer to:

Order Number	Date Entered	Date Shipped	Invoice Date	Terms of Sale
95231	6/7/--	6/8/--	6/10/--	2/10, 1/30, n/60

Shipping   *FOB Minneapolis*
Sold to: *Lagmeyer's Hardware*
          1575 Arrowhead Road
          Fargo, ND 58103-2537

Ship to: *Same address*

Quantity	Unit	Description	Unit Price	Amount
72	*Rolls*	*Transparent tape*	*$1.10*	*$79.20*
48	*Bottles*	*Rubber cement*	*1.25*	*60.00*
36	*Rolls*	*Masking tape*	*1.50*	*54.00*
24	*Cans*	*Wood glue*	*1.75*	*42.00*
		Total		*$235.20*
		Less 5% Trade Discount		*$ 11.76*
		Net Invoice		*233.44*
		Shipping		*6.00*
		Total Due		*$ 229.44*

PLEASE PAY ON INVOICE U.S. FUNDS ONLY
NO STATEMENT WILL BE SENT UNLESS REQUESTED

If paid by
6/20 Deduct $4.67
7/10 Deduct $2.33

Rate	5%	10%	15%	20%	25%	30%
5%	0.9025	0.855	0.8075	0.76	0.7125	0.665
5%, 5%	0.85738	0.81225	0.76713	0.722	0.67688	0.63175
10%	0.855	0.81	0.765	0.72	0.675	0.63
10%, 5%	0.81225	0.7695	0.72675	0.684	0.64125	0.5985
10%, 10%	0.7695	0.729	0.6885	0.648	0.6075	0.567

SELLING
PRICE

_____ %

$ _____

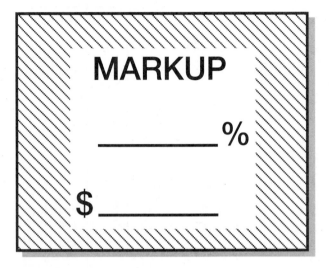

MARKUP

_____ %

$ _____

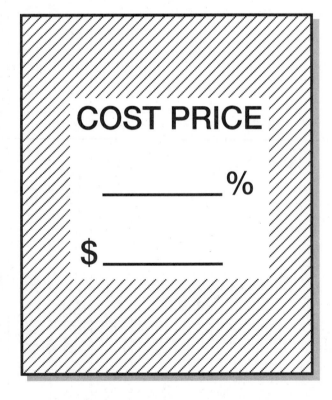

COST PRICE

_____ %

$ _____

MARKED PRICE

_____ %

$_____

DISCOUNT

_____ %

$_____

SELLING PRICE

_____ %

$_____

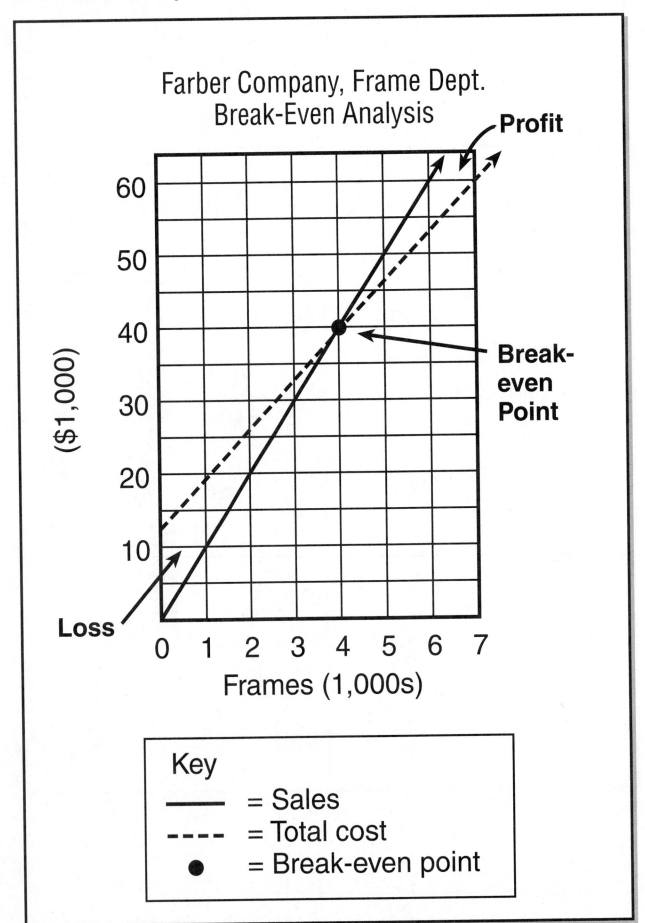

Cash Proof				
Date _____				
Change Fund				
+ Register total of cash received				
Total				
− Register total of cash paid out				
Cash that should be in drawer				
Cash actually in drawer				
Cash short				
Cash over				

Cash register No. _____

Cash Register Operator

_____

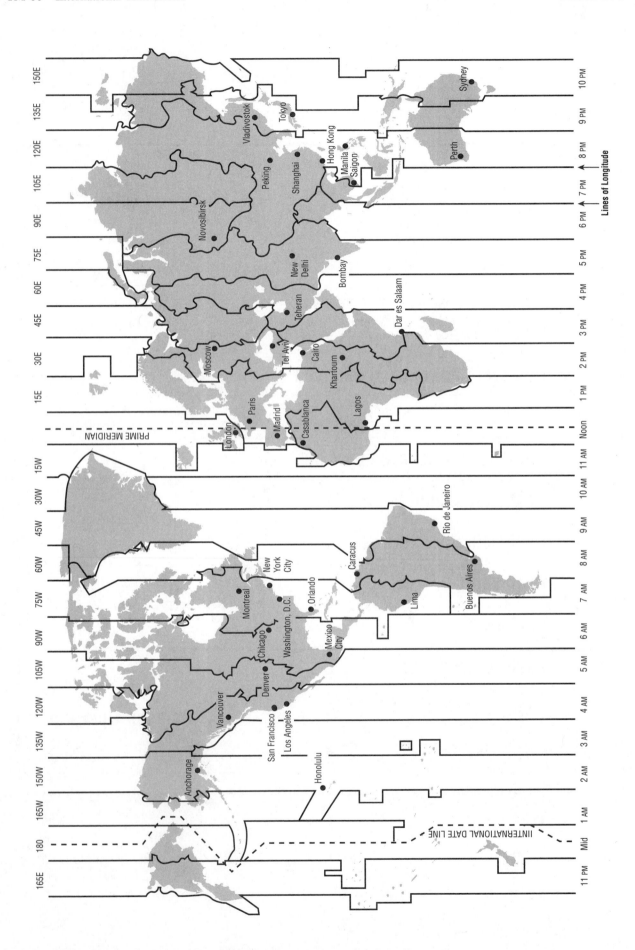